Get the eBook FREE!

(PDF, ePub, Kindle, and liveBook all included)

We believe that once you buy a book from us, you should be able to read it in any format we have available. To get electronic versions of this book at no additional cost to you, purchase and then register this book at the Manning website.

Go to https://www.manning.com/freebook and follow the instructions to complete your pBook registration.

That's it!
Thanks from Manning!

Web Components in Action

BEN FARRELL
Foreword by Gray Norton

MANNING
SHELTER ISLAND

For online information and ordering of this and other Manning books, please visit www.manning.com. The publisher offers discounts on this book when ordered in quantity. For more information, please contact

Special Sales Department
Manning Publications Co.
20 Baldwin Road
PO Box 761
Shelter Island, NY 11964
Email: orders@manning.com

♾ Recognizing the importance of preserving what has been written, it is Manning's policy to have the books we publish printed on acid-free paper, and we exert our best efforts to that end. Recognizing also our responsibility to conserve the resources of our planet, Manning books are printed on paper that is at least 15 percent recycled and processed without the use of elemental chlorine.

Manning Publications Co.
20 Baldwin Road
PO Box 761
Shelter Island, NY 11964

Acquisitions editor: Brian Sawyer
Development editors: Kevin Harreld, Kristen Watterson, and Rebecca Rinehart
Technical development editor: Douglas Duncan
Review editor: Ivan Martinović
Production editor: Anthony Calcara
Copy editor: Rebecca Deuel-Gallegos
Proofreader: Tiffany Taylor
Technical proofreader: Matthew Welke
Typesetter: Dottie Marisco
Cover designer: Marija Tudor

ISBN 9781617295775
Printed in the United States of America

To my amazing wife,
who writes way more exciting books than those about web development,
involving dragons and disasters.

contents

foreword

The web has come a long way. What started three decades ago as a relatively simple means of publishing, sharing, discovering, and consuming content has evolved into a powerful and flexible application platform supporting a dizzying array of use cases. Meanwhile, its footprint has expanded from desktop computers to devices of all types.

As a result of this gradual transformation, we web developers have been chasing an ever-moving target. Today's websites are orders of magnitude more complex than their early predecessors, and UI expectations have shot through the roof.

Thankfully, our toolbox has also evolved. The web platform itself has gained hundreds of new capabilities, and successive generations of libraries, frameworks, and tools have steadily advanced the state of the art, helping us meet rising demands.

One major enabler of the web's transformation in recent years has been the widespread adoption of component-based UI development. Factoring our work into components—each one responsible for the structure, style, and behavior of a slice of the user experience—has helped us manage complexity and build more ambitious sites.

Components can be reused throughout a project or shared across projects, increasing our efficiency. Design systems can be expressed as collections of ready-to-use components, ensuring consistency and freeing teams to focus on product-specific needs.

Popular frameworks have helped lead the component revolution, and indeed most components today are specific to a given framework or library. But in parallel, a multiyear effort has been underway to bring a first-class, native component model to the web platform.

Web Components is an umbrella term for a new family of web platform features offering direct support for component-based development. Custom Elements let you extend the vocabulary of HTML, defining your own tags that work seamlessly with the browser's built-in tags and can be used in all of the same places, regardless of what framework you might be using. The Shadow DOM lets you opt into native style encapsulation, ensuring that a component's CSS rules don't unintentionally break—and aren't broken by—the styling of the containing page.

You may be wondering what benefits Web Components bring over framework-specific component models. For one, Web Components promise to increase interoperability, making it simple to share components even across tech stacks. A common component model also lowers the risk of lock-in, allowing you to carry more work forward as your toolbox changes over time.

The book you're holding in your hands right now is exceptionally well-timed. The road to standardizing and landing Web Components has taken some twists and turns, but I'm happy to say that the destination is in sight: all but one of the major browsers have now shipped Web Components, and when the next version of Microsoft Edge is officially released, the puzzle will be complete.

Custom Elements, the Shadow DOM, and the other Web Components features are, by design, low-level primitives. Some developers will use these features only indirectly, as framework support for Web Components has spiked with increasing browser support. Many of the most popular frameworks now make it easy to develop and share Web Components, and a whole new class of Web-Components-centric tools has begun to emerge.

But you can also use the Web Components features directly, either individually or in combination. Reading this book will give you a deep understanding of each feature and how they relate to one another, equipping you to make smart choices for yourself and your team.

Ben Farrell has been using Web Components since the early days, in a wide range of applications. Along the way, he has amassed a wealth of valuable knowledge and discovered numerous effective patterns, all of which he'll share with you in these pages.

Ben teaches by example, demonstrating concepts through compelling projects that illuminate realistic use cases. You'll certainly learn a lot, but you're also bound to find ideas and code here that you can apply directly to your own projects.

In deciding to pick up Web Components and this book, you've chosen well. Enjoy the journey!

—Gray Norton,
Technical Lead/Manager for the
Polymer Project, Google

preface

Web Components, for me, began in 2013. I remember that I was working on a fun little Angular v1 side project and nerding out on some aspect of managing CSS and classes that Angular didn't handle well at the time. I knew I could have easily done what I needed in plain HTML/CSS/JavaScript, but Angular was making it difficult just because what I was doing was a bit off the beaten path.

Around this time, I felt like I was really starting to master Angular, so I wrote a few blog posts around some interesting, nontypical approaches. But this was also when Angular excitement felt like it was waning, and React excitement was just starting.

Honestly, I was disappointed. I took a long look at a cycle I felt trapped in. In the span of just two or three years, I was constantly learning and getting good at JS frameworks. None of these frameworks were compatible with each other. I'd get to a point where I felt like I could really focus on my project, with the framework off in the background, and then suddenly something new was released that made me feel like I had to go back to square one.

At the same time, Google's Polymer Library had been released as a very early and unstable version. Creating individual components that could live anywhere sounded like an amazing promise. Initially, I liked what it was trying to achieve, but a pre-v1 API that was in flux and the fact that I was replacing my workflow with yet another framework made me rethink things. I started looking at the proposed web standards that made the Polymer Library possible and saw enormous potential. I realized that it wasn't the Polymer Library I was excited about—it was really Web Components.

I started blogging and giving talks about Web Components. I also joined Adobe at around this time. This was significant because my team was working on small prototypes with one, maybe two, developers for a project. This meant that I could experiment with the technology and tools of my choice. For almost every project, I continued to push on

Web Components while experimenting and continually improving a workflow for working with them.

It certainly wasn't easy, of course. Sometimes the rug was completely pulled out from under me! As Web Components became the standard that they are today, we saw the API change and features become deprecated, but I stuck with it. I did so because I really do enjoy working as close to the browser as I can with just HTML/JS/CSS and saw Web Components as the vehicle to provide structure to my projects and not have them end up as code spaghetti.

I wasn't totally convinced yet of Web Components' viability. For one, I wasn't using the Shadow DOM quite yet. I didn't want to get lured into something only Google supported and that had questionable polyfill support. But then Web Components landed in Safari, and Mozilla promised support as well. The icing on the cake was when browsers started supporting JS modules/imports natively, and I could properly separate out code and, more importantly, HTML and CSS. When all this happened, I knew Web Components were starting to fulfill their potential.

This was all very slow going over several years, of course. Many developers who were initially excited about Web Components lost their patience, and I don't blame them. I initially approached Manning about a Web Components book prior to some important key things happening, like the major browser vendors coming together to finalize v1 of the specification. Manning wasn't confident with Web Components at the time, especially with books in the industry being cancelled due to unknowns about where Web Components would go.

Whether I was overly optimistic or had just spent enough time with them to know Web Components' potential, Manning contacted me a year later for another proposal. Even then, in early 2018, Web Components still could have taken a bad turn if the other browser vendors decided to back out. Also at the time, I wasn't approaching Web Component development in the same way as most others were—using HTML Imports as an entry point. However, during the course of the book, LitElement from the Polymer team started approaching things much like I was, using template literals to hold markup and style. This, coupled with Web Components landing in the fall of 2018 with Microsoft working on them as well, let me breathe a sigh of relief knowing that the approaches in my book are lockstep with the present and future of Web Components. I'll definitely continue to improve my workflow as new features come to the browser and are invented in the community, but I'm extremely excited with where Web Components are right now, as *Web Components in Action* is about to be published. And, of course, I can't wait to share everything with readers of this book!

acknowledgments

This book wouldn't have been possible without all the amazing people who helped me along the way. I want to thank my friends in North Carolina and the awesome folks running and attending NCDevCon for listening to me yammer on about Web Components on a near-constant basis. More specifically, I'd like to thank Adrian Pomilio for blowing my mind in his 2011 talk showing Custom Elements before they were really a thing.

I'd also like to thank the GE Design System team for being my Web Component co-conspirators at a time when they were so new and we weren't quite sure if everyone else thought we were insane. Specifically, I'd like to thank Martin Wragg, Jeff Reichenberg, and John Rogerson for nerding out with me about this new way to create for the web. I'd also like to thank the Google Polymer team for help and guidance during this time, as well as their technical lead/manager Gray Norton for writing the foreword for this book.

At Adobe, I'd like to thank the entire Adobe Design team (and beyond) for being so supportive and genuinely excited for me publishing my first book.

Of course, my wife Rebecca Gomez Farrell has not only supported me through this whole thing, but also happens to be an amazing writer and editor herself. In addition to getting me a stiff drink when I needed one, she helped a new writer be way better, with actual, professional advice.

I'd like to thank the Manning editorial team, including development editors Kristen Watterson, Kevin Harreld, and Rebecca Rinehart, as well as technical development editor Douglas Duncan, technical proofreader Matthew Welke, production editor Anthony Calcara, copyeditor Rebecca Deuel-Gallegos, and text proofreader Tiffany Taylor. Lastly, I'd like to thank the reviewers, whose feedback and insight were instrumental in shaping this book, including Alberto Ciarlanti, Alicia Baker, Birnou Sébarte, Clive Harber, Daniel Couper, Hernan Garcia, James Carella, John Larsen,

Juan Asencio, Justin Calleja, Oliver Kovacs, Pietro Maffi, Ronald Borman, Russel Dawn Cajoles, Ryan Burrows, Sergio Arbeo, Stefan Trost, Thomas Overby Hansen, Timothy R. Kane, and Kumar S. Unnikrishnan (TR Technology & Ops).

about this book

Web Components in Action isn't about dictating what approaches developers should take. Instead of telling readers what to do, I take a more exploratory approach to cover the basics of Web Components. You should recognize that, while experts may tell you what a good workflow is today, the exciting thing about standards is that they can be built upon in ways nobody expects.

In *Web Components in Action,* I aim to arm you with great ideas and workflows to get started. I also hope to empower you with the knowledge to take Web Components further, in ways I haven't considered yet and for types of projects I haven't encountered.

Who should read this book

Web Components in Action is for web developers who are curious about Web Components and want to know more about the standards behind them and how they come together with other web technologies to create standalone components or applications.

It's also for developers who want ideas about how to break free of complicated frameworks or libraries and get back to writing plain HTML/JS/CSS without needing any build steps.

How this book is organized: a roadmap

This book is in three parts covering 15 chapters and an appendix.

Part 1 covers the first steps in getting a simple component off the ground:

- Chapter 1 outlines what people mean when they talk about Web Components and the different standards that come together to create one.
- Chapter 2 walks through creating your very first Web Component, while introducing the bare-minimum concepts needed to create something useful.
- Chapter 3 brings a minimal component to the next level by making it reusable.

- Chapter 4 details the Web Components API and lifecycle, comparing them with others you may have encountered.
- Chapter 5 introduces modules for better code reuse and project organization.

The second part builds on a minimal component and covers concepts to improve developer workflow and project organization:

- Chapter 6 details using modules to separate out and import view logic like HTML and CSS to organize your component better.
- Chapter 7 covers an alternate, but nonpreferred, way to organize your component with HTML Imports, while breaking it down into pieces that are relevant to other aspects of Web Components as well.
- Chapter 8 introduces the Shadow DOM and how it's useful for protecting and encapsulating your component.
- Chapter 9 continues with exploring the Shadow DOM to cover its CSS aspects.
- Chapter 10 explores some trouble that Web Component developers may have with CSS in the Shadow DOM and ways in which to avoid or overcome it.

The third and final part covers working with multiple components together to build something larger:

- Chapter 11 reviews the previously covered concepts and uses them to build a brand-new, more polished component, built on child components already created.
- Chapter 12 takes this brand-new component forward to be more ready for production by using build tools that allow it to be used in older browsers that don't support Web Components.
- Chapter 13 furthers the same component by writing tests for it that run in three different contexts, to explore the various options available for Web Component developers.
- Chapter 14 discusses passing messages between your components and dives into some common design pattern when event bubbling doesn't cut it.
- Chapter 15 speculates on the future of Web Components and also the power they can enable today by hiding complexity and making everything from live video effects to mixed reality easier to use.

Lastly, the appendix covers newer JS features (ES6/ES2015) and how they help Web Components.

About the code

Source code is provided for all the examples in this book and is available for download from the Manning website at www.manning.com/books/web-components-in-action and in a GitHub repo found at https://github.com/bengfarrell/webcomponentsinaction. The repo is organized into folders for each chapter, and in those there are typically subfolders for each section. Exceptions are when working on a big example that encompasses the entire chapter.

Code can be run with just a browser and doesn't need to be compiled until the later chapters on build tooling. Generally, a simple HTTP server will be needed to run the associated HTML file that drives the example, but only to deal with cross-origin issues.

This book contains many examples of source code, both in numbered listings and inline in normal text. In both cases, source code is formatted in a `fixed-width font like this` to separate it from ordinary text. Sometimes code is also **`in bold`** to highlight code that has changed from previous steps in the chapter, such as when a new feature adds to an existing line of code.

In many cases, the original source code has been reformatted; we've added line breaks and reworked indentation to accommodate the available page space in the book. In rare cases, even this was not enough, and listings include line-continuation markers (➥). Additionally, comments in the source code have often been removed from the listings when the code is described in the text. Code annotations accompany many of the listings, highlighting important concepts.

liveBook discussion forum

The purchase of *Web Components in Action* includes free access to a private web forum run by Manning Publications where you can make comments about the book, ask technical questions, and receive help from the author and from other users. To access the forum, go to https://livebook.manning.com/#!/book/web-components-in-action/discussion. You can also learn more about Manning's forums and the rules of conduct at https://livebook.manning.com/#!/discussion.

Manning's commitment to our readers is to provide a venue where a meaningful dialogue between individual readers and between readers and the author can take place. It is not a commitment to any specific amount of participation on the part of the author, whose contribution to the forum remains voluntary (and unpaid). We suggest you try asking the author some challenging questions, lest his interest stray! The forum and the archives of previous discussions will be accessible from the publisher's website as long as the book is in print.

About the author

Ben Farrell is a senior experience developer at Adobe, working on the Adobe Design Prototyping Team. Ben, alongside his team, helps shape and realize the UX of products and features in the middle ground between design and engineering. Ben has been primarily web-focused his entire career but has worked on award-winning projects using a wide variety of platforms and languages.

about the cover illustration

The figure on the cover of *Web Components in Action* is captioned "Bourgeois de Londre," or a bourgeois man from London. The illustration is taken from a collection of dress costumes from various countries by Jacques Grasset de Saint-Sauveur (1757–1810), titled *Costumes Civils Actuels de Tous le Peuples Connus,* published in France in 1788. Each illustration is finely drawn and colored by hand. The rich variety of Grasset de Saint-Sauveur's collection reminds us vividly of how culturally apart the world's towns and regions were just 200 years ago. Isolated from each other, people spoke different dialects and languages. In the streets or in the countryside, it was easy to identify where they lived and what their trade or station in life was just by their dress.

The way we dress has changed since then, and the diversity by region, so rich at the time, has faded away. It is now hard to tell apart the inhabitants of different continents, let alone different towns, regions, or countries. Perhaps we have traded cultural diversity for a more varied personal life—certainly for a more varied and fast-paced technological life.

At a time when it is hard to tell one computer book from another, Manning celebrates the inventiveness and initiative of the computer business with book covers based on the rich diversity of regional life of two centuries ago, brought back to life by Grasset de Saint-Sauveur's pictures.

Part 1

First steps

You've probably been hearing more and more about Web Components lately. Much of this has to do with all the major, modern browsers now supporting them in recent months. This includes Microsoft Edge, because you can already download a developer preview while we wait for the official Chromium-backed release. It can get a bit confusing when you look deeper to see what Web Components actually are, though!

Not only has the collection of standards that make up Web Components changed a little over time, but, in reality, a Web Component can be created with Custom Elements alone! You can create your very own element that sits on your HTML page just like any other browser-provided one. More importantly, by using the Custom Element API, your element can be given custom logic to be a made a fully featured, tiny interactive component that looks simple from the outside and can work together with any other element on the page.

The first part of this book will zero in on how to create your first custom elements, as well as explore some best practices around them. At the end of the first part, even just exploring this one concept, you'll be making Web Components that are actually useful in real-world situations, even allowing them to be wrapped up as a single piece managing its own dependencies, perhaps including other nested Web Components, ready to be dropped onto an HTML page.

First Steps

1 The framework without a framework

This chapter covers

- What a Web Component is
- The Shadow DOM
- Custom Elements
- Polymer Library and X-Tags
- ES6/ES2015 language features

Hello, and thanks for reading *Web Components in Action!* I've been using Web Components for a few years now on just about every web development project I've had.

As web developers, it's our job to choose the right tools for any given project. This can get complicated, because it's not just the project's immediate needs that matter. Your team's needs do as well, as do whether the project is part of a bigger ecosystem at your company, how it will be maintained, and how *long* it will need to be maintained. The list goes on.

Of course, these decisions aren't unique to web developers, but one major difference between us and many software developers is that the web community has put out an astounding number of tools, libraries, and frameworks. It can get difficult to keep up with all of them—so much so that "framework fatigue" has been a topic of conversation for some time now.

Adoption of these new tools seems to happen at lightning speed. Putting aside frameworks for a moment, even something as niche as task runners for building your JavaScript (JS) projects has changed dramatically over the past few years. I've seen the switch from Grunt in 2012 to Gulp just a couple of years later, and now there's a tendency to go minimal by using the Node.js NPM (Node Package Manager) to run build scripts. Speaking of package managers, we developers have waffled between NPM, Bower, and Yarn for running our frontend dependencies.

Build tooling and package managers are one thing. They are small but significant pieces of our web development workflow. Yet this same churn is happening with how we actually build our applications and UI, which is arguably the most central and important part of web development.

For individual developers, this can definitely be hard to keep up with, although it's exciting to learn a new framework or library. Some have a steeper learning curve than others, and, in many cases, you're learning the framework's "system" as opposed to fundamental HTML/JS/CSS concepts.

As a developer on a team or in a company, there are additional challenges. At the start of a project, you'll need to agree on what tools you'll use to develop with over the lifecycle of the project. This includes build tools, testing tools, and, of course, any frameworks or libraries. Not everyone will agree on the best choice. If the team is large and working on many projects, it can be tempting to let developers on each project pick their own tools. After all, it's good to analyze the needs of the project and use the appropriate tools. But this also ignores the inevitable, when developers must work together to create common pieces of UI or integrate a newly adopted design system that is mandated companywide. Eventually, using different tools and frameworks may come back to bite your team.

If everyone agrees, begrudgingly or not, on the same framework, things can be great for a while. Even then, two or three years down the line, the framework can become dated. Using older technology begins to feel a little stifling, especially to junior developers on your team who want to keep their skills up-to-date with the rest of the web community. At this point, your organization is faced with the choice of redoing the entire technology stack using a new framework or keeping the old one and facing the perception of not being an innovative place to work.

It's a difficult problem and decision for sure! The question that begs asking, of course, is "What's the alternative?" I've talked to quite a few people who want to break free of the constant framework churn for a variety of reasons. "Why can't we just use plain HTML, JS, and CSS?" is a common question. One of the biggest benefits of not buying into a framework is being able to focus on core web development concepts rather than learning framework-specific skills that may or may not transfer to the next popular framework. Another huge benefit is being able to try small libraries and microframeworks that solve specific needs in your project. The barrier of entry to these, and even new frontend build tools, is much lower given that you aren't fighting a specific development environment provided by the latest popular framework.

Modern frameworks are extremely useful and solve some big problems, but why don't we hear more about using so-called "vanilla JavaScript," given developers' desire to try other things? We do, to some extent. Consider this poll by the State of JavaScript, conducted in 2017: https://2017.stateofjs.com/2017/front-end/results/. You'll note that no-framework development is second in popularity, behind only React.

However, we don't know specifics on why folks claim to prefer no framework, or vanilla JS. What kinds of things are those developers building? What tools/processes are they using? I'd be curious to know if they build a framework of sorts themselves to make up for the lack of structure and code organization that modern frameworks usually provide.

This last point about structure and code organization is why no-framework web development has been a nonstarter for me in the past, and it's why I've always turned to the latest framework. Without structure, your code becomes spaghetti. Maintaining and writing new features can be madness without predictable project organization. Nevertheless, I wanted to break free of big, all-encompassing frameworks; when I saw Web Components for the first time, I saw a huge opportunity to do just that.

So . . . how? To really tackle this question, we need to understand what Web Components really are. Before I get into the specifics, we'll use a browser's date picker as an example we've all likely come across. While it's not a Web Component, per se, it's a similar concept if you peek inside.

1.1 What are Web Components?

The popular modern frameworks of today largely offer code reusability in the form of *components* or *modules*. Generally speaking, these are shareable and standalone pieces of code (HTML/JS/CSS) that offer visual style and interactivity, and possibly have an API or options you can set to offer customization.

Think about what's already in your browser. And consider that we already have reusable, modular pieces that offer style and interactivity, and come with an API.

Of course, I'm talking about HTML tags or DOM elements. These are rendered in the DOM and have a specific type of functionality. A `<div>` tag or `<span>` tag is fairly generic and is used to hold text or a mixture of elements. A `<button>` or an `<input>` element is more specific in functionality and style. When you place a button in your HTML, it looks like a standard button, and when you click it, it acts like a button. This is similar to the different styles of `<input>`, whether you mean to create a date picker, slider, or text input field.

1.1.1 The date picker

Take the date picker, for example. To create a date picker, you'd simply put the following tag in your HTML:

```
<input type="date">
```

Seems easy, doesn't it? It is! What you actually get from this simple tag is fairly complicated, but it's all handled for you by your browser. This tag (when using the type `"date"`) offers a text input field, and you can click on the month, day, or year and step up or down through any of them. Also, if you click the down arrow to the side, it will pop open a calendar view that the user can interact with to choose a date, as figure 1.1 shows. Additionally, when on mobile, it acts slightly differently. It will not pop open as it does in a desktop browser, but instead shows a modal window.

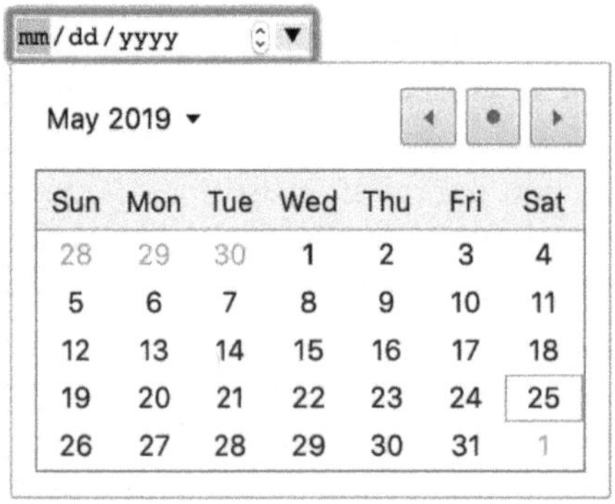

mm/dd/yyyy

May 2019

Sun	Mon	Tue	Wed	Thu	Fri	Sat
28	29	30	1	2	3	4
5	6	7	8	9	10	11
12	13	14	15	16	17	18
19	20	21	22	23	24	25
26	27	28	29	30	31	1

Figure 1.1 Expanded date picker UI

What's more, the date picker has *properties* you can query, including value. We can see this by logging the property in the JS console:

```
console.log( document.querySelector('input').value );
```

When I log this, I see the picker's current value in my console. It also dispatches *events* that I can listen to when the value changes or is submitted. I can also call *methods* on the picker for stepping through dates.

The date picker is a great example of reusable components or modules with fairly complex visual style and interaction patterns that need to be programmed by the browser vendors. They work in a variety of situations. The date picker is also a great example of a popular Web Component concept called the Shadow DOM.

1.1.2 The Shadow DOM

The Shadow DOM is a way to isolate your Web Component and guard against unintentional consequences from your larger application. When you open the dev tools to look at the DOM, you'll just see the `<input type="date">` tag. However, if you use Chrome and enable "Show user agent shadow DOM" in the dev tool settings, the same input tag expands to look like figure 1.2.

Lots more markup is revealed in this hidden *shadow root*! Personally, the first thing I'd look for when inspecting this is the calendar pop-up. While it would be great to see that piece in HTML and CSS, it's not there because that piece of UI is part of your native OS that your browser simply exposes through the element. That said, we have a

```
▼<input type="date" name="bday">
  ▼#shadow-root (user-agent)
    ▼<div pseudo="-webkit-datetime-edit" id="date-time-edit" datetimeformat=
    "M/d/yy">
      ▼<div pseudo="-webkit-datetime-edit-fields-wrapper">
         <span role="spinbutton" aria-placeholder="mm" aria-valuemin="1"
         aria-valuemax="12" aria-label="Month" pseudo="-webkit-datetime-edit-
         month-field">mm</span>
         <div pseudo="-webkit-datetime-edit-text">/</div>
         <span role="spinbutton" aria-placeholder="dd" aria-valuemin="1"
         aria-valuemax="31" aria-label="Day" pseudo="-webkit-datetime-edit-
         day-field">dd</span>
         <div pseudo="-webkit-datetime-edit-text">/</div>
         <span role="spinbutton" aria-placeholder="yyyy" aria-valuemin="1"
         aria-valuemax="275760" aria-label="Year" pseudo="-webkit-datetime-
         edit-year-field">yyyy</span>
       </div>
     </div>
     <div pseudo="-webkit-clear-button" id="clear" style="opacity: 0;
     pointer-events: none;"></div>
     <div pseudo="-webkit-inner-spin-button" id="spin"></div>
     <div pseudo="-webkit-calendar-picker-indicator" id="picker"></div>
  </input>
```

Figure 1.2 Enabling shadow root settings in the Chrome dev tools allows us to see the input tag's hidden Shadow DOM.

fair number of elements hidden away in our Shadow DOM that all appear in the input field element.

Looking closely, you might notice that our Shadow DOM hosts a mix of `<div>` and `<span>` tags. It might occur to you that this is dangerous! Why? Well, in my application's CSS, I could very well define all `<div>` tags to have a blue background with a super-large font size and all `<span>` tags to display with an opacity of 10%. If you didn't know that this additional markup existed, you might accidentally ruin all your date pickers—except for one major thing: the Shadow DOM protects the inner workings of your Web Component from the outside. Your blue/large div styles won't penetrate the Shadow DOM. What's more, you would not be able to write some JS to try to get and manipulate the date picker's `clear` button:

```
let myElement = document.getElementById('clear');
```

When we attempt to get this element, because it is within the bounds of the Shadow DOM, the element is not found, and our `myElement` variable is null. Figure 1.3 shows various attempts with both CSS and JS.

So, the Shadow DOM protects your shadow root scope. Yes, you can use this shadow root anywhere. But it makes a ton of sense in a custom element that you built to avoid unintended breakage when a developer sets a CSS rule that happens to have the same name as something you used in your component—or when that same developer

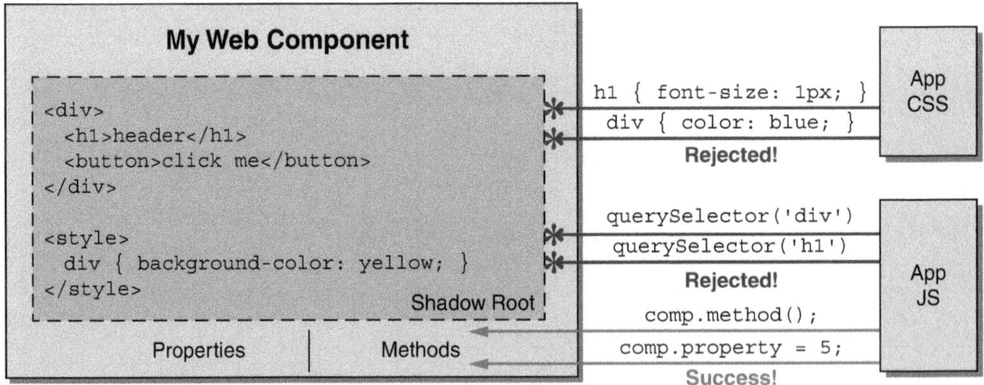

Figure 1.3 The Shadow DOM protects your component from unintended consequences when CSS or JS might affect styles and nodes inside that aren't meant to be altered. Instead, your component would have a custom-defined API to interact with using methods and properties.

happens to query an element by class, and something in your custom element gets picked up accidentally.

As you can imagine, the date picker is a useful element for complementing several other useful elements that we use on a daily basis. Many elements are used for semantic purposes, like the `<footer>` tag, but others have a specific API and style, like the `<button>`, `<option>`, and `<video>` tags.

1.1.3 What do people mean when they say Web Components?

As nice as the date picker, and any other element, might be, wouldn't it be amazing if we could create our own elements with our own visual style, internal logic, reusability, and encapsulation?

This is what folks mean when they refer to Web Components. In addition to the encapsulation provided by the Shadow DOM, we can use the Custom Element API to create our own components that do things specific to our own needs.

To me, that's the promise of Web Components. I want to take something I'm interested in and create a reusable piece that I can share with the world, my team, or just myself to use in multiple projects where I need it. Alternately, there might be a piece of UI that I find boring to create over and over and over again. With Web Components, I can create it once, use it in multiple projects, and flesh it out as I need more features. Even better, maybe someone else created a Web Component for something I need, and I don't have the time or expertise to re-create it. They can share it with me, and I can just use it like a normal DOM element.

1.1.4 The problematic history of HTML Imports

Unfortunately, some in the web development community regard the promise of Web Components as a broken one. I certainly can't blame them for feeling this way. When talking about the specific technical features that Web Components offer, the vision started to fall apart after the initial hype around Web Components settled down a few years ago.

Around 2015, it was widely understood that a standard Web Component would be built using three new features:

- Custom Elements
- The Shadow DOM
- HTML Imports

I haven't even mentioned HTML Imports yet. That concept was never adopted as a standard. In fact, in the beginning, Google was largely responsible for creating working drafts of Web Components. Google took it upon itself to create APIs and ship them in Chrome as a hopeful experiment to see if Web Components would take off. HTML Imports never made it; the other browser vendors at the time had no plans to ship the feature. Firefox, specifically, wanted to hold off to see how big a splash ES6/ES2015 modules would make and—perhaps, possibly, someday—import not only JS, but HTML as well.

HTML Imports were a pretty big loss. From the beginning, Google's plans for delivering Web Components hinged on them. The HTML Import, as figure 1.4 shows, was a snippet of HTML for declaring the component's markup or structure, and it also included the JS that defined the component's logic. HTML Imports were the main entry point for Web Components, and without them, we were at a loss as to how to use Web Components with markup and style at all.

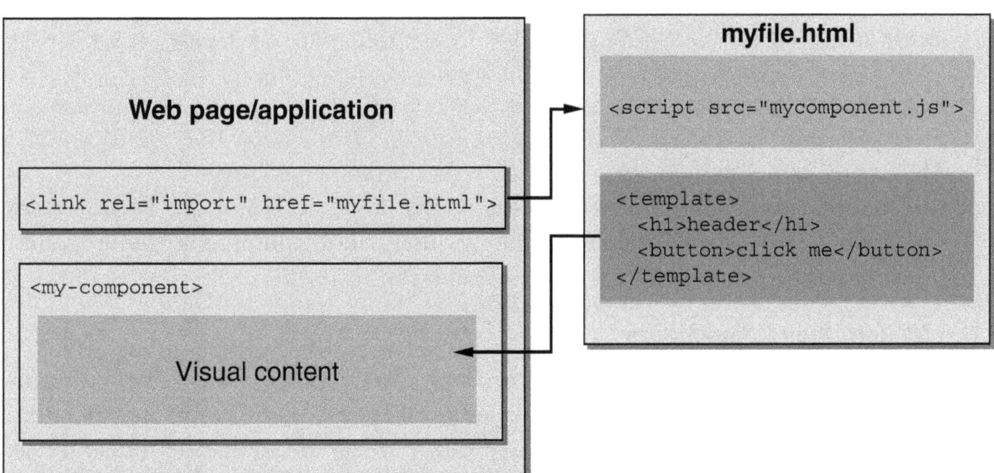

Figure 1.4 With HTML Imports, a file containing your component definition and your component's markup could be imported right into your document.

The Shadow DOM wasn't much better at the time. Chrome was the only browser to adopt it. It took until October 2018 for Firefox to adopt, and we're waiting for Microsoft Edge to ship it, though it is available as a developer preview right now.

Both the Shadow DOM and the Custom Element API have gone from version 0 to 1 as well. For Custom Elements, this was a bit troubling, given that developers who were familiar with Web Components during that shaky time were told to switch over to the new API.

Given all this, developers who called Web Components a "broken promise" and moved on to a framework can hardly be criticized. I can vouch that it was a bit tricky around 2015 to properly work with them, especially when targeting browsers other than Chrome.

1.1.5 Polymer Library and X-Tags

Another aspect of what people meant when they talked about Web Components then were the libraries that emerged at the time, which used Web Components as their basis. With the instability surrounding plain, no-framework components at the time, Google's Polymer Library (https://polymer-library.polymer-project.org) and Mozilla's X-Tags (https://x-tag.github.io) were what people thought of as Web Components, or at least the only way to work with them.

The Polymer Library did a great job pushing the standards and workflows forward, and it now looks like 3.0 is the last official feature release, as the Polymer Library goes into maintenance mode. The team is instead breaking off some of the core tools and features into much smaller and more targeted solutions like lit-html and LitElement as part of the Polymer Project. These core tools and features are well-aligned with the no-framework approach I outline in this book.

Even though the team did great work on a series of solid releases and is working now to focus on smaller and more opt-in features, the Polymer Library's early days prior to v1.0 were a little shaky. As expected with any pre-v1.0 library, the APIs changed a fair bit, especially as it tried to keep up with the changing specifications and lack of Shadow DOM on every browser except Chrome. The Shadow DOM was especially hard to deal with. Full-featured polyfills that included CSS encapsulation were too difficult and affected performance. To compensate, the "Shady DOM" was invented as a lightweight implementation that could be polyfilled.

It was a rocky time for Web Components in general, and the Polymer Library seemed like yet another framework/library that had to compete with more-solidified ones that didn't deal with in-flight web standards.

1.1.6 Modern Web Components

Despite these rocky times, I stuck with Web Components. I was successful at using them for projects but wasn't fully satisfied until I started using some new JS language features. The fat-arrow function turned out to be an amazing way to manage scope when working with mouse events or timers. More importantly, the `import` keyword and the concept of modules were huge.

With `import`, I was able to move away from the fragile mess of making sure every JS file I wanted to use was linked in a script tag on my main HTML page. Each Web Component could be completely responsible for importing its own code. This meant that on the main HTML page, I could have a single module-based script tag import a Web Component that contained my entire application. Each child component would just import whatever it needed.

This opened the door to reusable code modules written in pure JS and gave me the ability to create multiple levels of inheritance when I wanted my components to share an API and be a little smarter than the base `HTMLElement` API. Lastly, I could keep my HTML/CSS in a separate template.js file that I could import, separating my visual concerns from the component's controller logic.

The last huge JS feature that made Web Components a pleasure to work with was the *template literal*. Not only could I keep my HTML/CSS in a separate template file, but I could replace placeholder expressions in my markup with variables, and nest multiple templates together using JS functions.

These ES6/ES2015 features suddenly made Web Components a joy to work with. Even having previously worked with the now-deprecated HTML Imports, I think the combo of modules and template literals is a much better way to go, by comparison.

As I stated before, the Shadow DOM is 99% here. It's taken some time, but all the major browser vendors are in. We're just waiting for Microsoft to release the Edge developer preview to everyone. Personally, I've only now gone all in on working with the Shadow DOM after Firefox shipped.

At the same time, as nice as the Shadow DOM is, it's also optional. True, it does give our component's child elements some nice protection against style and JS creeping in and having adverse effects, but this is a new solution to a problem we've always had. So, if we need to wait a few months for browser support, or just opt out of it altogether for the short term, it's not the end of the world. That said, I've tempered my excitement on the Shadow DOM long enough due to previous browser support; now that we're about to cross the finish line, I'm thrilled because it's proving to be such a joy to use.

As excited as I am for the future of Web Components, I haven't heard of any sort of modern vision for them, especially for developers who were confused by them before. If I had to redefine the "promise of Web Components" for 2019 onward, it wouldn't be the three mandatory features of Custom Elements, Shadow DOM, and HTML Imports anymore.

To me, the 2019 vision for Web Components is shaping up to be a toolbelt of ES6/ES2015 features and the `<template>` tag when and if you need it, all in service of the Custom Element as the core feature. Once the Shadow DOM ships everywhere in the near future, it will also be a major addition to our toolbelt. This vision is how I'll be approaching Web Components in this book. We'll dive deep into the Custom Element and then explore workflows around all the optional tools in our toolbelt.

1.2 The future of Web Components

It's never easy to predict the future, especially on the web, where things change at an insane pace. That said, we have some strong clues indicating where Web Components might go beyond 2019.

We've already seen experiments with React, Angular (https://angular.io/guide/elements), and Vue (https://vuejsdevelopers.com/2018/05/21/vue-js-web-component/) on compiling components in each of these frameworks to a standalone Web Component, running completely independently of the framework that made those components. Additionally, tools like StencilJS (https://stenciljs.com) and Svelte (https://svelte.technology) allow you to create with a framework and compile to standalone Web Components.

What does this mean? Soon, we might all create components with no framework or with the framework of our choice. We'll use a React-created Web Component in Angular or a Vue-created Web Component in a no-framework web page. The artificial walls we have between developers and their frameworks may be coming down relatively soon, as depicted in figure 1.5. And this is all thanks to Web Components.

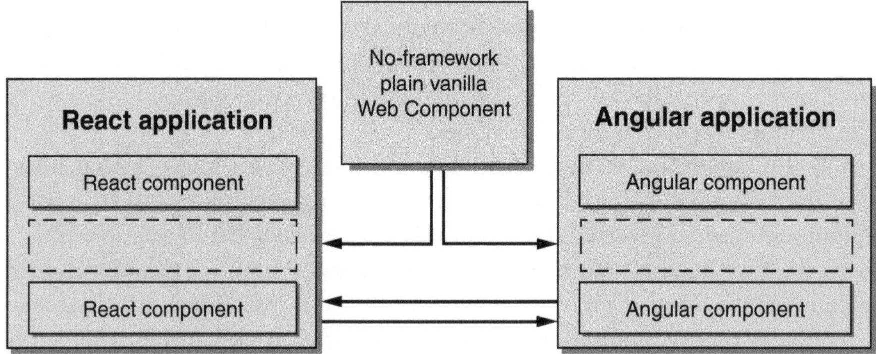

Figure 1.5 Web Components could bridge the gap in the future between popular frameworks. Not only can no-framework Web Components be used in these frameworks, but there are already experimental projects to compile a component in React, Angular, or Vue to independently run components that can be used anywhere.

This concept might even extend to allowing completely different languages to operate together. One application could have different components developed in JS, Typescript, and CoffeeScript; given that each is a modular component providing an API, this wouldn't matter. Even crazier, with the advent of WebAssembly, we could see languages like C++, Lua, Go, and so on compiled to bytecode and wrapped by a Web Component, looking like a completely normal element from the outside while simultaneously allowing high-performance graphics that can run faster than JS would normally run.

I also think that using ES6/ES2015 modules and imports will change the way we think about libraries and frameworks. Already, we are seeing two similar tools, lit-html and hyperHTML, for advanced markup management. Both of these have modules that developers can import instead of loading an entire library to target a specific problem. You're allowed to opt in or out whenever you want during your project.

In this regard, I think we'll see lots more amazing libraries. You'll import only what you need, when you need it. People might get bored with Web Components as a shiny new paradigm, but I can see us building on these fundamentals with importable scripts and libraries. The Polymer Project's new approach, as the team moves their original library into maintenance mode, seems to match this exactly. Time will tell if the major frameworks will break off features, as the Polymer team did with lit-html, into separate imports we can use outside the framework. But it seems inevitable to me, especially looking at other languages that have had import functionality forever.

1.3 Beyond the single component

So far, I've talked a lot about Web Components as individual components, but as much as I love standalone Web Components, they wouldn't be much use if they didn't work together to create your application.

Long before Web Components were a thing, we had great ways to interact with normal DOM elements. We can use these same methods to give structure to whatever we build with Web Components, just like we do with an ordinary `<div>`, `<video>`, or `<input>` tag.

1.3.1 Web Components are just like any other DOM element

For starters, every element has some sort of public API. By this, I mean that you can get and set properties on your element and call functions. For example, with the video element, you can call `pause()` and `play()` functions to control video playback. You can also check how long a video is by checking the `duration` property. Lastly, to jump to a specific point in your video, you can set the `currentTime` property.

Obviously, methods and functions on objects are common everywhere in programming. DOM elements are no different, as you may be able to tell from figure 1.6; furthermore, custom Web Components are no exception, either.

Somewhat similar to properties are *attributes*. You see these all the time in HTML. Something as simple as an `<img>` tag has a `src` attribute that points the element to the image's location. Attributes are a simple concept, but they are handy for giving your Web Component different behaviors depending on how you want it to act. Even better, Web Components have an API such that you can internally listen for attribute changes.

In the previous example of the video element, the attributes exposed by the tag don't match the properties that the API exposes. While we can set the `currentTime` property, we can't set the same attribute on the tag. Counter to this, many times with

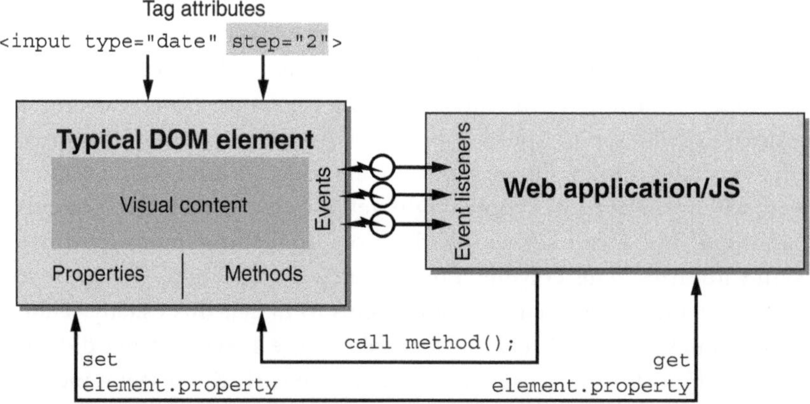

Figure 1.6 DOM elements have various properties, methods, events, and attributes that are used to tell the element how to act and communicate with the outside world.

Web Components you create, you'll want to use the best practice of *reflection*. When setting properties, you'll want to update the attribute (and vice versa), so these attributes and properties are in sync. Of course, this isn't a hard-and-fast rule, just a widely accepted best practice. Prior to Web Components, reflection wasn't necessarily adhered to. A good example of when things can go wrong is the `value` attribute on an `<input>` tag. A `value` attribute here sets the initial value, but when it changes, this `value` attribute stays the same. Querying the `value` property through JS will return the most recent value, assuming it's been changed. This is confusing! But we just accept it because that's how the `<input>` tag has always worked. When creating new Web Components, it's likely best to avoid this confusion and reflect attributes and properties. To this effect, the `video` element's `muted` attribute/property is a good example of reflection.

Lastly, you might want to listen for changes from your custom Web Component. We use events all the time in other scenarios. Think about clicking a button. Typically, we'd do the following to listen for the click:

```
mybutton.addEventListener('click', functionToCall );
```

You can also create and dispatch your own Custom Events. You can do this from anywhere, but they are especially handy when you need your application or other components within it to listen to events coming from your Web Component.

1.3.2 From individual component to application

Talking about individual components is one thing, but what about when you need to build an entire web application? Web Components can be as big or as little as you need them to be. You might build some extremely granular components, like buttons, and then nest those inside a bigger Web Component, like a custom toolbar.

Your toolbar component might handle the finer details of working with the buttons, perhaps toggling them on and off or disabling certain ones under specific circumstances. Our toolbar, alongside other components shown in figure 1.7, could be further nested inside another parent component, and so on. This can keep going all the way up until a single, solitary Web Component is the only thing in your `<body>` tag.

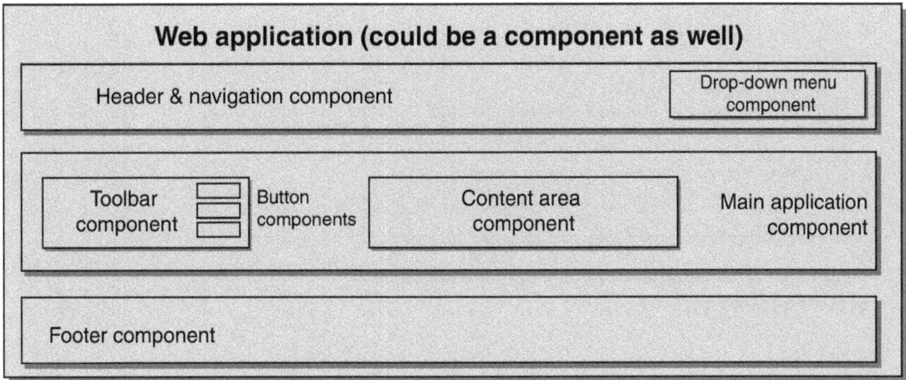

Figure 1.7 Example web application consisting of Web Components, which are themselves made up of more Web Components. The hierarchy can extend to something small, like a custom button, or be as large as the entire application wrapped as a Web Component.

Web Components, and no-framework JS, have much to offer you for web application development. But as your application grows, it will grow in complexity. It can get more and more difficult to coordinate how your components interact with each other.

Sometimes, you'll find that even with the inherent structure that Web Components give you, this just isn't enough to build your complex application. You might be tempted to turn to popular frameworks and libraries to help structure things. Frameworks like Angular offer data binding, MVC patterns, and more. Certainly, they can be helpful when building a traditional web application. On the other hand, we can write and import simple JS code based on tried-and-true design patterns that have been around for ages, avoiding these larger frameworks.

For example, native DOM events might fall short for you. Often, you'll want one part of your web application to message a completely different part of your application, and you won't want to worry about how the event bubbles through the DOM. You *could* turn to a library like RXjs or Redux, but it might be overkill. Instead, you could write a simple event bus with a small amount of code. Figures 1.8 and 1.9 contrast these two approaches.

In figure 1.8, you might, for example, have form-input components contained in a Web Component. These input components could trigger text input changes, drop-down changes, and more, all to that parent component. A good example of this might be a color picker component with RGB text input and sliders. The parent Web

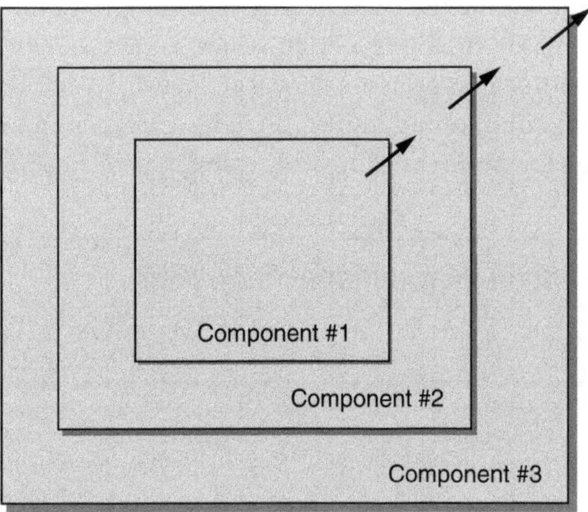

Figure 1.8 Events naturally bubble from the inside out of nested elements.

Component (the color picker) that hosts these input components would then have to pass the color on to its parent Web Component in another event to report the color's hex value.

This natural event bubbling could break down if the thing whose color you've decided to change is all the way on the other side of your DOM in a different section of the DOM tree. In this case, you'll need to use a different strategy, such as an event bus (figure 1.9).

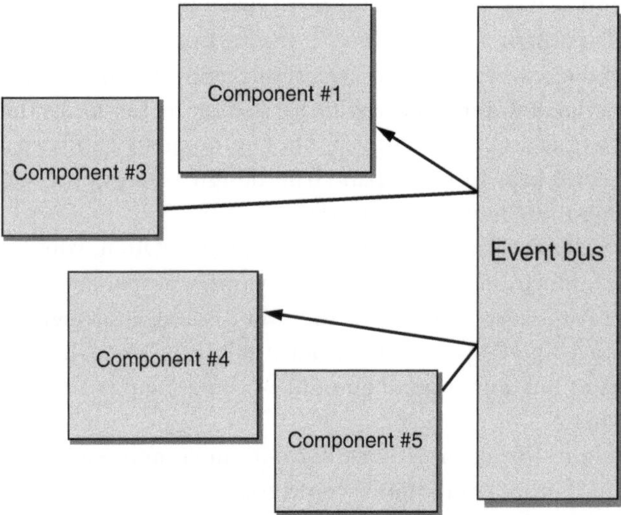

Figure 1.9 If normal event bubbling is not desirable, with a bit of code, you can create an event bus system to route events where you want.

There's also a middle ground with microframeworks. Microframeworks can be a great, minimalist way to organize your application and add specific functionality without getting too opinionated about it like a larger framework would. Worrying about finer details in your custom-built Web Components, while orchestrating your larger application with these smaller libraries, can be a nice way to go. Even minimalist solutions for data binding and routing can be found through NPM as well.

1.4 Your project, your choice

In the end, even though there's a great case to be made for no-framework Web Components, your project and your team will ultimately influence what you use to create for the web. Like any emerging standard, Web Components don't offer all the answers just yet. Then again, no popular framework does.

There will be cases where your web application is extremely straightforward, and a modern framework might be the perfect answer because it handles everything you need to do. Other times, you might be working on the type of project in which frameworks just get in the way. The solutions you can choose from cover a wide spectrum of options, with some of those options overlapping.

Even if no-framework Web Components aren't the right answer for you, your favorite framework will likely be built with them one day, although it may not be apparent. Getting acquainted with the web standards-based underpinnings of any framework is always a great idea, even if you don't use them directly.

Despite the somewhat confusing half-start of Web Components a few years back, we're at a place right now where they are a real option for making your next project. I'm sure we'll see new ideas and methods for your Web Component workflow in the years to come, but these new ideas will be based on the standards I'll cover in this book, along with the latest and emerging current workflows. We'll cover Web Components on an atomic level, all the way up to applications built with many components, as well as how to manage your HTML/CSS, organize your projects, and more. I hope you're as excited as I am about the future of the web!

Summary

In this chapter, you learned

- How Web Components have evolved in the past few years from a Google-owned working draft to a real web standard adopted by all the modern browsers
- About the Shadow DOM as an optional yet important feature, while being on the verge of widespread browser adoption
- Web Components' place in modern frameworks, as well as an agnostic part of any ecosystem
- The potential future of Web Components, with an ever-expanding community of JS modules in the spirit of Polymer Project libraries like lit-html and lit-element, as well as non-Polymer Project ones like hyperHTML
- About the individual Web Component versus an entire Web Component application

2 Your first Web Component

This chapter covers

- The basis for almost every element you use: `HTMLElement`
- Extending classes to make your own custom elements
- Giving your custom elements logic and interactivity
- Using custom elements after defining them with `customElements.define`

As I promised in the beginning of this book, we're going to start small. Luckily, with Web Components, even when we do start small, we can still make something meaningful. After this chapter, you'll have the know-how to make your first Web Component and be able to view it right in your browser! Subsequent chapters through this book will explore key concepts in more detail, but the basics start here. At the end of this chapter, we'll discuss options when your browser doesn't support custom elements, as in the case of the latest consumer Edge release (at the time of writing) or IE. For now, though, please use Chrome, Firefox, or Safari if you'd like to follow along with the code examples.

2.1 Intro to HTMLElement

Prior to learning the basics of Web Components, I didn't really know what an `HTMLElement` was. You might not either—it's an easy thing to never come across, because while it's a core concept in how the DOM works, we've typically never worked with it directly until now.

This is because when you add an element to your page, it just works. You don't necessarily need to know how an `<input>` tag is related to a `<button>` or how a `<div>` is related to an `<img>`.

To explain, we'll have to get a bit into the concept of inheritance. It's a popular concept in object-oriented programming, and one we'll run with later in the book as we explore code reusability, but to quickly explain, let me start with an example.

2.1.1 Crash course in inheritance

> **NOTE** If you are already familiar with inheritance in object-oriented programming, please skip to section 2.1.2 to explore inheritance in relation to your favorite DOM element.

Pretend you're at a zoo. While you're there, you notice that all the animals have some specific things in common. *Animals* need to eat, breathe, sleep, and move around. Of course, some animals are different than others. *Mammals* have fur, have babies instead of laying eggs, and are warm blooded. Mammals have all the base characteristics of animals, but there are extra rules when you call something a mammal. You could even go further and consider mammals like tigers, lions, and panthers as types of *felines*. Felines also have some specific things in common, like whiskers, claws, and eating meat.

In object-oriented programming, we can say that a feline inherits from a mammal, and a mammal inherits from an animal. If you were writing code, you might start by defining an `Animal` object (or *class* to be more specific), as figure 2.1 shows. Your `Animal` might have functions that you can call to make it `breath()`, `sleep()`, and `eat()`.

Next, you might want to create a `Mammal` object. It would be tiresome and repetitive to write code for `breath()`, `sleep()`, and `eat()` again for the `Mammal` object. Because this is all similar to `Animal`, we can use inheritance; when creating that `Mammal` object, we say `Mammal` extends `Animal`. `Mammal` automatically gets all the functionality of `Animal`, but we can add more specific functionality, like `growFur()`. We can even create a `Feline` object that inherits from `Mammal`, and because `Mammal` inherits from `Animal`, `Feline` will have all the functionality of `Mammal` and `Animal`.

Inheritance is a core feature of object-oriented programming, typically used in other languages, and now JavaScript (JS), via classes. If you are not familiar with this newer JS feature, read up on it in the appendix, "ES2015 for Web Components."

2.1.2 Inheritance in your favorite elements

Our zoo inheritance example is a lot like `HTMLElement`. With a few exceptions, like SVG, any element that you put in your HTML/DOM is inherited from `HTMLElement`.

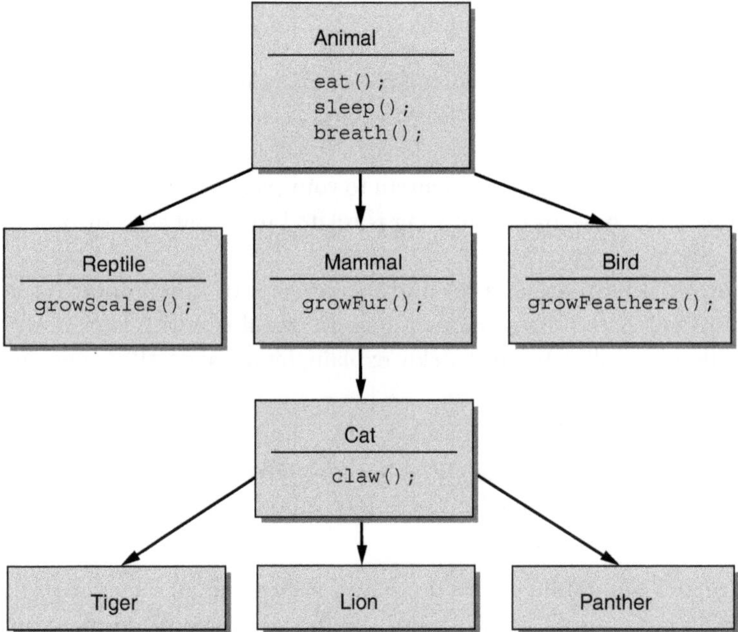

Figure 2.1 A not-so-scientific example of inheritance in the animal kingdom

While `HTMLElement` isn't the bottom rung of the inheritance chain as far as the browser is concerned (just like we can keep going with "Animal" to "Multicellular organism," to "Living thing," and so on), it serves as our starting point for Web Components.

To give some real examples of inheritance on actual elements, `<span>`, `<div>`, and `<button>` are created from `HTMLSpanElement`, `HTMLDivElement`, and `HTMLButtonElement`, respectively. In turn, all of these inherit from `HTMLElement`. In fact, you can see for yourself. Open up the browser console and type the following:

```
document.createElement('div').constructor
```

The console will return

```
ƒ HTMLDivElement() { [native code] }
```

What we're doing here is creating a new `<div>` element and asking it what the constructor is. The constructor is what's called first when you create an object like this. It's telling you that the constructor is the creator function on a specific class—in this case, `HTMLDivElement`.

Feel free to play around with your favorite elements! Button is another we can try:

```
document.createElement('button').constructor
```

which gives us

```
ƒ HTMLButtonElement() { [native code] }
```

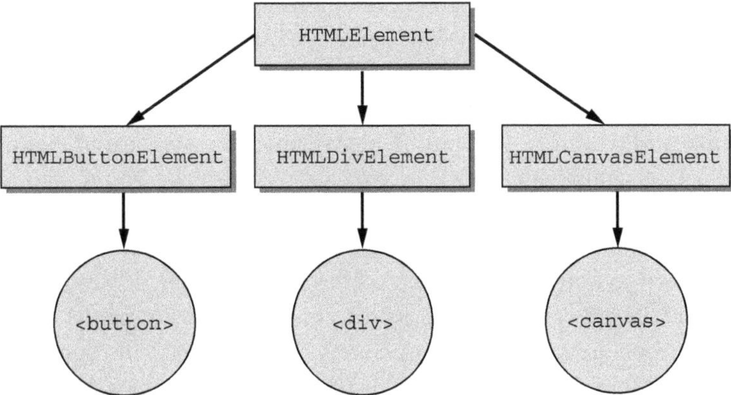

Figure 2.2 While there are a large number of classes that inherit from `HTMLElement`, here are three that produce common DOM elements that we use all the time, with the actual tags we write in our HTML.

As you can tell from our experiments and from figure 2.2, elements we use all the time are derived from a common source: `HTMLElement`.

2.2 Rules for naming your element

One interesting thing about HTML is that you can actually make up any name for a tag and drop it on your page, and it acts like a `<div>`.

Try it in your page:

```
<randomElement>Hi!</randomElement>
```

You'll see the text "Hi!", just like if you were using a `<div>`. Now, the question is, what are we inheriting from, here? Let's try it in our console:

```
document.createElement('randomElement').constructor;
```

We get back

```
f HTMLUnknownElement() { [native code] }
```

Were you expecting `HTMLUnknownElement`? Probably not! We just created an invalid element. Because it's invalid, it inherits from a special `Unknown` class, and we can't extend its functionality.

Why is it invalid? It's not because we can't invent our own element names when we create our own components; it's because there's a naming convention to follow. This naming convention is a simple hard requirement for the custom element specification, and that is to use a dash (`-`) in your element name. Under the hood, it allows the browser to differentiate between custom and native elements. It makes sense when you think about it.

Not only will readers like you be creating their own custom components, but browsers themselves will likely come out with new elements as well. A common use of

Web Components will likely be tiny pieces of common UI. If something useful, like a progress bar, was created not only by you, but also by other Web Component developers, *and* made it into browsers as a native feature, you can imagine how much of a mess it would be if everyone created something named `<progressbar>`.

Again, simply add a dash (`-`) in your element name. If your desired element name is `<progressbar>`, try again with a dash: `<progress-bar>`. Ideally, you'd want to give it a *namespace.* A namespace is used to indicate some sort of group that your component belongs to. For example, in Google's Polymer Elements Collection, any UI component built with the design system Material has a namespace of `paper`. If you go to Google's Web Component GitHub repo (https://github.com/PolymerElements), you can find `paper-tooltip`, `paper-dropdown-menu`, and `paper-toggle-button` (figure 2.3). Some of these have two dashes, and that's perfectly OK. You need one or more to be valid. The important takeaway here is that Google defines a namespace to indicate a set of related components, and then names the specific component after the dash. You certainly aren't required to follow the same logic—you just need that dash.

Let's revisit our `randomElement`, but name it with a dash this time to follow proper conventions:

```
document.createElement('random-element').constructor;
```

Good news! This prints the following in our console:

```
ƒ HTMLElement() { [native code] }
```

Element	Description	Stars	Forks
paper-badge	Material Design status descriptors for elements	34	22
paper-button	A button à la Material Design	116	64
paper-card	A Material Design piece of paper with unique related data	90	64
paper-dropdown-menu	A Material Design browser select element	64	113
paper-icon-button	A Material Design icon button	45	42

Figure 2.3 A small sampling of Google's `paper` elements. Note that these related UI Web Components have the prefix `paper`. Google also uses the prefix `iron` for core elements and `neon` for animation-related elements.

2.3 Defining your custom element (and handling collisions)

It's one thing, of course, to invent a name for a tag and create it versus actually giving the tag logic and definition before creating it. It would be fairly useless to create your own tag without giving it some custom behavior. We'll need to go beyond `HTMLElement` and override it with our own logic.

Thankfully, it's easy to do just that! This brings us to, in my opinion, the biggest and most useful piece of the Web Components API. With one simple line of JS and using an empty class that extends `HTMLElement`, we can take our desired element name and give it meaning:

```
customElements.define('my-custom-tag', class extends HTMLElement {});
```

There is a catch, though—and it's one that won't really affect you until you get into more complex things. All the same, it's good to bring this up now: `customElements.define` will throw an error if you've already defined a tag. This will definitely come up later when we use a newer JS feature called `import`, where we include our element anywhere we need to reference something in it.

For now, we can mimic this bad behavior by calling `customElements.define` twice in a row:

```
customElements.define('my-custom-tag', class extends HTMLElement {});
customElements.define('my-custom-tag', class extends HTMLElement {});
```

We get the following error:

```
Failed to execute 'define' on 'CustomElementRegistry': this name has already
    been used with this registry
```

Thankfully, this is easy enough to handle. We can determine if our custom element has already been defined by asking if `customElements.get('my-custom-tag')` returns something. By wrapping it in an `if/then` statement, we ensure that our element is defined only when we first call it:

```
if (!customElements.get('my-custom-tag')) {
   customElements.define('my-custom-tag', class extends HTMLElement {});
}
```

Now, extending `HTMLElement` to define a custom element is super powerful, but don't go too crazy yet. You might think that extending `HTMLDivElement` or `HTMLButtonElement` would work too. It could be nice to build off of a button for features it already has, like being able to disable it or working with forms easily. Unfortunately, this isn't possible yet in all browsers. While the `customElement` specification says this is OK, Safari has not yet implemented this functionality, and therefore it's best to approach extending other elements cautiously, or not at all. `HTMLElement` is the only native element definition we're currently allowed to extend and create custom elements from everywhere. Anything else will look like it works, but when you actually use your element, you'll get an error:

```
Uncaught TypeError: Illegal constructor: autonomous custom elements must
     extend HTMLElement
```

Note the "must extend" part of the error as well. Even passing `HTMLElement` without extending it into `customElements.define`, as in `customElements.define('my-element', HTMLElement)`, will result in this behavior when you use your new element.

2.4 Extending HTMLElement to create custom component logic

The easiest way to write your custom component, as you've just seen, is to use a newer JS feature called a *class*. JS classes provide a great and readable way to express how our custom element works and also how it inherits from an `HTMLElement`.

Let's start with a very much empty class, which inherits from `HTMLElement`. To make something simple that will get more useful as we progress throughout the book, we'll start with a slider. A slider is simple to use and make. When finished, it will allow a user to drag a thumbnail over a track to select a value:

```
class Slider extends HTMLElement {}
```

In thinking about an element name, `slider` is the most obvious choice, but we do need a namespace! Because this book is called *Web Components in Action*, and the slider should be a general UI component that can be used anywhere, lets brand our slider a `wcia-slider`. Now, with your new element definition seen juxtaposed against other common elements in figure 2.4, you can create something custom:

```
customElements.define('wcia-slider', Slider);
```

Of course, there is no custom logic because our element is based off an empty class. For now, it will act just like `HTMLElement` does, but we can fix this using the `connectedCallback` method in this class. This `connectedCallback` method is the first

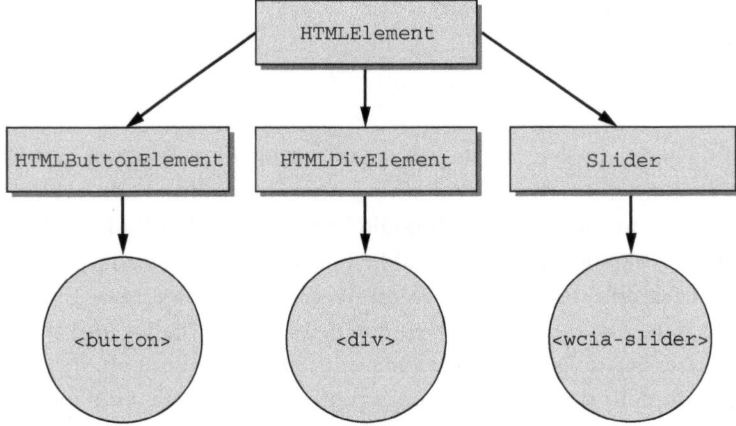

Figure 2.4 Our `HTMLElement` inheritance diagram modified to include your own custom elements at the same level as the native ones

of several lifecycle methods offered by the Custom Element API and fired when the component is added to the DOM.

Let's modify our class in the following listing to give some indication that we have an effect on it. Here's a snippet we can include on our page to define our element.

Listing 2.1 Giving our custom tag some custom logic

```
<script>
    class Slider extends HTMLElement {
        connectedCallback() {
            alert('hi from Slider');
        }
    }
    if (!customElements.get('wcia-slider')) {
       customElements.define('wcia-slider', Slider);
    }
</script>
```

An alert to signal us that the component is on the page and running

To see this in action, simply drop your custom tag in the body of your HTML:

```
<body>
    <wcia-slider></wcia-slider>
</body>
```

When you try this out, you actually won't see anything visible on your page except for the alert dialog that pops up. Now that we've verified that we can inject logic into our new Web Component, let's build up our Web Component to be something a bit more visible.

To do this, I should mention scope and how it can work for us in our Web Component. It can be easy to lose track of what scope `this` is referring to in a typical JS context. With Web Components and classes, we can use `this` in some dead simple and easy to read ways. With a few notable exceptions, like callback events and timers, `this` in your component will refer to the element itself. This includes custom methods and properties you introduce on the element, but also any methods or properties that the element already has. To put it another way, any method or property you might use from an ordinary, noncustom element can be used in this scope and referenced by `this`. The keyword `this` is the scope of our new custom element.

Examples for what you can call from `this` inside your custom element class include everything inherited from `HTMLElement`, like getting the element's CSS with `this.style`, getting the element's height with `this.offsetHeight`, or adding an event listener when the user clicks on your component with `this.addEventListener ('click', callback)`.

To give our element some content—specifically, a background and a thumbnail—let's start with the `innerHTML` property. Again, `innerHTML` can be used on any element and serves to set the HTML content inside the element. We can use it similarly here:

```
this.innerHTML = '<div class="bg-overlay"></div><div class="thumb"></div>';
```

While it's not incredibly readable to just throw HTML in a string like this in one line, for our purposes, to demo something small, let's run with it. We'll definitely improve on this later in the book.

Let's also add some style to the slider component. When styling and defining how a component works, it's important to think about how it will be used and why we're creating it. Given that we already have a slider natively provided by the browser, as figure 2.5 shows, and created with an `<input type="range">` element, ours should serve a slightly different purpose.

Figure 2.5 The native slider provided by the `input` element

Our slider will function the same way, with a draggable thumb over a track. However, we'll make our track much bigger. In fact, it'll be more of a background than a track. The reason for the bigger track is so we can visualize what a user would slide through better. This slider will be used to change the transparency of a specific color. Figure 2.6 shows the transparency slider we'll create.

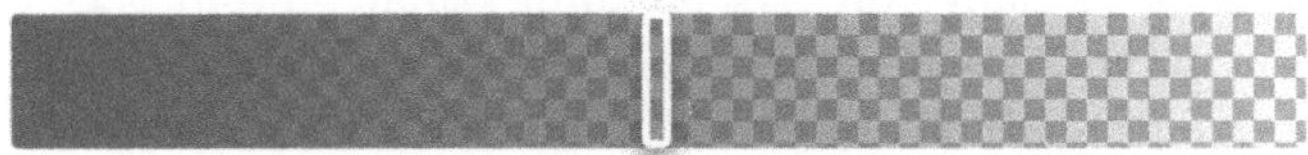

Figure 2.6 Our new transparency slider component

With this particular look for the slider decided, we can start adding some style! As mentioned previously, `this` can be used as the scope for our component, which we can then tap into the `style` property, just like any other element:

```
this.style.display = 'inline-block';
this.style.position = 'relative';
this.style.width = '500px';
this.style.height = '50px';
```

In addition to accessing the `style` property on the component's scope, we can use another `HTMLElement` property: `querySelector`. Normally, we might use `querySelector` on our `document` to find a child element inside. For example, if we needed to find an element with a class of `myelement` on the page somewhere, we might do the following:

```
let myElement = document.querySelector('.myelement');
```

The `querySelector` function doesn't have to search as wide as `document`. Instead, it can be scoped to any normal element to query-select its children. Given that our component is a normal element, we can query-select its children and apply some style to them as well. The following listing shows how we can reach into the Web Component using the scope of `this` to change style on the component's children.

Listing 2.2 Query-selecting inner components and setting their style

```
this.querySelector('.bg-overlay').style.width = '100%';
this.querySelector('.bg-overlay').style.height = '100%';
this.querySelector('.bg-overlay').style.position = 'absolute';
this.querySelector('.bg-overlay').style.backgroundColor = 'red';

this.querySelector('.thumb').style.marginLeft =
  '100px';
this.querySelector('.thumb').style.width = '5px';
this.querySelector('.thumb').style.height = 'calc(100% - 5px)';
this.querySelector('.thumb').style.position = 'absolute';
this.querySelector('.thumb').style.border = '3px solid white';
this.querySelector('.thumb').style.borderRadius = '3px';
```

Adding style to the background overlay element inside the component

Adding style to the thumbnail element inside the component

Putting it all together, we have what's shown in the following listing.

Listing 2.3 A complete but simple Web Component example

```
<html>
<head>
    <title>Slider</title>

    <script>
        class Slider extends HTMLElement {
            connectedCallback() {
                this.innerHTML =
                  '<div class="bg-overlay"></div><div class="thumb"></div>';

                this.style.display =
                 'inline-block';
                this.style.position = 'relative';
                this.style.width = '500px';
                this.style.height = '50px';

                this.querySelector('.bg-overlay').style.width = '100%';
                this.querySelector('.bg-overlay').style.height = '100%';
                this.querySelector('.bg-overlay').style.position = 'absolute';
                this.querySelector('.bg-overlay').style.backgroundColor = 'red';

                this.querySelector('.thumb').style.marginLeft = '100px';
                this.querySelector('.thumb').style.width = '5px';
                this.querySelector('.thumb').style.height = 'calc(100% - 5px)';
                this.querySelector('.thumb').style.position = 'absolute';
                this.querySelector('.thumb').style.border = '3px solid white';
                this.querySelector('.thumb').style.borderRadius = '3px';
            }
        }

        if (!customElements.get('wcia-slider')) {
            customElements.define('wcia-slider', Slider);
        }

    </script>
```

Setting the HTML contents of our Web Component

Setting the overall style of our Web Component

```
</head>
<body>
    <wcia-slider></wcia-slider>
</body>
</html>
```

Of course, now instead of simply having an alert, we can see our component in place on the page with some proper content!

2.5 Using your custom element in practice

At this point, if you're following along, you have your own custom element running on your page. In addition to the rule stating you need to have a dash contained in your custom tag, there *used to be* an additional rule concerning how to use the tag. Custom elements fell under the type of element that can't be expressed as a void or self-closing tag. In other words, the following variations of HTML wouldn't have worked until recently:

`<wcia-slider />` or `<wcia-slider>`

Now, however, in the latest browser versions, even these variations work. So, other than the dash requirement, your element can be used in all the ways other elements can be used. When you get into more complex components, you'll probably have click logic inside your component, but we can certainly wire a click event to our Web Component, just as with any other element:

```
<wcia-slider onclick="alert('clicked')"></wcia-slider>
```

Attributes are also great to use, but, of course, there aren't many situations where they'd be helpful without logic in your component to use the attribute. Let's alter how our component renders with a couple different attributes: color and value. These attributes can be written inline on the component tag:

```
<wcia-slider backgroundcolor="#0000ff" value="180"></wcia-slider>
```

Then, we can change the color of the background element by trading the "red" color for the value of the attribute:

```
this.querySelector('.bg-overlay').style.backgroundColor =
    this.getAttribute('backgroundcolor');
```

Meanwhile, the value attribute can change the position of the slider thumb:

```
this.querySelector('.thumb').style.marginLeft = this.getAttribute('value') +
    'px';
```

With these small changes, we can now change the color and slider position to anything we want. Unfortunately, the component is a bit ugly, as figure 2.7 shows, and not exactly what I showed at the start.

You might have also noticed that I used JS to set style properties instead of what I should have used: CSS. As with any element, we can target our element and inner children with a `<style>` block and make things look like I originally promised.

Figure 2.7 Slider (now blue with the thumb further to the right) affected by value and color attributes

Some of the CSS we're using looks pretty complicated. For this reason, I removed the attributes for now—we'll revisit this in later chapters with actual code to get the component functional as something you'd really use.

We'll add a checkered pattern behind the component with some semi-crazy-looking CSS (background image, position, and size). To be honest, I didn't create it myself, either—I found it online! The rules for the linear gradient on the color and the box shadow on the thumb are also a bit lengthy, but these finer CSS details in the following listing can lead to some nicer looking UI details.

Listing 2.4 Trading inline styles for CSS

```
<html>
<head>
    <title>Slider</title>

    <script>
        class Slider extends HTMLElement {
            connectedCallback() {
                this.innerHTML =
                  '<div class="bg-overlay"></div><div class="thumb"></div>';
            }
        }

        if (!customElements.get('wcia-slider')) {
            customElements.define('wcia-slider', Slider);
        }

    </script>

    <style>                              <-- Adding some fairly complex
        wcia-slider {                        CSS to our component to get
            display: inline-block;           the style just right
            position: relative;
            border-radius: 3px;
            height: 50px;
            width: 500px;
            background-image: linear-gradient(45deg, #ccc 25%,
              transparent 25%),linear-gradient(-45deg, #ccc 25%,
              transparent 25%),linear-gradient(45deg, transparent 75%,
              #ccc 75%),linear-gradient(-45deg, transparent 75%, #ccc 75%);
            background-size: 16px 16px;
            background-position: 0 0, 0 8px, 8px -8px, -8px 0px;
        }

        .bg-overlay {
            width: 100%;
```

```
            height: 100%;
            position: absolute;
            border-radius: 3px;
            background: linear-gradient(to right, #ff0000 0%, #ff000000 100%);
        }

        .thumb {
            margin-top: -1px;
            left: 250px;
            width: 5px;
            height: calc(100% - 5px);
            position: absolute;
            border-style: solid;
            border-width: 3px;
            border-color: white;
            border-radius: 3px;
            pointer-events: none;
            box-shadow: 0 4px 8px 0 rgba(0, 0, 0, 0.2),
                        0 6px 20px 0 rgba(0, 0, 0, 0.19);
        }
    </style>
</head>
<body>
    <wcia-slider></wcia-slider>
</body>
</html>
```

In this case, we can easily set all of the style right in our CSS. You might notice that we're getting a bit disorganized just placing script and style blocks in our HTML. Don't worry, we'll lock this down to be much cleaner as we explore more throughout this book. For now, even for a simple component, it's looking like a pretty stylized slider (figure 2.8) that could be great to dive deeper on later.

Figure 2.8 Styled slider using CSS

2.6 *Making a (useful) first component*

Let's face it, as much as we've learned so far about custom elements and creating some custom logic in your first component, it hasn't been a terribly useful component so far (for one, it doesn't slide). Don't worry! We'll build on the slider as we go along in this book, adding interactivity, exploring some standard practices, and allowing it to operate with other components.

For now, though, it's time to take what we've learned so far, as well as some of our prior web development knowledge, and create a simple Web Component that can be immediately useful and meaningful as a standalone component.

The first thing that comes to mind for a simple use case is something that web creators have needed for ages, has been made and remade countless times in jQuery, and is useful in all web contexts, from blogs to web applications. I'm talking about a photo or image carousel.

The idea here is to create a component that we can drop anywhere on a page, and that lets us specify an album title and author, and flip through an album of photos using forward and back buttons. To pull this off, I've chosen some photos from the popular image-hosting site imgur.com (copied to my GitHub repo so they don't disappear over time) as places I think would be fun to visit, and put them in an album. My "future vacation photos" component ended up looking like figure 2.9.

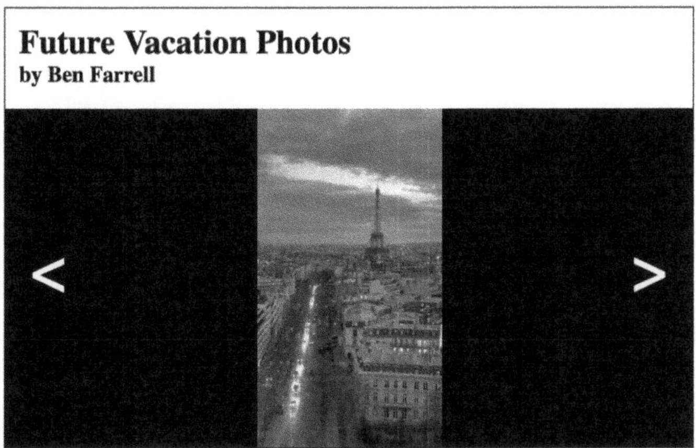

Figure 2.9 Result of the next demo, where we create a photo carousel

No doubt I could spend more time styling and creating graphics, especially for those forward and back buttons, but we're keeping it simple, here. Let's dive in and go step-by-step through creating this photo carousel.

2.6.1 *Setting up our web server*

There are simple things we can do without using a web server. Loading up a plain HTML file on your local filesystem in the browser of your choice gets you only so far. When you try to load assets, CSS, or JS files without a server, these files will be blocked. What to do?

Personally, I like using an integrated development environment (IDE) like JetBrains' WebStorm, which automatically creates a server for you when you load your HTML file through its UI. Many web developers live and die by a simple text editor and HTTP server. Because this is the free option, let's do it! Node.js is a great choice, especially because we use it for so many other things in regard to frontend tooling. If you haven't installed Node.js yet, go to https://nodejs.org, download, and install it.

Once installed, we can use the Node.js package manager, NPM, to install modules of our choice. Usually with Node, you'll install modules for your project specifically. This time around, we're going to pass the `-g` flag to install an `http-server` module we can use from anywhere. Open up your command line terminal (it doesn't matter what directory you happen to be in), and type

```
npm install http-server -g
```

When finished, assuming no errors, you'll have a simple web server you can run from anywhere on your machine. Now that you have the tooling installed, you can create a project folder wherever you like. I'm going to call mine "photocarousel" and create an empty folder for it on my desktop. Once the folder is created, I'm going to create a dummy HTML file named test.html to be sure that my server works and my file loads. In your favorite text editor, write the HTML in the following listing (again, just to create something you can look at in your browser).

Listing 2.5 A simple web page to test our server

```
<html>
    <head>
        <title>Photo Carousel Demo</title>
    </head>
    <body>
        <h3>Hi, from your webserver</h3>
    </body>
</html>
```

Now, in your terminal, navigate to the project folder you made and type

```
http-server
```

Since you have the `http-server` module installed globally, anywhere you issue this command from will start a web server. When successful, you'll see the following results:

```
Starting up http-server, serving ./
Available on:
  http://127.0.0.1:8080
  http://10.0.0.17:8080
Hit CTRL-C to stop the server
```

Now, in your browser (let's use Chrome or Safari), you can hit either one of these addresses, adding /test.html, and see your barebones HTML file in action.

Awesome! If you see something like figure 2.10, you now have a development environment!

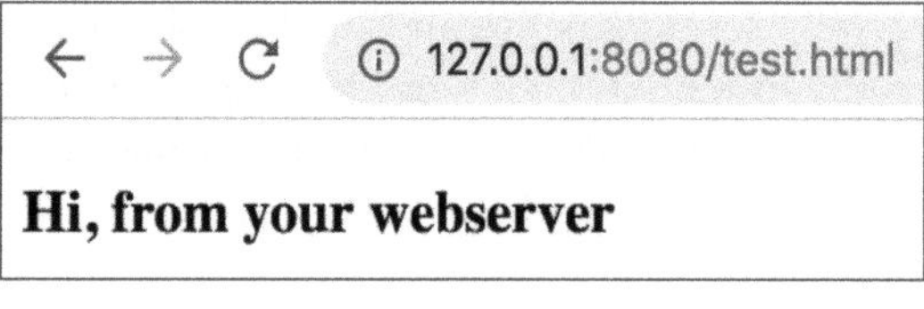

Figure 2.10 Running our simple HTML page from a web server

2.6.2 *Writing our HTML tag*

OK, so, we're going to write our custom photo carousel tag in the body of our HTML page. It won't actually work, but this will help us think about what features we want to implement when it comes down to the Web Component work.

I'm going to pick the namespace wcia, short for *Web Components in Action*, for this component. So, my tag name will be wcia-photo-carousel. I could just add that one tag to my body like this:

```
<body>
    <wcia-photo-carousel></wcia-photo-carousel>
</body>
```

We have the opportunity now to think about the different things we might want to change when it comes to our component from the outside. Personally, I think we'll want to give our carousel an album title to display above the photo, and also an author name for who created the photo album. Most important, though, are the actual photos we want displayed in our album. For this, we'll pass in a list of comma-separated URLs. This means our tag goes from looking like the previous empty one to what's shown in the following listing.

Listing 2.6 Our photo carousel component used on a web page

```
<body>
    <wcia-photo-carousel
            title="Future Vacation Photos"      <- Title attribute
            author="Ben Farrell"                <- Author attribute
            photos="images/fBmIASF.jpg,images/3zxD6rz.jpg,images/
            nKBgeLOr.jpg,images/yVjJZ1Yr.jpg"   <- Another attribute containing a comma-separated list of photos to show
    ></wcia-photo-carousel>
</body>
```

Now that we've thought about the inputs to our Web Component, we can start thinking about implementation.

2.6.3 *Creating our class*

Like I said earlier in this chapter, there are better ways to organize your code. For now, though, we'll just add a <script> tag to our HTML header to register our component and start our connectedCallback method.

Right after our <title> tag in our header, we can add the script block shown in the following listing.

Listing 2.7 Adding a script block with a class to define our component

```
<head>
    <title>Photo Carousel</title>

    <script>
        class PhotoCarousel extends HTMLElement {     <- Class to define our component
            connectedCallback() {
```

```
            }
        }
        if (!customElements.get(                    <-- Defining the tag for our
          'wcia-photo-carousel')) {                     component if it was not
            customElements.define('wcia-photo-carousel', PhotoCarousel);   already defined
        }
    </script>
</head>
```

Right here, we've created a class that extends `HTMLElement` called `PhotoCarousel`. We've created an empty `connectedCallback` method that we can fill out in a moment. Below our class definition, we are checking if our `wcia-photo-carousel` is already defined and, if not, defining it as a custom element.

2.6.4 *Adding content to our component*

We can now start thinking about what kinds of elements to put into our component to get the carousel we're after. Personally, I thought that a title and an author subtitle would make sense. Those can be header tags `<h2>` and `<h4>`, respectively. We'll also need two buttons—one for going to the next photo and one to go to the previous photo. Lastly, we'll need a `<div>` to contain our photos.

We'll talk about template literals later in the book, which will help us construct our HTML a better way, but for now, we'll just set the `innerHTML` property to a long string containing all those elements just mentioned. We'll do this when our component is added to the page, inside our `connectedCallback`, as the following listing shows.

Listing 2.8 Setting the HTML contents of our component

```
this.innerHTML = '<h2>'+ this.getAttribute('title') + '</h2>' +
    '<h4>by '+ this.getAttribute('author') + '</h4>' +
    '<div class="image-container"></div>' +
    '<button class="back">&lt</button>' +
    '<button class="forward">&gt</button>';
```

Note that we're using our `title` and `author` tag attributes here to display this custom information. As you can tell from figure 2.11, we're off to a good start.

You'll notice almost everything we added here—the title, the subtitle, the two buttons—just not the image container. This is because, while the image container has been added, there's nothing inside the container, and we haven't specified its size. So,

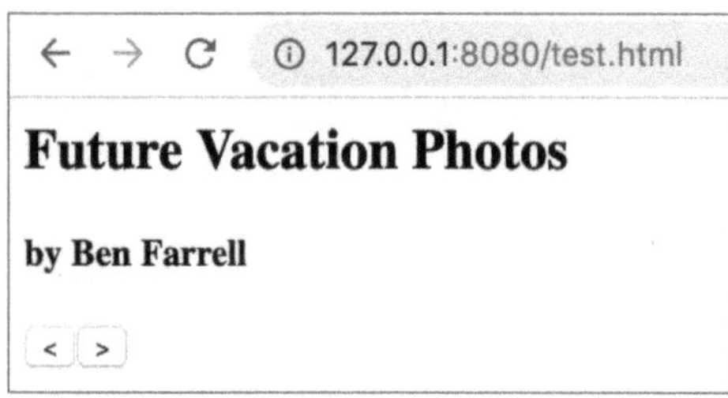

Figure 2.11 Our carousel component so far, with title, author, and forward/back buttons

although it's been added to the DOM, it just isn't visible. This is a good time to start styling our content.

2.6.5 Styling our component

Right after our `<script>` tag in the following listing, we'll add a style block.

Listing 2.9 Adding some CSS to style our component

```
. . .
</script>
<style>
    wcia-photo-carousel {                          <-- Styling the overall component
        width: 500px;
        height: 300px;
        display: flex;
        padding-top: 10px;
        flex-direction: column;
        border-color: black;
        border-width: 1px;
        border-style: solid;
    }

    wcia-photo-carousel h2, h4 {                   <-- Styling the two headers (title and author)
        margin-bottom: 0;
        margin-top: 0;
        margin-left: 10px;
    }

    wcia-photo-carousel .image-container {         <-- Styling the div element that contains our images
        margin-top: 15px;
        flex: 1;
        background-color: black;
    }
</style>
```

First, we set the overall style of our photo carousel component container. I decided, arbitrarily, that it will be 500 pixels by 300 pixels. You can change this to whatever you like. I also want some easy-to-use layout, so I used CSS Flexbox with a column direction to lay my elements out vertically. I also put a border around my component, as well as a padding on the top to give the header some breathing room.

Next, I reset the margins on my headers `h2` and `h4`. Headers usually have some pretty big spacing on the top and bottom, and I don't want that here. I also shifted my headers 10 pixels to the left, so they don't butt up against the left side of my component.

Last, I set the image container's `<div>` top margin to 15 pixels to give some vertical breathing room from the headers and gave it a black background. Setting `flex` to 1 here means that this image container will take up whatever remaining space I give it around the elements that already have height, like my buttons and headers.

Now things are starting to take form! Our limited styling gives us something that looks like figure 2.12.

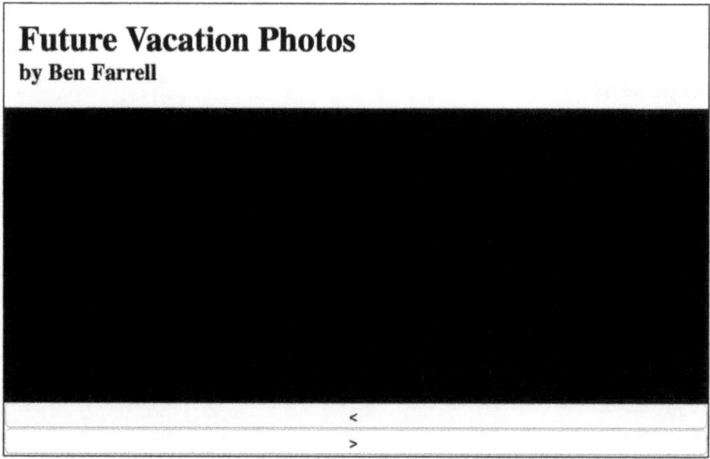

Figure 2.12 Progress so far after adding CSS to style

There's enough layout here that we can focus on some component logic now.

2.6.6 Component logic

Thinking about what to do next, you might remember that we haven't used the list of image URLs yet that we have on our tag in the body of our page. We also don't have some sort of counter that starts at 0 and increments and decrements with our buttons to use as the index of which photo we are on.

Let's start there. In our `connectedCallback`, prior to setting the `innerHTML` as we've done, let's add the following:

```
connectedCallback() {
    this._photoIndex = 0;
    this._photos = this.getAttribute('photos').split(',');
    this.innerHTML = '<h2>'+ this.getAttribute('title') + '</h2>' + . . .
```

Here, we're grabbing our photo list and turning it into an array using the commas as delimiters. Along with the index of which photo we are on, this array of photos is set to internal properties on the "instance" of our class. The scope within each method on our class can be accessed with `this`.

Let's also create a method to show our photo in the following listing, as well as calling it after we've set our `innerHTML`.

Listing 2.10 Adding a showPhoto method

```
connectedCallback() {
    this._photoIndex = 0;
    this._photos = this.getAttribute('photos').split(',');

    this.innerHTML = '<h2>'+ this.getAttribute('title') + '</h2>' +
        '<h4>by '+ this.getAttribute('author') + '</h4>' +
```

```
        '<div class="image-container"></div>' +
        '<button class="back">&lt</button>' +
        '<button class="forward">&gt</button>';
                                                        Call showPhoto as soon
    this.showPhoto();     <-                            as the component starts.
}
                                    The showPhoto method, which sets the
showPhoto() {       <-              background image of a div element
    this.querySelector('.image-container').style.backgroundImage =
       'url(' + this._photos[this._photoIndex] + ')';
}
```

Our `showPhoto` method finds the image container by query-selecting anything with a class of `image-container`, but only within the scope of our component, because we are using `this.querySelector` instead of `document.querySelector`, which you might normally use. It then sets the background image to our current photo. To see this in action, be sure to have an images folder with the images named the way you have specified in the initial `photos` attribute on the component. This book's GitHub repo has this folder already set up for your convenience.

There is a problem, though. While this technically works and shows the correct photo, my photos are too big! All I see is a blue sky, and the rest is off the component's canvas and unseen. In the following listing, let's add a couple more style properties to our image container.

Listing 2.11 Adding CSS to allow the current image to display correctly

```
wcia-photo-carousel .image-container {
    margin-top: 15px;
    flex: 1;                                    Makes our image fit inside
    background-color: black;                    the containing element
    background-size: contain;       <-
    background-repeat: no-repeat;   <-          Don't repeat the image
    background-position: 50%;   <-              and fill the container.
}
                                  Centers the image
```

Let's dig into those three CSS rules we just added. The `background-size: contain;` means that we are setting the size to be whatever allows the image to fit inside the container we give it, making sure we show the entire photo. Specifying `no-repeat` for the `background-repeat` will override the behavior of duplicating the image over and over. Usually, with the default action of repeating, it fills any space left over because the image isn't exactly the same size as the container we give it (unless we're lucky). Here, a `no-repeat` disables that space-filling behavior. Lastly, that 50% for the position means that we're centering the image both vertically and horizontally in our image container. With this done, we can see the first photo in the album, nicely sized and centered as figure 2.13 shows.

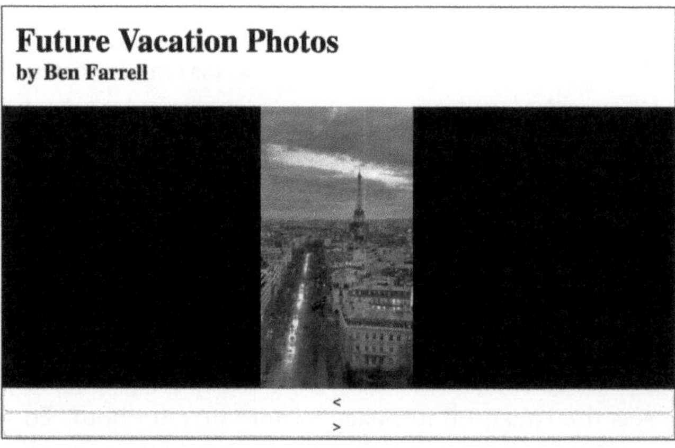

Figure 2.13 Progress so far to include showing the current image

2.6.7 *Adding interactivity*

I think that the obvious next step is to get our buttons working to show the next or previous photo. We'll begin by adding two lines to the end of our `connectedCallback` in the following listing.

Listing 2.12 Adding click listeners to our buttons

```
. . .'<button class="back">&lt</button>' +
      '<button class="forward">&gt</button>';

this.showPhoto();

this.querySelector('button.back').addEventListener('click', event =>
      this.onBackButtonClick(event));

this.querySelector('button.forward').addEventListener('click', event =>
      this.onForwardButtonClick(event));
}
```

Listens to clicks on the previous/back button

Listens to clicks on the next/forward button

With these lines, we are finding the back button and forward button and adding an event listener to them, such that when clicked, they will call the `onBack` or `onForwardButtonClick` methods.

You might notice the fat arrow: =>. Don't worry if you've never seen it. It's a newer JS feature and covered in the appendix. Typically, you might do the following:

```
this.querySelector('button.forward').addEventListener('click',
      this.onForwardButtonClick));
```

The fat arrow lets us keep the same scope as our class instance when the function is called. We can access properties and methods of the class instance (`this`) from the callback, shown in the following listing.

Listing 2.13 Handling our click event listeners

```
/**
 * handler for when user clicks the back button
 * @param event
 */
onBackButtonClick(event) {   <-- Handler for the back button
    this._photoIndex --;
    if (this._photoIndex < 0) {
        this._photoIndex = this._photos.length-1;   <-- If on the first image, loop around to the last
    }
    this.showPhoto();
}

/**
 * handler for when user clicks the forward button
 * @param event
 */
onForwardButtonClick(event) {   <-- Handler for the forward button
    this._photoIndex ++;
    if (this._photoIndex >= this._photos.length) {
        this._photoIndex = 0;   <-- If on the last image, loop around to the first
    }
    this.showPhoto();
}
```

These methods increment or decrement our photo's current index and then test if the index is out of the bounds of our array. If it is out-of-bounds, then we'll loop to the beginning or end of our array. Finally, we call our previous method to show the current photo given our new `this._photoIndex`.

Even though the look of our component hasn't changed, we can now click those buttons to advance or move back through our photo album!

2.6.8 Finishing touches

Done? Not quite. I'm not happy with the forward and back buttons yet. Let's put them on the sides to make our Web Component look like a real carousel.

First, let's add some more styles in the following listing, this time targeting our buttons.

Listing 2.14 Adding button styles

```
wcia-photo-carousel button {   <-- Common CSS for both buttons (buttons won't be visible just yet)
    cursor: pointer;
    background: transparent;
    border: none;
    font-size: 48px;
    color: white;
    position: absolute;
    top: 50%;
}

wcia-photo-carousel button.back {   <-- Style for the back button
```

```
    left: 10px;
}

wcia-photo-carousel button.forward {    <-- Style for the forward button
    right: 10px;
}
```

Back or forward, we want our buttons to display the pointer cursor when we hover over them. We also want to get rid of the default browser button look, so we'll remove the background and border from our buttons. Next, we'll make the font size really big and make the text white. Lastly, we'll allow the buttons to break free of the flex column and appear over the image by setting `position: absolute;`. We'll also center them vertically by setting the `top` value to 50%. For each button specifically, we'll inset it from the left or right by 10 pixels.

If you were to look at your progress now, you probably wouldn't even see your buttons anymore! That's because, if you're like me, your browser window is open fairly big, and your `position: absolute;` buttons are centered on the whole page itself instead of the component. Because they are white buttons against a white page, you won't see them. We need to add one more CSS property to position the buttons relative to the component rather than the page:

```
<style>
    wcia-photo-carousel {
        position: relative;
```

Here, we are setting the position of our entire component to `relative`. It doesn't do anything to our component, but any element inside with a position of `absolute` is now relative to the component instead of the page.

Just in case you missed a step here or there, our entire demo code can be seen in the following listing.

Listing 2.15 Demo code recap

```
<html>
<head>
    <title>Photo Carousel</title>

    <script>
        class PhotoCarousel extends HTMLElement {    <-- Class that defines our component
            connectedCallback() {
                this._photoIndex = 0;
                this._photos = this.getAttribute('photos').split(',');

                this.innerHTML = '<h2>'+ this.getAttribute('title') + '</h2>' +
                    '<h4>by '+ this.getAttribute('author') + '</h4>' +
                    '<div class="image-container"></div>' +
                    '<button class="back">&lt</button>' +
                    '<button class="forward">    <-- Component's HTML content
                      &gt
                    </button>';

                this.showPhoto();
```

```
            this.querySelector('button.back').addEventListener('click',
               event => this.onBackButtonClick(event));

            this.querySelector('button.forward').addEventListener('click',
               event =>
            this.onForwardButtonClick(event));
        }

        /**
         * handler for when user clicks the back button
         * @param event
         */
        onBackButtonClick(event) {
            this._photoIndex --;
            if (this._photoIndex < 0) {
                this._photoIndex = this._photos.length-1;
            }
            this.showPhoto();
        }

        /**
         * handler for when user clicks the forward button
         * @param event
         */
        onForwardButtonClick(event) {
            this._photoIndex ++;
            if (this._photoIndex >= this._photos.length) {
                this._photoIndex = 0;
            }
            this.showPhoto();
        }

        showPhoto() {
            this.querySelector('.image-container').style.backgroundImage
              = 'url(' + this._photos[this._photoIndex] + ')';
        }
    }

    if (!customElements.get(
      'wcia-photo-carousel')) {
        customElements.define('wcia-photo-carousel', PhotoCarousel);
    }

</script>

<style>
    wcia-photo-carousel {
        position: relative;
        width: 500px;
        height: 300px;
        display: flex;
        padding-top: 10px;
        flex-direction: column;
        border-color: black;
        border-width: 1px;
        border-style: solid;
    }
```

Button click event listeners

Back button click handler

Forward button click handler

Shows the current photo by setting the background image of the container element

Assigns the component class to a tag

Component styling with CSS

```
        wcia-photo-carousel h2, h4 {
            margin-bottom: 0;
            margin-top: 0;
            margin-left: 10px;
        }

        wcia-photo-carousel .image-container {
            margin-top: 15px;
            flex: 1;
            background-color: black;
            background-size: contain;
            background-repeat: no-repeat;
            background-position: 50%;
        }

        wcia-photo-carousel button {
            cursor: pointer;
            background: transparent;
            border: none;
            font-size: 48px;
            color: white;
            position: absolute;
            top: 50%;
        }

        wcia-photo-carousel button.back {
            left: 10px;
        }

        wcia-photo-carousel button.forward {
            right: 10px;
        }
    </style>
</head>
    <body>
        <wcia-photo-carousel    <-- Photo carousel component on our HTML page
                title="Future Vacation Photos"
                author="Ben Farrell"
                photos="images/fBmIASF.jpg,images/3zxD6rz.jpg,images/
                nKBgeLOr.jpg,images/yVjJZ1Yr.jpg">
        </wcia-photo-carousel>
    </body>
</html>
```

We'll now turn to figure 2.14 to see our component's final look.

2.6.9 Improving the carousel

Despite creating a fairly useful first Web Component, there are lots of ways we can improve. Most importantly, we need to package up our carousel as a standalone Web Component. As it stands right now, using it in a larger project would be a bit of a mess with the HTML, CSS, and JS embedded right in the main HTML. In chapter 5, we'll detail how to package it all up as a single JS module.

Figure 2.14 The finished photo carousel component

Second, it would be fantastic to make our component customizable. We could turn on and off features with an API or attributes in addition to our images list. We'll cover those in chapter 3.

Lastly, there are much better ways to organize our HTML and CSS for inclusion in the component, and even protect them from unintended style creep and DOM changes. Template literals and the Shadow DOM will be covered later in the book.

2.7 Notes on browser support

I mentioned at the start of this chapter that we're excluding some browsers. This is because even though custom elements are supported in Chrome, Firefox, and Safari, Edge development is still in progress. However, you can use the developer preview. I'm hopeful we'll see a final Edge release soon, which would cover all the major browsers.

This just leaves IE without custom element support. Luckily, we have polyfills for this! One such polyfill can be downloaded here: https://unpkg.com/@webcomponents/custom-elements@1.2.4/custom-elements.min.js.

Alternately, if you have Node.js and can use NPM, you can use the following:

```
npm install @webcomponents/custom-elements
```

Whichever method you choose, once you have the polyfill, simply include the script on your page:

```
<script src="path/to/custom-elements.min.js"></script>
```

In addition to the custom element specification, IE doesn't support newer JS language features like classes. Don't worry, this is all easily solvable, but we won't get into it until we talk about build processes later in this book. To be exact, I'll show you a way to transpile your ES2015/ES6 JS to ES5 JS for support in older browsers, or just those that don't support it yet.

Using Custom Elements v1

In this chapter and throughout the book, we'll be using the Custom Elements v1 specification. Don't worry, this is the latest and greatest, and I doubt the basics will change for years to come. I mention this because v1 is fairly recent, and searching for info about Web Components might tell you that to create a custom element, you'd use

```
document.registerElement('my-custom-tag', MyCustomTag);
```

Just know that Web Components, in general, have gone through a recent change and are now more solidified in their v1 specification. For more details on this point, and specifically what's changed, refer to chapter 4, which details the component lifecycle.

Summary

In this chapter, you learned

- How tags we use every day in basic web development are derived from `HTMLElement` (even if we never knew it!)
- Rules for naming and using your custom element on the page (which are required), as well as standard practices (which you aren't required to follow) for naming your element with a namespace
- A small taste of the Web Components API with `connectedCallback`
- Adding onto, or customizing, `HTMLElement` by using a common object-oriented programming technique called *inheritance* and creating some samples that use our new custom element

3 Making your component reusable

This chapter covers

- Using getters and setters to work with data in your component
- Using `attributeChangedCallback` to listen for attribute changes
- Identifying which attributes to listen for changes on using `observedAttributes`
- Working with attributes using `hasAttribute()`, `getAttribute()`, and `setAttribute()`

In the last chapter, we talked in great depth about simple ways to create your first Web Component. Specifically, we looked at creating your own custom element and assigning some minimal custom logic so your component acts a certain way. But what if you want your component to act differently depending on what parameters you use to set it up? What if you want your component to be adaptable? Usually, the goal in any platform, language, or framework is to create reusable code that can be simply configured to match the widest range of use cases.

Of course, saying we want to create reusable and configurable Web Components is one thing. It's almost meaningless unless we can talk about a concrete example!

3.1 A real-world component

One of my recent interests is 3D on the web. I'm especially interested in how virtual reality (VR) and augmented reality (AR) are making their way into browsers. Delving into WebGL and Three.js or Babylon is a bit too much to get into here (and off-subject), but we can do something simple to demonstrate reusable and configurable components.

3.1.1 A 3D search use case

3D has a bit of a content problem. I love experimenting with the 3D web, but I'm definitely not an expert in creating assets with complex 3D software. My favorite thing in VR lately is the explosion of 3D painting and modeling tools. Notably, Google has been doing some awesome things with Blocks and TiltBrush, its VR tools for modeling and painting in 3D. Even better, Google has created a hub that creators can publish to called Poly.

When you go to poly.google.com, you can browse around, search for 3D models, and pick your favorite to use in your application (many are free to use and modify). What's great for our purposes is that Poly has a REST-based API that we can tap into and use to make a 3D search Web Component of our own! Again, going all in on 3D is a little much, especially for a Web Components book—but the results we get back are all image thumbnails, so we don't have to get complicated at all in order to search and browse.

As with many services like Poly, we'll need to get an API key for access. If you'd rather not do this, you're still welcome to follow along, as I'll provide a JSON file you can use in its place, and you can run the example from your own server.

First things first. Head over to https://developers.google.com/poly/develop/web and follow the instructions for the API key. Once you have it, put it in a safe place for later.

3.1.2 Starting with an HTTP request

Let's now test the service and create an HTTP request in the following listing (in which we search for a parrot).

Listing 3.1 Creating an HTTP request to Google's Poly service

```
const url =
     'https://poly.googleapis.com/v1/assets?keywords=parrot&format=OBJ&key=
           <your_api_key>';                          <-- The Poly search API (insert your own API key)
const request = new XMLHttpRequest();                <-- Creates a new HTTP request
request.open( 'GET', url, true );
request.addEventListener( 'load', (event) => {
   console.log(JSON.parse(                           <-- Callback where we log the API response
     event.target.response
```

```
    ));
});
request.send();
```

When running this, you should see all of the results that come back right in your dev tools console. It will also be nicely formatted, given that we turned the raw text of the response back into JSON, as it was intended to be: `JSON.parse(event.target.response)`.

When we look at the `console.log` output, we'll see a JSON object returned from the service. Of course, over time, these results will change, but I do see a lot of parrots in the results! Exactly what we specified in the keyword search. If we expand the `assets` object and look at the array of 3D assets returned in figure 3.1, we see that each asset has a thumbnail object, which we can expand to look at the thumbnail URL. This URL is what we're after!

There's certainly lots of other data that you could use, especially if you opened up the "formats" array to reveal actual 3D object links. For our purposes, we're just going to use and display those thumbnails.

```
▾assets: Array(20)
  ▸0: {name: "assets/fBXvsC6pe_V", displayName: "Penguin",…
  ▸1: {name: "assets/cnimalnLIEA", displayName: "Vines", a…
  ▾2:
     authorName: "Poly by Google"
     createTime: "2017-10-23T00:28:27.763221Z"
     description: "#tropical #bird #avian #flying"
     displayName: "Parrot"
    ▸formats: (2) [{…}, {…}]
     isCurated: true
     license: "CREATIVE_COMMONS_BY"
     name: "assets/dfNjMLt00pd"
    ▸presentationParams: {orientingRotation: {…}, colorSpac…
    ▸thumbnail: {relativePath: "dfNjMLt00pd.png", url: "htt…
     updateTime: "2019-05-06T09:57:19.143415Z"
     visibility: "PUBLIC"
    ▸__proto__: Object
  ▸3: {name: "assets/frVFwZAW6z3", displayName: "Macaw", a…
  ▸4: {name: "assets/35EeLqGHH1y", displayName: "Parrot", …
  ▸5: {name: "assets/7sfRRUS5F_v", displayName: "Scarlet m…
  ▸6: {name: "assets/dpl7B31PqWX", displayName: "Parrot", …
  ▸7: {name: "assets/fFVqukPnc62", displayName: "Toco Touc…
```

Figure 3.1 Our HTTP response from Google Poly featuring assets and asset details

3.1.3 Wrapping up our work in a custom component

Let's wrap the HTTP request we just made into a new Web Component that allows us to search for assets by keyword and display the results. We should keep it simple, though. There's no need to overburden each Web Component to do too much—I like to think that we can be extremely granular with every component, and for bigger pieces of functionality, we can combine two or more components. This is why we're going to keep the keyword/search input out of the component. Our Web Component will *only* display search results based on data we pass it from the input.

To make our HTTP request snippet into a Web Component, we can use what we've already learned about custom elements and the `connectedCallback` method of the Web Components API.

Listing 3.2 Creating a Web Component from our HTTP request

```
<html>
<head>
   <meta charset="UTF-8">
   <title>Google Poly Search</title>
   <script>
       class PolySearch extends HTMLElement {
           connectedCallback() {
               this.doSearch();     <-- Calls the search function when component is added
           }

           doSearch() {
               const url =
     'https://poly.googleapis.com/v1/assets?keywords=parrot&format=OBJ&key=
            <your_api_key>';
               const request = new XMLHttpRequest();
               request.open( 'GET', url, true );
               request.addEventListener( 'load', (event) => {
                   console.log(JSON.parse( event.target.response ));
               });
               request.send();     <-- HTTP request from last example
           }
       }

       customElements.define(
'poly-search', PolySearch);     <-- Defines our Poly search component
   </script>
</head>

<body>
<poly-search></poly-search>     <-- Uses the Poly search element on the page
</body>
</html>
```

Hopefully, there's nothing earth-shattering in this listing. I *did* separate out the actual HTTP request into a `doSearch()` method. For now, I call it on `connectedCallback` when the component is added to the DOM. Because I don't have a big project that involves many components in this one example, I chose a simple element name that

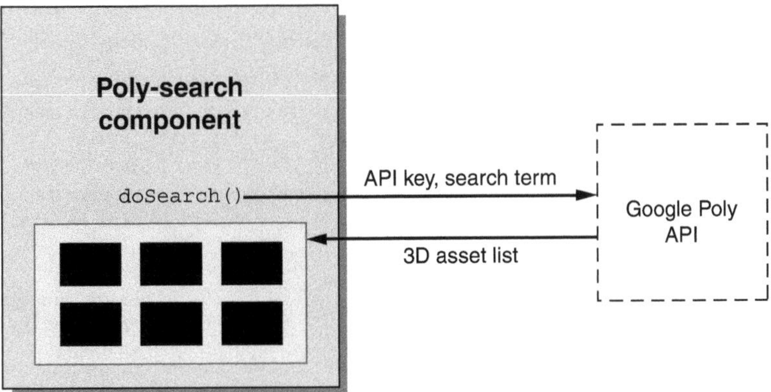

Figure 3.2 Our custom `poly-search` Web Component calling out to the Google Poly API with an API key and the search term "parrot." We'll get back a list of assets and thumbnails to display.

reflects the task I'm doing: `poly-search`. If I were doing multiple components for a large app, maybe I'd name it something like `<myappname-poly-search>`.

You might notice that our component only searches for parrots right now. I agree, this isn't incredibly useful. First, however, let's display our results. Figure 3.2 shows our component reaching out to the Google Poly API and returning an asset list, which our component then renders.

3.1.4 Rendering search results

We can start by swapping our `console.log(JSON.parse( event.target.response) );` with a call to another method that accepts all of the assets we requested:

```
this.renderResults(JSON.parse( event.target.response ).assets);
```

Then, inside our class, we'll add that render method to display all of the thumbnails on our page, as the following listing shows.

Listing 3.3 Render results of the HTTP request in our component

```
renderResults(assets) {
   let html = '';
   for (let c = 0; c < assets.length; c++) {
       html += '<img src="' + assets[c].thumbnail.url + '" width="200"
       height="150" />';
   }
   this.innerHTML = html;
}
```

- **The list of results is passed into our render function.**
- **Loops through the result list**
- **For each asset, adds a thumbnail image**
- **After the HTML string is built, adds it all to the component**

All we're doing here is looping through our asset array, grabbing the thumbnail URL, making it the source of an image element, and adding that to a long string of HTML. Once finished, we set this long HTML string to our component's `innerHTML`.

Of course, there are other ways to do this, rather than constructing strings. We could create a new image element with each loop.

Listing 3.4 Alternate way to render results

```
renderResults(assets) {
   for (let c = 0; c < assets.length; c++) {          <-- Loops through our asset results list the same way as before
      const img = document.createElement('img');      <-- Creates an image element each time, rather than using an HTML string
      img.src = assets[c].thumbnail.url;
      this.appendChild(img);                          <-- Appends each element to the DOM, one at a time
   }
}
```

I personally like the string approach for these cases better. You can create a big chunk of HTML and have it hit your DOM at the same time, rather than having one element per loop iteration. Also, HTML is a bit easier to read, especially when we get into template literals later on. A big downside to creating each element one by one in the loop is that with each one, you are causing the browser to re-parse and re-render that entire block. The same would happen if you were adding each image one at a time and setting `innerHTML` after each. It will likely be better to stick with an HTML string that gets built up over time and then set all at once to `innerHTML`.

3.1.5 *Styling our component*

If you run the example now, you'll see some fairly large images in a vertical list, as figure 3.3 shows. This is not what we necessarily want for a visual results display, so let's make the images smaller and place them in nice wrapping rows using some CSS, as in the following listing.

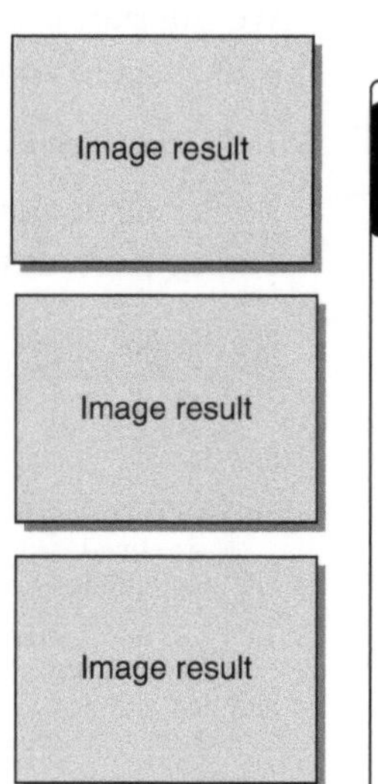

Figure 3.3 Our image results from poly.google.com before styling. They just flow down the page and force scrolling to see more than a few, because they are too large.

Listing 3.5 CSS to style our poly-search component

```
<style>
  poly-search {
      border-style: solid;          <-- Gives a nice subtle border around our entire element
      border-width: 1px;
      border-color: #9a9a9a;
      padding: 10px;                <-- A gap between the edges of our element and the inner results we are displaying
      background-color: #fafafa;    <-- A background color to pair with the border, separating the element from the page
      display: inline-block;        <-- Allows elements to flow horizontally and wrap to the next line when out of room
      text-align: center;
  }

  poly-search img {
      margin: 5px;                  <-- Spacing between images
  }
</style>
```

For this listing, I've simply put the style in our <head> tag, as you would normally do with CSS. Coupling style within the scope of each Web Component is definitely something we'll get to later on, but we'll just go simple right now.

Already, though, we are targeting our poly-search element with a CSS selector. This is perfectly valid! When you create your own custom element, you are really creating a custom element that works just like any other element would.

Running the example will give you the best picture of what this style is doing, but figure 3.4 is a visual approximation of what we accomplished, followed by some explanation of what we did with our CSS.

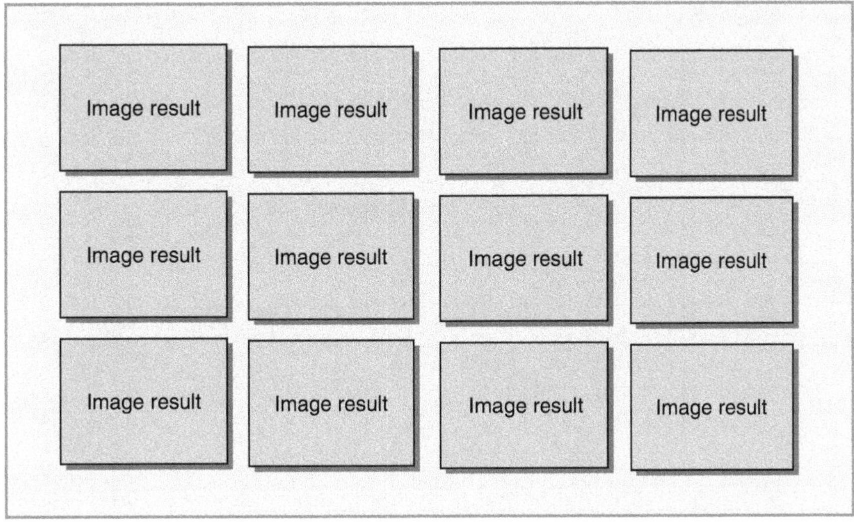

Figure 3.4 Our nicely styled and centered image grid. Images are smaller, have a nice gap between them, and are set against a subtle, off-white background with a gray border.

Here's our entire styled example.

Listing 3.6 Our entire working Web Component, fully styled

```
<html>
<head>
   <meta charset="UTF-8">
   <title>Google Poly Search</title>
   <script>
       class PolySearch extends HTMLElement {    <-- Web Component definition
           connectedCallback() {
               this.doSearch();
           }

           doSearch() {        <-- Search function call
               const url =
     'https://poly.googleapis.com/v1/assets?keywords=parrot&format=OBJ&key=
            <your_api_key>';
               const request = new XMLHttpRequest();
               request.open( 'GET', url, true );
               request.addEventListener( 'load', (event) => {
                   this.renderResults(JSON.parse
                     ( event.target.response ).assets);
               });
               request.send();
           }

           renderResults(assets) {       <-- Renders the results
              let html = '';
              for (let c = 0; c < assets.length; c++) {
                  html += '<img src="' + assets[c].thumbnail.url +
                  '" width="200" height="150" />';
              }
              this.innerHTML = html;
           }

       }
       customElements.define('poly-search', PolySearch);
   </script>

   <style>                <-- Component CSS
       poly-search {
           border-style: solid;
           border-width: 1px;
           border-color: #9a9a9a;
           padding: 10px;
           background-color: #fafafa;
           display: inline-block;
           text-align: center;
       }

       poly-search img {
           margin: 5px;
       }
   </style>
</head>
```

```
<body>
<poly-search></poly-search>        <-- Uses the component on the page
</body>
</html>
```

The basics are now in place, and we have something that works visually, but it isn't very useful yet as a search component.

3.2 Making our component configurable

Now, let's revisit our glaring problem, and the whole point of this chapter. This component isn't reusable at all. For one, even if I gave you my API key, there's no way to properly set it in the component. Second, we're always searching for "parrots." There's no way to pass this search term to our component, so if someone on your team used this component you built, they would have to go in and directly modify the URL string:

```
const url =
    'https://poly.googleapis.com/v1/assets?keywords=parrot&format=OBJ&key=<y
    our_api_key>';
```

3.2.1 Creating our component API with setters

Let's start by breaking that URL string up a little. We're going to do this in two different ways, which will eventually complement one another. The first method we'll explore is to make getters and setters for the API key and search term.

Inside our class, we can add this listing.

Listing 3.7 Getters and setters for our component's configurable options

```
set apiKey(value) {        <-- Setter for API key
   this._apiKey = value;
   this.doSearch();
}

set searchTerm(value) {        <-- Setter for search term
   this._searchTerm = value;
   this.doSearch();
}
```

Without a matching getter, JS would throw an error if we tried to read, or "get," the property. However, we could easily create a getter as well:

```
get searchTerm() {
   return this._searchTerm;
}
```

So far, though, getters aren't really necessary; we just need to inject the search term and API key variables *into* our component, as shown in figure 3.5.

Breaking things up like this makes sense. You'll likely need to set the API key only once, but as the user keeps searching for different things, the search term will be updated quite a bit.

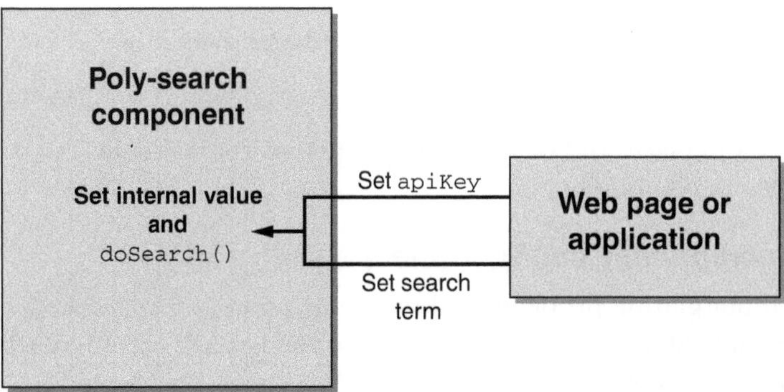

Figure 3.5 Using setters on our component from outside-in lets us perform logic and set a value, but also keep the component API simple.

3.2.2 *Using our API from the outside looking in*

With the code in listing 3.7 in place, when we set that property from the outside, it will run the function. In this regard, if you didn't know the code in this class, you'd think you were working with a simple variable, thanks to our setter methods. You also might notice that I'm using underscores (_) in my variable names. This doesn't mean anything special, but since JS doesn't have the notion of "private" variables (aside from the exciting new class fields feature in the latest version of Chrome), or variables that you're not allowed to access from outside your class, I use underscores to indicate that we don't intend for these variables to be accessed from the outside. Using underscores can be a point of contention for some and is regarded as an older practice. If you'd like to dive deeper on this concept, please refer to the appendix. Regardless, in this case, `_searchTerm` is our internal variable that we're using, while `searchTerm` is the setter for that variable.

By using a setter, we're not just setting this `searchTerm` property. When setting it from outside our component class here, that's just what it looks like to the user of our component's API. Instead, by using a setter method, we inject some logic to both set that internal property and run our `doSearch()` method to fire the HTTP request.

Now, if you were to write some JS in your script tag outside the component class, you could write the following to first select your component and then set each property (only after the component has been properly created, of course):

```
document.querySelector('poly-search').apiKey = '<your_api_key>';
document.querySelector('poly-search').searchTerm = 'parrot';
```

Of course, if we ran a search without an API key or without a search term, our search would fail, so in the following listing, we can wrap our search method in an `if` statement to make sure both variables are present before we search.

Listing 3.8 Wrapping the search method with an `if` statement

```
doSearch() {
   if (this._apiKey && this._searchTerm) {
       const url = 'https://poly.googleapis.com/v1/assets?keywords=' +
         this._searchTerm + '&format=OBJ&key=' + this._apiKey;
       const request = new XMLHttpRequest();
       request.open( 'GET', url, true );
       request.addEventListener( 'load', (event) => {
           this.renderResults(JSON.parse( event.target.response ).assets);
       });
       request.send();
   }
}
```

Checks that both API key and search term are present

Giving our components an API like this is a good exercise, but for this particular use case, there is another method for passing data: attributes. We use attributes all the time in web development. In fact, that `src` attribute to set the thumbnail URL in each image is just one example. Even just setting the style of an element using `class` or the `href` link for a link tag are attribute examples.

3.3 Using attributes for configuration

Using attributes on Web Components is so obvious, you might overlook it in favor of the getter/setter approach. We use attributes so often that we might not think of them as something that can be used for the inner workings of your Web Component.

3.3.1 An argument against a component API for configuration

With the getter/setter API approach, there is some complexity involved that isn't really needed. For one, having to wrap the search method with an `if/then` to check that the `apiKey` and `searchTerm` are set is good practice when a developer forgets to set one or the other, but it would be nice if both properties were immediately available when the component is used as intended.

The other annoyance is having to use JS at all to set these properties. If these properties were attributes on the HTML tag, we wouldn't have to set the `apiKey` and `searchTerm` over two separate lines. In more complex applications, it can be hard to track down where you set these in your code. Also, there may be timing issues with your component. Perhaps your component hasn't been properly created yet when you happen to call these setters. If this happened, it's possible that your values would just be lost!

These are definitely manageable concerns—but let's focus on attributes now.

3.3.2 Implementing attributes

Let's change things up a bit. First, let's get rid of our setters and our JS to use those setters. We don't need them. Next, we'll add our attributes to our custom element tag:

```
<poly-search apiKey="<your_api_key>"
             searchTerm="parrot">
</poly-search>
```

Now, we'll swap in some JS to get our attributes in place of using our variables. Let's keep the `if/then` check in the next listing just in case the user of our component forgets to use one attribute or the other.

Listing 3.9 Using attributes for configurable options in our search method

```
doSearch() {
   if (this.getAttribute('apiKey') && this.getAttribute('searchTerm')) {
       const url = 'https://poly.googleapis.com/v1/assets?keywords=' +
     this.getAttribute('searchTerm') + '&format=OBJ&key=' +
     this.getAttribute('apiKey');     <- Uses attributes instead of properties
       const request = new XMLHttpRequest();   for the configuration options
       request.open( 'GET', url, true );
       request.addEventListener( 'load', (event) => {
           this.renderResults(JSON.parse( event.target.response ).assets);
       });
       request.send();
   }
}
```

Lastly, since attributes are available as soon as the element is created, we can do an initial search right away when our component is added to the DOM using `connectedCallback`:

```
connectedCallback() {
   this.doSearch();
}
```

For brevity's sake, I'll leave out our CSS as we look at the current state of our component in the following listing.

Listing 3.10 Our complete (minus styling) component example using attributes

```
<html>
<head>
   <title>Google Poly Search</title>
   <script>
       class PolySearch extends HTMLElement {
           connectedCallback() {        <- When the component is added,
               this.doSearch();            runs the search function
           }

           doSearch() {
                if (this.getAttribute('apiKey') &&
                this.getAttribute('searchTerm')) {
                   const url =
     'https://poly.googleapis.com/v1/assets?keywords=' +
     this.getAttribute('searchTerm') + '&format=OBJ&key=' +
     this.getAttribute('apiKey');
                   const request = new XMLHttpRequest();
                   request.open( 'GET', url, true );
                   request.addEventListener( 'load', (event) => {
                       this.renderResults(
                                JSON.parse( event.target.response ).assets);
                  });
```

If both search term and API key are set, adds them to the search endpoint

```
                request.send();   <-- Send the HTTP request
            }
        }

        renderResults(assets) {
            let html = '';
            for (let c = 0; c < assets.length; c++) {
                html += '<img src="' + assets[c].thumbnail.url +
                '" width="200" height="150" />';
            }
            this.innerHTML = html;
        }
    }

    customElements.define('poly-search', PolySearch);
  </script>
</head>

<body>
<poly-search apiKey="<your_api_key>"
searchTerm="parrot">
</poly-search>

</body>
</html>
```

Appends an image element to the HTML string for every asset

Sets our component's HTML to the generated string

Declares the component on the page with the API key and search term

The component is now pretty functional, but the customization we've done only goes so far. That search term will likely change frequently; we'll need to watch for changes.

3.3.3 Case sensitivity

Note that while I used an uppercase "K" in `apiKey`, and an uppercase "T" in `searchTerm`, attributes themselves are not case-sensitive. We could absolutely rewrite our tag like this, and it wouldn't affect things at all (though there is a good reason for keeping things all lowercase, which we'll get to in a bit):

```
<poly-search apikey="<your_api_key>"
             searchterm="parrot">
</poly-search>
```

3.4 Listening for attribute changes

There's one remaining problem in regard to our use case, though. It's true that our API key will likely never change in our web app, but we do want users to input text and search for things. Before we get into solving that problem, let's create a typical text input that lets a user enter a search term. This aspect is outside of our Web Component, so it's not a lesson in Web Components per se, just something to help us demonstrate and solve our attribute problem.

3.4.1 Adding text input

With this in mind, let's change the contents of our <body> tag.

Listing 3.11 Text input for our component

```
<body>
    <label>Enter search term: </label>
    <input type="text" onchange="updatePolySearch(event)" />
    <br /><br />

    <script>
       function updatePolySearch(event) {
           document.querySelector('poly-search').setAttribute('searchterm',
             event.target.value);
       }
    </script>

    <poly-search apikey="<your_api_key>" searchterm="parrot">
```

We've now added a text input with an onchange event listener. Preceding that, we have a simple label, just to give context in our UI on what that text input is actually doing. I don't typically have inline JS like this on a tag, but for such a simple demonstration, it's easier to show it this way. The onchange event occurs only when the user "submits" the text, meaning when they press the Enter key or click off the field.

The function that it calls, updatePolySearch, captures the event that gets sent, which includes the *target*, or which element sent the event. We can query event.target .value to get the new search term that the user typed in. From there, we can set the searchterm attribute of our Web Component.

Feel free to try this out right now! If you open your browser's development tools to show the live view of the elements on the page, you can see our <poly-search> searchterm attribute changing in real time after we change our text input.

Unfortunately, just updating the attribute doesn't cause the search to rerun and update our results. We have to do this ourselves. This brings us to our second Web Component lifecycle method: attributeChangedCallback. Our first lifecycle method, of course, was connectedCallback, but now we're ready to get a bit deeper.

3.4.2 The attribute changed callback

The attributeChangedCallback method is like any other Web Component lifecycle method. You simply add the method in your class to override HTMLElement's empty method, and it will be fired when an attribute is changed.

This method accepts three parameters: the name of the attribute that changed, the old value of the attribute, and the new value of the attribute:

```
attributeChangedCallback(attrName, oldVal, newVal)
```

Let's integrate this into our Web Component and see what happens. I'm going to be a little evil here, but warn you up front. We're going to integrate this, but it's not going to work because of one missing detail that I'll explain afterward.

The first thing to do is to get rid of the connectedCallback method in our class. We do this because, in our specific case, our connectedCallback method triggers a search. However, now our attributeChangedCallback will actually do this as well. Technically speaking, our attribute *does* change from nothing to something when our component starts up, so the attributeChangedCallback triggers. Also, we don't have any logic to cancel our HTTP request before triggering it again in our component—to keep things simple and bug free when both of these callbacks fire at virtually the same time, let's just get rid of that connectedCallback.

Next, let's add our attributeChangedCallback method.

Listing 3.12 AttributeChangedCallback to listen for changes to our searchterm

```
attributeChangedCallback(name, oldval, newval) {
   if (name === 'searchterm') {
       this.doSearch();
   }
}
```

Our callback here is really simple. If the attribute name being changed is searchterm, then run our search again. This aspect *is* case-sensitive. The name coming in will always be lowercase. This can be a bit confusing if you write your attribute in HTML in camel case, and then just write the name over here the same way. To avoid confusion, it's wise to write our attributes in lowercase all the time.

As I was writing this, I accidentally made things a bit more complicated before I caught myself. I initially wrote the following code:

```
attributeChangedCallback(name, oldval, newval) {
   if (name === 'searchterm' && oldval !== newval ) {
       this.doSearch();
   }
}
```

I thought that I only wanted to call the search if the old value was different than the new value. There's no sense in rerunning a search and wasting a network request if the value doesn't change, right? Well, if the value didn't change, this method wouldn't get called in the first place, so doing this extra step is redundant.

Now that we've captured attribute changes and taken action when they change, it should work, right? Not yet! This is the part where I left out one little detail of how this method works. Before I explain what this is, let me give a little context and history.

3.4.3 Observed attributes

At the start of this chapter, I talked a bit about how common attributes are to everything we do in HTML. Each element has numerous potential attributes it can use that actually mean something. At minimum, elements will likely always have a class element for styling. And, of course, we can make up any attribute we want. With all of these potential attributes everywhere, it could be a huge waste of code execution to call `attributeChangedCallback` every single time something changes if we don't care that it changed.

Back in v0 of the Web Components API, the `attributeChangedCallback` did just that: it was called each and every time something as common as a CSS `class` attribute changed. Early Web Component adopters thought this was a bit annoying and wasteful. So now, in v1 of the Web Components API, we need to tell our component what specifically to listen for.

Listing 3.13 Telling our component what attributes to watch changes for

```
static get observedAttributes() {
   return ['searchterm'];
}
```

If you're not familiar with the `static` keyword for a class method, please refer to the appendix. In short, it's a method called on the class definition, rather than on the created instance.

In this static method, we've set our `observedAttributes` to an array containing `searchterm`. If we wanted more attributes to be observed, we could simply add more elements to the array:

```
static get observedAttributes() {
   return ['searchterm', 'apikey', 'anotherthing', 'yetanotherthing' ];
}
```

With this last piece added to our example in listing 3.14, our example should run. This new code for watching our `searchTerm` attribute is depicted in figure 3.6. We now automatically load our results with the first search term of "parrot," but when the user submits other terms, the results will update.

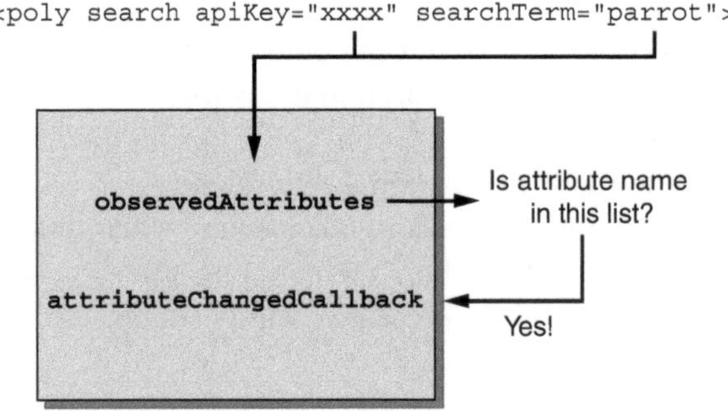

Figure 3.6 Before an `attributeChangedCallback` is fired inside your component as a result of an attribute change on your component's markup, that attribute name must be in the `observedAttributes` list.

Listing 3.14 Complete component with attributes that respond to a text input field

```
<html>
<head>
   <title>Google Poly Search</title>
   <script>

       class PolySearch extends HTMLElement {   <-- Component class
           static get observedAttributes() {
               return ['searchterm'];   <-- Watched attribute
           }

           attributeChangedCallback(name, oldval, newval) {
               if (name === 'searchterm') {
                   this.doSearch();   <-- When watched attribute changes,
               }                          runs the search request
           }

           doSearch() {   <-- Search request, which uses the API key and search term
               if (this.getAttribute('apiKey') &&
     this.getAttribute('searchTerm')) {
                   const url =
     'https://poly.googleapis.com/v1/assets?keywords=' +
     this.getAttribute('searchTerm') + '&format=OBJ&key=' +
     this.getAttribute('apiKey');
                   const request = new XMLHttpRequest();
                   request.open( 'GET', url, true );
                   request.addEventListener( 'load', (event) => {
                       this.renderResults(JSON.parse
                         ( event.target.response ).assets);
                   });
                   request.send();
               }
           }

           renderResults(assets) {   <-- Renders all assets
               let html = '';
               for (let c = 0; c < assets.length; c++) {
                   html += '<img src="' + assets[c].thumbnail.url +
                    '" width="200" height="150" />';
               }
               this.innerHTML = html;
           }
       }

       customElements.define(
             'poly-search', PolySearch);   <-- Map tag name to component class
   </script>

   <style>   <-- Component CSS
       poly-search {
           border-style: solid;
           border-width: 1px;
           border-color: #9a9a9a;
           padding: 10px;
           background-color: #fafafa;
           display: inline-block;
           text-align: center;
```

```
        }

        poly-search img {
            margin: 5px;
        }
        input {
            font-size: 18px;
        }
    </style>
</head>

<body>

<label>Enter search term: </label><input type="text"
        onchange="updatePolySearch(event)" />
<br /><br />

<script>
    function updatePolySearch(event) {
        document.querySelector('poly-search').setAttribute('searchTerm',
          event.target.value);
    }
</script>
<poly-search apikey="<your_api_key>"
            searchterm="parrot">
</poly-search>

</body>
</html>
```

Input field to allow user to type a search term

As input field changes, sets the searchTerm attribute on our component

Component added to page with API key set and starting search term set

With that, we've allowed our component to react to changes. It doesn't really make sense for us to react to API key changes because the API key is typically something that never changes. That search term is going to change all the time, though, so we definitely needed a way to react to it.

3.5 Making more things even more customizable

Let's now up our customization game! We can do some small style things, such as set the image size and component background color.

3.5.1 Using hasAttribute to check if an attribute exists

In listing 3.15, I'm being a bit of a lazy developer. I don't expect that the image sizes or background color will need to change at runtime—only when we're initially writing the HTML. So, I'm not listening for attribute changes; instead, I'm simply setting these style properties when the component is added to the DOM.

Listing 3.15 Adding attributes for size and background color

```
connectedCallback() {
    if (this.hasAttribute('thumbheight')) {
        this._thumbheight = this.getAttribute('thumbheight');
        this._thumbwidth = (this.getAttribute('thumbheight') *
          1.3333 /*aspect ratio*/);
    } else {
```

If the thumbheight attribute is set, uses it for image-sizing, and calculates the width as well

If not set, uses default/hardcoded values.

```
        this._thumbheight = 150;
        this._thumbwidth = 200;
    }
    if (this.hasAttribute('backgroundcolor')) {
        this.style.backgroundColor = this.getAttribute('backgroundcolor');
    }
}
```

If the background color attribute is set, adjusts the style of the component right away.

I'm also not forcing the component's user to have these attributes. Instead, I'm checking if the developer used the attribute in their markup by using `hasAttribute` and, if so, set these properties. If not, we have fallback values either with JS for the size or using the pre-existing style in CSS for background color.

To use my size properties, I've edited the image-rendering method as in the following listing.

Listing 3.16 Rendering our thumbnails with configurable sizes

```
renderResults(assets) {
    let html = '';
    for (let c = 0; c < assets.length; c++) {
        html += '<img src="' + assets[c].thumbnail.url + '" width="' +
         this._thumbwidth + '" height="' +
         this._thumbheight + '"/>';
    }
    this.innerHTML = html;
}
```

Uses the height and width properties to control the image size

As we've added stylistic customization, you can probably imagine so much more! Certainly, we could customize borders, spacing, and so on. There's one last thing we'll customize, and that's the search endpoint.

3.5.2 *Fully customizing the HTTP request URL for development*

This is also the point at which I'm going to make readers who didn't want to sign up for an API key happy. We're going to break up the HTTP request URL in the following listing. We'll do this by separating out the base of the URL as well as the 3D object format for good measure.

Listing 3.17 Breaking apart our HTTP request URL to be even more configurable

```
doSearch() {
    if (this.getAttribute('apiKey') && this.getAttribute('searchTerm')) {
        const url = this.getAttribute('baseuri') +
'?keywords=' + this.getAttribute('searchTerm') + '&format=' +
 this.getAttribute('format') + '&key=' + this.getAttribute('apiKey');
        const request = new XMLHttpRequest();
        request.open( 'GET', url, true );
        request.addEventListener( 'load', (event) => {
            this.renderResults(JSON.parse( event.target.response ).assets);
        });
        request.send();
    }
}
```

Adds base URI as a configurable option to allow calling a different search destination

With the following tag, we can start using all of our customization options.

Listing 3.18 Adding the `baseuri` attribute to the component tag

```
<poly-search apikey="<your_api_key>"
             format="OBJ"
             thumbheight="50"
             backgroundcolor="red"
             baseuri=
               "https://poly.googleapis.com/v1/assets"   <-- Specifies the search endpoint in the component's attributes
             searchterm="parrot">
</poly-search>
```

We can now tweak the baseuri attribute to be something else. Of course, different search services will have different APIs and result formats, but we can test our setup without Google by pointing to a JSON file that we host:

```
baseuri="http://localhost:8080/assets.json"
```

This will differ, of course, depending on how you've set up your development server (it could be localhost, it could be something else, and port 8080 is common, but it differs wildly depending on your setup).

3.5.3 Best practice guides

Because we've now covered both getters/setters and attributes for working with data, which one should we use? Really, it's up to you, but there are some emerging best practices. It's a bit too early to take these best practices as mandates, but there are some good ideas, especially if you intend to share your components with other people. One resource is an incomplete working draft: https://github.com/webcomponents/gold-standard/wiki. Google has also published some best practices that are further along: https://developers.google.com/web/fundamentals/web-components/best-practices.

3.5.4 Avoiding attributes for rich data

Within the Google Web Components guide, there are a few best practices for attributes. One such practice is to not use attributes for rich data such as arrays and objects.

Let's say, for example, that you have a very complex application, and for some of your Web Components, setup is insanely complex. Perhaps you have 50 or more properties to use for configuration—or your configuration data needs to be represented as a nested structure:

```
{
    Tree: {
        Branches: [
            { branch: {
                leaves: [
                 { leaf: "leaf"},
                 { leaf: "leaf"},
                 { leaf: "leaf"},
```

```
                    ]
                  }
               }
         ]
   }}
```

Either way, separating out these properties for individual attributes would be overwhelming or impossible.

We can actually stringify a JSON object and shove it into an attribute on our tag:

```
<my-element data="{"Tree": {"Branches": [{"branch": {"leaves": [{"leaf":
    "leaf"},{"leaf": "leaf"},{ "leaf": "leaf"}]}}]}}
    " my-element>
```

It's probably easier to do this through code, however:

```
myElement.setAttribute('data', JSON.stringify(data));
```

To pull the data out, you'd then have to serialize that string to JSON:

```
JSON.parse(this.getAttribute('data'));
```

In the end, though, when you have this massive, ugly string in your DOM, your development tools get that much harder to read and put up roadblocks for understanding your DOM structure. In this case, perhaps it's better to use a method or setter to pass your data to your component and avoid rich data attributes.

3.5.5 Property and attribute reflection

Another Google-suggested best practice is to do something called *reflection* for your attributes and properties. Reflection is the practice of using both getters and setters as well as attributes for your data, and always keeping them in sync with each other. Especially when handing your component off to other developers or sharing it with the world, users may expect a consistent component API.

Attributes are generally easier to work with when writing HTML, while with JS code, setting properties on the component is more concise and easier to use. In other words, JS developers will prefer writing `yourcomponent.property = 'something';` and likely won't prefer writing `yourcomponent.setAttribute('property', 'something');`. At the same time, someone writing HTML would prefer to just set the attribute in the markup.

When these two methods don't do the same thing, or one is supported and not the other, it can get a bit confusing for your component's consumer. That's why, when setting a property through JS, the corresponding attribute should change on the element, and vice versa. When an attribute changes, getting the property after that should reflect the newest value.

One trap that Google has identified with its best practice guide is using `attributeChangedCallback` to update the setter, which Google is calling *re-entrancy*; it's implemented as follows.

Listing 3.19 A pitfall for reflection from Google's Web Components best practices guide

```
// When the [checked] attribute changes, set the checked property to match.
attributeChangedCallback(name, oldValue, newValue) {
  if (name === 'checked')
    this.checked = newValue;       <-- When the attribute changes,
}                                      the setter is called.

set checked(value) {
  const isChecked = Boolean(value);
  if (isChecked)
    // OOPS! This will cause an infinite loop because it triggers the
    // attributeChangedCallback() which then sets this property again.
    this.setAttribute('checked', '');    <-- When the setter is called,
  else                                       the attribute is updated,
    this.removeAttribute('checked');         causing an infinite loop.
}
```

In this example, taken straight from Google's developer documentation, an infinite loop is caused. The setter is used and sets the attribute, but this causes the `attributeChangedCallback` to fire, which again uses the setter, which then changes the attribute . . . you get the point—it's an infinite loop, and the flow can be seen in figure 3.7.

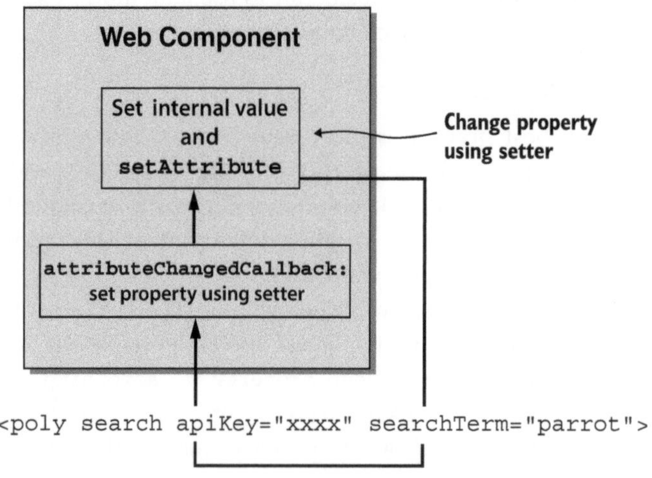

Figure 3.7 Re-entrancy is a bad way to implement property/attribute reflection. Setting the attribute when your getter is used causes an `attributeChangedCallback` to be fired, which can then set the property again, continuing on in an infinite loop.

A better way might be to use the attribute as the so-called "source of truth." I've added reflection to the `searchTerm` property in our Poly search example with just an additional getter and setter, shown in the following listing.

Listing 3.20 Adding a getter/setter in addition to existing attributes for reflection

```
static get observedAttributes() {
    return ['searchterm'];
}

get searchTerm() {
    return this.getAttribute('searchTerm');    <-- Getter will simply return access and return the attribute.
}

set searchTerm(val) {
    this.setAttribute('searchTerm', val);    <-- Setter will set the attribute.
}

attributeChangedCallback(name, oldval, newval) {
    if (name === 'searchterm') {
        this.doSearch();    <-- When setting, the attributeChangeCallback fires and runs the search.
    }
}
```

In this example, our getter simply returns the current attribute, while our setter sets the attribute. There are, of course, additional ways to accomplish reflection, but the important takeaway is that if you want to maximize the developer experience with your component, keep your attributes and properties consistent and synced with each other!

3.6 Updating the slider component

Now that we understand how to work with attributes to make a reusable component, and know about using attribute reflection to our advantage, it's time to update the slider component from the last chapter to make it interactive and reactive to the attributes we give it or JS properties we set on it. Right now, our component class is pretty slim, especially after moving all of the CSS outside the component into a `<style>` tag. All it does is render HTML (two `<div>` tags); the next listing shows the slider minus the lengthy CSS.

Listing 3.21 Slider component (without CSS)

```
<html>
<head>
    <title>Slider</title>

    <script>
        class Slider extends HTMLElement {
            connectedCallback() {
                this.innerHTML = '<div class="bg-overlay"></div>
                <div class="thumb"></div>';
            }
        }

        if (!customElements.get('wcia-slider')) {
            customElements.define('wcia-slider', Slider);
        }
```

```
    </script>

    <style><!-- CSS was here --></style>
</head>
<body>
    <wcia-slider></wcia-slider>
</body>
</html>
```

Recall that we temporarily used two properties to control some of the component's functionality, or, in other words, its API. Let's formalize this API and list those properties here:

- `value`—The current percentage value of the slider from 0–100
- `backgroundcolor`—A hexadecimal color of the topmost background layer

With those now defined, we can do two things. The first is to listen for changes to those attributes. We'll be adding all of these functions right inside the `Slider` class.

Listing 3.22 Listening for attribute changes

```
static get observedAttributes() {
   return ['value', 'backgroundcolor'];     <-- Listens for both value and backgroundcolor attribute changes
}

attributeChangedCallback(name, oldVal, newValue) {
   switch (name) {
       case 'value':
           this.refreshSlider(newValue);     <-- Reacts to changes in the slider value if set from outside the component
           break;

       case 'backgroundcolor':
           this.setColor(newValue);     <-- Reacts to background color changes
           break;
   }
}
```

The second thing to do is to intertwine those attributes with a proper JS API using reflection, as we've just learned. When one of these properties is set through the JS setter, the attribute is updated on the component. Likewise, when the attribute is set on the tag, this value can be retrieved through the matching getter. The next listing shows reflection in our component for these two attributes.

Listing 3.23 Getters and setters for the `backgroundcolor` and `value` properties

```
set value(val) {
   this.setAttribute('value', val);
}

get value() {
   return this.getAttribute('value');
}

set backgroundcolor(val) {
   this.setAttribute('backgroundcolor', val);
```

```
}

get backgroundcolor() {
   return this.getAttribute('backgroundcolor');
}
```

Remember, with reflection, our attributes are the "source of truth," so these getters and setters simply set or get the attribute directly.

We're almost ready to demo the slider for real! Referring back to listing 3.22, which holds the component class definition, remember the `attributeChangedCallback`. We have two methods that don't exist yet. When receiving a new slider value, we see

```
case 'value':
   this.refreshSlider(newValue);
   break;
```

Likewise, with a new background color value, we have

```
case 'backgroundcolor':
   this.setColor(newValue);
   break;
```

Just so we can start seeing the results of our work, we should create these functions in the component class.

Listing 3.24 Functions to set the background color and slider value

```
setColor(color) {       <-- Sets the background color (a gradient from an opaque solid color to the same transparent color)
    if (this.querySelector('.bg-overlay')) {
           this.querySelector('.bg-overlay').style.background =
             `linear-gradient(to right, ${color} 0%, ${color}00 100%)`;
    }
}

refreshSlider(value) {    <-- Sets the current location of the slider thumb based on its value
    if (this.querySelector('.thumb')) {
            this.querySelector('.thumb').style.left = (value/100 *
              this.offsetWidth - this.querySelector('.thumb').offsetWidth/2)
              + 'px';
    }
}
```

Both functions likely need a bit of explanation, even though they are tiny. First, we're checking to see if the DOM element we're changing exists. There's a bit of a timing issue with the `attributeChangedCallback`. Namely, it will fire first before `connectedCallback` if there are attributes on the component at the start. So, these DOM elements may not exist yet. Once we update this component to use the Shadow DOM later in the book, this problem won't exist. This is also the reason we need to add a couple of lines to the `connectedCallback`, to make sure the initial attributes are acted on:

```
this.setColor(this.backgroundcolor);
     this.refreshSlider(this.value);
```

Next, when setting the color, the color value we get is a hexadecimal value (complete with the hash at the beginning). At the beginning, or 0% stop of the gradient, we can use this color value as normal. In our demo, it's red, or #ff0000. The second color stop, at 100%, should be the same color but completely transparent. With the exception of Edge, every modern browser supports adding an additional "00" at the end to indicate the transparency to complement the red, green, and blue two-digit values in the larger hexadecimal code. We'll worry about Edge later!

The `refreshSlider` function is pretty easy math. We calculate the thumbnail's horizontal location by taking the fraction (percent divided by 100) of the component's overall width. The slightly tricky part here is that we don't actually want to position from the leftmost edge of the thumbnail. Instead, the dead center of the thumbnail should indicate the value. To center it, we need to subtract by half the width of the thumb graphic.

With these last updates, even though we don't have interactivity, at least our attributes cause updates to the component. We can now load the HTML file and see something that looks like figure 3.8.

Figure 3.8 The slider component so far

What's cool is that, even if we don't have interactivity yet, the attributes on the demo can be changed. When the page is refreshed, you'll see the new color and slide percentage. How about a blue background at 70%?

```
<wcia-slider backgroundcolor="#0000ff" value="70"></wcia-slider>
```

We're almost done! The next step is to make that thumbnail draggable.

Let's finish our component by adding some mouse listeners to the components. These three listeners can be seen in the next listing.

Listing 3.25 Adding three event listeners to handle mouse move, up, and down

```
connectedCallback() {
    this.innerHTML = '<div class="bg-overlay"></div><div
     class="thumb"></div>';

    document.addEventListener('mousemove',
            e => this.eventHandler(e));       <-- Mouse listeners for enabling slider dragging

    document.addEventListener('mouseup', e => this.eventHandler(e));
    this.addEventListener('mousedown', e => this.eventHandler(e));
```

```
        this.refreshSlider(this.value);        ◁— Due to timing issues with
        this.setColor(this.backgroundcolor);      attributeChangedCallback firing first,
}                                                 refresh the slider and color now.
```

For mouse-down events, we only really care when the user clicks on the slider component. Even when clicking outside the thumbnail, it should snap to the horizontal location in the slider. Mouse-up events need to be caught everywhere on the overall web page. If the user clicks inside the component, but then the mouse drags outside, the user should still be able to release the mouse button, releasing the thumbnail. Likewise, for the mouse-move events, even when our mouse is dragging outside of the component, the thumbnail should still follow (the best it can within the confines of the slider).

All that's left now is to add some code for our new `eventHandler` method.

Listing 3.26 Function to handle events and a function to update the slider percentage

```
updateX(x) {                              Offsets the horizontal position to
   let hPos =          ◁————————————       use the center of the thumbnail
   x - this.querySelector('.thumb') .offsetWidth/2;
   if (hPos > this.offsetWidth) {  ◁—
       hPos = this.offsetWidth;         Restricts horizontal position to
   }                                    confines of component bounds
   if (hPos < 0) {
       hPos = 0;
   }
   this.value = (hPos / this.offsetWidth) * 100;  ◁— Calculates the percentage
}                                                    horizontal position and sets
                                                     the value attribute through
eventHandler(e) {                                    the setter API
   const bounds = this.getBoundingClientRect();
   const x = e.clientX - bounds.left;  ◁— Calculates horizontal position relative
                                          to left edge of the component
   switch (e.type) {
       case 'mousedown':        ◁————————
           this.isDragging = true;           On mousedown, sets a boolean to indicate
           this.updateX(x);                  the user is dragging, updates the "value"
           this.refreshSlider(this.value);   attribute, and updates the slider position
           break;

       case 'mouseup':    ◁————————————
           this.isDragging = false;          On mouseup, sets the boolean to false to
           break;                            indicate the user is no longer dragging

       case 'mousemove':        ◁————————
           if (this.isDragging) {              On mousemove, if the boolean
               this.updateX(x);                indicates the user is dragging,
               this.refreshSlider(this.value); updates the "value" attribute and
           }                                   updates the slider position
           break;
   }
}
```

With this last addition, our slider component is fully functional! We can even crack open the dev tools, like in figure 3.9, to watch the `value` attribute change as we drag the thumbnail.

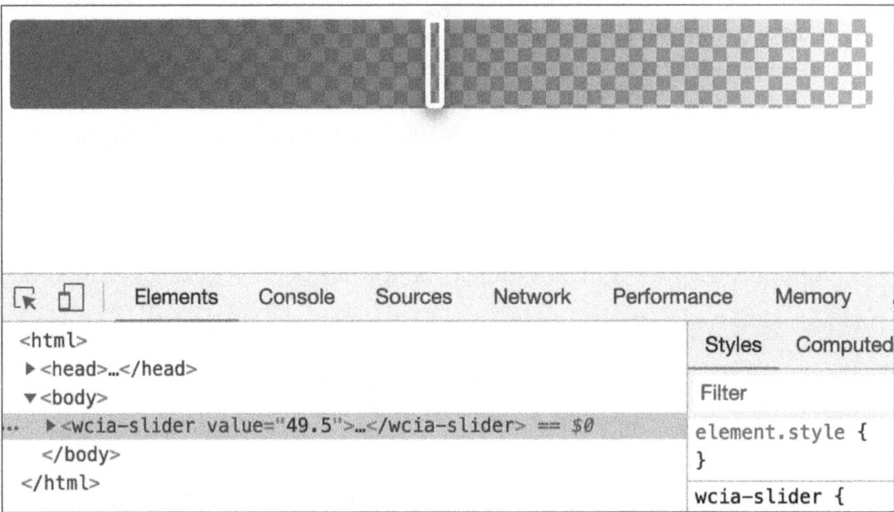

Figure 3.9 Using the slider component and watching the `value` attribute update in the dev tools

The slider component isn't done yet! It's really not shareable if someone else on your team wanted to use it. This will involve bringing the relevant CSS into the component (as real CSS, not the JS style setting like in the last chapter) and separating out these visual concerns from the main component class.

Summary

In this chapter, we've expanded our Custom Element API methods repertoire to both `connectedCallback` and `attributeChangedCallback`. In the next chapter, we'll talk through the rest of the Web Component lifecycle in depth and compare it to similar component lifecycles on both the web and beyond. Also in this chapter, you learned

- How to use attributes to call an endpoint for a search service, with ideas on which attributes need to be watched and which don't, including how to actually watch the attributes in practice using the Web Components API
- What reflection is and how it can make your component more robust, such that it can be used through its tag as well as through a custom JS API, and how to avoid the problem of re-entrancy
- Strategies for when to use attributes versus a custom API and when to use both for a better developer experience for your component's consumers

4 The component lifecycle

> ***This chapter covers***
> - Using the `connectedCallback` Web Components API method to listen when your component is added to the DOM
> - Knowing when and how to use the constructor method, especially because it occurs before the component has access to the DOM
> - Utilizing the `disconnectedCallback` Web Components API method to clean up after your component
> - The seldom-used `adoptedCallback` Web Components API method

4.1 The Web Components API

Up to now, we've explored a couple different methods from the Web Components API, but we really didn't talk about the API as a whole. These methods are the basic building blocks for building everything from custom components to entire applications. So, it's a good idea to take a look at all of them in detail. In the last chapter, we looked at the `attributeChangedCallback` and the `observedAttributes` static getter. In this chapter, we'll cover the rest in the same amount of detail.

Additionally, we need to consider that now that Web Components are shipping in browsers, the specification should be considered a permanent part of the web development workflow for years to come. With this in mind, we should have some confidence that Web Components can be used in a variety of situations.

The most obvious use case for Web Components intersects with those use cases that big frameworks such as Angular, React, and Vue are targeting. Generally speaking, this use case is a data-centric web application that might interact with a REST-based API. On the other side of the spectrum, as we see more graphic-intensive uses for the web, like games, 3D, video, and so on, we need to know that the Web Components API can handle those too.

To have this confidence, I want to cover the entire API in detail but also compare it to a couple different component lifecycles. For more traditional web applications, we can look at a typical React component lifecycle. For more graphic-intensive applications, we can look at the component lifecycle for an extremely successful 3D/game engine (not web-based) called Unity.

4.2 The connectedCallback handler

We've previously tapped into the `connectedCallback` method in examples from the last couple of chapters, but let's revisit it. This time, however, let's add back an alert inside a generic component to alert us exactly when our component starts up.

Listing 4.1 Testing when our `connectedCallback` is called

```
<script>
  class MyCustomTag extends HTMLElement {
      connectedCallback() {
          alert('hi from MyCustomTag');
          this.innerHTML = '<h2>'+ this.getAttribute('title') +
            '</h2><button>click me</button>';
      }
  }

  if (!customElements.get('my-custom-tag')) {
      customElements.define('my-custom-tag', MyCustomTag);
  }
</script>

<style>
  my-custom-tag {
      background-color: blue;
      padding: 20px;
      display: inline-block;
      color: white;
  }
</style>

<body>
<my-custom-tag title="Another title"></my-custom-tag>
</body>
```

Alert added to our previous example's connectedCallback

Of course, what we should see when running this code in our browser is even more basic than what we had in the last couple of chapters: a simple, ugly Web Component with a header and a button that says "click me." With the alert added back in, you'll also see a modal box pop up immediately that says "hi from MyCustomTag."

The question now, based on the limited amount of code we have here, is when does `connectedCallback` get called? The name of this method is a clue, but let's explore by removing the `<my-custom-tag title="Another title"></my-custom-tag>` from the body of our page.

Now, visually we have a completely empty page, but we're still doing things on this page. Our script block is still running, so we're still registering this custom component as something we could use. We're just not putting it on the page yet.

With this in mind, and our element removed from the body, let's refresh the page: no element, and no alert. Let's use our component's constructor to poke at this a bit more. If you recall from chapter 2, we identified the constructor as the function that runs when the class is instantiated.

Note that because we're using a constructor in an inherited class, we must call `super();` as the first line. By doing this, `HTMLElement`'s constructor is called as well. Usually, when calling the inherited method, you might call `super.myInherited-Method()` on any line, but here in the constructor, it's just `super();` on the first line in the constructor.

Listing 4.2 Alerting from both our constructor and our `connectedCallback`

```
<script>
  class MyCustomTag extends HTMLElement {
      constructor()  {
             super();
             alert('hi from MyCustomTags      ◁— Alert added to constructor
             ➥ constructor');
      }                                        Alert remaining in
      connectedCallback() {                    connectedCallback to
          alert('hi from MyCustomTag       ◁— compare timing
          ➥connected callback');
          this.innerHTML = '<h2>'+ this.getAttribute('title') +
            '</h2><button>click me</button>';
      }
  }

  if (!customElements.get('my-custom-tag')) {
      customElements.define('my-custom-tag', MyCustomTag);
  }
</script>
```

OK, so if we refresh this page . . . well, nothing happens—again. Note that while we fully defined our element, we haven't instantiated or called it into action yet! To test our theory that the constructor is called on creation, and `connectedCallback` happens when added to the DOM, let's do a bit of manual DOM manipulation with JS.

With the blank page loaded, we'll open up the browser dev tools and open the console. In the console, enter

```
x = document.createElement('my-custom-tag');
```

Great! Our constructor alert is fired, and we see the message "hi from MyCustomTags constructor." By creating the element, we've implicitly called `new MyCustomTag();` and, as a result, the constructor is called. At the same time, however, the `connectedCallback` method has not been called because we haven't added it to our DOM. Let's do that now! In the same console, now that our x variable is set, run the following:

```
document.body.appendChild(x);
```

As expected, the alert from the `connectedCallback` is called. Also, you should now see the component in the page's body. This flow, from creation to `connectedCallback`, is captured in figure 4.1.

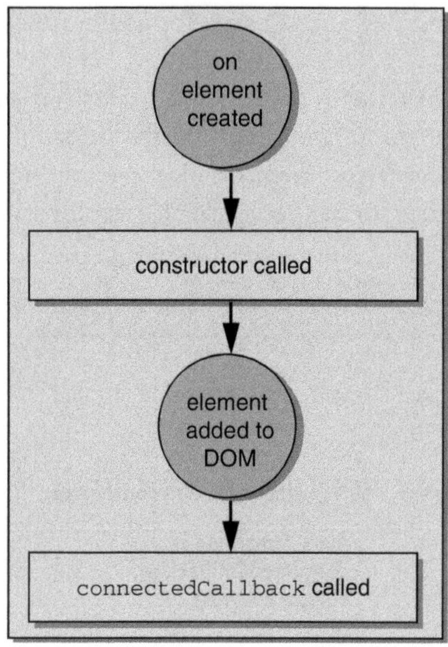

Figure 4.1 The start of a Web Component's lifecycle: constructor first, and then `connectedCallback` after adding to the DOM

What if we tried something a little more indirect? What we just did begs the question of whether `connectedCallback` was fired because we added it to *any* element or if it was a matter of adding it to our page's DOM. Let's test this by refreshing the page and creating our element again in the console:

```
myEl = document.createElement('my-custom-tag');
```

Of course, the constructor alert will still fire and show us the message. Next, let's create yet another element to act as a container:

```
myContainer = document.createElement('div');
```

Now comes the moment of truth. Will our `connectedCallback` alert us when we add `myEl` to `myContainer`? Let's try:

```
myContainer.appendChild(myEl);
```

And the answer is no! Adding the custom component to just any element not yet attached to the DOM will not trigger the `connectedCallback` method. We have an isolated node held in the `myContainer` variable. The node looks like this:

```
<div>
        <my-custom-tag></my-custom-tag>
</div>
```

Although we've proven that our `connectedCallback` method is not fired when adding it to something that's not connected to the DOM, we haven't yet proven that indirectly adding to the DOM will fire that method. Let's continue in the console and try:

```
document.body.appendChild(myContainer);
```

Confirmed! Instead of adding our custom element directly to the page, we've first added it to another container (a `<div>`). We then added that container to our DOM, and our `connectedCallback` method is still called, proving that the callback is called only when it's added to the page and nowhere else, even if not directly added to the page.

Additionally, if we remove the element and then re-add it, we see that our `connectedCallback` is called each time:

```
document.body.removeChild(myContainer);
document.body.appendChild(myContainer);
```

This actually means that if you add, remove, and then add your component again, you should be careful to do any one-time setup you intend only once.

Figure 4.2 recaps our explanation with four scenarios. A component can be directly on the page, or even inside another component. If either the component or

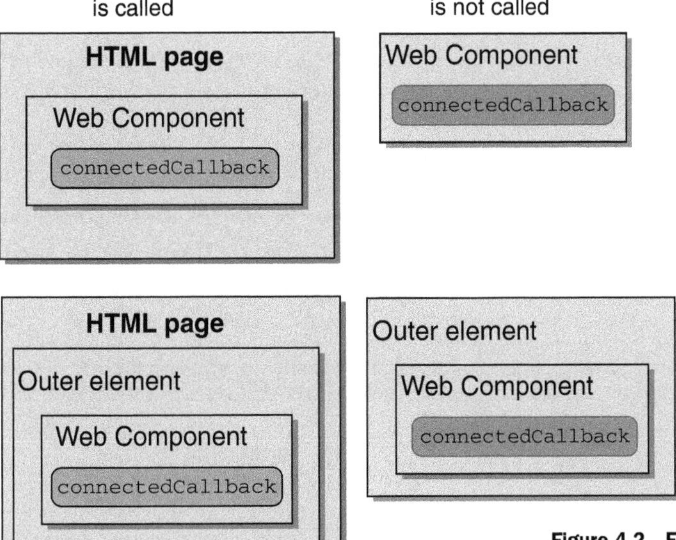

Figure 4.2 Four different scenarios for creating your Web Component

the outer component (and it could be the outer, outer, outer component) is on the main HTML page, the `connectedCallback` will be called.

Alternately, even if the component is added inside another element, its `connectedCallback` won't be fired if the outer element is not on the main page. Generally speaking, for that `connectedCallback` to fire, the component must have an ancestor on the main HTML page.

4.2.1 Constructor vs. connected

What does this all mean for practical purposes? What logic belongs in the constructor versus the `connectedCallback` method? It would be reasonable to think that we can shove everything into the constructor and keep the `connectedCallback` method empty. Unfortunately, no—there is a bit of nuance here.

A big aspect of what you'll want to do when creating a component is to set the content of your element. You'll likely want to set `innerHTML` to some markup. It's how, in our simple example, we're adding the header and button. You might also want to get an attribute of your component. Unfortunately, when the constructor is fired, the element isn't yet ready to be interacted with in this way.

We can prove this by moving the `innerHTML` line to the constructor, as follows.

Listing 4.3 Trying (and failing) to set `innerHTML` from the constructor

```
class MyCustomTag extends HTMLElement {
   constructor()  {
       super();
       this.innerHTML = '<h2>'+ this.getAttribute('title') +
         '</h2><button>click me</button>';
   }
   connectedCallback() {}
}
```

When our page reloads, we can try creating the element again with the `createElement` function, but the following error is seen in our console:

```
DOMException: Failed to construct 'CustomElement': The result must not have
     children
```

Our browser is telling us that when our custom element is initially created, it's not allowed to have children. Furthermore, we can check on our `title` attribute that we've been using to populate our header tag in the constructor versus the `connectedCallback`.

Listing 4.4 Attempting to access attributes on the constructor vs. `connectedCallback`

```
class MyCustomTag extends HTMLElement {
   constructor()  {
       super();
       console.log('From constructor',        <-- Accessing an attribute on this component from the constructor (failed)
                 this.getAttribute('title'));
   }
```

```
   connectedCallback() {
       console.log('From connectedCallback',
                    this.getAttribute('title'));   <-- Accessing an attribute on this component from the connectedCallback (success)
   }
}
```

When we change to the previous listing and reload our page, our console will indicate that the constructor doesn't know the title yet, logging `null`. Our `connectedCallback` is just fine, though.

Just by looking at what works and what doesn't here, we can start to feel out how we should organize our component. The `connectedCallback` should contain all the logic to populate our element visually. For a typical component, lots of logic within, like adding events, interactions, and so on, will depend on these visuals being present. This can leave the constructor fairly empty or devoid of meaningful code for many situations.

Depending on your component, however, there are likely to be exceptions that should live in the constructor. One such exception is logic that you may want to happen after your element is initialized, but prior to it being added to the page. You may want, for example, to create the element in advance and do a network request to pull information off the internet before you append your component to the DOM. In this fashion, if your component has all the data it needs to render, it can do so instantly when on the page. In this case, because there are no dependencies on the visual elements within your component, the constructor can be a good place for this code.

Listing 4.5 A nicely formatted property list in a constructor

```
class MyCustomTag extends HTMLElement {
   constructor()  {   <-- Constructor method
          super();

   /**
    * URL to fetch data to populate our hypothetical list
    */
   this.serviceURL =    <-- Adds human-readable properties to the constructor
'http://company.com/service.json';

   /**
    * internal counter to track something
    */
   this.counter = 0;

   /**
    * last error message displayed
    */
   this.error;
   }
   connectedCallback() { . . . }
}
```

As I mentioned at the start of the chapter, one great use of the constructor can be to contain property declarations. It's really handy to have a constructor at the top of your class and be able to easily read all the properties that you use within, as seen in listing 4.5. I've found that even if you don't set your properties to anything yet, it's still great for component readability. I should mention again, however, that with the latest version of Chrome supporting public and private class fields, we can declare our properties in the class itself, which is nicer and more inline with every other language that supports classes. Once other browsers pick up support, the approach I just outlined will likely be something of a bad practice.

One big caveat to using the constructor versus the `connectedCallback` for DOM-related logic arises if you are using the Shadow DOM, which will come up in chapter 7. When using the Shadow DOM, you're creating a separate mini DOM that's internal to your component. In this case, the Shadow DOM is available whenever you create it—even in the constructor.

This caveat is why you'll see many modern Web Components use the constructor for most everything in the component, while the `connectedCallback` might not be used much at all.

Will you use the Shadow DOM? Up until recently, I wouldn't have recommended it, but Firefox just shipped an update with support for it (along with all Web Component features), and Edge should ship a release beyond its development preview soon.

As awesome as the Shadow DOM is, you'll need to weigh whether you need it and whether it's supported in the browser of your choice. There will certainly be situations where the Shadow DOM just doesn't make sense for your project—knowing the nuances of the `connectedCallback` versus constructor methods will be important.

4.3 The remaining Web Component lifecycle methods

We've discussed four of the six methods of our component lifecycle (constructor, `connectedCallback`, `attributeChangedCallback`, and `observedAttributes`). There are just two remaining methods: `disconnectedCallback` and `adoptedCallback`.

4.3.1 Disconnected callback

The `disconnectedCallback` serves a very important purpose, which is to give the component an opportunity to clean up after itself. This callback is fired when the component is removed from the DOM.

The reason for cleanup is twofold. First, you don't want stray code running when you don't need it. Second is to give garbage collection a chance to run. If you're not familiar with garbage collection, consider a language like C++. When you store data in a variable, it will never go away, or get *released,* to use proper terminology. As a developer, it is your job to properly release it when you are done. If you're not careful, all the variables you're not using anymore can start adding up and consuming tons of memory! Luckily, with more modern languages like JS, your unused variables will get "garbage-collected." Every once in a while, when the engine (in our case, the JS engine) knows it has enough idle time to clean up, it will go in and release the variables you aren't using. It's not psychic, though, and can't predict what you don't need.

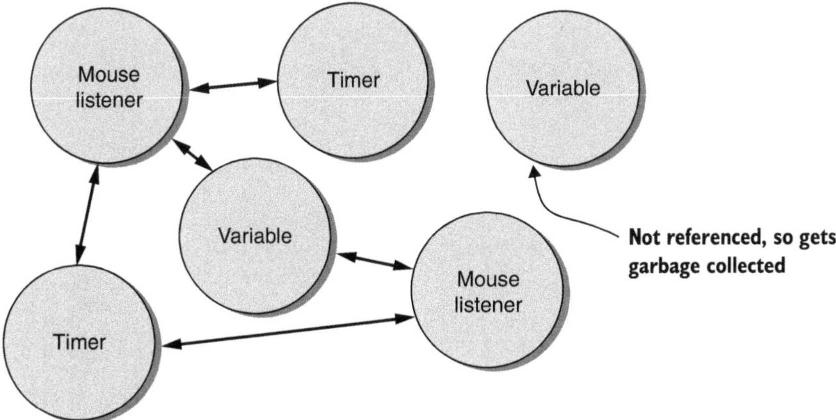

Figure 4.3 Memory references inside a Web Component

Instead, if it sees that you don't reference or link to something in memory, as in figure 4.3, it will release it. This is why the `disconnectedCallback` is a good opportunity to reset or null any variables that might link to other objects.

It can definitely be a chore to worry about these finer details when your component just works. Occasionally, if we know exactly how we are using our component, we can ignore some of this. For example, if you know that your application will never be removed from the DOM, you might be able to ignore cleanup. Of course, the scope of projects can change, and that component you never expected to be removed might need to be.

To cite an example of much-needed cleanup, say you query a server every 30 seconds to get updated data. If you `removeChild(yourelement);` from its parent container, it will still run that timer and still query the server. Let's try a simplified experiment using a countdown timer example.

Listing 4.6 A demonstration of code running after the element has been removed

```
<html>
<head>
   <meta charset="UTF-8">
   <title>Cleanup Component</title>
   <script>
       class CleanupComponent extends HTMLElement {
           connectedCallback() {
               this.counter = 100;
               setInterval( () =>
                   this.update(), 1000);       <-- Starts the countdown timer
           }

           update() {
               this.innerHTML = this.counter;
               this.counter --;
               console.log(this.counter);      <-- Console logs the current timer value (still running after component is removed!)
```

```
            }
        }

        customElements.define('cleanup-component', CleanupComponent);
    </script>
</head>

<body>
    <cleanup-component></cleanup-component>
    <button onclick="document.body.removeChild(document.querySelector
                    ('cleanup-component'))">remove</button>    <-- Button to remove the component
</body>
</html>
```

In this example, we're also logging our counter value with

```
console.log(this.counter);
```

I've also added a button with some inline JS code. When you click the Remove button, the countdown timer component is removed from the DOM.

When you run the example, the timer counts down as usual. After clicking Remove, you don't see the timer anymore, but if you open the console log, you'll see that it's *still* counting down! It's bad enough to leave that timer running—even worse that we're muddying up the console log with elements we don't want anymore. It would be still worse if we were making network requests we don't care about or doing something computationally expensive for an element we don't need.

So, we can use the `disconnectedCallback` to clean up our timer. We'll likely want to clean any event listeners added as well, such as mouse events. Let's try cleaning up our timer when the element is removed in the following listing.

Listing 4.7 Using `disconnectedCallback` to clean up a timer

```
class CleanupComponent extends HTMLElement {
    connectedCallback() {
        this.counter = 100;
        this.timer = setInterval( () => this.update(), 1000);
    }

    update() {
        this.innerHTML = this.counter;
        this.counter --;
        console.log(this.counter);
    }

    disconnectedCallback() {
        clearInterval(this.timer);    <-- When component is removed (on disconnectedCallback), removes the timer
    }
}
```

We've now captured our timer in a variable:

```
this.timer = setInterval( () => this.update(), 1000);
```

This way, when we need to clean up using `disconnectedCallback`, we can clear it using the same variable:

```
disconnectedCallback() {
    clearInterval(this.timer);
}
```

Checking our logs again, we have no more messages, and our element should be properly garbage-collected on the next pass.

4.3.2 Adopted callback

Despite the fact that even I need to buckle down and use `disconnectedCallback` more to write better and more versatile components, this last lifecycle method I truly can't see most people ever needing. The `adoptedCallback` lifecycle method fires when your Web Component moves to a different document.

Don't worry if this doesn't make sense, because it doesn't usually happen. Usually, you'll have only one document per HTML page. The exception to this is when using iframes (or inline-frames), which have really fallen out of favor for most uses. Basically, with an iframe, you have a mini HTML page in a frame on your master HTML page.

Elements can be stolen from the iframe and placed into the surrounding page, or vice versa. To do this, you'd grab a reference to the element and then move it to the new document:

```
const frame = document.getElementsByTagName("iframe")[0]
const el = frame.contentWindow.document.getElementsByTagName(
      "my-custom-component")[0];
const adopted = document.adoptNode(el);
```

Once done, the `adoptedCallback` lifecycle method will fire. But again, on the rare occasion I've found myself working with iframes, I've never had to move nodes from one document to the other. Maybe you'll find a use for this method, and if you do, know that your component can listen!

4.4 Comparing to React's lifecycle

Let's now talk about the Web Component lifecycle in relation to the React lifecycle. After all, with only a handful of lifecycle methods, it can feel like Web Components might be lacking. Given how popular React is, and its wide audience of developers, it's great for measuring Web Components against to see how they stack up.

React is a bit opinionated, like all frameworks and libraries tend to be. It offers a specific component lifecycle that works for React developers and their use cases. Of course, there's absolutely nothing wrong with this, but the point is that we're looking at a lifecycle that may or may not apply to how you want to work. I'd like to reiterate that this is exactly what I love about working with Web Components—they have just enough features to cover the bare minimum of what you need, and anything beyond that can be built up with your own code or existing microframeworks or libraries.

The React documentation breaks down its lifecycle methods into four main categories: mounting, updating, unmounting, and error handling. The error-handling method is one we haven't gotten into yet, and indeed, there is nothing similar in Web Components. React's philosophy here (at least as of v16) is to establish "error boundaries" such that if you have an error in one component, it doesn't take the rest of your components or the application down with it.

While it is true that a JS error has the potential to do some really bad and unexpected things anywhere in a Web Components-based application, with React, it was a little worse. Prior to v16, an error promised to unmount your entire application! Errors in vanilla JS are usually tamer—unexpected things will happen, but usually your application won't be brought to its knees. As a result, in v16, React created error boundaries so that each component could handle any badness and not affect the rest. Web Components are a little more decentralized, so React's problems aren't so similar.

In React, *mounting* means creating a chunk of HTML that represents your component and then inserting that HTML into the DOM. For mounting, there are several relevant methods.

Like Web Components (and most everything else), React lets you override the constructor. The types of things you'd do are very similar to Web Components, in that you'd likely not want to put tons of component logic here, and you'd ideally initialize things that you'd use later. The methods `componentWillMount` and `componentDidMount` let you do stuff before and after the component is added to the DOM.

While `componentDidMount` is a lot like Web Components' `connectedCallback`, there doesn't seem to be lots of purpose for `componentWillMount`. There's nothing here you couldn't just do with the constructor. In fact, React v16 is already showing warning messages that this method will be deprecated in the next major version.

Prior to `componentDidMount` (or when the component changes in some way), you are allowed to override the `render` method. With this method, you would mainly return HTML to represent your component's inner markup.

With Web Components, `render` just isn't necessary as a standard lifecycle method, though LitElement and others have added this to their Web Components to make updating HTML more streamlined. With the basic lifecycle as is, we can control our component's `innerHTML` at any time and aren't limited by our component lifecycle for when to set our component's contents, or even which pieces are updated. In this regard, we are better off being unbound by stiff rules that say where or when we can create the inner workings of our component! With LitElement and various frameworks, you're buying into a design pattern and making the choice to be bound by some rules that dictate when your component renders. Great, if that's what you choose, but as a standard that needs to fit a variety of use cases, I think it's much better to opt-in to something like a `render` method.

For updating the component, React has several methods as well: `componentWillReceiveProps`, `shouldComponentUpdate`, `componentWillUpdate`, `getSnapshotBeforeUpdate`, and `componentDidUpdate`. In addition to `componentWillReceiveProps` being deprecated soon, the rest are helpers for when something changes in your component, and it needs to update. They are less relevant to Web Components because React, as a system, keeps track of a bunch of stuff outside the scope of your actual

HTML element. State, properties, and so on are all things that change and trigger your component to change. In fact, React has a different suggested usage altogether. You are supposed to change state or properties, and your component is supposed to . . . well . . . "react" to these changes.

When you interact with Web Components, on the other hand, you'll likely do so much like you'd interact with a normal DOM element: through a custom API or using attributes. With this difference, the need for these extra methods melts away. Some might argue that the way React works offers more of a helping hand, but with Web Components, you have more freedom to do things how you want, specific to your own project.

4.5 Comparing to a game engine lifecycle

Speaking of freedom to implement how we want depending on the project, we shouldn't regard traditional web applications as the only use case for building something on the web. More and more graphics-intensive projects are being built all the time. A good use case to consider is a game engine. In this regard, I think it's fair to compare the Web Component lifecycle to Unity. Unity 3D is one of the most popular tools for making real-time 3D for games, applications, and even AR/VR.

In Unity, a developer typically works with a 3D object of some sort that has a `Monobehavior` attached. Much like our Web Component extends `HTMLElement`, a custom Unity behavior extends `Monobehavior`.

`Monobehavior` has two lifecycle methods used for starting a behavior. `Awake` is like our Web Component constructor. It gets called when the `Monobehavior` is created, regardless of whether it's enabled or not. With Unity, behaviors aren't necessarily active and running if they are disabled.

Likewise, our Web Component isn't really "enabled" if it hasn't been added to the DOM, because it's not visually on the page. Unity has `OnEnable` and `OnDisable` methods to watch for this. A behavior can get enabled multiple times, just like our Web Component can get added to the DOM multiple times. So here, `OnEnable` is a lot like our Web Component's `connectedCallback`.

Unity's `Start` method gets called the first time the behavior is enabled, including if it's enabled when the application starts. Web Components don't have a similar call, and like I said, if we add the same element to our DOM more than once, we need to guard against any re-initialization if it hurts our components. Luckily, this is easy to overcome—we can just set a variable to true the first time going through our `connectedCallback` and avoid calling the same initialization with an `if/then`.

These subtle distinctions only matter if you choose to not use your Web Component in the simple way of just writing markup in your HTML, as in when creating, adding, and removing elements with JS. For example, when prototyping or building a specific application, you'll probably know exactly how your Web Components are to be used and be able to adjust as needed. If you're building a library of Web Components you intend to share, you may want to consider all of these use cases.

Next, Unity 3D has several methods in its `Monobehavior` lifecycle that are called each render frame, which means they are called many times per second to give the developer an opportunity to update what gets drawn on screen when graphics are updated. These methods handle specific things like physics, different render passes, and so on. For our purposes, I'll condense them down to Unity's `update` method because unless we get into WebGL or other specific cases, they really don't apply to Web Components.

While Web Components don't have a similar update method as part of the lifecycle API, or even the variety of update methods I've described previously, we arguably don't need one. We aren't necessarily doing games or graphics-intensive things that need to run every frame with JS, so in those cases, we don't need it. On the occasion we do need an update method, there are a couple of ways we can do it.

The first thing we can try is a timer. Let's take that timer example we had before, and start there.

Listing 4.8 A countdown timer component

```
<html>
<head>
  <meta charset="UTF-8">
  <title>Countdown Timer</title>
  <script>
      class CountdownTimer extends HTMLElement {
          connectedCallback() {
              this.counter = 100;
              setInterval( () =>          // Creates our internal timer (calls update every second)
                      this.update(), 1000);
          }

          update() {                                      // Displays the timer's current value
              this.innerHTML = this.counter;
              this.counter --;                 // Decrements every timer update
          }
      }

      customElements.define('countdown-timer', CountdownTimer);
  </script>
</head>

<body>
  <countdown-timer></countdown-timer>
</body>
</html>
```

In listing 4.8, we've created a simple example countdown timer component (virtually the same as earlier in this chapter). When our component is added to the DOM, we use our `connectedCallback` to initialize a property called `counter` and set it to 100. We also start a standard JS timer and attach that to an internal method called `update`:

```
setInterval( () => this.update(), 1000);
```

If you have used the timer before, you know the last parameter of 1,000 makes the timer fire every 1,000 milliseconds (or every second). On the `Update` method itself, we simply set the contents of our component with `innerHTML` and decrement our variable by one.

What you'll see in your browser when you run this is a numeric display that starts at 100 and counts down by 1 every second. `setInterval` is great for situations like this where you just need a normal timer; but for animation or graphics that need to change every 1/30th of a second, for example, JS's newer `requestAnimationFrame` will produce smoother results that are actually tied to the browser's render cycle.

Let's swap our `setInterval` for `requestAnimationFrame` and do something a little more animated in the next listing.

Listing 4.9 Swapping `setInterval` for `requestAnimationFrame`

```
<html>
<head>
    <title>Visual Countdown Timer</title>
    <script>
        class VisualCountdownTimer extends HTMLElement {
            connectedCallback() {
                this.timer = 200;
                this.style.backgroundColor = 'green';
                this.style.display = 'inline-block';
                this.style.height = '50px';
                requestAnimationFrame( () =>
                        this.update());
            }

            update() {
                this.timer --;
                if (this.timer <= 0) {
                    this.timer = 200;
                }
                this.style.width =
                        this.timer + 'px';
                requestAnimationFrame( () =>
                        this.update());
        }

        customElements.define('countdown-timer', VisualCountdownTimer);
    </script>
</head>

<body>
    <countdown-timer></countdown-timer>
</body>
</html>
```

Using requestAnimationFrame instead of setInterval (annotates the first `requestAnimationFrame` call)

Smoothly animates the width of our component (annotates `this.style.width =`)

Keeps requestAnimationFrame going by calling it every update (annotates the second `requestAnimationFrame` call)

With the exception of `requestAnimationFrame` happening only once, thereby forcing us to call it on every `update` call, the implementation is mostly the same as `setInterval`:

```
requestAnimationFrame( () => this.update());
```

Again, I have a counter, but I call it `timer` now, because we'll be making our component shrink with each animation frame to simulate a countdown timer. I also have some CSS styling to set the background color, height, and inline-block style of the component. It's not awesome that I'm setting style with code here when I could use CSS, but I want to keep this example dead simple:

```
this.style.backgroundColor = 'green';
this.style.display = 'inline-block';
this.style.height = '50px';
```

On the `update` method, we decrement our `timer` and also check if it's equal to or smaller than 0. If so, then we reset it to 200, just to keep our component in an infinitely demo-able loop. After all that, we set the component height and width to the `timer` property. Lastly, we call the next animation frame and run our `update` method again. We end up with a green visual countdown component that shrinks every frame until it gets to nothing and then resets to 200 pixels wide again.

In addition to `setInterval` and `requestAnimationFrame`, other frameworks and libraries we may want to use might have their own ways to call a timed `update` method like this. For example, if you use a 3D library like Three.js or Babylon, they both have their own render hooks you can tap into, so you'd implement your component a bit differently.

The point is that the Web Component lifecycle doesn't come with an `update` method like many other component lifecycles you might see. Because web technology can be used for so many different things, it's not wise to dictate how you should do it. Most of the time in my own work, I never need that `update` method. Even simple UI animation can be handled through CSS. And of course, when I do, I like having the choice of which method to use.

Maybe you, in your own personal use cases, *always* need some sort of `update` method like Unity has. It certainly makes sense if you are a game developer or similar and need a `render/update` method to drive your game and animation.

If this is the case, you're still covered. Web Components support inheritance, and we can go one level deeper and just add on to the existing component lifecycle. Let's steal code from our visual countdown timer animation example and use our `requestAnimationFrame` call to power it.

Listing 4.10 Creating an inheritable base for components to update every frame

```
<html>
<head>
  <script>
       class GameComponentBase
               extends HTMLElement {
           constructor() {
               super();
               this.onUpdate();
           }

           update() {}
```

- Class provides a base for building game-style components
- Update method to be filled out by component using the base class

```
        onUpdate() {
            this.update();
            requestAnimationFrame( () => this.onUpdate());
        }
    }

    class VisualCountdownTimer
            extends GameComponentBase {
        connectedCallback() {
            this.timer = 200;
            this.style.backgroundColor = 'green';
            this.style.display = 'inline-block';
            this.style.height = '50px';
        }

        update() {
            this.timer --;
            if (this.timer <= 0) {
                this.timer = 200;
            }
            this.style.width = this.timer + 'px';
        }
    }

    customElements.define('countdown-timer', VisualCountdownTimer);
  </script>
</head>

<body>
  <countdown-timer></countdown-timer>
</body>
</html>
```

Internal update method to keep requestAnimation frame going (annotation on `onUpdate()`)

Actual component class, which extends the base component (annotation on `extends GameComponentBase {`)

So, in the example in listing 4.10, we're still doing the exact same simple animation: making a countdown indicator graphic shrink. But we've pulled the logic that deals with creating an update event every frame out into its own class. Note that I say *class* and not *component* because we've done everything to create a new component except define a custom element and map that to a tag.

Instead, we're creating a base class, `GameComponentBase`, that components can inherit from. Figure 4.4 shows this chain of inheritance, all originating from `HTMLElement`. I did

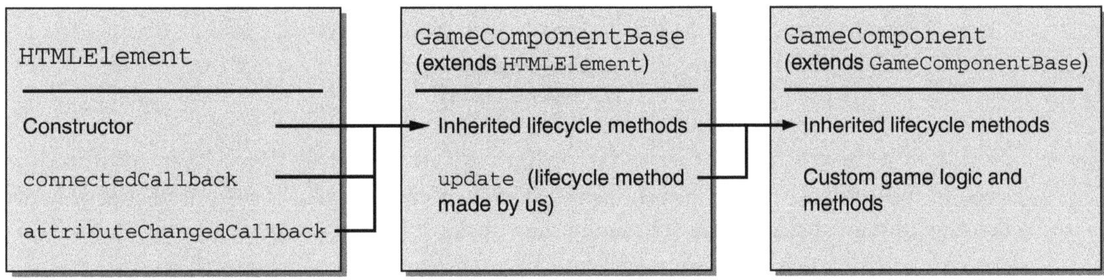

Figure 4.4 Using inheritance to create a subclass of `HTMLElement` to enable frame updates like a game engine

something a bit tricky, though. Instead of directly calling the `update` method, I have a different method—`onUpdate`:

```
onUpdate() {
   this.update();
    requestAnimationFrame( () => this.onUpdate());
}
```

The reason is best explained by doing it a way I would not suggest first. Let's not use both, and only use `update`.

Listing 4.11 Simpler example with just one overridable update

```
class GameComponentBase extends HTMLElement {
    constructor() {
        super();
            this.update();
        }

        update() {
            requestAnimationFrame( () =>
               this.update());      <-- Single update method
        }
    }
```

This new `GameComponentBase` is still good and can be used in pretty much the same way, but let's take a look at how we'd use it.

Listing 4.12 Using the simpler base class

```
class VisualCountdownTimer extends GameComponentBase {
    connectedCallback() {
        this.timer = 200;
        this.style.backgroundColor = 'green';
        this.style.display = 'inline-block';
        this.style.height = '50px';
    }

    update() {
        this.timer --;
        if (this.timer <= 0) {
            this.timer = 200;
        }
        this.style.width = this.timer + 'px';
        super.update();      <-- Now required to
    }                            call super.update()
}
```

Notice we've simplified our `GameComponentBase` class a bit. We've condensed the two `update` methods into one, but in our `VisualCountdownTimer` component, we're now forcing anyone using `GameComponentBase` to call `super.update();` every time! Of course, with inheritance, we don't call `update` on our underlying `GameComponentBase` unless we use `super.update()`. I don't know about you, but I'd make a new component and forget to call `super.update()` most of the time. A little planning like this up front can make the developer experience happier.

Unity has two more lifecycle methods, `OnDisable` and `OnDestroy`, which serve the same purpose as Web Components' `disconnectedCallback`: to clean up after disabling or destroying the component.

4.6 Component lifecycle v0

The Web Components API seems pretty solid now, doesn't it? We've compared and contrasted it to other component lifecycles, and I hope you have a pretty good feel that it'll work well for anything you throw at it. I don't expect that you'll know each and every method by memory, especially when starting out. We all have to Google syntax occasionally. One caveat when you do look up usage with Web Components is that it's a relatively new standard, and it's already gone through one revision.

What this means is that when you look up syntax, you might accidentally stumble on the old methods. Currently, we are using v1 of the Web Components API. What came before was dubbed v0, and v0 won't work anywhere except for where it was originally implemented: Chrome. Even there, as time moves on, it will be more and more spotty.

IMPORTANT The Web Components API has changed!

Not much has changed really (see table 4.1), though the first thing to note is that instead of letting you use the constructor in v1, you use the `createdCallback` method.

Table 4.1 Custom Element/Web Components API changes

Method calls	How it changed
Deprecated: `createdCallback` Current: `constructor`	In v1, the more standard constructor replaces the `createdCallback`.
Deprecated: `AttachedCallback` Current: `connectedCallback`	In v1, to listen for when your element has been added to the DOM, you use the `connectedCallback;` in v0, it was the `attachedCallback`.
Deprecated: `detachedCallback` Current: `disconnectedCallback`	The old way of listening for when the element is removed from the DOM, now the `disconnectedCallback` in v1, was the `detachedCallback` in v0.
Former: `AttributechangedCallback` Current: `attributeChangedCallback` and `observedAttributes`	The last change is the `attributeChangedCallback` in v1. The name actually hasn't changed here, but the usage has. Now you need to make sure to define those `observedAttributes`, as we discussed in the last chapter, to tell the component what attributes you'd like to listen for. Previously, this callback would just listen to everything.

Table 4.1 Custom Element/Web Components API changes *(continued)*

Method calls	How it changed

Deprecated:
`document.registerElement`
Current:
`customElements.define`
	Lastly, outside of the component lifecycle API, the way you register your element has changed as well. Currently, we use
	`customElements.define('my-web-component', MyWebComponent);`
	Formerly, in v0, we would use
	`document.registerElement('my-web-component', MyWebComponent);`

Summary

In this chapter, you learned

- How to round out the lifecycle methods you've already learned with the remaining two methods: `disconnectedCallback` and `adoptedCallback`
- The concept of garbage collection, and why you would clean up after your component
- How to subclass a Web Component and use it as a base to provide common functionality, like frame-by-frame animation, to other components
- Differences for and similarities to the React and game engine lifecycle methods, and how even though both have more methods to their APIs, Web Components don't fall short

5 Instrumenting a better web app through modules

This chapter covers

- ES2015 modules as an alternative to `<script>` tags in your HTML
- Creating self-reliant Web Components
- Using a Web Component to contain your entire application
- Scope management for callbacks with the ES2015 fat-arrow feature

So far in exercises throughout this book, we've been putting our classes and component definitions inside the `<head>` tag in our main HTML page. Typically, you'd never want to do this on a real project and might want to be a bit more organized with a `<script>` tag pointing to a JS file for each component you have. At first glance, this is perfectly fine. If your project uses Web Components only in a limited way, this works! CSS is similar—each component can have its own CSS file as well, which can be linked from the main page. With many components to manage in your project, however, this could get a little out of hand. In this chapter, let's explore ES2015 modules for a better way.

5.1 Using the <script> tag to load your Web Components

To explain why linking to multiple JS/CSS files in our main HTML page can be problematic, let's revisit our Web Component from chapter 2. If you recall, this component was a photo carousel that allowed us to set a list of photos to navigate through as well as some metadata for display, such as title and author, as figure 5.1 shows.

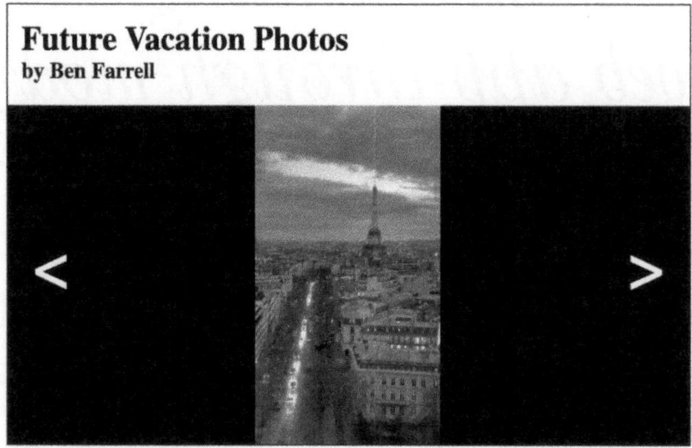

Figure 5.1 Revisiting the photo carousel component from chapter 2

With this component example, all of our JS and CSS code was in the index.html file with no external references. Of course, things get more maintainable by moving this code to external files that we can simply link to and bring in. This is fairly typical for a no-frills web project. When we do this, our HTML file gets more manageable and easier to read, as shown in the following listing.

Listing 5.1 Example of loading Web Components with the `<script>` tag

```
<html>
<head>
   <meta charset="UTF-8">
   <title>Script Source for Loading Web Components</title>
   <script src="photocarousel.js"></script>      <-- JavaScript has been pulled out to a linked file.
   <link href="photocarousel.css"
         rel="stylesheet"
         type="text/css"/>      <-- CSS has been pulled out to a linked file.
</head>
<body>
   <wcia-photo-carousel
           title="Future Vacation Photos"
           author="Ben Farrell"
           photos="https://i.imgur.com/fBmIASF.jpg,https://i.imgur.com/
           3zxD6rz.jpg,https://i.imgur.com/nKBgeLOr.jpg,https://
           i.imgur.com/yVjJZ1Yr.jpg">
```

```
    </wcia-photo-carousel>
</body>
</html>
```

5.1.1 Having to deal with many JS and CSS references

Now, if you had more Web Components in this project, you might add more and more `<script>` tags and more and more `<link>` tags. There's nothing wrong with this. Lots of times when we develop a big project, we pull in a bunch of libraries, and as a final step before releasing, we concatenate to one file for JS and one file for CSS.

Often, when relying on script references in my HTML, I maintain two separate HTML files. One is for development, and the other is for releasing my actual project. In a case where we have many Web Components we intend to pull in, our dev HTML head tag might look like the following listing, which shows an example of many hypothetical JS and CSS references in a more fully featured photo album application.

Listing 5.2 Example of index.html for development

```
<head>
    <meta charset="UTF-8">
    <script src="photocarousel.js"></script>
    <link href="photocarousel.css" rel="stylesheet" type="text/css"/>

    <script src="photoalbumbrowser.js"></script>
    <link href=" photoalbumbrowser.css" rel="stylesheet" type="text/css"/>

    <script src="loginpanel.js"></script>
    <link href="loginpanel.css" rel="stylesheet" type="text/css"/>

    <script src="socialsharing.js"></script>
    <link href="socialsharing.css" rel="stylesheet" type="text/css"/>

    <script src="photouploader.js"></script>
    <link href=" photouploader.css" rel="stylesheet" type="text/css"/>
</head>
```

Photo carousel component (CSS/JS)

Hypothetical photo album browser component (CSS/JS)

Hypothetical login panel component (CSS/JS)

Hypothetical social sharing component (CSS/JS)

Hypothetical photo upload component (CSS/JS)

Meanwhile, our goal would be to pull in fewer dependencies on our production-ready HTML file. We could run a task via Grunt, Gulp, or even just NPM to concatenate all JS and all CSS so that our production-ready HTML head tag looks like this:

```
<head>
    <meta charset="UTF-8">
    <script src="build.js"></script>
    <link href="build.css" rel="stylesheet" type="text/css"/>
</head>
```

To be honest, I'm still not perfectly happy here. For one, I have to worry about two imports for every Web Component I use (CSS and JS). Second, this doesn't do anything to maximize code reusability. Yes, I can point to external files containing code for my Web Components, but what if those files themselves need to point to external files? For example, in chapter 4, we explored extending `HTMLElement` to create a game-oriented base component that gives us an `update` method that is fired every frame. We need to import that `GameComponentBase` somehow.

You might say, "Well, importing that `GameComponentBase` class is easy: we'll just add it to the list of JS files we link to in our `<head>` tag." Again, depending on your use, this might be manageable. The counterargument here is that you're accepting the challenge to keep track of every single dependency in your project. If you just have one or two dependencies, great! If you have 10 or 20 or more, it can get problematic.

5.1.2 Tiny scripts are more organized, but make the reference problem worse

Dependencies can come in many forms. Our `GameComponentBase` is a major one, but you can also consider smaller dependencies. Dependencies can be as small as helper methods to manage your HTML, or even a super-tiny configuration object. For example, we could maintain a project-wide data model that we import into any Web Component or JS file that needs it:

```
appConfig = {
   rootURL: 'yourserver.com',
   apiVersion: 2,
   login: 'username'
}
```

This is just a simple object that contains some data about how we want to log in to our server (if we're using one), but it could potentially be used in any Web Component that gets data from this server. It's a piece of reusable code that we need everywhere. It's also such a tiny piece of JS—which might be linked to along with 20 or 50 other tiny pieces of JS—that remembering to include all of these in your `<head>` tag can get a bit daunting.

5.1.3 Including CSS for self-reliant components

Before we address this, let's make our Web Component class even more self-reliant by making it manage the CSS itself. We're simply eliminating the need to point to an external CSS file by inserting the `<style>` rules into the `innerHTML` along with the HTML markup. This example, as seen in the next listing, doesn't change anything about our component except to leave us with only one file to reference when using the component in our project.

Listing 5.3 Adding CSS to our component's `innerHTML`

```
this.innerHTML = '<h2>' + \
  this.getAttribute('title') + '</h2> \
  <h4>by '+ this.getAttribute('author') + '</h4> \
  <div class="image-container"></div> \
  <button class="back">&lt</button> \
  <button class="forward">&gt</button> \
  <style> \
      wcia-photo-carousel { \
      width: 500px; \
      height: 300px; \
      display: flex; \
      padding-top: 10px; \
      flex-direction: column; \
      position: relative; \
      border-color: black; \
      border-width: 1px; \
      border-style: solid; \
  } \
  wcia-photo-carousel h2, h4 { \
      margin-bottom: 0; \
      margin-top: 0; \
      margin-left: 10px; \
  } \
  wcia-photo-carousel .image-container { \
      margin-top: 15px; \
      flex: 1; \
      background-color: black; \
      background-size: contain; \
      background-repeat: no-repeat; \
      background-position: 50%; \
  } \
  wcia-photo-carousel button { \
      cursor: pointer; \
      background: transparent; \
      border: none; \
      font-size: 48px; \
      color: white; \
      position: absolute; \
      top: 50%; \
  } \
  wcia-photo-carousel button.back { \
      left: 10px; \
  } \
  wcia-photo-carousel button.forward { \
      right: 10px; \
  }\
</style>';
```

HTML markup that was previously in our component

CSS added to our component, previously in an external CSS file

For now, we've accomplished something pretty good—a completely self-reliant component that only needs to be included via a single `<script>` tag. To be fair, our `innerHTML` is getting a bit long. A criticism could be that we've just moved some complexity from the outside to the inside and made the inside a bit less manageable. Don't worry, we'll clean this up in the next chapter by expanding on the concept of modules that we are learning here.

Listing 5.4 Reducing dependencies with no more CSS references

```
<head>
   <meta charset="UTF-8">
   <script src="photocarousel.js"></script>.     <-- Reduced component dependencies from two lines (CSS and JS) to just JS
</head>

<body>
   <wcia-photo-carousel
           title="Future Vacation Photos"
           author="Ben Farrell"
           photos="https://i.imgur.com/fBmIASF.jpg,https://
          i.imgur.com/3zxD6rz.jpg,https://i.imgur.com/nKBgeLOr.jpg,https://
          i.imgur.com/yVjJZ1Yr.jpg">
   </wcia-photo-carousel>
</body>
```

Honestly, though, when looking at listing 5.4, things look pretty clean. You'd never know the complexity of the component on the inside; you're just using it. With only a single `<script>` tag for including the Web Component definition, there's really not much to manage here. Even if there was just a separate CSS file like there was before, for someone using this component, it might be a bit confusing. They wouldn't necessarily know that the CSS file was required, or even where it is or what its file name is. Again, having a single script dependency to use your component and having it just work, managing its own dependencies, makes things simple for component consumers.

5.1.4 *Dependency hell*

Now, if you think our goal to have our Web Component be completely self-reliant is adding up to more problems than it's worth, I wouldn't blame you. Prior to this next feature that I'm going to show you, using `<script>` tags and linking to CSS files was exactly what I did. It worked fairly well.

The problems start when you need to make your Web Components a little smarter and more organized. In addition to the small JS dependencies I brought up before, how do you best manage your HTML inside your component? It would be ideal, especially if there's a lot of it, to have it outside your class and bring it in. It can be helpful to keep the markup as a separate concern, not only so it doesn't clutter your Web Component class, but also so that multiple team members can work on a single component and not all have to work in the same file when working on different concerns like markup, controller logic, or style.

Another big concern is when you have a custom Web Component inside your custom Web Component. How do you best deal with this? Consider what would happen if you made an application driven by a single component in your index.html page. This component might have eight components within, and then each of those components could have several components as well.

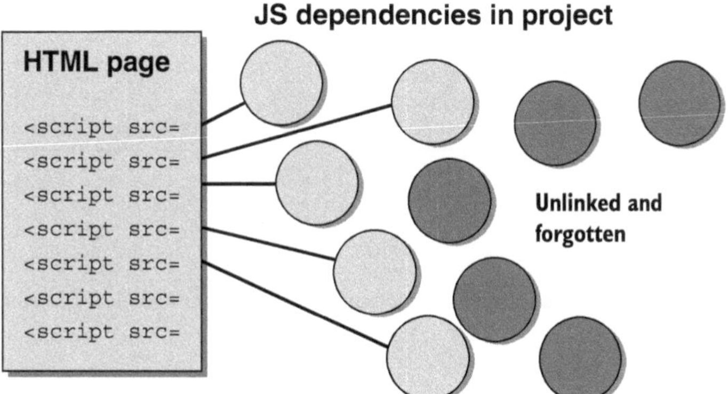

Figure 5.2 Using `<script>` tags on the main HTML page means having to remember to add every single JS file you use throughout.

In this situation, it's suddenly your job to

- Monitor every single component used in your project
- Make sure you have `<script>` tags for each component in your index.html file
- Delete references to any components no longer used
- Keep a complete list of any and all component dependencies, including them in the index.html file
- Manage the load order of every component and component dependency, ensuring that scripts load before they're needed
- Stay in close contact with team members, given that you will all be editing the same index.html file to manage all of this

There are lots of reasons for a better way than the mess figure 5.2 depicts, and, thankfully, in every major modern browser, we can use JS modules!

5.2 *Using modules to solve dependency problems*

If you are unfamiliar with the concept of modules and want a bit of a deeper dive, please see the appendix. In short, however, we're going to forgo our mess of `<script>` tags that we need to maintain and instead load scripts and components using the new `import` keyword. With this, we can reduce the fragility of including JS in our main HTML file and make our Web Components responsible for managing their own dependencies. It's an extremely clean and organized way of working with custom components. To demonstrate, let's create a simple Web Component-based application comprising a few different custom components to highlight this shift in strategy. In the end, we'll have an architecture similar to figure 5.3, which is a lot easier to manage than figure 5.2 and solves our many concerns.

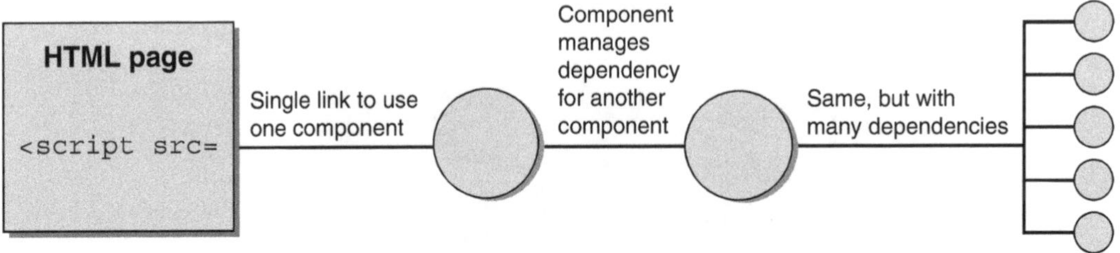

Figure 5.3 The index.html page only references a single component, simplifying our code but still allowing many dependencies.

5.2.1 Creating a musical instrument with Web Components and JS modules

In this demo, I want to create a stringed instrument in our browser. I call it a Web Harp! Each string is made by a Web Component, and, when strummed, it vibrates and makes some sound. To keep it simple, it won't be much to look at, as depicted in figure 5.4, but functionally it should be fun to play with.

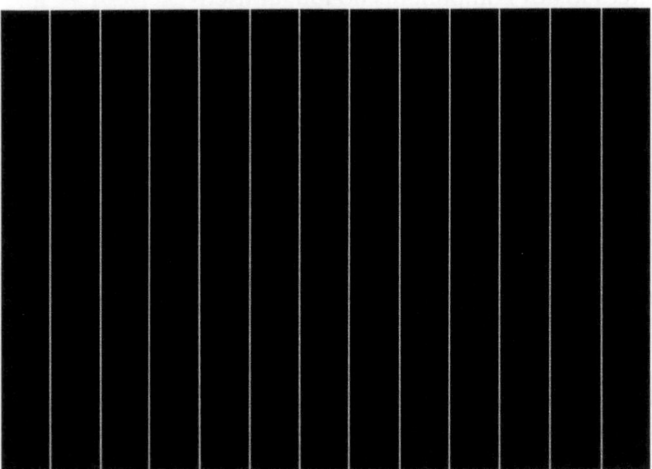

Figure 5.4 Output of our Web Harp demo. Each white line is a strummable string that vibrates and makes some noise.

We will use JS modules to manage all of our dependencies such that we'll load only a single JS file in our index.html, despite the fact that we're using a few Web Components. We won't write our own audio engine, though—instead, we'll import an existing one right into the Web Component that needs it.

Another great thing about decentralizing our dependencies is that our initial HTML page is dead simple, with only one referenced component, as depicted in the following listing.

Listing 5.5 A minimal application HTML file for our Web Harp demo

```
<html>
    <head>
        <title>Web Harp</title>
        <script type="module"
                src="./components/app/app.js">
        </script>
        <link href="csshake.min.css"
              type="text/css" rel="stylesheet">
        <link href="main.css"
              type="text/css" rel="stylesheet">
    </head>
    <body>
        <webharp-app strings="8"></webharp-app>
    </body>
</html>
```

- Our single Web Component dependency, which itself is responsible for all other component dependencies in the app (the `<script>` tag)
- A third-party CSS shake library to give our strings a vibrate effect (the `csshake.min.css` link)
- Some light CSS to manage style on our overall HTML page (the `main.css` link)

Now, I'm cheating a bit with the CSS because I'm using a library to manage animation. So, the components for this project aren't self-reliant in that regard, but they are in every other aspect. The HTML in each component is super simple, too. Since we're just making some vertical lines to represent the strings in our harp, there's very little markup. All of this simplicity lets us focus on exploring JS dependencies using modules. We'll explore using modules for managing HTML and CSS in the next chapter to make everything much cleaner when a project requires lots of style and markup, unlike this one.

In this project, we'll be managing three components:

- `<webharp-app>` will contain our entire application and manage our mouse input.
- `<webharp-strings>` will hold the strings in our application.
- `<webharp-string>` will be each individual string that we can strum.

These components will each be contained in their own folder, inside a master components folder. This is depicted in figure 5.5, where you'll also notice some extra files to help us manage sound and animation. We'll get to those extras as we progress.

Also note that we'll be building up all of these components first to establish our application's minimalistic visual layout. Once done, we'll finally put the `<webharp-app>` in an index.html page, at which point we can preview the application before we move on to add interactivity, animation, and sound.

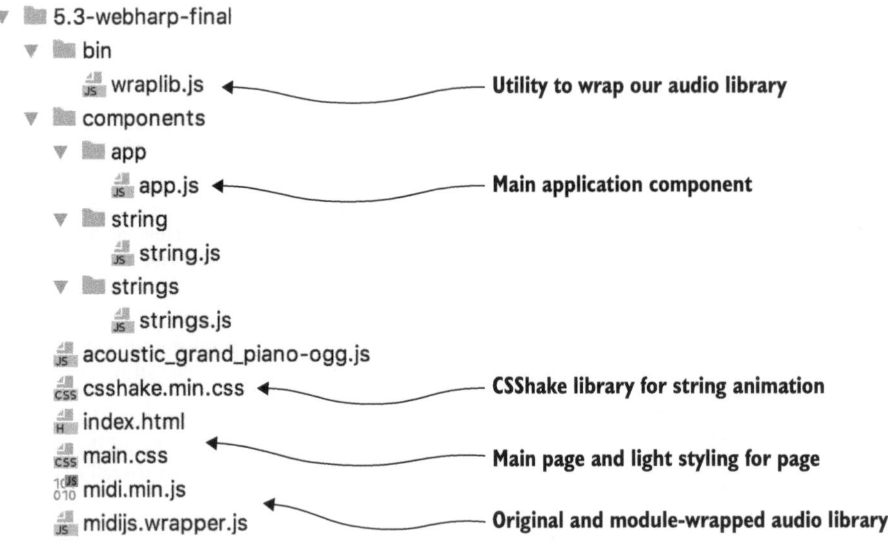

Figure 5.5 Web Harp example file structure

5.2.2 *Starting with the smallest component*

Let's start at the smallest level and focus on the <webharp-string> component. It's going to be a simple vertical line that we create using a <div> tag, which we'll style to be as tall as the container and 2 pixels wide with a color of white, as depicted in figure 5.6. Our component begins in the next listing.

Figure 5.6 A single `<webharp-string>` component centered over a black background

Listing 5.6 A Web Component that defines an individual string for our instrument

```
// file: components/string/string.js

export default class WebHarpString
extends HTMLElement {
   strum(params) {}

   stopStrum() {}

   connectedCallback() {
       this.innerHTML = '<div class="line"></div> \
                        <style>\
                            webharp-string > .line { \
                                background-color: white;\
```

- Exports class as a module
- Empty function placeholders to fill in later
- Inner HTML of our string component

```
                                    height: 100%; \
                                    width: 2px; \
                                }\
                            </style>';
    }
}

if (!customElements.get('webharp-string')) {
    customElements.define(                    ⊲ Registers our custom
'webharp-string', WebHarpString);               <webharp-string> element
}
```

Note that we're using the `export default` keywords prior to the class definition. This marks our class as a JS module, which has the ability to be imported elsewhere. Our `connectedCallback`, which happens when our component is added to the DOM, should be no surprise given what you've already read in the other chapters. We are simply setting our `innerHTML` to have a `<div>` with the style I mentioned earlier.

We vaguely know that we want to be able to strum this string. If you've ever watched a guitar string, you might remember that it vibrates for a little while, but eventually stops. So, without a real plan, let's just stub in a `strum` method. We can guess that it takes some parameters based on what note it plays and how forcefully it was strummed. We'll circle back to that later, but we can also guess that after a certain amount of time, we'll need to stop strumming; hence we can add an empty `stopStrum` method.

5.2.3 *Importing and nesting a Web Component within a Web Component*

Let's move on to the `<webharp-strings>` component (listing 5.7). This component will serve as the layout container for the several strings we plan to place horizontally across the application. Given that our `<webharp-app>` component is just a thin wrapper around this main visual component, the `<webharp-strings>` component is how the entire end application will look, as seen in figure 5.4.

Listing 5.7 A Web Component that contains multiple Web Harp strings

```
// file: components/strings/strings.js

import WebHarpString from '../string/string.js';        ⊲ Imports the individual
                                                           <webharp-string> component
export default class WebHarpStrings extends HTMLElement {
    connectedCallback() {
        let strings = '<div class="spacer"></div>';
        for (let c = 0; c < this.getAttribute('strings'); c++) {
                    strings +=                              ⊲ Loops through and
                        `<webharp-string></webharp-string>`;   adds the number of
        }                                                      strings we want as
                                                               specified by the
            strings += '<style>\                               strings attribute
             webharp-strings { \
                height: 100%; \
                display: flex; \
```

```
                } \
                webharp-strings > webharp-string, div.spacer { \
                    flex: 1; \.
                } \
            </style>';

        this.innerHTML = strings;
        this.stringsElements =
                this.querySelectorAll('webharp-string');
    }
}
if (!customElements.get('webharp-strings')) {
   customElements.define('webharp-strings', WebHarpStrings);
}
```

Each <webharp-string> is laid out via a CSS flex container.

Gets a list of all of our strings through a querySelector

In our `connectedCallback`, we'll create our `<webharp-string>` components in a `for` loop, where the number of times we loop is how many strings we want. This component takes an attribute named `strings`, which feeds into this `for` loop. As a result, we can make a harp with as many or as few strings as we want!

Thankfully, we have CSS flexbox, which allows us to lay out our container very easily. Giving each string a rule of `flex: 1`, our strings will evenly space horizontally across our container, which we've sized as 100% of the size of our application. I've also added a spacer `<div>`; otherwise our first string would start at the very edge of our container and be virtually invisible. We also use `querySelectorAll` to put all the `<webharp-string>` elements we just added into an array we can use later when we flesh out interactivity in our component.

Most importantly, our very first line is

```
import WebHarpString from '../string/string.js';
```

We've learned a lot of exciting things so far in this book about Web Components, but I really feel like this notion of importing another Web Component into this one, entirely with JS, is a true level-up for the whole ecosystem. With this import, we've enabled our application to know what a `<webharp-string>` is, and when we add it to our `innerHTML`, our custom element acts exactly as it should. What's more, we don't have to do anything in our index.html file to link to our Web Component or register it in any way. It just works as a dependency of the component that needs it.

Despite this example being simple, there may be situations where we'd like to use our `<webharp-string>` here as well as inside another component. With `import`, even if importing the same file in multiple places, the request happens only once, with the subsequent import request simply using the first result.

Additionally, we can safeguard our Web Components by not trying to register them again if they've already been used elsewhere, like this:

```
if (!customElements.get('webharp-string')) {
   customElements.define('webharp-string', WebHarpString);
}
```

With this in mind, we can import our Web Components wherever we want with ease. Let's now wrap our `<webharp-strings>` with the final application component, `<webharp-app>`, which will hold the entirety of our application and will be the one component that gets included on our index.html page.

5.2.4 Using a Web Component to wrap an entire web application

When making a web application like this, it can be easy to put your individual components in your main HTML page. Perhaps you might put them in your `<body>` tag and write some light application logic in a `<script>` tag to tie it all together.

Likely, your app will grow in size, you'll keep adding components, and your application logic will grow. As this happens, your index.html will get harder and harder to maintain. When it's time to start pulling major pieces out and repackaging them as smaller components, there will likely be some refactoring.

I'd like to suggest something else. Create a Web Component that represents your entire application. This component will have the same structure and lifecycle as the rest of your components and import whatever dependencies you need. When this component starts to become too big over the course of developing your app, you can easily break pieces off into smaller Web Components. Because they'll have a similar structure to the rest of your components, there will likely be minimal refactoring to do.

Listing 5.8 The Web Harp application Web Component

```
// file: components/app/app.js

import Strings from '../strings/strings.js';

export default class WebHarpApp extends HTMLElement {
   connectedCallback() {
        this.innerHTML = '<webharp-strings strings="' +
          this.getAttribute('strings') + '"></webharp-strings>';
   }
}

if (!customElements.get('webharp-app')) {
   customElements.define('webharp-app', WebHarpApp);
}
```

Our Web Harp application component is fairly simple. Like our last component, we import any child components we need. In this case, we're importing `<webharp-strings>`, which, again, is the container that holds all our Web Harp's strings. Similar to the last component, we're accepting an attribute called `strings` to specify how many strings our Web Harp has and passing that on to the `<webharp-strings>` component. Again, we are using `export default` prior to our class definition to define this component as one that can be imported. Meanwhile, our index.html file is always clean and easy to look at, as seen in the following listing.

Listing 5.9 The Web Harp HTML file so far

```
<html>
   <head>
       <title>Web Harp</title>
       <script type="module"   <— Single app component dependency
               src="./components/app/app.js">
       </script>
       <link href="main.css" type="text/css" rel="stylesheet">
   </head>
   <body>
       <webharp-app strings="12"></webharp-app>   <— Application component
   </body>
</html>
```

When looking at this index.html file, note that the only thing we are linking to with our `<script>` tag is our `<webharp-app>` component. Everything else is a dependency of components downstream from the app component, as seen in figure 5.7, and we thankfully don't need to worry about them here. It's again important to note that this is possible because our `<script>` tag has a type of `module`. This is what enables module loading, which in turn allows us to use the `import` keyword within anything that is loaded as a result.

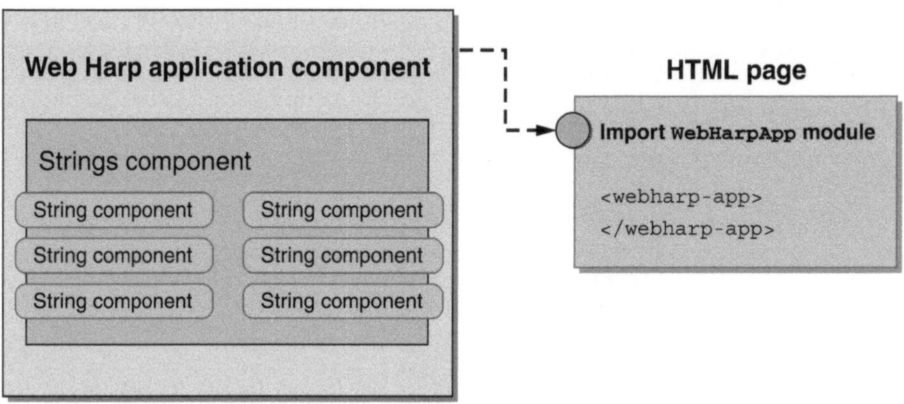

Figure 5.7 Nested Web Components inside an application Web Component, all imported as a module from our main HTML page

There's really nothing special in the main.css file: just the code to set the size and color of our app and remove margins so that our app runs to the edges of our browser window, as seen in listing 5.10 and rendered in our browser in figure 5.8.

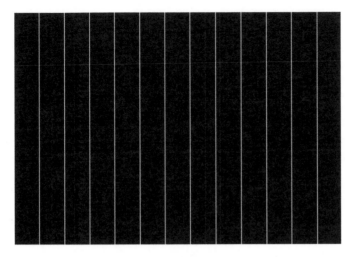

Figure 5.8 The current state of our Web Harp

Listing 5.10 Simple CSS for basic body and application style

```
body {
   background-color: black;
   margin: 0;
   padding: 0;
}

webharp-app {
   height: 100vh;
   width: 100vw;
}
```

As of now, we've created the main structure of our application. The required components are in place, so we can preview it in our browser (remember to use some sort of local web server, as these modules may be blocked from loading if you just use your filesystem). The look actually won't change from now on, but we do need to add some functionality and interactivity!

5.3 Adding interactivity to our component

The next step is to make our application work! Going forward, our goal is to add animation and sound by strumming the harp strings with our mouse. To do this, we're going to listen for mouse input by adding on to our `connectedCallback` in `<webharp-app>`, defined in components/app/app.js.

Listing 5.11 Adding an event listener with the fat arrow

```
// file: components/app/app.js
connectedCallback() {
```

```
    this.innerHTML = '<webharp-strings strings="' +
        this.getAttribute('strings') + '"></webharp-strings>';
    this.stringsElement =
        this.querySelector('webharp-strings');
    this.addEventListener('mousemove',
        e => this.onMouseMove(e));
}
```

Saves a reference to the <webharp-strings> element for later use

Adds a mousemove listener to our application component

To use this element later, we're querying and saving a reference to our <webharp-strings> component using `this.querySelector('webharp-strings');` as seen in listing 5.11. Most importantly, we're adding an event listener to the component itself (`this`) to listen for mouse movement:

```
this.addEventListener('mousemove', e => this.onMouseMove(e));
```

This listener we've added is using the fat arrow to preserve class instance scope in our new `onMouseMove` callback.

5.3.1 Listening for mouse movement

Of course, the function we're pointing to doesn't exist yet. We'll need to add `onMouseMove` to our class in order to capture this event:

```
onMouseMove(event) {
    this.stringsElement.points = {
        last: this.lastPoint,
        current: { x: event.pageX, y: event.pageY } };
    this.lastPoint = { x: event.pageX, y: event.pageY };
}
```

In this callback, we're both capturing the current mouse coordinates in a variable and, before that, sending both the current and last mouse coordinates to our <webharp-strings> element. Sending both of these coordinates enables us to get the distance traveled between our moves, which we can then use to guess how forcefully or fast our strings are being strummed with the mouse.

5.3.2 Passing data to child components

Note that we are sending these points through a getter method in our <webharp-strings> component, so let's populate a setter in components/strings.js with the code in the following listing.

Listing 5.12 Sending points to the Web Harp strings component

```
// file: components/strings/strings.js

set points(pts) {
    if (!this.stringsElements) { return; }
    if (!pts.last || !pts.current) { return; }
    let magnitude =
        Math.abs(pts.current.x - pts.last.x);
```

Checks if our query-selected stringsElements exist

Checks that the current and last coordinates are populated

Captures the speed of the strum

```
    let xMin =                                     <-- Captures the lowest and
        Math.min(pts.current.x, pts.last.x);           highest values of the
    let xMax = Math.max(pts.current.x, pts.last.x);    current and last points

    for (let d = 0;                                <--
            d < this.stringsElements.length; d++) {
        if (xMin <= this.stringsElements[d].offsetLeft && xMax >=
            this.stringsElements[d].offsetLeft) {
            let strum = {                              Loops through the
                power: magnitude,                      strings and strums the
                string: d                              relevant ones
            };
            this.stringsElements[d].strum(strum);
        }
    }
}
```

Ok, so this listing is a little complex, but we can break it down. First, you might recall in the first steps of this example that we looked up each one of our <webharp-string> components, or each visual string, and saved them all to an array we could use later. Well, now is when we use them.

First, we should probably acknowledge that we could potentially get a mouse event coming in before everything is set up, so we'll test if our string array is populated first and bail out of the function if not:

```
if (!this.stringsElements) { return; }
```

We'll also check that both current and last coordinates are populated, especially because during the first mouse-move event, we won't have that last coordinate:

```
if (!pts.last || !pts.current) { return; }
```

Next, we'll capture the speed of the strum by getting the distance between our two *x*, or horizontal, mouse coordinates, as well as capturing the lowest and highest values of our current versus last coordinates:

```
let magnitude = Math.abs(pts.current.x - pts.last.x);

let xMin = Math.min(pts.current.x, pts.last.x);
let xMax = Math.max(pts.current.x, pts.last.x);
```

With these three helpful values, we can loop through the array of <webharp-string> components. If the leftmost edge of our string falls in between the last and current *x* coordinates, then we know to strum that particular string. We can send the numeric index of which string was strummed, as well as the *magnitude*, or how forcefully it was strummed:

```
for (let d = 0; d < this.stringsElements.length; d++) {
    if (xMin <= this.stringsElements[d].offsetLeft && xMax >=
      this.stringsElements[d].offsetLeft) {
        let strum = {
            power: magnitude,
            string: d
        };
```

```
        this.stringsElements[d].strum(strum);
    }
}
```

And with this, we have some interactivity! Unfortunately, while we do successfully strum our string at this point, our string doesn't actually do anything when strummed yet. We can test that things actually work, however, by adding a `console.log` to components/string/string.js

```
strum(params) {
    if (this.timer) { clearTimeout(this.timer); }
    this.timer = setTimeout( () => this.stopStrum(), 1000);
    console.log(params);
}
```

Now, if you run the experiment and open your console log, you should be able to see exactly which string is being strummed as well as how hard, right in your console.

5.3.3 Making your components shake with CSS

As you might expect, there are two last things to add: visual and audio feedback (it is an instrument, after all). Let's add the visual first, with the caveat that it's not really a lesson in Web Components or JS modules, just something we want to add to make this demo work. To do this, we'll pull in a CSS-related project called CSShake, which you can find at http://elrumordelaluz.github.io/csshake/.

The purpose of CSShake is to make your elements look like they are shaking, which I've done my best to depict in figure 5.9. There are tons of different ways the library allows you to shake things. It's one of those well-built libraries you never thought you'd use, but now that we need it, it's great how well-thought-out it is! For the purposes of this demo, we'll just link to the CSS file and allow style to affect elements in our component as normal. In chapter 7, we'll turn this notion around and protect our Web Component from style creeping in with the Shadow DOM.

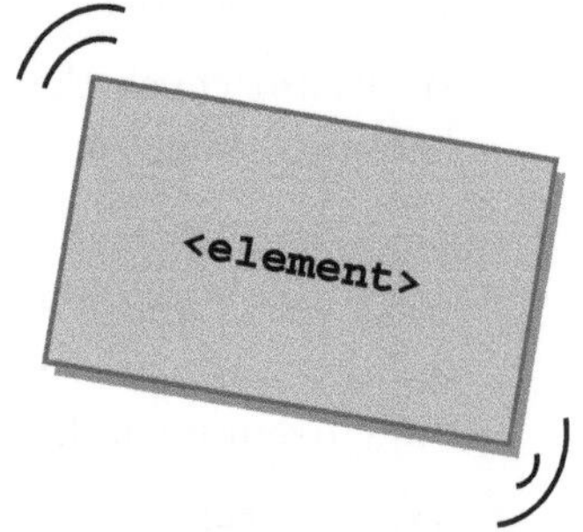

Figure 5.9 CSShake takes an element on your page and animates it with various ways of shaking.

First, let's add it to our HTML file:

```
<head>
    <title>Web Harp</title>
    <script type="module" src="./components/app/app.js"></script>
    <link href="main.css" type="text/css" rel="stylesheet">
    <link href="csshake.min.css" type="text/css" rel="stylesheet">
</head>
```

To use CSShake, we simply add classes to and remove them from the elements we want to shake, as follows.

Listing 5.13 Adding CSShake classes to shake our strings when strummed

```
// file: components/string/string.js

strum(params) {
   if (this.timer) { clearTimeout(this.timer); }

   let dur = params.power * 10 + 250;
   this.classList.add(              <-- Adds shake classes: a base "shake," a class to indefinitely shake, and a horizontal shake type
       'shake',
       'shake-constant',
       'shake-horizontal');
   if (dur < 500) {
       this.classList.add('shake-little');   <-- If the strum isn't strong, only shakes a little bit
   }
   this.timer = setTimeout( () => this.stopStrum(), dur);
}

stopStrum() {
   this.classList.remove('shake', 'shake-constant', 'shake-horizontal',
     'shake-little');   <-- Removes all the classes once the strum stops
}
```

Here, as already mentioned, we begin by clearing a timer if one exists. We're also calculating a `duration` variable in milliseconds by factoring in the strum power (or how fast the string was strummed) and adding a minimum baseline of 250 milliseconds, or a quarter of a second.

For the visual strum, we can add a few CSS classes to describe the string shaking. It's using the base `shake` class, and we want it to shake constantly and horizontally. If the strum isn't very strong, we'll add a `shake-little` style to slightly differentiate a big versus little strum.

Our strum will be as long as our calculated duration. We'll stop the strum when the timer runs out, at which point we'll remove all the classes we've added to the `<webharp-string>` component.

5.4 Wrapping third-party libraries as modules

We need one last thing to complete our Web Harp experiment, and that is sound! The Web Audio API is a complex subject, and the same can actually be said for any real-time audio and tone generation. Luckily, we have JS libraries we can use to hide all that complexity from us. One such library I've enjoyed playing with is MIDI.js (https://github.com/mudcube/MIDI.js/). If you're familiar with MIDI, you know that it's mainly used to connect music devices and not actually generate sound itself, but this library offers real-time tone generation as well. If you look at the commit history, you might notice that the last commit date was in 2015. There's definitely nothing wrong with authoring a good library like this and then moving onto other things after it's sufficiently good. The downside is that this project isn't using the latest JS language features like modules, so we can't import the library into our Web Component.

5.4.1 Frontend tooling for wrapping a module with Node.js

Or can we? Though it doesn't appear to be a proper project on its own, Owen Densmore published a Medium article in 2017 discussing wrapping JS dependencies as modules. Inside one of his projects lives a script called wraplib.js (https://github.com/backspaces/as-app3d/blob/master/bin/wraplib.js). As seen in figure 5.10, the script takes a third-party library and wraps it up as a module that can be imported into your project.

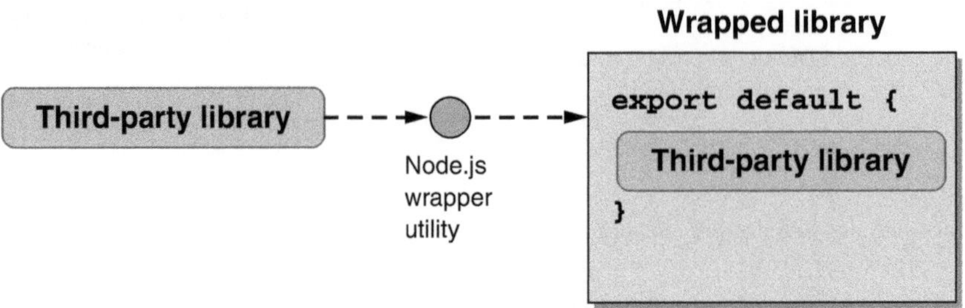

Figure 5.10 Using a Node.js utility to wrap a third-party library as an importable module

I've pulled this script into the project's bin folder. Also required is the actual MIDI.js library. Typically, we would have installed MIDI.js from npm, which you can certainly do by running

```
npm install midi.js
```

For convenience's sake, however, I've put a minified MIDI.js into the project folder in this book's GitHub repo, and we can use it directly from there. Assuming you have Node.js installed from before, navigate to your project directory in the terminal and do

```
node ./bin/wraplib.js midi.min.js MIDI > midijs.wrapper.js
```

At only 33 lines of code, the wraplib.js script is pretty simple if you open it up. Basically, with the first argument, you're telling it what file you'd like to wrap; the second is what global variable name the library is stored under, and then it pipes to an output file.

5.4.2 Not perfect, but does the job

You may have done a double take when I described the second parameter. Wraplib is a bit of a hack, and a common argument is that it shouldn't clutter the global namespace like it does. With our example, once we start the library, if you opened the dev tools and console logged `window.MIDI`, you'd see the library we are wrapping. This pattern of putting things in the global namespace is a bit messy; but, on the other hand, it's a hack that enables us to import a library that hasn't been updated for a few years. And of course, this node script to wrap the library could easily make it into your frontend build process with Gulp, Grunt, or even just `npm run`, as we'll explore in chapter 12.

5.4.3 Using the wrapped module to play some notes

With midi.js wrapped up as a module, let's import and use it! In /string/string.js, we'll initialize and load a piano soundfont in addition to our previous string markup.

Listing 5.14 Initializing MIDI.js, preparing to play piano notes

```
// file: components/string/string.js

connectedCallback() {
   MIDI.loadPlugin({                     <-- Initializes the MIDI plugin with an
       soundfontUrl: './',                   acoustic grand piano instrument
       instrument: 'acoustic_grand_piano',
       onsuccess: () => this.onLoaded()
   });

   this.innerHTML = '<div class="line"></div> \
                    <style>\
                        webharp-string > .line { \
                            background-color: white;\
                            height: 100%; \
                            width: 2px; \
                        }\
                    </style>';
}
onLoaded() {
    this._ready = true;     <-- Sets flag to indicate we are ready when
}                               the plugin has been initialized
```

Like midi.js, I've included it at the root of the project. Alternately, you may find it and copy it from the original source repo: https://github.com/mudcube/MIDI.js/tree/master/examples/soundfont. In the same file, we'll add a `playSound` function and trigger it from our `strum` method.

Listing 5.15 Adding note playback from the `strum` function

```
// file: components/string/string.js

strum(params) {
   if (this.timer) { clearTimeout(this.timer); }

   let dur = params.power * 10 + 250;
   this.classList.add('shake', 'shake-constant', 'shake-horizontal');
   if (dur < 500) {
       this.classList.add('shake-little');
   }
   this.timer = setTimeout( () => this.stopStrum(), dur);
   this.playSound(params);      <-- Calls playSound function when strumming
}

playSound(params) {                        Returns early from function if
   if (!this._ready) { return; }       <-- third-party library isn't ready yet

   let note = 60 + params.string * 5;  <-- Sets the note we want to play
   MIDI.setVolume(0, 127);                 depending on the string strummed
```

```
    MIDI.noteOn(0, note, params.power, 0);   <-- Starts note playback with same power as how hard the user strummed
    MIDI.noteOff(0, note, 0.75);   <-- Sets the duration of the playback to ¾ of a second
}
```

There are some minor details here that deal with the note we're playing. Namely, we'll start on a C note in the fourth octave and go up in increments of five half steps for each string index plucked. As we're venturing into a bit of music theory here, don't worry if you don't understand, but feel free to play with the numbers a bit. Also, when turning on the note, we're using the strum power as the note's velocity (think of a piano key and how hard you hit it as the velocity). Finally, we'll set a duration of 0.75 seconds for the note delay (or how long it sounds after pressing). I'm using a constant number here because a piano sound doesn't have a lot of variability in length before it drops off.

5.4.4 No more audio autoplay

Unfortunately, after I initially wrote this chapter, Chrome started shipping versions in which background audio could not be played until a user took action, like with a mouse click. While I can certainly understand how annoying audio playing without you requesting it is, it's a bit of a downer for fun experiments like this.

Nevertheless, we need to address it to make the Web Harp work! To do this, we'll simply force the user to start the experience by clicking a screen that lives as a `<div>` tag covering the initial page. The next listing shows our modified index.html file.

Listing 5.16 Clickthrough covering the page to address Chrome's autoplay feature

```
<html>
    <head>
        <title>Web Harp</title>
        <script type="module" src="./components/app/app.js"></script>
        <link href="csshake.min.css" type="text/css" rel="stylesheet">
        <link href="main.css" type="text/css" rel="stylesheet">

        <script>
            function clicktostart() {
                document.querySelector('.audio-fix').style.display = 'none';
                document.querySelector('webharp-app').style.display =
                  'inline-block';   <-- When clicked, makes the clickthrough display as none and the Web Harp app display normally
            }
        </script>
    </head>
    <body>
        <webharp-app strings="12"></webharp-app>
        <div class="audio-fix"   <-- Adds the clickthrough div that covers the entire page, forcing the user to click to take action
            onclick="clicktostart()">
            Click Me To Start
        </div>
    </body>
</html>
```

Lastly, we just need to style the clickthrough <div>, as well as allow both that <div> and the application to stack on top of each other by absolutely positioning both via CSS. The next listing shows this CSS added to what we previously had.

Listing 5.17 New CSS to style and overlay the clickthrough

```
body {
    background-color: black;
    margin: 0;
    padding: 0;
}

.audio-fix {        <-- Styles and positions the clickthrough element
    position: absolute;
    width: 100vw;
    height: 100vh;
    background-color: #2a2a2a;
    color: white;
    font-size: xx-large;
    display: flex;
    justify-content: center;
    align-items: center;
}

webharp-app {
    height: 100vh;
    width: 100vw;
    display: none;        <-- Initially sets the Web Harp app to not display
    position: absolute;        <-- Allows the Web Harp app to go underneath the clickthrough
}
```

With the clickthrough in, the user sees figure 5.11 before being able to start the Web Harp.

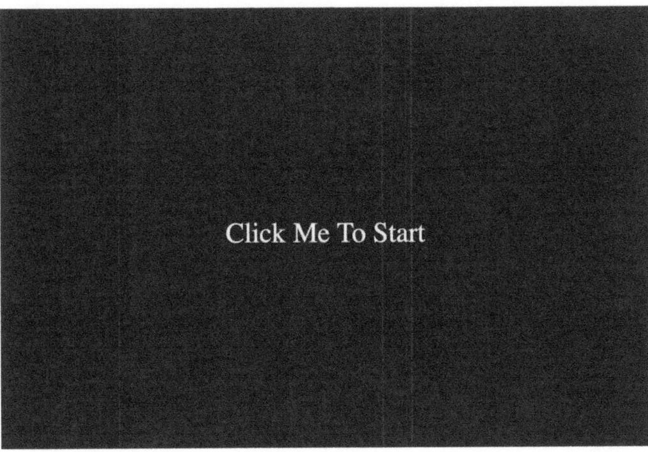

Figure 5.11 The user must click to start the Web Harp to enable audio and not be blocked by Chrome

5.4.5 *Playing the Web Harp*

Once done, we can reload our Web Harp, run our mouse across the strings, and play some music! Some things can definitely be improved with this example. Our inline HTML and CSS look pretty ugly with all of those slashes to continue the string over the line breaks. Also, it would be nicer if we could focus on our Web Component logic in the class and separate the CSS and HTML to somewhere else. These things would certainly make our component much more readable and organized. In the next chapter, we'll explore another ES2015 concept called template literals that will help us clean things up!

Summary

In this chapter, you learned

- How Web Components can manage their own dependencies, including other Web Components, by using modules, as well as how having a single import to use your Web Component can avoid confusion about how to include the component on your page
- How Web Components can be a bit more self-reliant by placing CSS inside the component, avoiding the need to have to manage many CSS files or manage rules for many components in the same CSS file
- Wrapping third-party libraries as a module using Node.js, even if the original author never intended the library to be used that way, avoiding having to make an exception for an otherwise self-reliant component
- Building a musical instrument in our browser using Web Components, with even the main application being a Web Component comprising Web Component children, keeping the index.html file tiny and manageable

Part 2

Ways to improve your component workflow

Creating your own HTML element through the Custom Element API is pretty amazing. From the outside, it looks like any other tag on the page, but inside, it's as complex or as simple as you need it to be! Now, though, it's time to set our sights inward and dive deep on the workflow for creating a great Web Component. This is where we go beyond Custom Elements and explore the rest of the collection of standards that make up Web Components.

As with any new technology, Web Components suffered some missteps, as with the now-deprecated HTML Imports; but this part will take that misstep and break it down into relevant pieces you can go forward with that do have great support. We'll compare one of those pieces, the template tag, with other ways of authoring your inner HTML and CSS to make up your component's UI.

Finally, this part of this book ends with the most renowned Web Component feature: the Shadow DOM. Though not a required part of Web Components, it is a huge shift in how we work with the browser's DOM. Creating a separate mini DOM just for your component is extremely powerful, as it removes frustrations that web developers have had for ages by creating a protective layer around your component where styles don't accidentally creep in, and your inner elements aren't tampered with via mistargeted JS.

Because the Shadow DOM is such a powerful feature and such a change from how we did things before, there are some important caveats to cover as well. These caveats include polyfilling in the increasingly rare situation where your browser doesn't support Web Components, as well as accommodating situations where you actually want style to creep in, like when using a design system. Much of this section is devoted to the Shadow DOM because it's such a game changer.

6 Markup managed

This chapter covers

- Multiline string syntaxes
- ES2015 template literals (with variables)
- Templating HTML/CSS using JS logic and functions
- Templating with lit-html
- Tagged templates

This chapter will keep building on what we've learned from previous chapters, especially the last one, where we learned about modules. So far, we've managed to create self-reliant Web Components that load their own dependencies, including other Web Components. With this, our index.html is minimal. Between this, learning to use attributes, and building our own component API in chapter 4, we essentially cleaned up our use of Web Components from the outside looking in.

We left off with a somewhat messy-looking component on the inside, however. Shoving lots of markup and CSS into the component's `innerHTML` works well but isn't very readable, especially the way we've been working with multiline strings. In this chapter, we'll address this problem, and, in the end, we'll have clean and organized components on the inside and out.

6.1 String theory

Strings are one of the most basic things in JS. You no doubt use them constantly in every aspect of web development. Why go over such a simple concept? The answer is that there is a new JS feature in ES2015 that greatly cleans up our Web Components.

So, what's the big deal? Prior to ES2015, there were a couple different string syntaxes that did the same thing—double quotes and single quotes:

```
"Hi I am a string"
```

or

```
'Hi I am a string'
```

If you recall from prior examples, we were trying to shove all of our HTML into a string and then set our component's `innerHTML` with that string. With a tiny amount of HTML, it's fine:

```
this.innerHTML = '<div class="someclass"></div>';
```

6.1.1 When inline HTML gets ugly

The problem is when the HTML you want to add starts getting bigger. Even this is semi-manageable:

```
this.innerHTML = '<div><input type="text"/><button>Submit</button></div>';
```

At some point, however, having everything on a single line becomes unreadable and hard to manage, so we start expanding our string to cover multiple lines. Let's examine an input form from Mozilla's MDN documentation.

Listing 6.1 Sample input form markup in a JS string

```
this.innerHTML = '<form> \          <-- Each line has a backslash to continue to the next.
             <div> \
                 <label for="example">Let's submit some text</label> \
                    <input id="example" type="text" name="text"> \
              </div> \
              <div> \
                 <input type="submit" value="Send"> \
              </div> \
        </form>';
```

The alternate way of doing multiline strings in this next listing is a little more verbose.

Listing 6.2 An alternate way of doing multiline strings

```
this.innerHTML = '<form>' +
                   '<div>' +
                     '<label for="example">Let's submit some text</label>' +
                       '<input id="example" type="text" name="text">' +
                   '</div>' +
                     '<div>' +
```

Each line is enclosed by single quotes and followed by a plus to continue.

```
        '<input type="submit" value="Send">' +
        '</div>' +
    '</form>';
```

Each of these examples is less than ideal. What's desirable is to let HTML look like it would on a real HTML page. This means multiple lines, indentation, and, most importantly, no added overhead from using something special like a backslash or + to extend over multiple lines.

6.1.2 String syntax with the backtick

Let me introduce a slightly different way of writing a string in the following listing: the backtick character (`).

Listing 6.3 Using the backtick to enclose HTML strings

```
this.innerHTML = `<form>
            <div>
            <label for="example">Let's submit some text</label>
              <input id="example" type="text" name="text">
            </div>
            <div>
            <input type="submit" value="Send">
            </div>
        </form>`;
```

Backticks allow multiline strings without extra formatting.

This way of string writing is called *template literals*, as opposed to the *string literal* way we've done it before. While the previous example solves our readability and workflow problems, template literals do much more that can help us! If you're not familiar with using template literals or using expressions within, please refer to the appendix.

6.2 Using template literals

With this better way of writing strings, you might imagine that there could be some great ways to pull HTML in from different sources. Perhaps you have some HTML you've written in a different HTML file. You've tweaked the markup and style to look exactly how you want—and then it's time to integrate it. We'll now explore a few ways of bringing this HTML in.

6.2.1 Business card creator

Let's try a little exercise and create a browser-based business card creator. The idea is that we'll provide a few different options that the user can customize; then, theoretically, they'd be done and ready to print. There won't be any logic or interactivity inside the card itself; we just want to display a static card with some values like name, job title, email, and so on that we can change depending on what variables are used. Unlike previous exercises, we're really going to focus on layout and style up front, as opposed to component logic. Once we finish up the next demo, we'll have results like those in figure 6.1.

Figure 6.1 End result of the next demo: a business card that allows us to customize values like name, job, title, and so on

Think about what we've done with Web Components up until now. Any visual treatment has been done by placing our HTML in JS and setting our component's `innerHTML` property. This is fine if we know the HTML and CSS we want to use, but if layout and style are a primary concern, this isn't the best way to create markup and iterate.

No, the best way to do this is to simply go back to web development basics and create something right in an HTML file with markup and CSS. It's easy to preview and tweak without worrying about any Web Component or JS complexities. In terms of values we want to replace, we can use our template literal syntax right in the HTML, as shown in listing 6.5 and rendered in our browser as figure 6.2.

${p.first_name} ${p.last_name}

${p.title}

phone: ${p.phone}

${p.email} / ${p.website}

Figure 6.2 Initial business card layout without style

Listing 6.4 Markup for business card with inline expressions

```
<div class="biz-card">
   <div class="logo"></div>
   <div class="top-text">
       <h1>${first_name} ${last_name}</h1>
       <h3>${title}</h3>
   </div>

   <div class="bottom-text">
```

Placeholders for first name and last name values

Placeholder for job title

```
        <h3>phone: ${phone}</h3>    ⊲— Placeholder for phone number
        <h3>${email} / ${website}</h3>     ⊲— Placeholders for email
    </div>                                     and website
</div>
```

6.2.2 Iterating design with just HTML and CSS

It's fairly simple markup for an HTML file, but it starts to be a bit much to throw in your Web Component class along with everything else. Our business card has a <div> container for the entire card, which is made up of a logo, followed by a name and job title. The text on the bottom of the card includes a phone number, email address, and website.

What really makes this come together is the CSS. The style rules can be seen in listing 6.5, while the end result is depicted in figure 6.3.

Figure 6.3 A business card made with HTML and CSS prior to Web Component integration

Listing 6.5 Style for the business card

```
<style>
    .biz-card {              ⊲— Main business card style
        font-size: 16px;
        font-family: sans-serif;
        color: white;
        width: 700px;
        height: 400px;
        display: inline-block;
        border-color: #9a9a9a;
        background-size: 5%;                    If copying this code, swap
        background-image:                       in your own background
      ➥url("background-pattern.png");   ⊲—   image here.
        box-shadow: 0 4px 8px 0 rgba(0, 0, 0, 0.2), 0 6px 20px 0 rgba
      ➥(0, 0, 0, 0.19);
    }
```

```
    .biz-card .logo {                    <-- Style for logo
        height: 100px;
        margin-top: 10%;
        text-align: center;
        background-image:
       url("biz-card-logo.png");         <-- If copying this code, swap
        background-size: contain;            in your own logo image
        background-position-x: center;       here.
        background-repeat: no-repeat;
    }

    .biz-card .top-text {                <-- Remaining styles for the
       text-align: center;                   rest of the text
    }

    .biz-card .top-text h1 {
        font-size: 2.5em;
        margin-bottom: 0;
    }

    .biz-card .top-text h3 {
        margin: 0;
    }

    .biz-card .bottom-text {
        text-align: center;
        margin-top: 10%;
    }

    .biz-card .bottom-text h3 {
        margin: 0;
    }
</style>
```

Of course, I spent some time iterating and tweaking my markup and style to get the final business card result, but that's the point! Keeping our visual design away from the Web Component and our overall project can keep us focused on really designing and styling it well.

With our browser rendering the raw template literal syntax—`${first_name}`, for example—these expressions are a little ugly to look at in context. Even so, we can try out a variety of different names, email addresses, and so on to make sure our design holds up in different contexts before ultimately putting the placeholder expression in. With this, we focused on our markup and style outside the scope of a hypothetical overall application and even the Web Component itself. With no JS in sight, we could even pass this off to a designer or front-ender who might be a little afraid of code. Once we're happy with our markup and style, how can we then use our business card in our Web Component?

6.3 Importing templates

This is the point where the new JS features we've been learning come together extremely nicely. Specifically, I'm talking about combining template literals with JS modules.

Let's start a new project to host a business card Web Component. Our index.html shown in the next listing will again be dead simple, just serving to place the Web Component in our DOM and load the component's JS definition.

Listing 6.6 New page to host our business card component

```
<html>
   <head>
       <title>Business Card</title>
       <script
            type="module"
            src="components/bizcard/bizcard.js">   <-- Includes the Web Component definition module
       </script>
   </head>

   <body>
       <biz-card></biz-card>   <-- Declares the Web Component on the page
   </body>
</html>
```

Once finished—and once our component does its job of hosting the HTML and CSS, and letting us specify the values we'd like to swap in for our placeholder expressions—we'll get the result depicted in figure 6.1 at the start of this chapter.

6.3.1 Keeping markup out of the main component logic

Next up, of course, is to work on our component definition class, but with a little bit of a twist: we won't include any HTML or CSS in the next listing because we are separating the concern to another module.

Listing 6.7 Business card customizer component

```
import Template from './template.js';   <-- Imports our template module

class BizCard extends HTMLElement {
   connectedCallback() {
       this.innerHTML = Template.render({   <-- Uses the template to render HTML/CSS into the component's innerHTML
           first_name: 'Emmett',
           last_name: 'Brown',
           title: 'Student of all Sciences',
           phone: '555-4385',
           email: 'emmett@docbrown.flux',
           website: 'www.docbrown.flux'
       });
   }
}

if (!customElements.get('biz-card')) {
   customElements.define('biz-card', BizCard);
}
```

As we don't have any interactivity right now, and we're simply displaying a business card—`<biz-card>` with some parameterized text—we just have to set our component's `innerHTML`.

Prior to this chapter, we'd simply set the innerHTML to an ugly-looking string in the component itself. If we had variables to put in the string like we do now, with name, email, and so on, it would be even uglier! In the spirit of making our projects cleaner and more organized, let's import our HTML via a JS module.

You might be asking yourself, why a JS module? Given that our goal here is to have our component render HTML, why not import HTML? Unfortunately, JS is the only valid module type supported right now, but perhaps in the future we'll be able to import other types. In fact, Chrome now appears intent on implementing both CSS and HTML modules, but we'll need to wait a bit for that. In the next chapter, I'll briefly get into the now-defunct HTML Imports as an early attempt to tackle this problem, though these were only imported from another HTML directive and not through JS, as we are trying to do now.

6.3.2 A module just for HTML and CSS

All that said, using JS to hold our HTML is pretty powerful and enables us to insert some logic when we need it. First, let's go simple and create the module that holds our template, shown in the following listing.

Listing 6.8 Defining our template module

```
export default {
   render(props) {
       return `${this.html(props)}
               ${this.css(props)}`;     <- Combined HTML and CSS to render
   },
                                        <- Function to return future HTML
   html(p) { return ``; },
   css(p) { return ``; }  <- Function to return future CSS
}
```

You'll note right away that I don't have HTML or CSS here yet, and that's because I want to talk about the structure without markup getting in the way.

First off, you might notice that this is not a class, unlike every other module we've been using. You are certainly free to use a class here if you'd like, but there's really no reason to do so, and it just adds the extra step of instantiation and storing the instance if you need to use this module multiple times throughout the class.

Instead, by not making it a class, we can use it right away in our Web Component by calling on the import and the function it contains:

```
Template.render( . . .
```

My render method combines both the HTML and CSS from their respective methods. I certainly could have just bundled all of the markup into one; but I think it's more maintainable to separate them out and offer a bit more flexibility on how we want to bring in and use either one, as figure 6.4 shows.

Now, how to fill those empty template literals with content? The obvious answer is to open up the HTML file we created earlier in this chapter and simply copy and

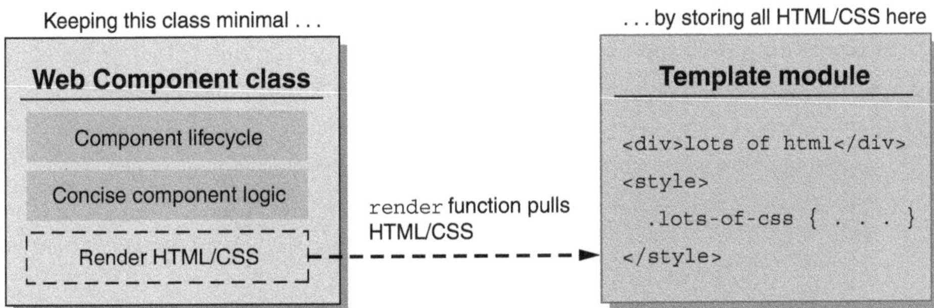

Figure 6.4 Keeping your Web Component class small by using another module

paste. If you're just working with one or a few pieces of markup like that, then copy and paste is pretty easy. However, what if you were working with a large team of production assistants who didn't touch JS code or source control and were churning out dozens of HTML/CSS templates and constantly iterating with a team of designers? This might sound far-fetched to some, but I've worked on projects where we were building an application shell to host many pages of something like a quiz, where each page had a different enough layout that we couldn't use a consistent template.

In these cases, you might want to automate the process of taking HTML that can be previewed standalone in a browser all the way to your JS-based module. I've done exactly this in the GitHub repo for this section. There, I've created an automated Node.js tool that takes an HTML source file and automatically fills the template module we'll use in our business card (figure 6.5).

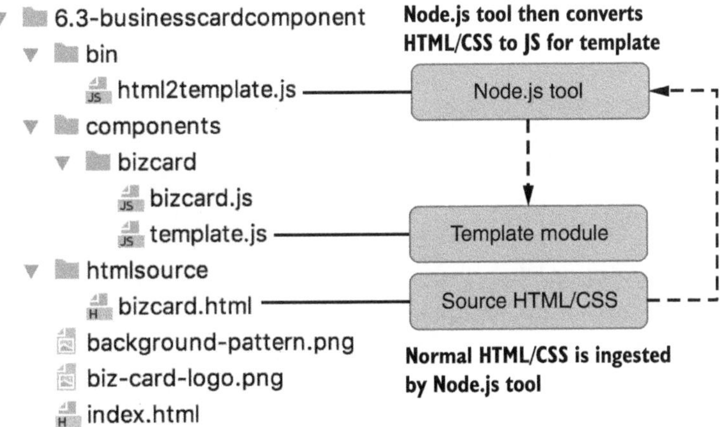

Figure 6.5 Example Node.js-based tool for automating JS module population with an existing HTML file

The downside is that these use cases are likely to be so different from each other that my example only serves as a starting point. Wherever the HTML/CSS comes from, automated tool or no, our business card ends up looking like figure 6.6.

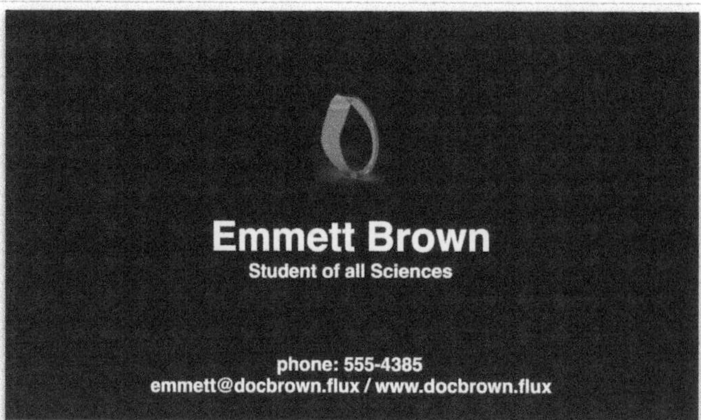

Figure 6.6 Results of integrated template so far

6.4 Template logic

JS-driven HTML and CSS has a lot of potential that can be left undiscovered when using large blocks of markup as is (whether automated or copy and paste). To explore what I mean, let's allow a bit of customization for our business card. We'll allow the user to select from a list of logos and tiled backgrounds to personalize their card, as shown in figure 6.7.

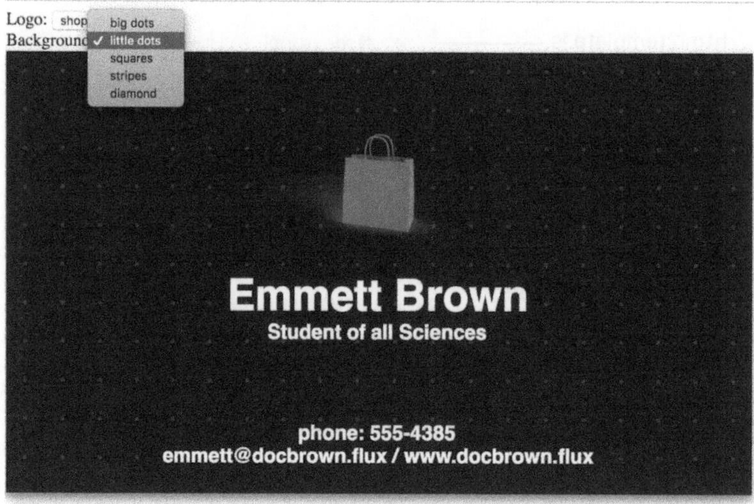

Figure 6.7 Allowing customization with the business card logo and background

For this, I'd like to briefly touch on a more DIY approach and then branch out to a more recent class of options with a lot of potential.

6.4.1 Creating menus from data

Let's start by writing some JS to generate the option lists shown in figure 6.8.

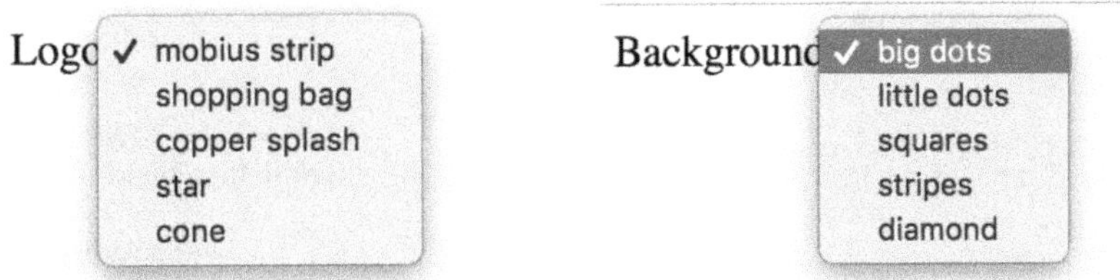

Figure 6.8 Two option lists we will be adding to our component in order to customize the business card

We're simply going to continue building on top of our business card component with the generated template.js left intact. To enable this, we'll add some additional data to pass into our `Template.render` method in our bizcard.js Web Component definition, as shown in the following listing.

Listing 6.9 Passing menu options to the template

```
this.innerHTML = Template.render({
   first_name: 'Emmett',
   last_name: 'Brown',
   title: 'Student of all Sciences',
   phone: '555-4385',
   email: 'emmett@docbrown.flux',
   website: 'www.docbrown.flux',
   backgroundChoices: [                          <-- Business card background options
       { name: 'big dots', uri: './images/big-dot-pattern.png'},
       { name: 'little dots', uri: './images/tiny-dot-pattern.png'},
       { name: 'squares', uri: './images/square-pattern.png'},
       { name: 'stripes', uri: './images/stripes-pattern.png'},
       { name: 'diamond', uri: './images/diamond-pattern.png'},
   ],
   logoChoices: [                          <-- Business card logo choices
       { name: 'mobius strip', uri: './images/mobius-logo.png'},
       { name: 'shopping bag', uri: './images/bag-logo.png'},
       { name: 'copper splash', uri: './images/splash-logo.png'},
       { name: 'star', uri: './images/star-logo.png'},
       { name: 'cone', uri: './images/cone-logo.png'},
   ],
});
```

To be specific, we've added two arrays: one for the tiled background of the card and one for the logo graphic in the center. We'll use these to populate two `<select>` drop-downs to customize our card.

To populate these drop-downs, we'll add some HTML to our template.js module, shown in the next listing.

Listing 6.10 Calling out to a function-based expression to render our menus

```
html(p) {
   return `
      <div class="logo-picker">
           Logo: ${this.options(p.logoChoices)}     ◁ Populating HTML with logo choices
      </div>
      <div class="background-picker">Background:
           ${this.options(p.backgroundChoices)}</div>     ◁ Populating HTML with background choices
      <div class="biz-card">
       <div class="logo"></div>
       <div class="top-text">
           <h1>${p.first_name} ${p.last_name}</h1>
           <h3>${p.title}</h3>
       </div>

       <div class="bottom-text">
           <h3>phone: ${p.phone}</h3>
           <h3>${p.email} / ${p.website}</h3>
       </div>
   </div>`;
},
```

Note that even though we're using these option arrays originally defined in the Web Component definition, just passing the array wouldn't do much besides render a raw array. That's where a custom `options` method comes in.

6.4.2 More generation logic, harder automation

With these new `<select>` menus, we're doing something a bit new with template literals. Instead of simply using a variable to populate, we're using a function from our template with a return value containing the string with the menu, as figure 6.9 shows. Not only that, but we're using the same function to generate both menus, only differentiated by the list of options we pass in, as shown in the following listing.

Listing 6.11 Function to convert an array of choices to menu options

```
options(list) {
   let choices = ``;
   for (let c = 0; c < list.length; c++) {     ◁ Loops through list of choices
       choices += `<option value="${list[c].uri}">${list[c].name}</option>`;     ◁ Appends option tag with choice to string
   }
   return `<select>${choices}</select>`;     ◁ Returns menu populated with menu items
}
```

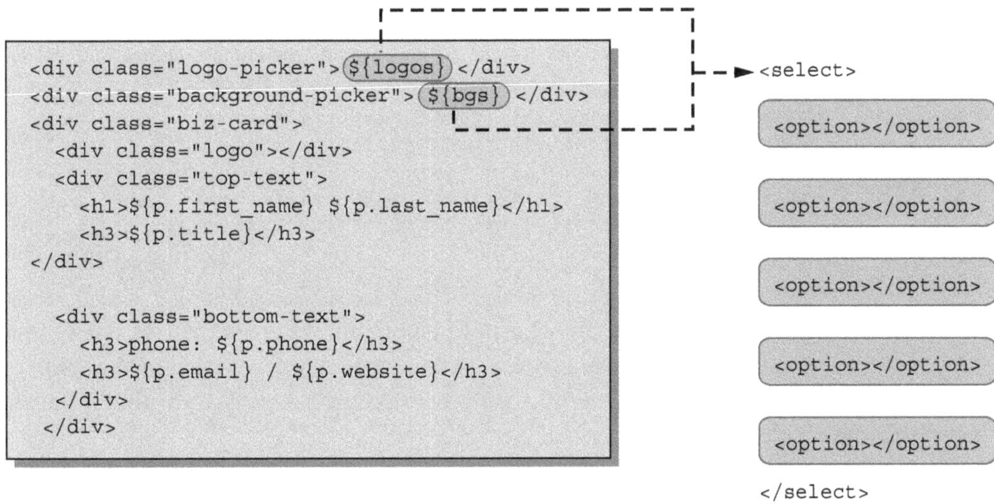

Figure 6.9 Calling out from an HTML template to a JS function to generate menu options from an array

Next, we need to have our business card component react to selections in the menu. This, in a roundabout way, brings us to a last helper function I like to put in my template.js files.

6.5 Element caching

Consider that we'll need to add event listeners to our `<select>` menus in order to listen for change selection. To do this, we'll naturally need to get references to them. It's of course easy enough in the `connectedCallback` function in our Web Component definition to do the following after setting the `innerHTML`.

Listing 6.12 Adding event listeners to react to drop-down changes

```
this.querySelector('.logo-picker select').addEventListener( 'change', e =>
     this.updateGraphics() );
this.querySelector('.background-picker select').addEventListener(
     'change', e => this.updateGraphics() );
```

Adds an event listener to watch for logo changes

Adds an event listener to watch for background changes

This method is less than ideal, however. First, query selection takes a bit of CPU time. These two lines are hardly a problem and happen only once to add the event listener. On the other hand, let's look at that `updateGraphics` function in the bizcard.js Web Component class, as seen in the following listing.

Listing 6.13 On logo/background changes, re-renders both

```
updateGraphics() {
   this.querySelector('.biz-card')            <-- Another query selector to get the card
       .style.backgroundImage = `url("${this.querySelector(
       '.background-picker select').value}")`;
   this.querySelector('.logo')                <-- Yet another query selector to get the logo
       .style.backgroundImage =`url("${this.querySelector(
       '.logo-picker select').value}")`;
}
```

These two lines of code occur when either of the <select> menus have changed. First, we query-select the business card container element and assign the value of the query-selected background menu to the `backgroundImage`. We do this yet again for the logo.

Yes, we're doing some extra processing by query-selecting four times with each menu change. If things were much more complicated, it would likely be a valid concern. There's no real problem with this example in particular, but when there are situations where you need to optimize, it's certainly worth looking into this extra processing!

6.5.1 Don't make me query-select in my component

But take note of the lack of readability in those statements and remember that the markup is in the template.js module and not here in the Web Component class. Also consider that markup is bound to change as we iterate on our project, and, worse, query selection can get more complex when there is more complexity in our HTML.

Because of all these concerns, I like to cache my DOM elements using a method inside the template.js module itself. As a function right next to the `html() { . . . }` function, I can easily reference the markup to create my selectors. A simple <form> example shows this mapping in figure 6.10.

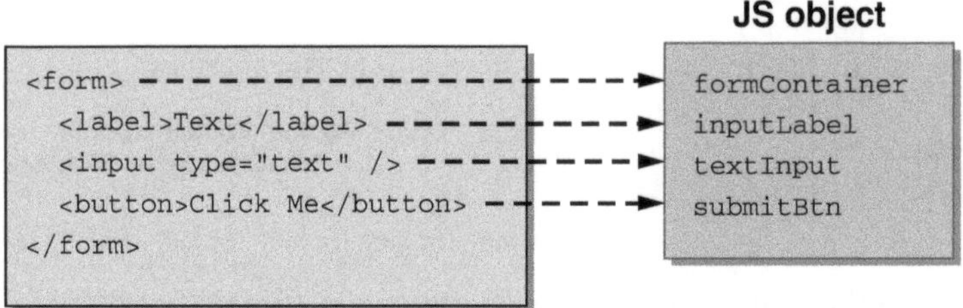

Figure 6.10 Mapping and caching elements from `querySelector` lookups to a JS object for easy reference

In our business card example, I can put the following inside the template.js module.

Listing 6.14 Query-selecting once and saving the references for later use

```
mapDOM(scope) {
   return {
       logoPicker: scope.querySelector(
               '.logo-picker select'),
       backgroundPicker: scope.querySelector('.background-picker select'),
       logo: scope.querySelector('.logo'),
       background: scope.querySelector('.biz-card')
   }
},
```

- Scope parameter is the Web Component reference
- One instance of query-selecting an element and saving to the object

With this, we are both caching the elements and creating easy references to them. Also, these easy references can be as permanent as you need them to be! Meaning, if I needed to change the selector to my `logoPicker`, for example, I could do it right here. Maybe it gets changed to `scope.querySelector('.card-container > div .logo-chooser select')`. My selector got a bit more complex, but my Web Component can continue referring to the `logoPicker` property.

The only slight complexity here is having to pass in our `scope`. Since this `mapDOM` function lives in another module, and it isn't a class instance, it doesn't have a reference to the Web Component class. To solve this, we can simply pass our Web Component reference, or `this`, into the `mapDOM` function, as done in the following listing.

Listing 6.15 Keeping query selection out of the component controller logic

```
import Template from './template.js';

class BizCard extends HTMLElement {
   connectedCallback() {
       this.innerHTML = Template.render({. . . });

       this.dom = Template.mapDOM(this);
       this.dom.backgroundPicker.addEventListener(
               'change', e => this.updateGraphics() );
       this.dom.logoPicker.addEventListener(
               'change', e => this.updateGraphics() );
       this.updateGraphics();
   }

   updateGraphics() {
       this.dom.background.style.backgroundImage =
               `url("${this.dom.backgroundPicker.value}")`;
       this.dom.logo.style.backgroundImage =
               `url("${this.dom.logoPicker.value}")`;
}

if (!customElements.get('biz-card')) {
   customElements.define('biz-card', BizCard);
}
```

- Options have not changed and have been left out for brevity.
- Maps our elements to a JS object
- Adds a listener to the logo picker element referenced by our element object
- Sets the background image of our logo element referenced by our element object

You can see that in our `connectedCallback` function, we are assigning the object that holds our cached elements to `this.dom`, and we can reference it anywhere in our class. With easy property names that make sense for our context here, we avoid the ugliness as well as the (minimal) performance hit of the query selections.

Lately, I'm in favor of more automated approaches, which use an attribute to "mark" each element and then use a script to iterate through and create a similar mapping for you without explicitly defining it in your code. You can find this approach in my GitHub repo for this section.

6.6 Smart templating

There's something very interesting happening on the Polymer Project front as I write this book. To recap, Google's Polymer Library ran from roughly 2013 to 2018 and was designed to work with Web Components. This was at a time when Web Components were so rough around the edges, you really needed a library or framework to help out and keep up with all of the changing advancements and specs.

The interesting bit is that the Polymer Library, after three major releases, is being deprecated and moved into maintenance mode. The Polymer Project as a whole lives on and is very active as the team splits off smaller and more targeted tools and libraries from the project.

Two prominent examples of this are lit-html and LitElement. Both are newly production-ready and 1.0 (though LitElement was technically listed as 2.0 so as not to conflict with the other LitElement project when the team took over the name on NPM). I won't get into LitElement because as nice as it is, it's a thin wrapper around everything we've learned in this book! So, the concepts are basically the same. The Polymer team has added some niceties, such as an expanded lifecycle API as well as automated reflection (where properties and attributes are always in sync).

One of the more complicated feature sets in LitElement is actually all done through lit-html. The lit-html project is a set of importable modules for managing your HTML and CSS, just like what we've been using since chapter 5. It's hard to call it a "library" because of this. When I think of a JS library like React or a framework like Angular, I usually think of a big monolithic file that I'd include that might take over my whole project, and that I would have to do things the React or Angular way throughout.

No, both lit-html and LitElement are opt-in per component. This means I might use them on one component, but perhaps all of my other components in my project wouldn't use them. With lit-html, if there's a feature I won't use, I simply wouldn't import that module, and it wouldn't add to my project's file size, unused.

I think this approach will be the future of Web Components (and maybe the web): light, opt-in libraries that can easily be replaced as opposed to big, monolithic frameworks or libraries that force you to do a number of things their way. There are many tools like this, in fact; but given how prominent the Polymer team is in the Web Component space, we'll likely see some major adoption for lit-html and LitElement by Web

Component developers, especially because they are paving the way for maximum cross-browser support of all Web Component features, even down to IE11.

6.6.1 Using lit-html

There is a learning curve with lit-html, just like any other JS library. What lit-html is good at is rendering HTML/CSS to your component that you've defined in a string, just like we've been doing so far. One benefit of using lit-html is that it replaces only what's changed on render, which can lead to better performance. Recall our previous examples of setting our component's `innerHTML`, where we replace the entire contents. With large DOM trees, this can lead to some performance hiccups if you're not smart about it. In addition to simple rendering of your HTML/CSS strings, lit-html offers some advanced templating features. Let's walk through a quick intro to some of these features.

To get started, usually you'd `npm install` the project:

```
npm install lit-html
```

However, for simplicity's sake here, I've just copied the whole thing into the bizcard-lithml Web Component directory in this book's GitHub repo.

6.6.2 Repeating with templates

The first thing to try with lit-html is to get rid of our custom JS function to create our `<select>` menus. For this, we'll use lit-html's `repeat` module, along with its standard `html` module. With this, we can pull from an array of data and repeatedly populate HTML, as depicted in figure 6.11. We'll do this by adding lit-html imports to our template.js module and changing our markup to include a repeating block of HTML, shown in listing 6.16.

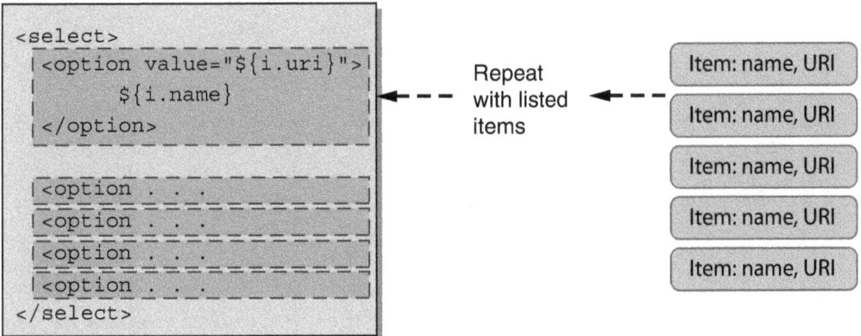

Figure 6.11 Using an array of items to repeat a snippet of HTML, populating a menu of options

Listing 6.16 Using lit-html to repeat HTML for a menu

```
import {html} from './lit-html/lit-html.js';
import {repeat} from './lit-html/directives/repeat.js';
export default {
   render(props) {
       return html`
               <div class="logo-picker">Logo:
                   <select>
                       ${repeat(                    <-- Repeats menu options to create a menu of logo choices
                           props.logoChoices,
                           (i) => i.id, (i, index) => html`
                             <option value="${i.uri}">${i.name}</option>`)}
                   </select>
               </div>
               <div class="background-picker">Background:
                   <select>
                       ${repeat(                    <-- Repeats menu options to create a menu of background choices
                           props.backgroundChoices,
                           (i) => i.id, (i, index) => html`
                           <option value="${i.uri}">${i.name}</option>`)}
                   </select>
               </div>
               ${this.html(props)}
               ${this.css(props)}`;
   },
```

Note that our structure really hasn't changed much! We're still pointing to the `html()` and `css()` functions to use our original markup. We did have to change those methods a tiny bit, however. To treat markup as HTML and not raw text within lit-html, we need to use a more advanced feature of template literals called *tagged templates*. These tagged templates mash together a template literal and a function in a concise syntax that allows the function to parse the template literal, as figure 6.12 shows.

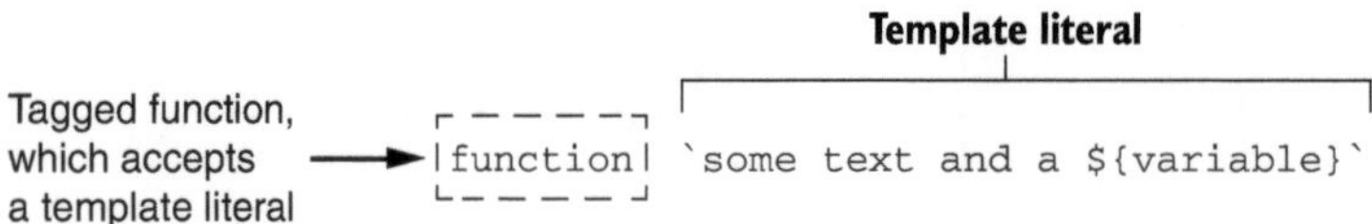

Figure 6.12 The parts of a tagged function and how it works with a template literal

For this example, `html` is the function provided by lit-html, and our template literal is our markup or CSS. You can see us nesting these tagged templates in our custom `render` function in figure 6.13.

6.6.3 *Should you use it?*

And with that, we've cut our custom menu generation function out completely! The question is, and this is a question you need to ask yourself when using any third-party module or library, was it worth it? You're now depending on an external project,

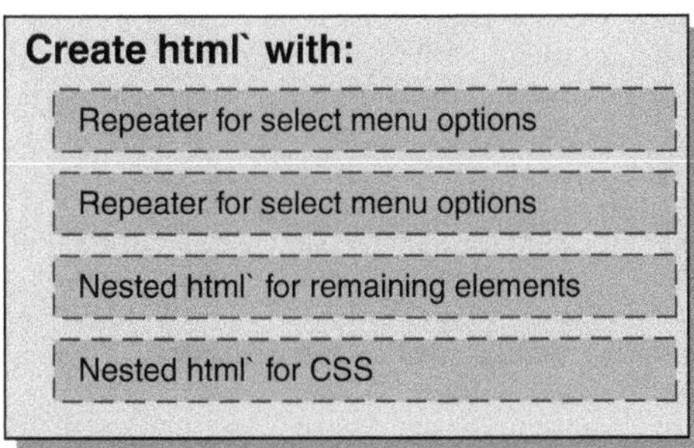

Figure 6.13 Our template module using lit-html, with nested HTML tagged functions for various content

though a newly stable one, given that it just reached 1.0. The syntax seems a bit error-prone until you've used it enough, and it's potentially a bit difficult to debug. That said, one big plus with lit-html is the simple `render` function. When using lit-html to render your HTML, only pieces that have changed get updated. Compare this to just setting the `innerHTML` as we've done before—there's a higher performance cost to slam all of this markup onto the DOM, so in circumstances where lots of HTML needs to be updated (especially if it happens often, or if you're not sure it needs to be updated), lit-html can be a real benefit.

As with any third-party module or library, the more you use it, the more it becomes second nature. Taken in isolation, lit-html definitely wasn't worth it for generating our `<select>` menus in this tiny Web Component. What if we had dozens or hundreds of Web Components, many of which had repeating elements generated with data? Also, what if you could pass off these markup templates to another front-ender who you don't want touching your application logic or writing custom JS code to handle these data-generated elements? These could be good reasons to use just this "repeat" functionality alone.

6.6.4 *Injecting event listeners into markup*

Another bit of functionality that lit-html offers is the ability to add listeners to your markup. In our business card example, you might recall that we add our event listeners manually in our Web Component class:

```
this.dom.backgroundPicker.addEventListener( 'change', e =>
     this.updateGraphics() );
this.dom.logoPicker.addEventListener( 'change', e => this.updateGraphics() );
```

If we had a long list of items that we needed to add event listeners to, this could be a fairly big chunk of code that serves no purpose other than setup. We can let lit-html help us with this by adding event listeners right inside our template and calling a function in our Web Component, as in figure 6.14.

To start, let's adjust our `connectedCallback` in our Web Component class, using the code from listing 6.17.

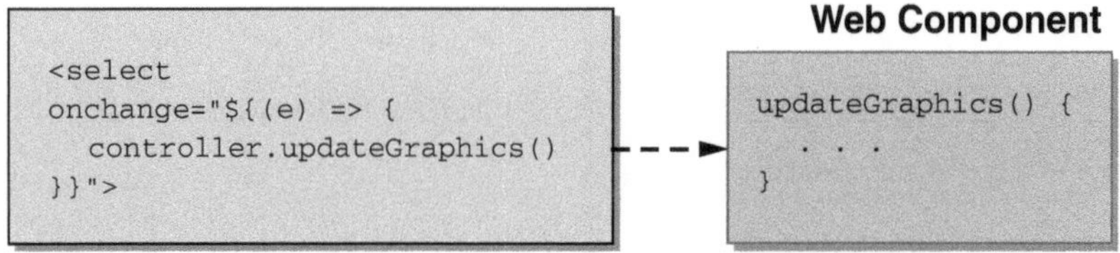

Figure 6.14 Inline event listener to listen for menu changes and calling a function in our Web Component

Listing 6.17 Removing event listeners in our component to prep for lit-html

```
connectedCallback() {
   render(Template.render(this, {
        first_name: 'Emmett',
        last_name: 'Brown',
        title: 'Student of all Sciences',
        phone: '555-4385',
        email: 'emmett@docbrown.flux',
        website: 'www.docbrown.flux',

        backgroundChoices: [
            { name: 'big dots', uri: './images/big-dot-pattern.png'},
            { name: 'little dots', uri: './images/tiny-dot-pattern.png'},
            { name: 'squares', uri: './images/square-pattern.png'},
            { name: 'stripes', uri: './images/stripes-pattern.png'},
            { name: 'diamond', uri: './images/diamond-pattern.png'},
        ],
        logoChoices: [
            { name: 'mobius strip', uri: './images/mobius-logo.png'},
            { name: 'shopping bag', uri: './images/bag-logo.png'},
            { name: 'copper splash', uri: './images/splash-logo.png'},
            { name: 'star', uri: './images/star-logo.png'},
            { name: 'cone', uri: './images/cone-logo.png'},
        ],
   }), this);

   this.dom = Template.mapDOM(this);
   this.updateGraphics();
}
```

Generates a template literal to pass to lit-html's render function

Passes our Web Component scope (this) to let lit-html know where to write the content

There are just two changes here. First, we removed adding the event listeners. After adding the event listeners into our markup using lit-html, as in listing 6.15, we won't need them anymore. Second, we want to give lit-html a reference back to our Web Component to run our `updateGraphics` function, so we pass `this` as the first parameter to the `Template.render` function, where the second parameter is all the data we are passing.

Now, on to the lit-html magic. In listing 6.18, we want to use the standard `change` event to listen for select menu changes; but with lit-html in the mix, we'll use its `@` expression to create the proper bindings. Following through, we can insert an inline function that points back to our Web Component, referenced with a variable named `controller`.

Listing 6.18 Injecting event listeners into markup using lit-html

```
render(controller, props) {
   return html`
          <div class="logo-picker">Logo:
              <select @change="${(e) => {
                controller.updateGraphics()} }">
                  ${repeat(props.logoChoices, (i) => i.id, (i, index) =>
                   html`<option value="${i.uri}">${i.name}</option>
              `)}</select>
          </div>
          <div class="background-picker">Background:
              <select @change="${(e) => {
                controller.updateGraphics()} }">
                  ${repeat(props.backgroundChoices, (i) => i.id, (i, index) =>
                    html`<option value="${i.uri}">${i.name}</option>
              `)}</select>
          </div>
          ${this.html(props)}
          ${this.css(props)}`;
},
```

Menu change listener for logo menu added with lit-html

Menu change listener for background menu added with lit-html

Again, though, in our simple example, we only reduced JS code in our Web Component by two lines when we removed the event listeners. Was it worth it? Probably not, but for larger-scale projects with a team, it could definitely be worth it!

Additionally, as the Polymer team rockets forward with the Polymer Project (www.polymer-project.org), we may see lit-html along with LitElement become a fairly commonplace solution for Web Components.

6.7 Updating the slider component

It's been a bit since we've updated the slider component we started back in chapter 2. Now, with our ability to import a template and cache elements, we can make the slider a little better, and shareable as a real component!

We can start by separating out a few files. Until now, the slider HTML, JS, and CSS were all wrapped up in a single HTML file. Our goal is to end up with a demo HTML file to show off the slider, a component source class JS file, and, lastly, a template module to hold the HTML/CSS for the component. Figure 6.15 shows the new project file structure.

It probably makes the most sense to start out with the template.js module. It's new to the slider and features ideas from this chapter that we just covered. We'll pull in the component HTML that was previously in the component class, and the CSS that was previously in the all-encompassing slider HTML file. The next listing shows this module in its entirety.

demo.html
slider.js
template.js

Figure 6.15 The three files for the slider component

Listing 6.19 Slider component's template module

```
export default {
    render() {
        return `${this.css()}
                ${this.html()}`;
    },
                                                    Caches the elements
    mapDOM(scope) {  <-                             of the component
        return {
            overlay: scope.querySelector('.bg-overlay'),
            thumb: scope.querySelector('.thumb'),
        }
    },
                                                    Moves the HTML from
    html() {                                        the component class
        return `<div class="bg-overlay"></div>  <-  into this module
                <div class="thumb"></div>`;
    },
                                                    Moves the CSS from the
    css() {                                         old HTML file into this
        return `<style>   <-                        component/module
                    wcia-slider {
                        display: inline-block;
                        position: relative;
                        border-radius: 3px;
                    }

                    .bg-overlay {
                        width: 100%;
                        height: 100%;
                        position: absolute;
                        border-radius: 3px;
                    }

                    .thumb {
                        margin-top: -1px;
                        width: 5px;
                        height: calc(100% - 5px);
                        position: absolute;
                        border-style: solid;
                        border-width: 3px;
                        border-color: white;
                        border-radius: 3px;
                        pointer-events: none;
                        box-shadow: 0 4px 8px 0 rgba(0, 0, 0, 0.2), 0 6px
                          20px 0 rgba(0, 0, 0, 0.19);
                    }
                </style>`;
    }
}
```

You may not have looked at the CSS for this component since chapter 2, so you may not notice that a few things are missing. Left out of the CSS here are the component's width and height, as well as the (kind of insanely complicated) CSS for the checkered background.

The reason for this is that it makes the component a bit more customizable from the outside. If you think about it, you'll want a generic UI component like this to show in a variety of sizes in different contexts. You'd use CSS do this with any other element, and this component should be no different. In terms of the checkered background, I'm planning ahead that we'll want to use this component in another context besides for setting transparency. Setting the background CSS from the outside allows us to swap in any other background super easily. The next listing shows the demo page for the slider component with the size and background CSS pulled out, as discussed.

Listing 6.20 Slider demo page

```
<html>
<head>
    <title>Slider Demo</title>

    <script    <— Component class module
        type="module"
        src="slider.js">
    </script>
    <style>
        wcia-slider {    <— Extra CSS to control component's size and background
            height: 50px;
            width: 500px;
            background-image: linear-gradient(45deg, #ccc 25%,
             transparent 25%),linear-gradient(-45deg, #ccc 25%,
             transparent 25%),linear-gradient(45deg,
             transparent 75%, #ccc 75%),linear-gradient(-45deg,
             transparent 75%, #ccc 75%);
            background-size: 16px 16px;
            background-position: 0 0, 0 8px, 8px -8px, -8px 0px;
        }
    </style>
</head>
<body>
    <wcia-slider    <— Slider component on page with some default settings
        backgroundcolor="#ff0000"
        value="50">
    </wcia-slider>
</body>
</html>
```

Last is the slider.js module. Yes, it's a module now! We can change `class Slider` to `export default class Slider`, so that it can be imported. The following listing shows the new module without the details that haven't changed.

Listing 6.21 Slider module (slider.js)

```
import Template from './template.js';   <-- Imports template.js

export default class Slider extends HTMLElement {   <-- Makes class an importable module
    connectedCallback() {
        this.innerHTML = Template.render();   <-- Offloads HTML to template module
        this.dom = Template.mapDOM(this);   <-- Caches elements

        document.addEventListener('mousemove', e => this.eventHandler(e));
        document.addEventListener('mouseup', e => this.eventHandler(e));
        this.addEventListener('mousedown', e => this.eventHandler(e));

        this.refreshSlider(this.getAttribute('value'));
        this.setColor(this.getAttribute('backgroundcolor'));
    }

    static get observedAttributes() { . . . unchanged . . . }
    attributeChangedCallback(name, oldVal, newValue) { . . . unchanged . . . }
    set value(val) { . . . unchanged . . . }
    get value() { . . . unchanged . . . }
    set backgroundcolor(val) { . . . unchanged . . . }
    get backgroundcolor() { . . . unchanged . . . }

    setColor(color) {
        if (this.dom) {   <-- Uses cached elements
            this.dom.overlay.style.background = `linear-gradient(
            ➥to right, ${color} 0%, ${color}00 100%)`;
        }
    }

    refreshSlider(value) {
        if (this.dom) {   <-- Uses cached elements
            this.dom.thumb.style.left = (value / 100 * this.offsetWidth -
            ➥this.dom.thumb.offsetWidth / 2) + 'px';
        }
    }

    updateX(x) {
        let hPos = x - this.dom.thumb.offsetWidth/2;   <-- Uses cached elements
        . . . unchanged . . .
    }

    eventHandler(e) { . . . unchanged . . . }
}

if (!customElements.get('wcia-slider')) {
    customElements.define('wcia-slider', Slider);
}
```

The slider component is now a shareable piece of UI that we can really use as part of any other project. We'll do one last thing in a future chapter, and that is to have it use the Shadow DOM. Using the Shadow DOM isn't entirely necessary, but it's an awesome feature to have in terms of component encapsulation. I'll let you be the judge when you read all about it and we update the slider one last time.

Summary

In this chapter, you learned

- A new way to write strings using the backtick (`) character, which allowed the creation of template literals. A new ES2015 feature, these template literals allow not only multiline strings with no awkward syntax, but also insertion of variables into the templated string—perfect for inserting HTML and CSS right into our JS with no tweaking required.
- How to use element caching as well as separation of code and markup for better component readability and maintainability.
- About logic-generated templates using custom JS as well as the Polymer Project's lit-html library for repeating markup from data, while additionally using lit-html to add event listeners in your HTML.
- How to build an example Web Component project featuring a business card customizer, focusing on visual layout and style, which enables us to examine workflows with more complex HTML and CSS.

7 Templating your content with HTML

This chapter covers

- Building on the concepts from (the now-deprecated) HTML Imports
- Document fragments
- The `<template>` tag
- Leveraging templates to replace HTML/CSS in a Web Component
- Loading templates from index.html or via a network request
- Named and unnamed slots

We've come a long way with Web Components so far! In addition to creating some moderately simple Web Component-based applications, we've gone fairly deep on some strategies for using HTML and CSS in our Web Components.

Of course, these strategies so far have revolved around storing markup in JS strings. Despite the great separation of concerns we get by storing our HTML/CSS in importable JS modules, as seen in chapter 6, there will no doubt be situations where keeping HTML as HTML is preferred.

7.1 R.I.P. HTML Imports

Web Components, in fact, started with an HTML-first strategy. What I mean by this is that if you started working with Web Components a few years ago, you wouldn't have expected to import JS modules to drive your components—you'd instead have expected to import actual HTML.

The imported HTML would hold a <script> tag, which itself holds your Web Component class definition. This class would pull HTML and CSS from the owner document to use for your custom component's contents. As this is a bit much to take in, take a look at figure 7.1, and let's also break down an example index.html file in the following listing.

Listing 7.1 Using HTML Imports from a sample project

```
<html>
     <head>
        <title>HTML Import Demo</title>
        <script src="html-imports.min.js"></script>
        <link rel="import" href="samplecomponent.html"></link>

        <style>
            button {
                background-color: #c09853;
            }
        </style>
     </head>

     <body>
          <sample-component></sample-component>
     </body>
</html>
```

HTML Import, which loads a sample Web Component (annotates the `<link rel="import">` line)

Sample Web Component is declared here (annotates the `<sample-component>` line)

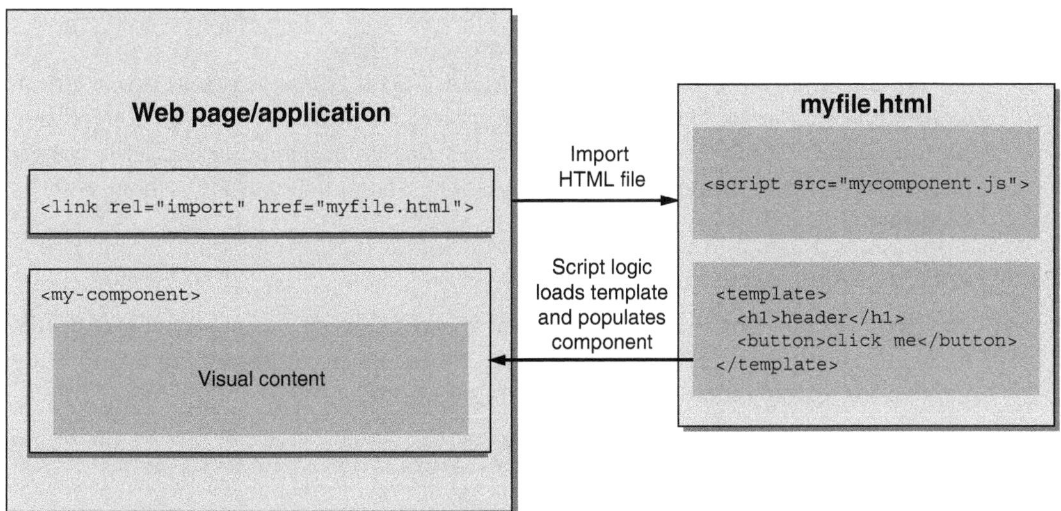

Figure 7.1 HTML Imports allow Web Components to be loaded via an HTML file.

You'll notice that the <sample-component> tag is used as we've normally used Web Components. It's just another custom element we've defined. The difference, of course, is how we go about defining this Web Component.

In the <head> tag, we are referencing two things. The first is the HTML Import polyfill:

```
<script src="html-imports.min.js"></script>
```

The second is the actual HTML file we're attempting to import:

```
<link rel="import" href="samplecomponent.html">
```

Of course, the reason for the polyfill is that, although Chrome was the only browser to ever support HTML Imports, the feature is now deprecated in the latest versions.

7.1.1 Polyfilling HTML Imports

Web Components in general were a Google-led invention. The working draft spec was implemented in Chrome to generate interest, paving the road in hopes that all browsers would follow. Custom Elements ended up being a fairly uncontentious specification. Other browser vendors worked with Google to add their two cents, and the spec morphed from v0 to v1 with collaboration from those other vendors. The Shadow DOM, while much more complicated and therefore a bit slower to be adopted, was on a similar track, and was ultimately accepted like Custom Elements were.

HTML Imports, on the other hand, don't appear to have any traction. Firefox, specifically, didn't want to adopt something so similar to JS modules when they were already so new at the time. It's a good guess that someday modules could import more than just JS. Perhaps someday, we could use modules to import other file types, like HTML, which Chrome is already looking into.

Despite the lack of support, the HTML Import-based Web Component has some decent ideas. With the polyfill, it's certainly a feasible workflow, even if most Web Component developers will likely not use the whole thing.

To add a bit more confusion, the official polyfill from Google (https://github.com/webcomponents/html-imports) has graduated from v0—now no longer supported natively in any browsers—to a very similar v1 implementation. This polyfill allows easy, drop-in support in any browser. The v1 implementation is what we'll be covering here.

7.1.2 What's inside the import

Now that we know what we're dealing with, let's peek inside the imported HTML file. Of course, it really could be any HTML, but for the purposes of creating a Web Component, we're doing some very specific things.

Listing 7.2 Contents of an HTML Imports-based Web Component

```
<script src="samplecomponent.js"></script>

<template>
```

```
    <style>
        span {
            padding: 20px;
            background-color: yellow;
        }
    </style>

    <span>Hi from an HTML Import component</span>
</template>
```

Notice the `<template>` tag in the previous listing. This tag has implications well beyond the dying HTML Imports and can be directly applicable to modern Web Component development, so I'm going to save the detailed explanation of this until the next section of this chapter. For now, just note that this `<template>` tag holds the content that we'd like to populate our component with.

Outside of the `<template>` tag, on the first line of listing 7.2, we have a script reference to our Web Component definition class:

```
<script src="samplecomponent.js"></script>
```

This Web Component definition looks extremely similar to other component definitions we've covered earlier in this book, with some minor exceptions.

Listing 7.3 Populating Web Component markup from an HTML Import template

```
class SampleComponent extends HTMLElement {      <-- Non-module (no export and not importable)-based Web Component class
    connectedCallback() {
        HTMLImports.whenReady( () => {
            const template =                   <-- Creates a reference to the template
                ownerDoc.querySelector('template');
            const clone =                      <-- Clones the content
                template.content.cloneNode(true);
            this.appendChild(clone);           <-- Adds the content to our component
        });
    }
}

const ownerDoc =                               <-- Gets a reference to the owning document
        HTMLImports.importForElement(document.currentScript);
if (!customElements.get('sample-component')) {
     customElements.define('sample-component', SampleComponent);
}
```

Like those other component definitions, with listing 7.3, we are defining a class that extends `HTMLElement`. Because we aren't importing it as a `<script type="module">`, it does not start with `export default SampleComponent`.

We're also still using the same Custom Element API to define the tag name as we have in every component we've created before. Right above that line, though, is something a bit odd. We're getting this script's "owner document." Remember, we're not working with our index.html page as usual. We're now talking about importing another HTML document entirely into our index.html page.

With another HTML page in play (the imported one), it would be nice for a script on that imported page to know which of the two pages it's actually running in. The use case here is that we can query-select the template from the imported HTML as we do in the `connectedCallback` method in listing 7.3. To do this, of course, the script needs to know what page it's running on—the owner document.

The general HTML Import flow consists of

1. Importing the HTML page
2. Having the imported HTML/JS find its owner document
3. Defining the Web Component in that imported page
4. Getting and cloning a template reference on the imported page
5. Adding the cloned template to the Web Component

Figure 7.2 represents this generalized HTML Import flow, and it's the same process we use in listing 7.3.

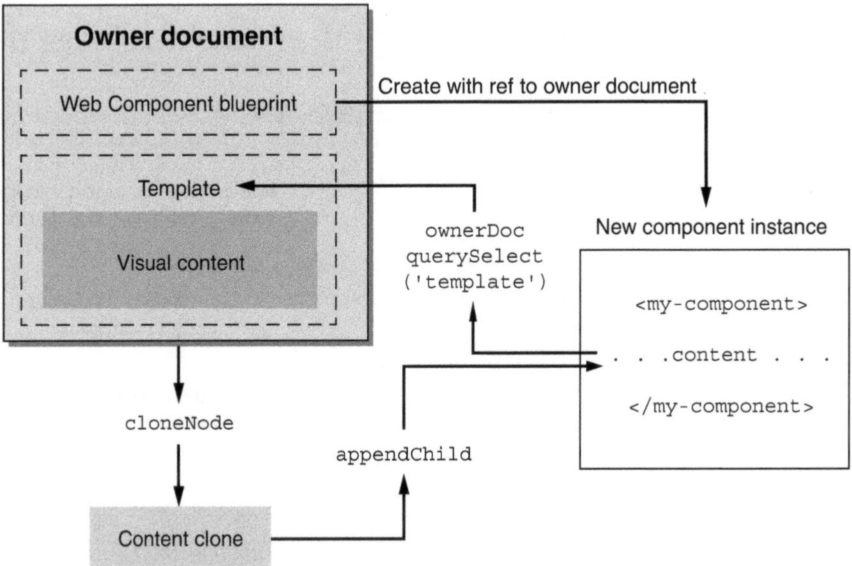

Figure 7.2 A typical HTML Import flow. The owner document contains our Web Component definition and a template of the desired HTML/CSS. The component is responsible for cloning this template and inserting the clone as its content.

Once our imported HTML is fully ready, as determined by our `HTMLImports.whenReady` callback, we can query-select the template from this owner document, copy it, and then append it as a child of our component. As a result, we see figure 7.3 when previewing in our browser.

Hi from an HTML Import component

Figure 7.3 Output from our simple HTML Import-driven component

So, that was fairly easy, right? If it weren't for the lack of browser support for HTML Imports, this would be a pretty nice workflow! For those who want to stay away from JS as a way to write HTML and CSS, this could have had potential.

Again, you'll notice that I completely breezed through some of the explanation of working with the `<template>` tag. That's because, even though HTML Imports don't have any traction, the `<template>` tag is available in all modern browsers, and some would consider it an important piece of the modern Web Component workflow. As such, it deserves some proper explanation away from HTML Imports.

7.2 The <template> tag

The `<template>` tag itself is extremely straightforward. That said, usage of it does require a little bit of explanation.

Let's look at some normal, everyday HTML:

```
<p>
   This is content that's not in a template tag.
</p>
```

Dropping this paragraph and its contents on an HTML page will simply render the contents. On the other hand, we could use a `<template>` tag:

```
<template>
   This is content that IS in a template tag.
</template>
```

Now, this content doesn't appear anywhere on the page! What happened? If you inspect the element in Chrome, as shown in figure 7.4, the element exists. Inside the element, we can see a "document fragment." You can then expand the fragment to see the actual text. Firefox shows an empty `<template>` tag, but if you right-click to view the DOM properties, you can see a `content` property, which holds a document fragment containing the text.

OK, so that doesn't really answer any questions, it just changes the question to what a document fragment is!

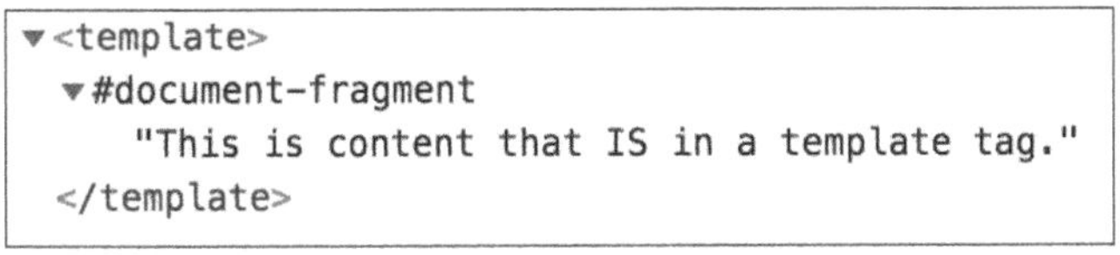

```
▼<template>
  ▼#document-fragment
     "This is content that IS in a template tag."
  </template>
```

Figure 7.4 Inspecting the <template> tag in Chrome

7.2.1 Document fragments

To find out what a document fragment is, let's just create one through JS, as in the following listing.

Listing 7.4 Using a document fragment

```
<html>
<head>
   <title>Document Fragment Demo</title>
</head>
<body>
<script>
   const fragment =                                    <-- Creates the document fragment
       document.createDocumentFragment();
   for (let c = 0; c < 5; c++) {
       const li = document.createElement('p');
       li.innerText = 'paragraph ' + c;
       fragment.appendChild(li);                       <-- Adds children to the fragment (paragraphs)
   }
   document.body.appendChild(fragment);                <-- Adds the fragment to the page body
</script>
</body>
</html>
```

Here, we are first creating a document fragment and then using a `for` loop to add five paragraphs containing some text. After appending to the body, our DOM tree looks like this:

```
<p>paragraph 0</p>
<p>paragraph 1</p>
<p>paragraph 2</p>
<p>paragraph 3</p>
<p>paragraph 4</p>
```

Pretty simple, as figure 7.5 shows, but why bother with a document fragment when we could just use `createElement`?

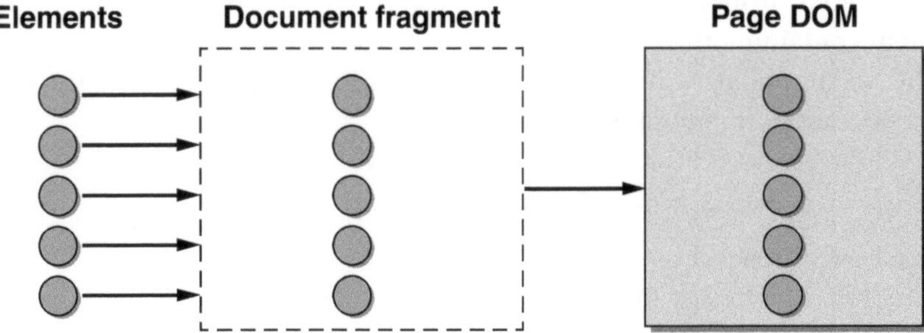

Figure 7.5 Adding elements to the DOM via a document fragment

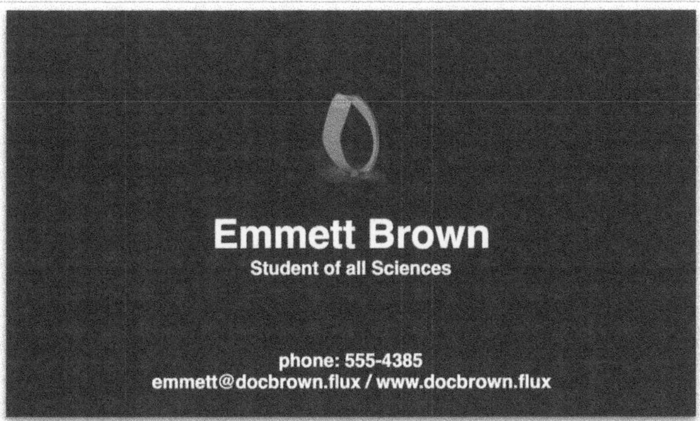

Figure 7.6 Adding elements to a parent element before adding to the page DOM

Well, for one, if we wanted to do the same operation, appending elements to the body all in one `appendChild` call with `createElement`, we'd need to create a parent element to hold our paragraphs, like in figure 7.6. Our DOM would look like this:

```
<div>
<p>paragraph 0</p>
<p>paragraph 1</p>
<p>paragraph 2</p>
<p>paragraph 3</p>
<p>paragraph 4</p>
</div>
```

If that's what we want, great; but if it's not, the other alternative would be to append each <p> one by one onto the body, like in figure 7.7. This is fine, but each time you append to the body, it causes the page's entire DOM to recalculate. The less you do this, the better your performance will be.

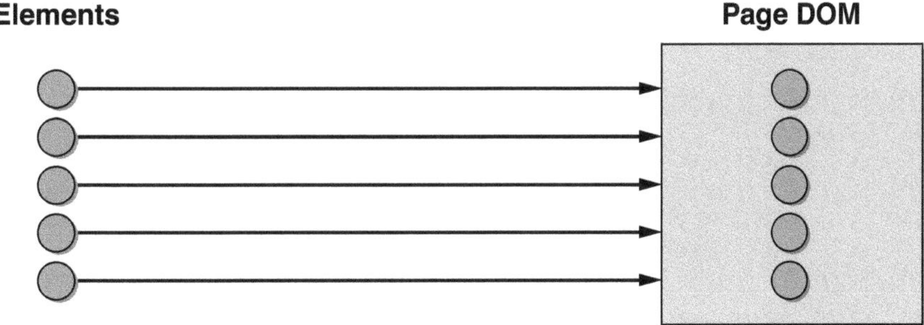

Figure 7.7 Adding elements one by one to the page DOM, with the unfortunate effect of re-rendering the DOM each time

One other nuance of document fragments is that after you've appended those elements to the DOM from the fragment, they disappear from the fragment itself. In the previous example, if we console-logged our `fragment` variable prior to `document.body.appendChild(fragment);`, we'd see `#documentFragment`, which can expand out and reveal its children. After appending, this logged `#documentFragment` would be empty. Keep this in mind, because it'll be important later as we get started working with templates.

The document fragment doesn't seem to be a well-known feature; it certainly wouldn't be shocking if you'd never used it before. It seems to fit a very narrow use case, but the `<template>` tag has taken document fragments a bit more mainstream!

7.2.2 Using template content

With all we've covered so far, you might be able to guess that the `<template>` is a kind of holding area for content that isn't actually rendered on the page. The idea is that your HTML page holds various `<template>` tags, each storing some snippet of HTML/CSS that you'd like to use later on by copying it and adding it to your main DOM.

Let's populate an HTML file with a few extremely simple templates, as shown in the following listing.

Listing 7.5 Adding a few templates to a page

```
<html>
<body>
   <template id="button">        <-- First example template of three
       <button>Click Me</button>
       <p>
           This is a template with a button
       </p>
   </template>

   <template id="textfield">
       <label>Enter</label>
       <input type="text">
       <p>
           This is a template with a text input
       </p>
   </template>

   <template id="list">
       <ul>
           <li>Item 1</li>
           <li>Item 2</li>
           <li>Item 3</li>
           <li>Item 4</li>
       </ul>
   </template>

<script>
   const template =        <-- Gets a reference to the "button" template
      document.getElementById('button');
   const clone =          <-- Clones the template
```

```
    template.content.cloneNode(true);
  document.body.appendChild(clone);
</script>

</body>
</html>
```

Adds the cloned content to our page

Of course, if we run this HTML page in our browser without that script block, nothing displays. But our templates are waiting and ready to use. With that script block, however, we can grab one of the templates, and content will appear on our page, as seen in figure 7.8.

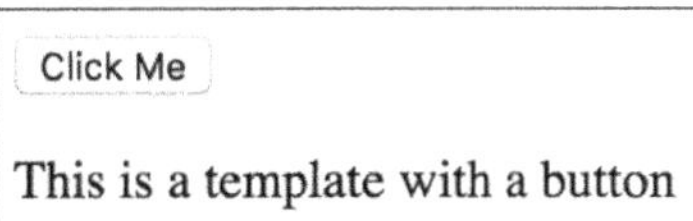

Figure 7.8 One of our sample templates added to the browser

Fetching the `<template>` we'd like to use is easy! It's the same as any other element. We can use `querySelector`, `querySelectorAll`, or `getElementById`. For this example, we'll do `document.getElementById('button');`. Go ahead and try selecting one of the other two templates and adding it to your page as well, if you're following along with code.

Once the `<template>` is stored in our `template` variable, we can get the document fragment through the `content` property. To use the template, we should actually clone it first, so the template is not empty after appending: `template.content.cloneNode(true)`. After that, we can add it to the page with `document.body.appendChild(clone)`. Passing `true` to `cloneNode` simply means that we want to *deep clone*, or clone the element as well as all its children.

Let's drill into that best practice of cloning first to explain how the template can be cleared out. For this limited example specifically, we don't have to clone anything. We can simply add the content to our page with `document.body.appendChild(template.content)`. After appending a document fragment to another element, however, your fragment will then be empty.

This means that we can add this `<template>` once, but only once! Subsequent tries would just result in us adding empty contents. Figure 7.9 shows our elements in motion, moving from document fragment/template to the page's DOM.

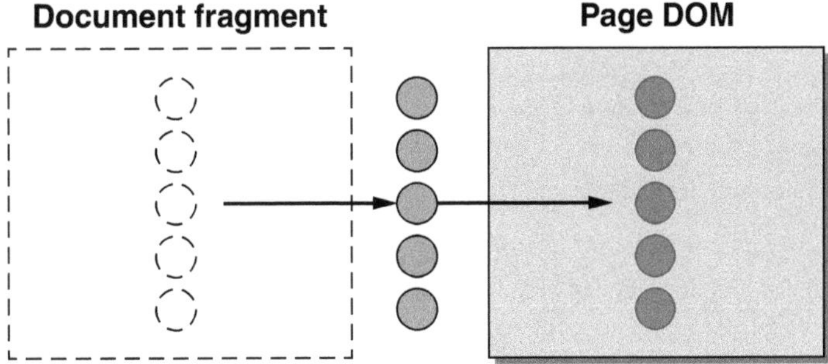

Figure 7.9 Appending to the page's DOM from a document fragment within a template means that these elements are actually moving out of the template/fragment.

If we clone our <template> instead of adding it directly, we can use the same one over and over again, as in the following listing.

Listing 7.6 Cloning multiple times to add to our page

```
const template = document.getElementById('button');
const clone = template.content.cloneNode(true);      <- Clones a first time
document.body.appendChild(clone);                     <- Adds the clone to our page the first time
const clone2 = template.content.cloneNode(true);     <- Clones a second time
document.body.appendChild(clone2);                    <- Adds to our page a second time
```

7.3 Choose your own template adventure

In the last chapter, we did some customization on a Web Component-based business card. If you recall, you could swap in different backgrounds and logos. What if we could choose between different card layouts entirely? Let's create three separate templates and layouts, as in figure 7.10.

Figure 7.10 Three different business card layouts (starting with a blank one)

To do this, let's simplify and strip out the logo and background customization that we previously had so we can focus on the general HTML and CSS of the card.

Listing 7.7 Simplified business card example using templates to drive HTML and CSS

```
export default class BizCard extends HTMLElement {
   static get observedAttributes() { return ['layout']; }

   attributeChangedCallback(                <- Simplified attributeChangedCallback focusing on content
       name, oldvalue, newvalue) {
       this.innerHTML = '';
       const template = document.getElementById(newvalue);
       const clone = template.content.cloneNode(true);
       this.appendChild(clone);
   }
}

if (!customElements.get('biz-card')) {
   customElements.define('biz-card', BizCard);
}
```

Keeping it simple and short, this Web Component class definition lives as bizcard.js in the same file structure we had previously in our business card customizer demo. To recap, here it is in figure 7.11.

- 7.3-businesscardtemplates
  - components
    - bizcard
      - bizcard.js
  - background-pattern.png
  - biz-card-logo.png
  - index.html

Figure 7.11 Template-driven business card creator

Also, in the spirit of simplicity, we'll simply wipe out all of the innerHTML for the component every time we want to load a new card layout. With this in mind, note that the card layout <template> tags live in the main index.html file, outside of this component. These templates are selected by their ID, cloned, and then appended to our Web Component. We're now appending to an empty node, given that we just cleared out the innerHTML of the component with this.innerHTML = ''. This simplicity of just replacing all of the innerHTML is exactly why our new menu in the next section to select the card's layout will not live in the component. If it did, this menu would be wiped out as well!

All this logic is contained on the component's attributeChangedCallback. This is done to hinge the layout name we'd like to use based on the component's layout attribute. This, of course, means that we need to declare the layout attribute in the observedAttributes getter:

```
static get observedAttributes() { return ['layout']; }
```

We will indeed seed the component with a blank layout called "none," as we are declaring on the component tag itself in the index.html. But this blank layout, shown in figure 7.12, isn't much to look at yet:

```
<biz-card layout="none"></biz-card>
```

Again, with the way attributes work in the Web Components life cycle, this initial value of "none" will trigger the attributeChangedCallback and populate the component with this particular layout. Aside from this, however, to actually change the layouts, we can implement a drop-down menu on the page, with a change event that updates the layout attribute (see listing 7.8).

Figure 7.12 Starting with an empty/blank card layout

Listing 7.8 Setting the `layout` attribute from a menu outside of our component

```
<body>
   <p>
       <select onchange="updateLayout(event)">      ◁ Menu to choose the
           <option value="none">none</option>          business card layout
           <option value="default-card">default</option>
           <option value="variation">variation</option>
       </select>
   </p>
   <biz-card layout="none"></biz-card>

   <script>
       function updateLayout(event) {
           document.querySelector('biz-card').setAttribute('layout',
           ➥event.target.value);    ◁ Change event to
       }                               update the Web
   </script>                           Component attribute
</body>
```

Of course, aside from the <head> tag, which contains our script module reference, there are the actual templates to use. Included in the next listing is the top part of the index.html file and placeholders for three different templates.

Listing 7.9 HTML page including a business card template

```
<head>
   <title>Business Card</title>      Web Component
   <script       ◁                    module import
        type="module"
        src="components/bizcard/bizcard.js">
   </script>
</head>

<template id="default-card"> . . . </template>    ◁ Our three templates
                                                     (placeholders)
```

```
<template id="variation"> . . . </template>
<template id="none"> . . . </template>
```

To condense code on the page here, most notably the long CSS in the templates, I've included only the `<template>` tags with no inner content. Please refer to my Github repo if you'd like to see it all (https://github.com/bengfarrell/webcomponentsinaction/blob/master/chapter7/7.3-businesscardtemplates/index.html). As shown in figure 7.13, our component reaches out to the document, fetches each template by this ID, and, as we've seen, populates the component.

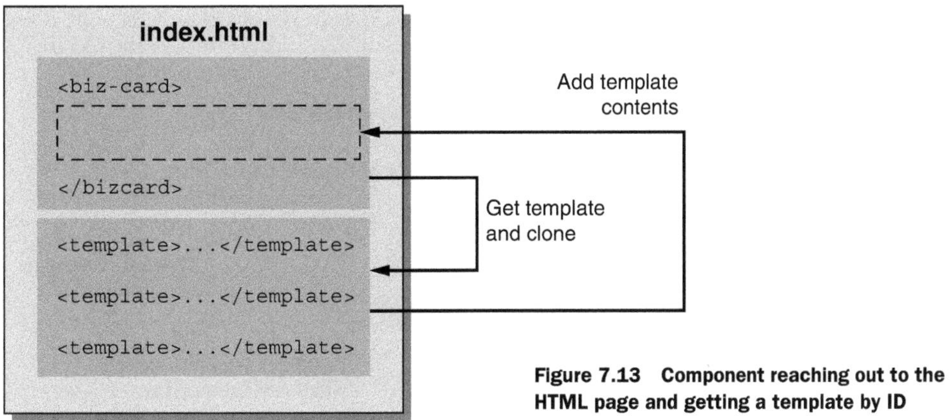

Figure 7.13 Component reaching out to the HTML page and getting a template by ID

Now, while it's perfectly fine to put all of this in our index.html, it feels a bit messy and long. I'm on the fence about whether it's really unorganized—a long list of `<template>` tags is easy to pick out because it doesn't interfere with the actual rendered DOM structure of the page. On the other hand, when there are multiple custom components, it's not clear which `<template>` belongs to which component. In this regard, it seems difficult to manage depending on your particular use case. Additionally, with many components used in a project, there could be way too many templates to keep your HTML page manageable.

Given my reservations, I'd like a way to keep this a bit cleaner. As you might recall, HTML Imports kept things super clean! Without them, can we come up with another way to dynamically load templates?

7.4 Dynamically loading templates

For this next demo, let's think about two things. First, I'd like to keep our various `<template>` tags inside our component as child nodes. By doing this, it will be clear that the templates actually belong to the Web Component in question. Second, I'd like to load our templates from somewhere else instead of cluttering up the component.

You might imagine that we could do this with template literals and modules, as we have in previous chapters, and we certainly could! Instead, I'm going to avoid this

HTML-in-JS approach, just because we've already done it. Additionally, it might be interesting to load our templates as another remote resource that we can fetch from a server.

The interesting thing about keeping our <template> tags inside our component is that we have to maintain some fairly permanent markup inside the component, while also clearing out large chunks of HTML/CSS whenever the layout is updated.

This means that setting `this.innerHTML` all at once isn't going to cut it. If we replace all of our HTML, we're essentially throwing away our loaded templates. Our our component's `connectedCallback` in the next listing needs to reflect this.

Listing 7.10 Loading templates with a network request

```
connectedCallback() {
   this.cardElement =        <-- Creates card layout container
        document.createElement('div');
   this.templates =          <-- Creates template container
        document.createElement('div');
   this.appendChild(this.cardElement);
   this.appendChild(this.templates);
   const request = new XMLHttpRequest();
   request.open( 'GET', 'templates.html', true );   <-- Network request to fetch templates
   request.addEventListener( 'load', (event) => {
       this.templates.innerHTML =        <-- Populates template container
               event.target.response;        with loaded templates
       this.populateCard();
   });
   request.send();
}
```

Right away, we're creating and adding two <div> elements, `this.cardElement` and `this.templates`. These will act as containers for the business card and our loaded templates, respectively.

Next, we're making a network request to load templates.html, which contains all of the <template> tags that lived in our index.html before. Once loaded, we can simply set the `innerHTML` of our `this.templates` <div>, as in figure 7.14. Both this callback

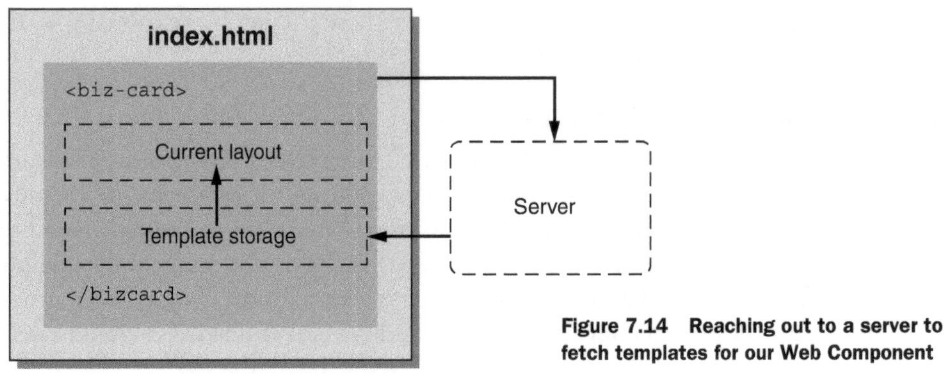

Figure 7.14 Reaching out to a server to fetch templates for our Web Component

and our `attributeChangedCallback` call the function `populateCard();` to load the current layout as specified via our `layout` attribute. But in this case it's good to check if `this.templates` exists yet, given that the `attributeChangedCallback` may fire before the `connectedCallback`, as shown in the following listing.

Listing 7.11 Calling a method to fill in our card layout

```
static get observedAttributes() { return ['layout']; }

attributeChangedCallback(name, oldvalue, newvalue) {
   if (this.templates) {
      this.populateCard();     <-- Calls the method to fill in our card container
   }                               in components/bizcards/bizcard.js
}
```

Either way it's called—a network request to load our template.html or the result of an attribute change—the `populateCard();` function in the next listing has a fairly easy method to add to the same class in order to swap in our new business card layout.

Listing 7.12 Contents of the `populateCard` function

```
populateCard() {                  <-- populateCard method in components/bizcards/bizcard.js
   const template = this.templates.querySelector(
   ➥ 'template.' + this.getAttribute('layout'));   <-- Gets reference to template
   if (template) {
      const clone =                                 <-- Clones template
            template.content.cloneNode(true);
      this.cardElement.innerHTML = '';     <-- Clears current template
      this.cardElement.appendChild(clone);    <-- Adds clone and fills in HTML/CSS
   }                                              for current layout
}
```

The first thing we do is grab the template from within the component. Recall that I moved the templates from the index.html to a separate templates.html file. I did one slightly different thing. Instead of using IDs for the template names, I'm now using classes. What was `<template id="default-card">` is now `<template class="default-card">`.

Typically, when you look online for how to use the `<template>` tag, you'll see folks using the `id` attribute to identify and fetch their `<template>` from the DOM. In this exercise, as we want to keep our templates as a child of the component, it doesn't make much sense to use `id`. Remember, each individual ID can be used only once on the entire HTML page. When templates live in the page outside of the DOM structure, IDs make sense because we're looking at a pool of templates on the entire page, each called up by their unique ID.

Now, instead of querying the entire page for a unique ID, we are querying not just our component's children, but specifically the children of the `this.templates` container. If found (and it might not be found due to the template.html file not being loaded yet), it will clear the contents of our card container with `this.cardElement.innerHTML = ''`, clone the template, and then append this new child to `this.cardElement`.

In terms of the templates, because the contents in them are the same as before, we've only traded IDs for classes:

```
<template class="default-card">
. . .
</template>
```

Of course, with our templates separated out, our index.html gets a lot simpler.

Listing 7.13 With templates removed, our index.html is once again manageable.

```
<html>
  <head>
      <title>Business Card</title>
      <script type="module" src=
      ➥"components/bizcard/bizcard-template-loading.js"></script>
  </head>
  <body>          <-- A much shorter body with templates being loaded by the component
      <p>
          <select onchange="updateLayout(event)">
              <option value="none">none</option>
              <option value="default-card">default</option>
              <option value="variation">variation</option>
          </select>
      </p>
      <biz-card layout="none"></biz-card>

      <script>
          function updateLayout(event) {
              document.querySelector('biz-card').setAttribute
              ➥('layout', event.target.value);
          }
      </script>
  </body>
</html>
```

With all of that, we have the exact same demo as before, just a lot cleaner. Also, we could take this further and specify a different HTML file to load. We could even use an attribute on the component to point to specific HTML files full of templates for a specific use case:

```
request.open( 'GET', this.getAttribute('templatefile'), true );
```

Done? Not quite. You've probably noticed one feature regression. Our new business cards in this chapter (as we've been using templates) don't inject custom information like first name, last name, job title, and so on.

One solution could be to more diligently ensure that each element that we'd like to replace content on is marked with the appropriate class. We could then query our layout for the element marked with the class and replace the `innerHTML`.

For example, if we ensured that every element that contained a placeholder for `firstname` had the class `firstname`, we could do the following:

```
this.cardElement.querySelector('firstname').innerHTML = someObject.firstname;
```

There is some complication with this method, however. Consider our default template, where it lists both email and website in an `<h3>` header tag:

```
<div class="bottom-text">
   <h3>phone: #xxx.xxx.xxxx</h3>
   <h3>email@email.com / http://website.com</h3>
</div>
```

How do you target and replace the contents of this combined field, especially when it may be split out to separate elements in other templates? Additionally, in this template, a slash separates the email and website values. Setting the `innerHTML` of this `<h3>`, you'd need to know that this slash is the design choice for this template and make sure to populate that as well!

It's starting to get complicated. One solution would be to insert `<span>` tags to mark each value you'd like to replace and use those for query selection:

```
<div class="bottom-text">
   <h3 class="phone">phone: #xxx.xxx.xxxx</h3>
   <h3><span class="email">email@email.com</span> / <span
     class="website">http://website.com</span></h3>
</div>
```

It's an OK solution, but we're adding a bit more complexity to our HTML when we really shouldn't have to. Fortunately, there is a newer solution just for this problem. Let's talk about the `<slot>` tag!

7.5 Entering the Shadow DOM with slots

Indeed the `<slot>` tag is the perfect solution to our custom field dilemma, but before diving in, there's something big to know. The `<slot>` tag only works in conjunction with the Shadow DOM. It's a big topic, and I think it's best to start exploring the Shadow DOM in depth in the next chapter. In the meantime, we'll ease in and explore the `<slot>` tag! Of course, the result of this will be a business card with our fields filled in with custom values, replacing our placeholder values, as figure 7.15 shows.

The `<slot>` tag is a bit like the `<template>` tag in that it doesn't actually get rendered in the DOM layout. Unlike the `<template>` tag, we aren't copying from it, but instead content is automatically placed inside. Slots are essentially targets for replacing content. Let's take one of our `<template>` layouts and create some slots to target content that we can swap in as shown in listing 7.14.

Figure 7.15 Business card using a templated layout and slots to insert custom values

Listing 7.14 Placing slot tags in our template to allow content replacement

```
<div class="biz-card">
   <div class="logo"></div>
   <div class="top-text">
       <h1><slot name="firstname">First</slot>
           <slot name="lastname">LastName</slot></h1>    <-- First slots containing firstname and lastname
       <h3>
           <slot name="title">Job Title</slot>    <-- Third slot containing job title
       </h3>
   </div>
   <div class="bottom-text">
       <h3>phone:
           <slot name="phone">#xxx.xxx.xxxx</slot>    <-- Fourth slot containing phone number
       </h3>
       <h3><slot name="email">email@email.com</slot> /
       <slot name="website">http://website.com</slot></h3>    <-- Last slots containing email and website
   </div>
</div>
```

Here, I've wrapped each individual placeholder value in a `<slot>` tag. Each slot has a `name` attribute, as well, to define how we can reference any given slot. So, how do we replace content? Like I said, for this to actually work, we need to use the Shadow DOM in our component. Luckily, there are only a few changes to make in the next listing to use it.

Listing 7.15 Altering the createdCallback to use the Shadow DOM

```
connectedCallback() {
   this.root = this.attachShadow({mode: 'open'});          ◁— Creates the Shadow DOM
   this.cardElement = document.createElement('div');           in order to use slots
   this.templates = document.createElement('div');
   this.root.appendChild(this.cardElement);       ◁— Appends elements to the Shadow
   this.root.appendChild(this.templates);              DOM instead of the component
```

In our connectedCallback, we are attaching a *shadow root*. Think of this like a separate and protected DOM tree only available to the internal workings of our component. We can then save that shadow root as this.root (or whatever variable name you'd like to use) and append any children to it. Despite this.cardElement and this.templates being inside the shadow root, they've already been added to this new Shadow DOM, so the usage doesn't change at all. We can use those element references just like always and set their innerHTML or append more children.

Now, to actually fill in our placeholder slots depicted in figure 7.16, we can put the relevant named values right inside our <biz-card> component, shown in the following listing.

Listing 7.16 Populating slots with values inside the component tag

```
<biz-card layout="none">
   <span slot="firstname">Ben</span>  ◁—— One of four slots we're
   <span slot="lastname">Farrell</span>     populating with the
   <span slot="phone">555.555.5555</span>   firstname value
   <span slot="email">ben@benfarrell.com</span>
</biz-card>
```

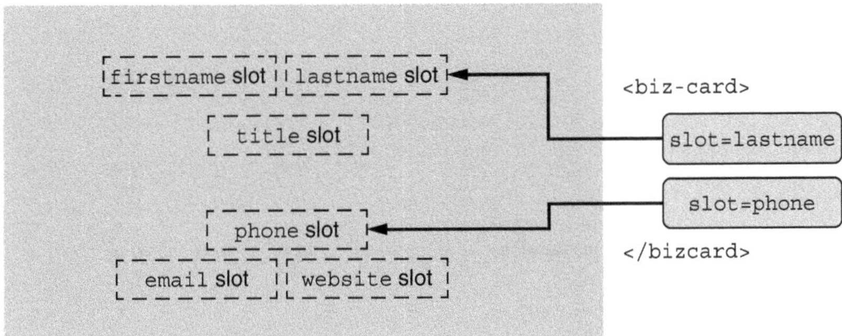

Figure 7.16 Using named slots as placeholders in the business card Web Component

Taking a look at one of the layout results in figure 7.15, we can see that we forgot to create a value for "website." Notice that instead of giving some kind of error, the website slot simply falls back to its default content. Keep in mind as well that the entire

<span> tag is being inserted into the <slot>. It could easily be a <button slot="firstname">Ben</button>, or even another <slot> tag, where only its contents will be rendered: <slot slot="firstname">Ben</slot>.

I'll end the business card example here with a couple of unresolved issues. The first is, of course, adding that website slot to fill in that last placeholder. More importantly, we've lost a good bit of functionality from the last chapter to this one. Our background and logo are no longer customizable. If you feel up to the challenge, perhaps you may want to try reincorporating those!

7.5.1 Slots without a name

Slots can even be a bit more generic. In our example, we're using *named slots*, but they don't have to be named at all—you'd just lose the ability to specify and use multiple slots in the same component, as in the following listing example, with browser results shown in figure 7.17.

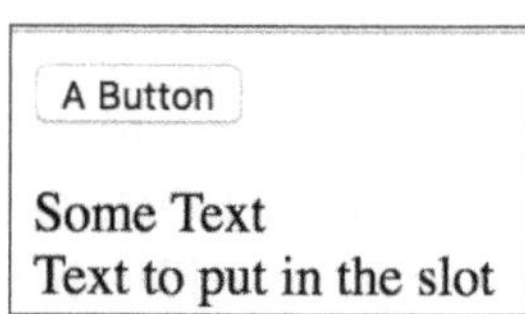

Figure 7.17 Browser screen to complement listing 7.17 using unnamed slots

Listing 7.17 Using generic, unnamed slots

```
<script>
   class SlotsDemo extends HTMLElement {
       connectedCallback() {
           this.root = this.attachShadow({mode: 'open'});
           this.root.innerHTML = `<div>
                  <button>A Button</button>
                  <p>
                       Some Text
                       <br />
                       <slot>placeholder text</slot>      ◁ Creates an unnamed slot placeholder
                  </p>
               </div>`;
       }
   }

   if (!customElements.get('slots-demo')) {
       customElements.define('slots-demo', SlotsDemo);
   }
</script>
<body>
   <slots-demo>     ◁ Fills in the unnamed slot placeholder
        Text to put in the slot
   </slots-demo>
</body>
```

Of course, named slots work better for our business card use case because we can insert multiple values in all the right spots. I do like the simplicity of using <slot> without the name, however. Adding simple text as the content of your tag couldn't be easier!

What's a bit weird is that we've created a protected DOM that's not accessible outside of our component, yet we are doing this to make placeholders with values that are replaced from the outside. It seems a bit counterintuitive, but it does make sense if you consider how the shadow root slightly changes the usage of our component.

I've been using the JS API in this book quite a bit for setting our component's `innerHTML` from the inside. Equally valid is setting the `innerHTML` right in your component's usage on the page:

```
<my-component>This text is the innerHTML</my-component>
```

When using the Shadow DOM, however, this `innerHTML` is no longer rendered because this type of outside content won't penetrate our Shadow DOM. Only the `innerHTML` inside our shadow root is rendered. This creates the perfect opportunity to use that content inside your tag in a different way. Of course, this different way is using slots. These slots are allowed to punch through the Shadow DOM in the very specific ways outlined here. If the Shadow DOM wasn't used, it might be a bit ambiguous if the content was meant to be rendered as the actual content of your component or to fill in your `<slot>`.

As we'll see in the next few chapters, the Shadow DOM is really powerful. Slots are a great feature to use in conjunction, but it's likely not the reason you'll want to use the Shadow DOM. In the next few chapters, we'll take an in-depth look at what the Shadow DOM is and what it can do for your component development workflow, because we've only scratched the surface so far.

Summary

Whether you plan to use templates or not, it's great to have one more tool in our toolbelts. I've personally had some great experiences using template literals to hold HTML/CSS in my JS, as we've discussed in previous chapters, but not every situation is the same. This business card creator is a great example of where templates can really help, especially when we want to create loads of interchangeable templates and not force front-enders on our team who might not know JS that well to help us out.

In this chapter, you learned

- How to work with HTML Imports despite them not being on a standards track anymore, along with a breakdown of how they work, which can be relevant to modern Web Component development
- A full explanation of the `<template>` tag, how you'll get repeated use from these tags when cloning their contents first, and how document fragments are the main driver behind them
- How to use templates with a hands-on example in which we completely swapped out HTML and CSS to introduce brand new layouts and style in the same component, loaded from either the index.html page or remotely via a server
- How to replace specific and multiple placeholder contents in the same component with the named `<slot>` tag, or a single placeholder in the `<slot>` tag, but without using names

8 The Shadow DOM

This chapter covers

- Component and class encapsulation
- How the Shadow DOM protects your component's DOM
- The open and closed Shadow DOM
- Shadow DOM terminology: shadow root, shadow boundary, and shadow host
- Polyfilling with the Shady DOM

In the last chapter, we peeked briefly at the Shadow DOM to introduce the concept of slots. If you recall, slots are a way of taking templated content and adding placeholder values that can be replaced by your Web Component's end user. We marked the areas that can accept new HTML content as slots.

While the `<template>` tag is a standalone concept and available in all modern browsers, the `<slot>` tag is not. In fact, the `<slot>` tag is dependent on the Shadow DOM. We've covered every core feature of Web Components so far, except for the Shadow DOM.

There's a reason I'm covering it last, and that's because I want to show that it's not entirely necessary to the Web Component story, as awesome as it is. In the past several chapters, we've covered Custom Elements, templates, and HTML Imports, as well as non-Web Component-based techniques to back them up, like ES2015 modules and template literals. All these concepts are either available now for all modern browsers or easily polyfilled.

The Shadow DOM is a little more complicated. In terms of browser adoption, we're only just now seeing near-universal coverage in modern browsers, with Microsoft releasing its Chromium-backed latest version of Edge as a developer preview. This is after Firefox's October 2018 release with full Web Component support.

Even with spotty adoption until recently, a lot of Web Component hype these past several years has been targeted squarely at the Shadow DOM. I agree that it's a groundbreaking browser feature for web development workflows, but Web Components are much more than this one feature. Regardless, part of the disappointment in the community around Web Components has been the slowness of Shadow DOM adoption, coupled with how problematic it is to polyfill.

And that's why I haven't gotten into the Shadow DOM until now in this book. For me, it's an optional feature in my daily work, used only when I'm not concerned about browser support, and I wanted to reflect that here. This concern has greatly diminished over the past few months, given that we're waiting for a single browser (Edge); meanwhile the Polymer team has been hard at work on LitElement and lit-html, which promise polyfill integration and support even in IE11.

You can be a Web Component developer and pick and choose which features you use, the Shadow DOM included. That said, once it's shipped with all modern browsers, I plan to use it all the time—and that day is quickly approaching and will likely have arrived by the time this book is published!

8.1 Encapsulation

In terms of hype for the Shadow DOM, the claims I've seen are that it removes the brittleness of building web apps, and that it finally brings web development up to speed with other platforms. Does it live up to those claims?

I'll let you decide, because like anything, the answer depends on your project and needs. However, both claims are made with one central theme in mind: *encapsulation.*

When people talk about encapsulation, they typically mean two things. The first is the ability to wrap up an object in a way that it looks simple from the outside; but on the inside, it might be complex, and it manages its own inner workings and behavior.

Thus far, everything we've learned about Web Components supports them being a great example of this encapsulation definition. Web Components offer

- A simple way to include themselves on an HTML page (custom elements)
- Multiple ways to manage their own dependencies (ES2015 modules, templates, and even the now-obsolete HTML Imports feature, which can be easily polyfilled)
- A user-defined API to control them, with either attributes or class-based methods, getters, and setters

This is all great, but often, when people talk about encapsulation, they attach a larger definition to it. Encapsulation is what we just discussed; but it can also mean that your encapsulated object is protected from end users interacting with it, even unintentionally, in ways you didn't intend, as figure 8.1 shows.

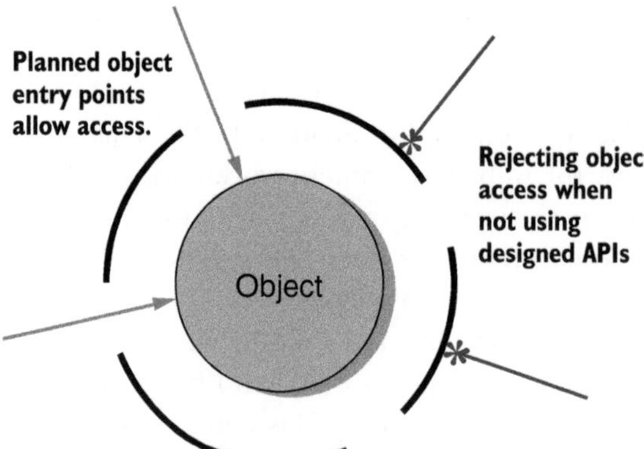
Planned object entry points allow access.
Rejecting object access when not using designed APIs
Object

Figure 8.1 Encapsulation means hiding the inner workings of an object, but it often includes choosing how and where to provide access from the outside in.

8.1.1 Protecting your component's API

In the appendix, I mention a couple ways to make your variables private in your Web Component class. What's important is that you, as a developer, have thought about how your class is used and made some effort to restrict outside usage of your properties and methods to only how you intend them to be used.

One important distinction is between actually restricting properties and methods and restricting them by convention only. A good example of restricting by convention is using the underscore on properties and variables in your class.

For example, someone on your team may hand you a component that has a method to add a new list item element to its UI:

```
addItemToUI(item) {
        this.appendChild(`<li>${item.name}</li>`);
}
```

When you use this component for the first time, you might think, "Hey, I'll just use this function to add a new item to my list!" What you don't know is that the component's class has an internal array of the item data. As a consumer of this component, you're supposed to use the `add()` method, which adds an item to the data model and then calls the `addItemToUI` function to then add the `<li>` element:

```
add(item) {
    this.items.push(item);
    this.addItemToUI(item);
}
```

When the component is resized or collapsed/hidden and shown again, these list elements are destroyed and then redrawn using the internal data model. As someone using this component for the first time, you didn't know that would happen! When you used addItemToUI instead of add, the component was redrawn, and that item you added is now missing.

In this example, the addItemToUI method shouldn't be used by the component consumer; it should be used only internally, by the component. If the original component developer took the time and effort to make the method private, it would have been impossible to call at all.

Alternately, the component developer could make the method private by convention. The most popular way of doing so is using the underscore, in which case the method would be named _addItemToUI. You could still call the method as a user of the component, but with the underscore, you'd know you really shouldn't.

There is more to Web Component encapsulation. This notion of protecting your component for real, or just doing so by convention, comes into play beyond your component's class definition.

8.1.2 *Protecting your component's DOM*

Protecting your custom Web Component class's methods and properties is likely the least of your concerns! What else in your component should be protected? Consider the component in the following listing.

Listing 8.1 A bare-bones, sample component

```
<head>
   <script>
       class SampleComponent extends HTMLElement {     <-- A dead simple Web Component placed on a web page
           connectedCallback() {
               this.innerHTML =
               ➥`<div class="inside-component">My Component</div>`
           }
       }

       if (!customElements.get('sample-component')) {
           customElements.define('sample-component', SampleComponent);
       }

   </script>
</head>
<body>
   <sample-component></sample-component>
</body>
```

As you might notice, there's not much to this component. It simply renders a <div> with the text "My Component" inside, shown in figure 8.2.

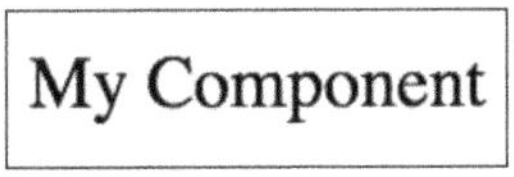

My Component

Figure 8.2 A simple Web Component rendering a short string in the browser

In terms of encapsulation, how protected is that <div> tag from the outside? It turns out, not at all. We can add a <script> tag right after our component:

```
<script>
   document.querySelector('.inside-component').innerHTML +=
   ' has been hijacked';
</script>
```

In figure 8.3, our browser output shows that our component's innerHTML has indeed been set from the outside. Breaking down what happened, an outsider successfully query-selected the <div> inside our component and set its innerHTML.

My Component has been hijacked

Figure 8.3 Setting the innerHTML of our component's DOM from the outside

Before we talk about what can be done to solve this problem, we should break it down into two parts. In part one, I'm pretending to have malicious intent when using this component in a way it shouldn't be used by deliberately breaking its functionality and structure from the outside. In this example, I specifically know there is a <div> with a class named inside-component, I know it has some text that it's displaying, and I'm purposely changing it.

Part two is of a less malicious nature. What if we did something similar accidentally? When a simple custom tag like <sample-component> is on the page, it's easy to forget it can contain any number of elements, like an additional button, all with class names you've used over and over again. For example, what if your page had the following HTML, and you wanted to add a click listener to the button when your component already has a button inside?

```
<sample-component></sample-component>
<button>Click Me</button>
```

Given that in this short snippet, the Click Me button is the button in the page source, you might be tempted to do this:

```
document.querySelector('button').addEventListener('click', . . .);
```

In the hypothetical situation depicted in figure 8.4, our <sample-component> already contains a button, and worse, it's styled to not even look like a button! As a result, you've query-selected the wrong button and are completely confused why your button click doesn't work when you try it in your browser.

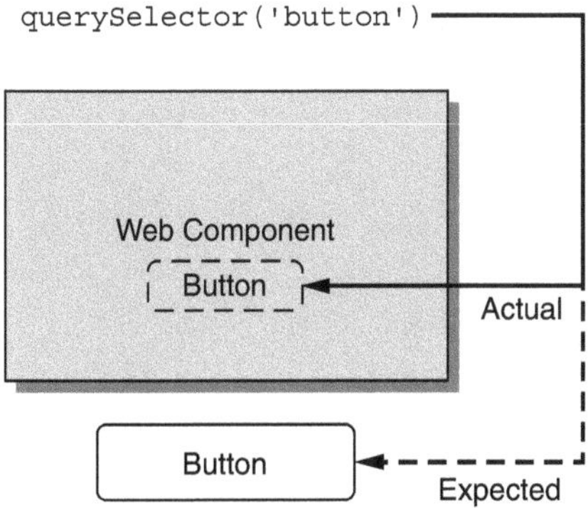

Figure 8.4 Query-selecting a button on the page, but unintentionally picking up a button in our Web Component

8.2 Enter the Shadow DOM

The Shadow DOM attempts to solve both problems but comes up a little short for malicious users. To explain, let's try it out!

What we can try first is not allowing the `<div>` in our previous example to be hijacked. Using the Shadow DOM, we can easily block normal access to this `<div>`, and for this, we just need to change two lines in our `connectedCallback`, as follows.

Listing 8.2 Using the Shadow DOM in a simple component

```
connectedCallback() {
   this.attachShadow({mode: 'open'});
   this.shadowRoot.innerHTML =
   `<div class="inside-component">My Component</div>`
}
```

- Creates an open Shadow DOM and attaches it to our component
- Sets our component's HTML

There's not much code here, but it does bear some explanation. The first thing we're doing is creating a shadow root and attaching that shadow root to our component. In this example, we're using a mode of `open` to create it. Please note that this is a required parameter. Because browser vendors couldn't agree on what the default should be, closed or open, they've passed this issue on to you rather than take a position themselves. It's easier to explain the difference between these modes after exploring what's going on in the code first.

Aside from being closed or open, what is the shadow root? Remember back to chapter 7 and our discussion of the `<template>` tag. Recall that the basis of the template was the document fragment. A document fragment is an entirely separate DOM tree that is not rendered as part of your main page. The shadow root is, in fact, a document fragment. This means that the shadow root is an entirely separate DOM! It's not actually the same DOM as the rest of your page.

We can view the shadow root in action in this example by opening Chrome's dev tools, as figure 8.5 shows. What you might not expect is seeing that elements you use every day have their own shadow root.

```
▼<sample-component>
  ▼#shadow-root (open)
      <div class="inside-component">My
      Component</div>
  </sample-component>
```

Figure 8.5 Viewing the Shadow DOM and associated shadow root in Chrome's dev tools

Let's take a peek at a video tag. We don't have to properly set it up with a video source to see its shadow root and the rest of its Shadow DOM. Simply drop a `<video></video>` tag in your HTML. Inspecting it in Chrome using the default settings won't reveal much. To reveal its Shadow DOM, you'll need to allow it to show the "user agent Shadow DOM," as in figure 8.6. Essentially, Chrome will reveal any Shadow DOM you create, but will hide it by default in the normal browser elements that use it. The `<select>` tag is another one that has its own Shadow DOM you can view in this manner.

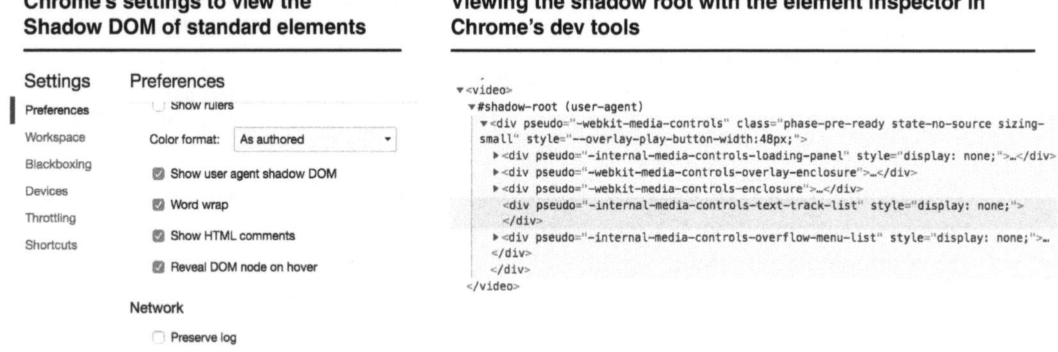

Figure 8.6 Viewing the user agent Shadow DOM/root for everyday elements

8.2.1 The shadow root

As we get into proper terminology like "shadow root," familiarize yourself with the related terms shown in figure 8.7:

- *Shadow root*—The document fragment containing the separate DOM.
- *Shadow tree*—The DOM contained by the shadow root.

- *Shadow host*—The node of your page DOM that parents the shadow tree/root. For our purposes, this is your Web Component, though it could easily be used outside of a custom element.
- *Shadow boundary*—Imagine this as a line between your shadow host and shadow tree. If we reach into the shadow tree from our component and set text on a button, for example, we could say we're crossing the "shadow boundary."

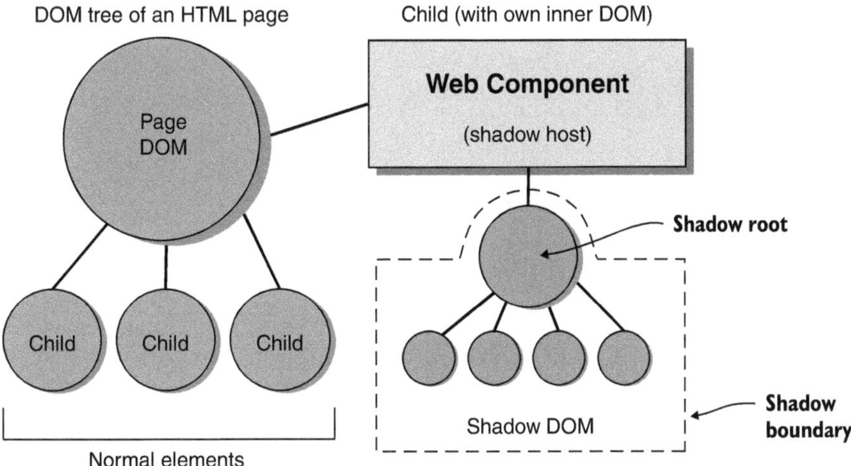

Figure 8.7 The Shadow DOM, host, root, and boundary (the dotted line)

Terminology aside, the important takeaway is that we're dealing with a new DOM inside a document fragment. Unlike a document fragment used by the `<template>` tag, however, this fragment is actually rendered in the browser, yet still maintains its independence.

Once created, we can use the new and automatically created property of our component, `shadowRoot`, to access any of our element's properties, like `innerHTML`. This is what we did in our example:

```
this.shadowRoot.innerHTML =
  `<div class="inside-component">My Component</div>`
```

With just this change, we've now protected our component from accidental intrusions. When we now run the same query selector and try to set the `innerHTML`, it fails:

```
document.querySelector('.inside-component').innerHTML +=
  ' has been hijacked';
```

Our error reads

```
Uncaught TypeError: Cannot read property 'innerHTML' of null
```

What happens now? Query-selecting our `inside-component` class comes up with nothing, and setting the `innerHTML` property is attempted on a null object, as figure 8.8 shows. That's because we've isolated the HTML inside our component with the Shadow DOM.

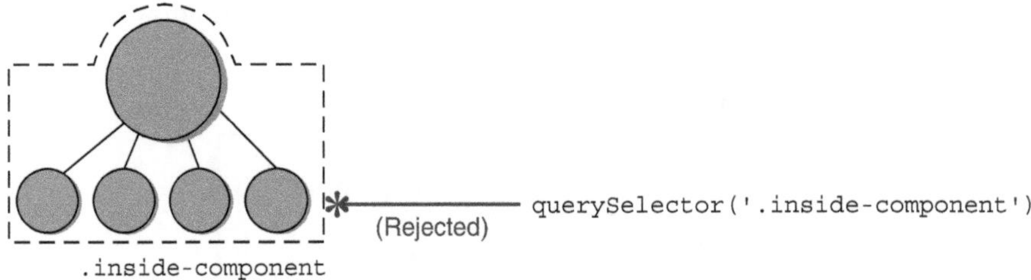

Figure 8.8 Attempting to query-select inside the Shadow DOM

8.2.2 Closed mode

Here's the thing, though. If we wanted to be malicious, we still could be. The same `shadowRoot` property is available from the outside. We could adjust our query selector to be more complex and still set the `innerHTML` of that `<div>`:

```
document.querySelector('sample-component').shadowRoot.querySelector
➥ ('.inside-component').innerHTML += ' has been hijacked';
```

Here, we're showing JS that easily sets our component's `innerHTML`. Can we stop those malicious users from coming in and manipulating our component in ways we don't want? The answer appears to be no, but that's where closed mode comes in. Curtailing malicious users is the intention behind having two modes. To explain, let's set `mode` to `closed` in the following listing.

Listing 8.3 Setting the shadow mode to `closed`

```
connectedCallback () {
   this.attachShadow({mode: 'closed'});        ◁── Sets the shadow mode to closed
   this.shadowRoot.innerHTML =
      `<div class="inside-component">My Component</div>`
}
```

This won't work as intended, however, without changing something else! With the shadow root closed, the `shadowRoot` property doesn't exist (it's `null`), so we can't set the `innerHTML` through it. How, then, can we interact with our own component when working from the inside?

The call to `attachShadow` does return a reference to the shadow root, whether you're in open or closed mode. If you only need a reference in the same function where you created the shadow root, you can simply declare a variable, as follows.

Listing 8.4 Using a variable to reference the shadow root

```
connectedCallback () {
   const root = this.attachShadow(      <-- Sets a variable to the newly created shadow root
      {mode: 'closed'});
   root.innerHTML = `<div class="inside-component">My Component</div>`
}
```

If that's the only interaction point with your component's Shadow DOM, problem solved! You've taken steps to close off your component from malicious users . . . except for one more thing. Let's pretend we are malicious and will stop at nothing to sabotage this component. We can change the function definition of `attachShadow` after the component class is declared:

```
SampleComponent.prototype.attachShadow = function(mode) { return this; };
```

This is being very tricky indeed, but what we've done is change the `attachShadow` function so that it doesn't actually create a shadow root and instead does nothing but pass back the Web Component's natural scope. The original component creator, who intended to create a closed shadow DOM, is not creating a shadow DOM at all. The shadow root reference is what they were supposed to get back, but it ended up really just being the component's scope. This trickery still works the same because `this`, and the shadow root, have approximately the same API.

And now we're back to our original, easy way of taking over the component:

```
document.querySelector('.inside-component').innerHTML +=
   ' has been hijacked';
```

Should you expect people who use your component to try to break in in this way? Probably not. But they could. It's not real security because it's so easily bypassed.

Recall at the start of this chapter when we talked about protecting your component for real or doing so by convention. There, we discussed using the underscore to protect private variables and methods in your class instead of using more secure ways. Here, it's the same thing, but instead of variable and methods, we're talking about your component's DOM.

That's why Google's own documentation on Web Components says you shouldn't use closed mode (https://developers.google.com/web/fundamentals/web-components/shadowdom). You're closing off the Shadow DOM to make it secure, but you're trusting that the folks who use your component won't bypass it in some very simple ways. In the end, you're protecting your component by convention regardless of what you do; it's just that closed mode makes it more difficult to develop with.

Google claims that closed mode will make your component suffer for two reasons. The first is that by allowing component users into your component's Shadow DOM through the `shadowRoot` property, you're at least making an escape hatch. Whether you're making private class properties with underscores or keeping the Shadow DOM open, it's protecting your class or component by convention.

Despite your best intentions for your component, you likely won't accommodate all use cases all the time. Having a way into your component allows some flexibility, but it's also important to recognize that this way in goes against your better judgement as a component developer. It's a signal to the developer who uses your component that they should do so at their own risk. That's ill-advised, of course, but when deadlines are tight, and a web app needs to be shipped tomorrow, it's nice to provide a path forward with an open Shadow DOM using the `shadowRoot` property to access things you don't intend to be accessed at present. You'll also see that an escape hatch with the open mode is rather nice for reaching in to perform automated testing, as we'll discuss in chapter 13.

Google's second gripe with closed mode is the claim that it makes your component's Shadow DOM inaccessible from inside your own component. But it's more complicated than that. The `shadowRoot` property is no longer available in closed mode, but we can easily make a reference to it.

Our current example has a locally scoped variable in the next listing.

Listing 8.5 Locally scoped shadow root variable

```
connectedCallback() {
   const root = this.attachShadow(          <-- Locally scoped shadow root variable
        {mode: 'closed'});
   root.innerHTML = `<div class="inside-component">My Component</div>`
}
```

Now let's change it to having a property on your class.

Listing 8.6 A public property containing the shadow root

```
connectedCallback () {
   this.root = this.attachShadow(          <-- The shadow root saved as a public property
        {mode: 'closed'});
   this.root.innerHTML = `<div class="inside-component">My Component</div>`
}
```

On the other hand, making it a public property defeats the purpose. Again, you're back to having a public reference to the Shadow DOM; it just happens to be named `root` (or any property name you choose) instead of the `shadowRoot` property, as created by an open Shadow DOM. And again, it's easy to access your component's DOM through it. That said, if you did use a stronger way of protecting your class properties, like using Weak Maps to make your properties private, it's still wouldn't be foolproof, but it would close things off pretty well and allow internal access to your closed DOM just fine. It might be worth speculating that a truly closed Shadow DOM might be achievable once we have native private class fields available in all browsers, but we just aren't there yet.

It's clear that a closed Shadow DOM isn't worth the trouble for most cases. There is no bulletproof way to completely lock down your component, and protecting your component by convention using the open Shadow DOM is the way to go.

8.2.3 Your component's constructor vs. connectedCallback

Back in chapter 4, when discussing the component API, I cautioned that the constructor wasn't very useful for many things in your component initialization. This is because when the constructor fires on your component, it doesn't yet have access to your component's DOM-related property and methods, like `innerHTML`.

Now, with the Shadow DOM, nothing has changed in relation to the page's DOM. Your component, when using the Shadow DOM, still does not have access to the DOM-related properties and methods for your element until it gets added to the page DOM with `connectedCallback`.

Despite this all being true, it's no longer actually a concern. We're no longer relying on the page's DOM. We're creating a separate mini DOM for our component when we call `attachShadow`. This mini DOM is immediately available, and we can write its `innerHTML` right away!

This is why you'll see most examples of Web Components using the constructor to do all of the initialization work instead of the `connectedCallback` method, as we've been using so far. Going forward in this book, I'll likely do everything in the constructor because I'll be using the Shadow DOM. But it's important to keep this distinction in mind, given that the Shadow DOM is just one piece of the Web Component puzzle and, as such, it is optional (even though you'll probably want to use it from here on in). Let's change our previous simple example slightly to reflect this.

Listing 8.7 Using the constructor instead of `connectedCallback`

```
<html>
<head>
    <script>
        class SampleComponent extends HTMLElement {
            constructor() {                          <-- Constructor method
                super();                             <-- Call to super() is required as we extend HTMLElement
                this.attachShadow({mode: 'open'});
                this.shadowRoot.innerHTML =
                 `<div class="inside-component">My Component</div>`   <-- Sets the innerHTML in the constructor
            }
        }

        if (!customElements.get('sample-component')) {
            customElements.define('sample-component', SampleComponent);
        }

    </script>
</head>
<body>
    <sample-component></sample-component>
</body>
</html>
```

8.3 The Shadow DOM today

Though the Shadow DOM sounds pretty amazing, it has a history of being a bit unreliable. I'm not knocking the implementation or the spec, just the slow inclusion of it as a supported feature in all modern browsers, as I mentioned at the start of this chapter. I've personally been in a holding pattern until very recently. When Firefox shipped Web Components this past October, and with the knowledge that Edge is on the way, I'm now happily using the Shadow DOM in my newer projects.

What happens when the browser of your choice doesn't have support for the Shadow DOM? The obvious answer is to use a polyfill, just like with any other feature. Unfortunately, this answer is a bit complicated for the Shadow DOM specifically.

The biggest problem when polyfilling is the subject of the next chapter. In terms of being defensive against accidental intrusions into your component, we've covered your component's API and its local DOM as accessed through JS. These are great to protect against through the encapsulation that the Shadow DOM gives us. I might argue, however, that protecting against CSS rules that bleed through is the absolute best use of the Shadow DOM. The reason I love this so much is that web developers have been struggling with this problem since CSS was a thing, and it's only gotten worse as web experiences have become more complex. There are some fairly novel workarounds, but the Shadow DOM completely negates this problem.

Currently, the effort to polyfill the Shadow DOM is divided up into these two use cases. We'll talk about CSS and its polyfill in the next chapter. Polyfilling JS access to your DOM is really easy, though. Back in chapter 2, when polyfilling custom elements, we specifically used the custom element polyfill.

We can go a little broader, though, and cover everything that's not supported. The polyfills found at www.webcomponents.org/polyfills offer some smart feature detection and fill in features where appropriate. That includes both custom elements and the Shadow DOM.

One option is to use

```
npm install @webcomponents/webcomponentsjs
```

and then add the `<script>` tag to your page:

```
<script src="node_modules/@webcomponents/webcomponentsjs/
    ➥webcomponents-bundle.js"></script>
```

Additionally, a CDN option is available. In the end, we should have something that works in all modern browsers, as in the next listing.

Listing 8.8 Component with polyfill

```
<html>
<head>
    <script src="https://unpkg.com/@webcomponents/webcomponentsjs@2.0.0/
     ➥webcomponents-loader.js"></script>     ◁ Polyfill loaded from CDN
    <script>
        class SampleComponent extends HTMLElement {
```

```
        constructor() {
            super();
            this.root = this.attachShadow({mode: 'open'});
        }

        connectedCallback() {
            if (!this.initialized) {
                this.root.innerHTML = 'setting some HTML';
                this.initialized = true;
            }
        }

    }

    if (!customElements.get('sample-component')) {
        customElements.define('sample-component', SampleComponent);
    }

    </script>
</head>
<body>

<sample-component></sample-component>

<script>
    setTimeout(function() {
        document.querySelector('sample-component').innerHTML =
        ➥ 'Component is hijacked';
    }, 500);    <-- Sets our component's innerHTML from the outside
</script>
</body>
</html>
```

We're using the polyfill and then testing it out by attempting to set our component's `innerHTML`. I used a timer here to set the `innerHTML` to make sure we try to hijack the component after it tries to set its own text in the `connectedCallback`. Using the Shadow DOM in most browsers, setting the `innerHTML` from outside the component fails. With the polyfill and the "Shady DOM," the same behavior happens in those that don't support the Shadow DOM, like Microsoft's Edge (with support coming soon) and IE.

As I alluded to before, however, the Shady DOM works pretty well for JS access to the DOM. Shady CSS is a different story, and one that we'll jump right into in the next chapter!

Summary

In this chapter, you learned

- What encapsulation is and how a self-contained object is only half the battle. Protecting and offering controlled access to your object is also important.
- That the Shadow DOM offers protection to your component's inner DOM and is most useful for accidental intrusions from the outside.

- That although the Shadow DOM offers a closed mode, it's impractical, and protecting your component by convention with an open Shadow DOM is the way forward, especially because it offers a way to bypass its protective boundary in a pinch.
- Differences between constructors and `connectedCallback` for working with your component's DOM when using or not using the Shadow DOM.
- How to use polyfill support with the Shady DOM and that there is a separate solution for CSS encapsulation.

9 Shadow CSS

This chapter covers

- Keeping external style out of your Web Components
- The Shadow DOM for CSS encapsulation
- Shadow DOM CSS selectors
- Rediscovering the ID attribute for Web Components

Let's continue on with our Shadow DOM exploration! In the last chapter, we zeroed in on a really nice aspect of the Shadow DOM. As awesome as DOM encapsulation is, the CSS aspect of the Shadow DOM is even better! Despite coming up with clever ways to mitigate style creep in our web development work over the years, it has always been a problem.

9.1 Style creep

Style creep can sometimes be a bit of a headache in web development work. To sum up, it's when CSS rules come in and affect elements you didn't intend to affect. You may be working to style an element in one place, but some style rules you've defined in your CSS for another element on your page are unintentionally picked up because the CSS selectors match. Although style creep isn't limited to Web Components, let's take a look at a Web Component example to see how it impacts us.

Figure 9.1 shows a simple little Web Component that is essentially a stylized numerical stepper.

Figure 9.1 A stylized stepper component comprising two buttons and a text span

For this hypothetical use case, let's say that no matter what the other buttons look like in our web application, it's important that this stepper be red, and that the plus and minus buttons are flush around the number in the middle. We're going for a very specific look here, and it needs to be perfect. The next listing shows us how this was achieved.

Listing 9.1 A stepper component without logic, just style

```
<html>
<head>
   <script>
       class SampleComponent extends HTMLElement {
           connectedCallback() {
            this.innerHTML = `
               <button class="big-button">-</button>
               <span class="increment-number">5</span>
               <button class="big-button">+</button>
               <style>
                 sample-component {
                    display: flex;
                 }
                 sample-component .increment-number {
                   font-size: 24px;
                      background-color: #770311;
                      color: white;
                      font-family: Helvetica;
                      display: inline-block;
                      padding: 11px;
                      border: none;
                   }

                   sample-component button {
                     border-radius: 0 50px 50px 0;
                     border: none;
                     width: 50px;
                     height: 50px;
                     font-size: 36px;
                     font-weight: bold;
                     background-color: red;
                     color: white;
                   }

                   sample-component button:first-child {
                     border-radius: 50px 0 0 50px;
                   }

                   sample-component .big-button:active {
                     background-color: #960000;
                   }

                   sample-component .big-button:focus {
```

Annotations: Stepper decrement button (at the `-` button line); Current stepper value (at the `<span>` line); Stepper increment button (at the `+` button line); Component styles (at `<style>`); Component styles, continued (at `sample-component button {`).

```
                    outline: thin dotted;
                }
                </style>`;
            }
        }

        if (!customElements.get('sample-component')) {
            customElements.define('sample-component', SampleComponent);
        }

    </script>
</head>
<body>
<sample-component></sample-component>       <-- Sample component on page
</body>
</html>
```

Notice how each style rule is prefaced with `sample-component`. In such a simple example with only one component on the page, specifying `.sample-component button` isn't strictly necessary. After all, our component has all of the buttons in the entire page here. A button is such a common element, however, that as soon as we start adding other content to our page, this button style will start affecting that other content. By making the rule specific to our `.sample-component`, we're avoiding style from this component leaking out into other elements we didn't intend.

It's good to have a refresher on how global styles like these work. In figure 9.2, we see that the CSS rules we define in our component become part of the page's global style space. In turn, these styles will affect any and all elements on our page.

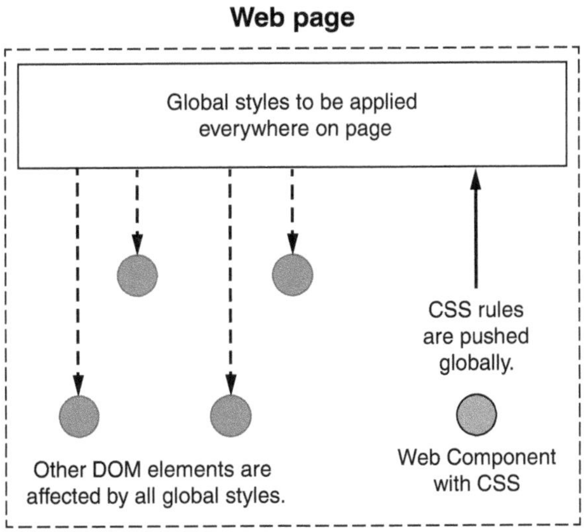

Web page

Global styles to be applied everywhere on page

CSS rules are pushed globally.

Other DOM elements are affected by all global styles.

Web Component with CSS

Figure 9.2 Without using the Shadow DOM, style defined in your Web Component will apply to the entire page.

9.1.1 Style creep into component descendants

Even with this specificity, our button rules could leak the other way as well. What if we had another component within this one with buttons of its own? Those buttons still have `<sample-component>` somewhere in their ancestry, so the CSS here would creep into any components downstream.

It's inevitable that you'll face some style creep, no matter how specific your selectors are, and you'll need to debug it. But again, web developers have faced this issue forever. That said, when using Web Components, it's easier to overlook these kinds of problems because we tend to treat the components we work with as standalone, encapsulated objects and skip over the inner content when scanning the DOM in our debug tools.

9.1.2 Style creep into your component

So, let's say you've covered all your bases. You've carefully planned your class names and CSS rules to be a good component developer and not let your styles leak out of your components. That's only half the battle—style can still creep into your component from the page and miscellaneous parent components.

Let's pretend your web app is driven by some sort of design system. Design systems, like Bootstrap, define a consistent look and feel in your web pages or applications. For example, you'd likely want most buttons in your application to adopt a single look, like in figure 9.3.

Figure 9.3 An example globally stylized button that could come from a design system

With the next listing, we'll add this button to our page with a simple button element and some page-level CSS to style it.

Listing 9.2 A styled button coexisting on our page with a Web Component

```
<head>
  <style>
    button {          <-- Non-component button styles
        border-top: 1px solid #96d1f8;
        background: #65a9d7;
        background: linear-gradient(90deg, #3e779d, #65a9d7);
        padding: 5px 10px;
        border-radius: 8px;
        box-shadow: rgba(0,0,0,.5) 0 8px 8px;
        text-shadow: rgba(0,0,0,.4) 0 2px 2px;
        color: white;
        font-size: 14px;
        font-family: Helvetica;
        text-decoration: none;
```

```
            vertical-align: middle;
        }
        button:hover {
            border-top-color: #28597a;
            background: #28597a;
            color: #ccc;
        }
        button:active {
            border-top-color: #1b435e;
            background: #1b435e;
        }
    </style>

    <script>
        . . . same component definition as before
    </script>
</head>
<body>
<sample-component></sample-component>
<br /><br />
<button>Button from Design System</button>
</body>
</html>
```

Non-component button element

Looking at the results in figure 9.4, we can already see how the button style is creeping into our component and doing some bad things.

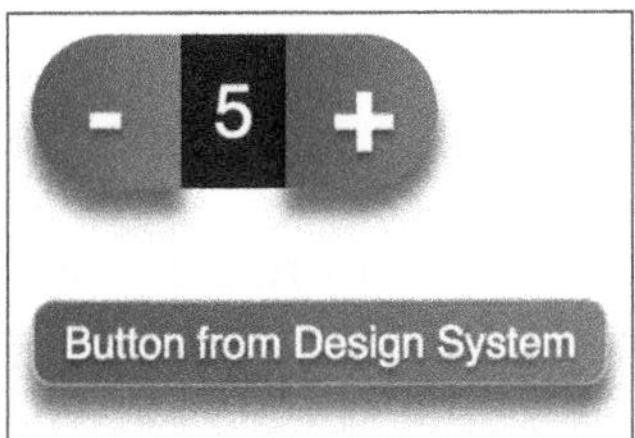

Figure 9.4 How a global button style can negatively affect our stepper component

We're starting to adopt some of the look of the button in our stepper. We have the drop shadow, and the blue gradient backgrounds, which of course don't match the numeric text in the middle anymore. Things are even more broken when you click the button—the background changes to red. In short, things are getting messy!

This is all caused by the generic button styles having just a few different rules than our stepper component button. The stepper's background color rule is overridden by the generic button's background rule. And of course, the stepper button shouldn't have a text shadow or box shadow rule like the generic button does.

We're not even getting into rule specificity here! Pretend that our generic button had a "big-button" variation as well, which just so happens to match the rule name inside our component.

Let's go back and make this variation by increasing the font size and padding of that button to make it a proper "big button." Our goal is to get something that looks like our previous generic buttons in figures 9.3 and 9.4, just bigger in context.

The reality, however, is that when we define this variation by changing all of our button rules in the CSS outside of the component from `button {}` to `button.big-button {}`, we get some unexpected results. With more rule specificity like this, and the coincidental naming of "big-button" for both buttons (inside our component and out), we've just created a situation in which rules we've defined outside of our component are more specific than those within. This really hurts the shape of our stepper buttons, shown in figure 9.5, that we've carefully defined with the `border-radius` rule.

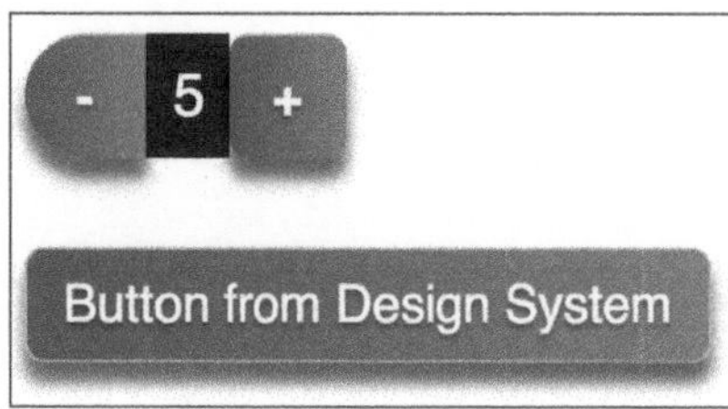

Figure 9.5 More specificity and same-named classes wreck the stepper component even more.

We can fix this, of course. We can add even more specificity in our CSS selectors inside the component, just like we did for the generic button. We can go from `button {}` to `button.big-button {}`. Also, though, we have to negate the properties that aren't covered in our component that are defined in our generic button:

```
sample-component button.big-button {
  box-shadow: none;
  text-shadow: none;
  padding: 0;
}
```

With these changes, we're back to our component looking just fine. It's obvious now that we have to be a little on guard for these types of problems. How much on guard really depends on how much you can control the surrounding application and anticipate how that style could creep in and affect you. The button versus stepper situation would have really been helped if rules for the `<button>` element as a whole weren't defined in the global CSS. Creating more unique names would be helpful as well.

As much as this sounds like a mess, and it is, it's something we as web developers have had to deal with forever. All that said, the Shadow DOM promises a fix!

9.2 *Style creep solved with the Shadow DOM*

In the last chapter, we saw that creating a shadow root on our component created a separate and independent DOM: access to this DOM was limited, and JS calls couldn't leak through to change elements or query-select components. When all was said and done, it was super easy!

We can protect our Web Component's DOM in the same way here. With the next listing, we can go back to our stepper component and use the Shadow DOM.

Listing 9.3 Using the Shadow DOM to protect our stepper component's style

```
class SampleComponent extends HTMLElement {
   connectedCallback() {
       const root =                              <-- Creates a shadow root to use the Shadow DOM
           this.attachShadow({mode: 'open'});
       root.innerHTML = `<button class="big-button">-</button>
                         <span class="increment-number">5</span>
                         <button class="big-button">+</button>
           <style>
                sample-component {
                   display: flex;
                }
                span {                           <-- With a smaller and more manageable DOM, CSS selectors don't need to be so specific.
                   font-size: 24px;
                   background-color: #770311;
                   color: white;
                   font-family: Helvetica;
                   display: inline-block;
                   padding: 11px;
                   border: none;
                }
                button {
                   border-radius: 0 50px 50px 0;
                   border: none;
                   width: 50px;
                   height: 50px;
                   font-size: 36px;
                   font-weight: bold;
                   background: none;
                   background-color: red;
                   color: white;
               }

               button:first-child {
                   border-radius: 50px 0 0 50px;
               }

               button:active {
                   background-color: #960000;
               }

               button:focus {
                   outline: thin dotted;
               }
           </style>`;
   }
}
```

Not only did I introduce the Shadow DOM into our stepper component, but I also got a little overly excited and removed all of my specific rules. My CSS selectors now specify only the rules for the generic <button> and <span> tags. After everything we've had to deal with in this example, as well as over the years of CSS pain in web development, this feels lazy and prone to breakage, doesn't it?

But the point is, now that we have a separate DOM, and we know that our component is this simple, as with our stepper component, we can absolutely style our elements generically here, and it's perfectly fine! Style won't creep in, as shown in figure 9.6, and style won't creep out and affect child components that also use Shadow DOMs.

Web page

Global styles applied everywhere on page

Style rejected

Other DOM elements

Web Component using Shadow DOM

Figure 9.6 Web Components using the Shadow DOM are unaffected by page-level CSS styling.

Listing 9.3 isn't perfect yet, though. For the most part, figure 9.7 looks OK, but the stepper component has some bad spacing in it.

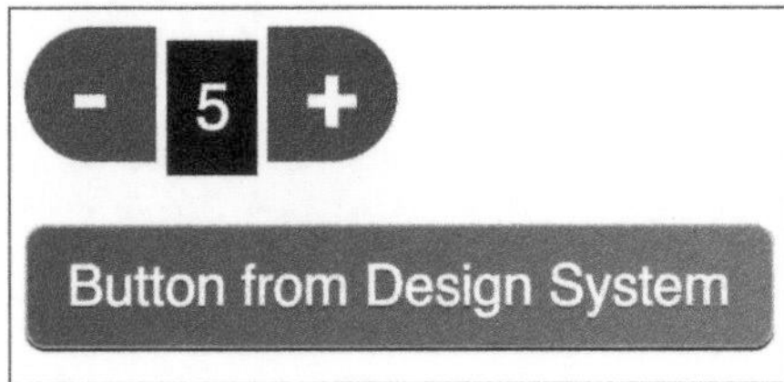

Figure 9.7 The stepper component, almost fixed, and living side by side with a globally styled button

What happened here? Well, our component used to have a display style of `flex`. The old rule is left in, but it's not working:

```
sample-component {
  display: flex;
}
```

That's because the `<sample-component>` tag is now outside of our Shadow DOM. Technically speaking, the tag that represents our component is the shadow host, and this host contains the shadow root, which contains our Shadow DOM. Since CSS can't leak into the Shadow DOM, this rule using `sample-component` is now meaningless for what we want to achieve here.

Instead, styling the Shadow DOM comes with a few new ways to use CSS selectors. The first is the new selector, `:host`. The `:host` selector is shorthand for styling what's inside the shadow host, as figure 9.8 shows. Changing our selector to

```
:host {
  display: flex;
}
```

puts our `display: flex` rule back in action.

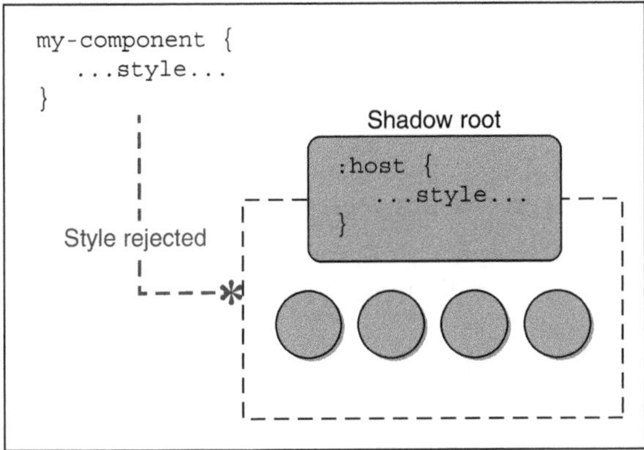

Figure 9.8 CSS on the shadow host (or using the component's tag as the selector) won't penetrate into the shadow root or into the Shadow DOM.

9.2.1 *When styles creep*

There *is* a bit of nuance to Shadow DOM CSS encapsulation, however. The Shadow DOM works pretty well to guard against outside styles coming into your Shadow DOM-guarded component. The nuance is that we're guarding against style creep when defined by a selector and not overall style. To explain what I mean, let's try another example in the next listing, where we define some style on the `<body>` of the page, outside the Shadow DOM.

Listing 9.4 Text rules affecting inside the Shadow DOM

```
<html>
<head>
    <style>
        .text {          <- Some text styling on the outer page
            font-size: 24px;
            font-weight: bold;
```

```
            color: green;
        }
    </style>

    <script>
        class SampleComponent extends HTMLElement {
            connectedCallback() {
                const root = this.attachShadow({mode: 'open'});
                root.innerHTML = `<span>Some Text</span>`;
            }
        }

        if (!customElements.get('sample-component')) {
            customElements.define('sample-component', SampleComponent);
        }

    </script>
</head>
<body class="text">
   <sample-component></sample-component>
</body>
</html>
```

A span containing text inside our component's Shadow DOM

Applies the text styling to the entire page body

So, what do you expect here? I promised that the Shadow DOM guards against styles coming into your component, yet when the example runs, as seen in figure 9.9, the <span> tag contains big, green, bold text!

Some Text

Figure 9.9 The large, green, bold text indicates that outside style is affecting the contents of our Shadow DOM.

This is because the nuance I'm talking about is that we're really guarding against CSS selectors from the outside being able to latch onto classes on the inside. Yet when an ancestor of your component (Shadow DOM or no) has some style applied to it that doesn't require selecting anything inside your component, that style will still affect the children. Now, if we removed that text class from the body like so,

```
<body>
```

and put that same class on the <span> inside our component like this,

```
root.innerHTML = `<span class="text">Some Text</span>`;
```

you'll see that the text style has no effect, as shown in figure 9.10.

Some Text

Figure 9.10 When we place the class directly on the `<span>` tag, the Shadow DOM successfully blocks the style.

The "text" selector from our example can't penetrate the Shadow DOM, yet those same rules as a style from the outside can. However, even something as simple as an outside <button> style won't creep in in the same way because "button" is still a selector (albeit a generic one). This can be pretty useful and makes a lot of sense. If all the text on your overall page is styled a certain way, or your page has a specific background color, you don't want your components to depart from these basic styles.

What if you didn't want even that style to creep in? We can do a bit of a trick with the `:host` selector.

Listing 9.5 Resetting the style in the Shadow DOM

```
<script>
    class SampleComponent extends HTMLElement {
        connectedCallback() {
            const root = this.attachShadow({mode: 'open'});
            root.innerHTML = `<span>Some Text</span>
            <style>
                :host {
                    all: initial;      <-- Applies initial styles
                }                          to all elements in the
            </style>`;                     shadow root
        }
    }

    if (!customElements.get('sample-component')) {
        customElements.define('sample-component', SampleComponent);
    }
</script>
```

While we certainly could set each individual style rule to `"initial"` to reset them, it's more encompassing to reset everything in our shadow root using the `all` CSS property and the brand-new `:host` selector.

To go beyond the `:host` selector and explore a little more, let's start a new demo project to properly give the Shadow DOM a try!

9.3 Shadow DOM workout plan

So, this demo has a bit of a dual meaning. Yes, we will be going through some Shadow DOM exercises to introduce some new concepts, but the demo we'll be making is also an exercise browser and workout creator.

The final product in this chapter won't be as interactive as it could be, and that's because we'll keep exploring this demo in chapter 14 as we cover events to implement the rest of the functionality. For this chapter, we'll end up with an exercise library on the left and your custom workout plan on the right, as shown in figure 9.11. Clicking each exercise in the library will add it to your plan.

Exercise types are either "strength" or "cardio" and are represented by a blue or green stripe, respectively. To keep things simple on the page, and because I don't personally own a bunch of exercise videos to share with you, my thumbnails and backgrounds are gray. However, in this book's GitHub repo, I've included GIF links in my data model, defined in components/exerciselibrary/exerciselibrary.js, so that each exercise renders with a motion thumbnail that will let you properly preview the exercise.

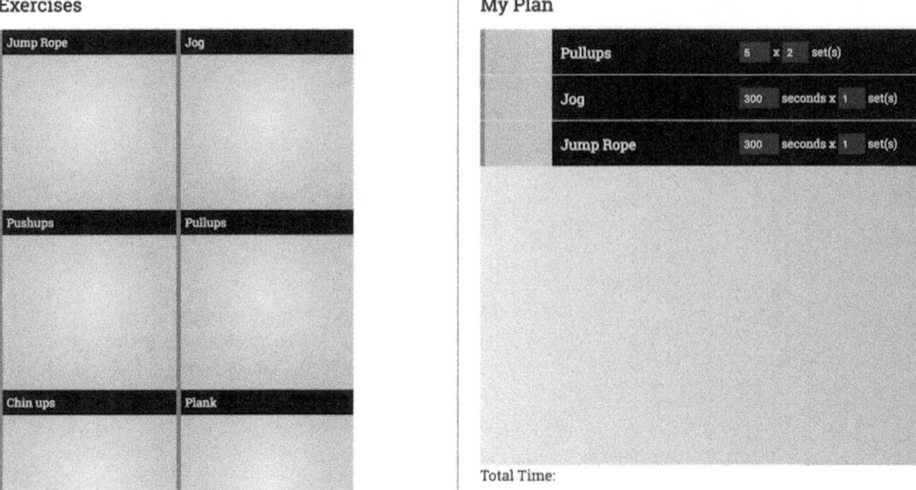

Figure 9.11 A demo app to browse exercises from a library and create a custom workout plan

9.3.1 Application shell

As a first step, let's create the overall application structure along with some placeholders for child components. Specifically, we'll create an HTML page, CSS file, and `<wkout-creator-app>` component, where the file structure looks like figure 9.12. If you are following along, please remember to use some sort of simple web server, given that we do have dependencies loaded from our index.html that may not work just using the file system.

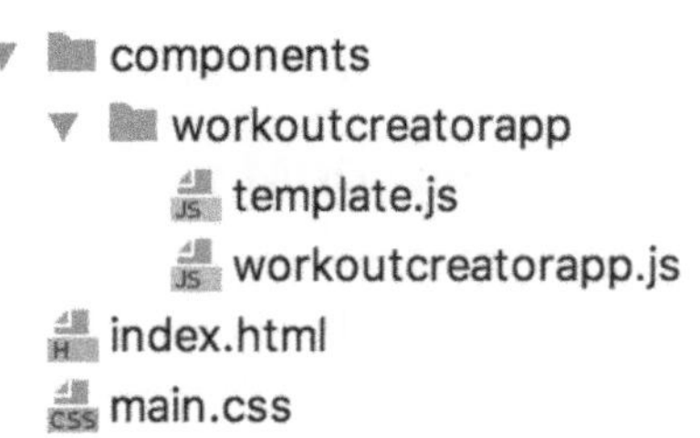

Figure 9.12 Basic file structure as we start our demo application

As with our other demos, our index.html will be extremely simple, as in the following listing.

Listing 9.6 The index.html for our demo application

```
<html>
<head>
   <title>Workout Creator</title>
   <script type="module"        <- Component import
         src="components/workoutcreatorapp/workoutcreatorapp.js">
   </script>
   <link rel="stylesheet" type="text/css" href="main.css">
</head>
```

```
<body>
   <wkout-creator-app></wkout-creator-app>    <-- Component declared in HTML
</body>
</html>
```

Our CSS is even simpler, and is just negating the margin and padding of the page body while sizing the <wkout-creator-app> to the entirety of the page with a bit of padding.

Listing 9.7 The main.css for our demo application

```
body {    <-- Resets margin and padding on page
   margin: 0;
   padding: 0;
}

wkout-creator-app {    <-- Sizes the application to take up the entire page
   height: calc(100vh - 20px);
   padding: 10px;
}
```

For the <wkout-creator-app> itself, the component's code, shown in the next listing, is also very simple.

Listing 9.8 The main application component for our demo application

```
import Template from './template.js';

export default class WorkoutCreatorApp extends HTMLElement {
   constructor() {
       super();
       this.attachShadow({mode: 'open'});    <-- Uses the Shadow DOM in our component
       this.shadowRoot.innerHTML = Template.render();
   }
}

if (!customElements.get('wkout-creator-app')) {
   customElements.define('wkout-creator-app', WorkoutCreatorApp );
}
```

Note that, unlike in past demos, we are now using the Shadow DOM. Also, unlike what we did earlier in this book, we are doing all of our component setup in the constructor and directly using the `shadowRoot` property to access our local Shadow DOM.

Lastly, I'm going to be using Shadow DOM CSS features as well as doing some things you'd never do without the Shadow DOM. Neither of these are easy to back out of! So, here I'm going all in on the Shadow DOM with no turning back.

9.3.2 Host and ID selectors

Continuing on from our `WorkoutCreatorApp` module that defines the <wkout-creator-app> component, let's take a peek at the template.js module that holds our HTML and CSS in the next listing.

Listing 9.9 Application template module that defines our HTML and CSS

```
export default {
   render() {
       return `${this.css()}
               ${this.html()}`;
   },

   html() {
       return `<wkout-exercise-lib>          <-- Left container for the exercise library
               </wkout-exercise-lib>
               <div id="divider-line"></div>   <-- Divider line with an ID attribute
               <wkout-plan></wkout-plan>`;     <-- Right container for workout plan list
   },

   css() {
       return `<style>
                   :host {
                      display: flex;
                   }

                   wkout-exercise-lib,
                   wkout-plan {
                       flex: 1;
                       height: 100%;
                       background-color: #eaeaea;
                   }

                   #divider-line {
                       width: 1px;
                       height: 100%;
                       margin-right: 25px;
                       background-color: black;
                   }
               </style>`;
   }
}
```

First off, we're creating three child elements. Two of them are components that aren't defined yet, so they'll just be rendered as empty `<div>` elements; they're styled with a background color, so we can visualize their placement thus far, as figure 9.13 shows. In the middle of these two sits a black divider line.

Even with just this, we have two points to discuss with the Shadow DOM. First, we're using the previously mentioned `:host` CSS selector to assign some style to our host component. In this case, we simply want to use a display type of `"flex"` to lay out our three elements.

The second point is an important one. It sounds like a small point, but it's actually kind of huge. Our divider line is assigned the ID `"divider-line"` in `<div id="divider-line"></div>`. We then use this ID to assign style with CSS: `#divider-line {}`.

Why is this so important? Well, ingrained in every web developer is that we should use the ID attribute sparingly. The reason is that there can be only one element with that ID in your entire DOM. If you make a mistake and assign a second element with

Figure 9.13 How our barebones application looks so far in a browser

the same ID, you're bound to get CSS or query-selection problems when you're only able to select or style one of the multiple elements with the same ID.

Typically, our selectors will be multiple classes together to get the specificity required to accurately select or style an element. For our divider line, we might use a CSS selector that looks like

```
wkout-creator-app div.divider-line.center.thin {}
```

Yes, I got a little ridiculous with the selector just now using `.center` and `.thin`, but I'm just trying to underscore the point of overdoing the specificity, which is usually needed.

Now, however, we can use the Shadow DOM. Coming back to the point that each ID in your entire DOM must be unique, remember we're now using multiple DOMs! Your ID needs to be unique only inside the scope of your Web Component. An element with an ID of `#divider` could easily exist elsewhere on the page or in other Web Components, and there would be no conflict.

Even better, given that there are only three elements in this Web Component, with just the divider line using a `<div>` tag, we could easily not bother with an ID, instead using a selector like this: `div {}`.

Personally, I think this is really exciting. Coming back to when I introduced the Shadow DOM in the last chapter, I said that it removes the brittleness of web development. This is a prime example. We can focus on the structure and style of our component and not worry about conflicts anywhere else. Our selectors can be as dead simple and easy to read as our component's internal structure allows.

9.3.3 Grid and list containers

We're going to continue on now with more of same concepts we just explored in order to get a grid of exercises and our workout plan list in place. That's two more components, which makes our project structure look like figure 9.14.

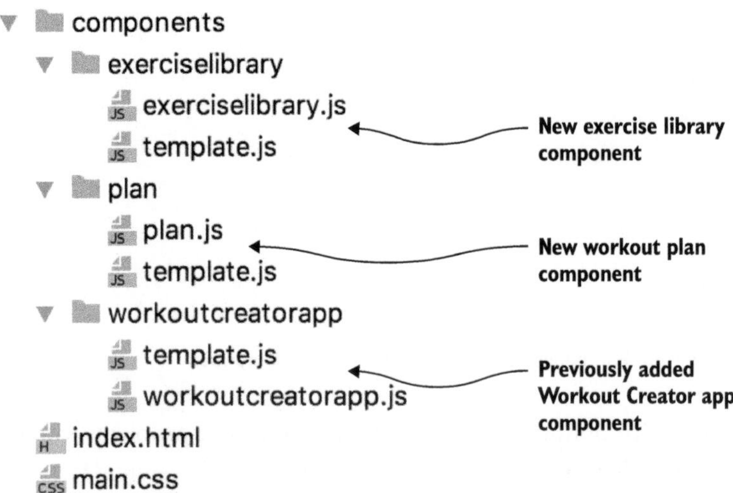

Figure 9.14 Project file structure as our two container components are added for the exercise library and workout plan

Remember, we are actually rendering those `<wkout-plan>` and `<wkout-exercise-lib>` components already in the application component; it's just that they aren't defined yet, so they render as `<div>` elements. As such, our first step after creating the new files and folders for the components is to import those modules at the head of workoutcreatorapp/template.js:

```
import ExerciseLibrary from '../exerciselibrary/exerciselibrary.js';
import Plan from '../plan/plan.js';
```

With those defined, let's get to work fleshing out these components!

Both are pretty simple, in fact. This is largely due to us not paying any attention to interactivity yet. The next listing shows our plan/plan.js and plan/template.js files.

Listing 9.10 Workout plan component files

```
// Plan.js
import Template from './template.js';

export default class Plan extends HTMLElement {
   constructor() {
       super();
       this.attachShadow({mode: 'open'});
```

```
        this.shadowRoot.innerHTML =        <-- Assigns HTML/CSS to
            Template.render();                 our component
    }
}

if (!customElements.get('wkout-plan')) {
    customElements.define('wkout-plan', Plan);
}

// Template.js
export default {
    render() {
        return `${this.css()}
                ${this.html()}`;
    },
                                          HTML to render
    html() {
        return `<h1>My Plan</h1>      <--
                <div id="container"></div>
                <div id="time">Total Time:</div>`;
    },
                                      CSS to render
    css() {
        return `<style>       <--
                    :host {
                        display: flex;
                        flex-direction: column;
                    }

                    #time {
                        height: 30px;
                    }

                    #container {
                        background: linear-gradient(90deg, rgba(235,235,235,1)
                            0%, rgba(208,208,208,1) 100%);
                        height: calc(100% - 60px);
                        overflow-y: scroll;
                    }
                </style>`;
    },
}
```

Since our workout plan list is empty at the start of the application, we aren't rendering anything except the container, header text, and a footer to show total plan duration.

Again, we're using a Shadow DOM, which enables us to use element IDs to target both the time and container `<div>` tags for styling. On both of these, we're just setting sizing and background fill color, as well as telling our exercise list container to scroll when it gets too tall. Also again, we're using the `:host` selector to tell our component's shadow root to display using a vertical flexbox.

The `<wkout-exercise-lib>` component is similar, except we actually do want to feed it with data. The purpose of this component is to show a list of exercises to choose from, so they should all be present when the application loads. As such, we'll be rendering a header and container, just like the last component, but we'll also be populating the container with all of our exercises. The next listing shows exercise-library/exerciselibrary.js and exerciselibrary/template.js.

Listing 9.11 Exercise library component files

```
// exerciselibrary.js
import Template from './template.js';

export default class ExerciseLibrary extends HTMLElement {
   constructor() {
       super();
       this.attachShadow({mode: 'open'});
       this.shadowRoot.innerHTML = Template.render([
           { label: 'Jump Rope', type: 'cardio', thumb: '', time: 300, sets: 1},
           { label: 'Jog', type: 'cardio', thumb: '', time: 300, sets: 1},
           { label: 'Pushups', type: 'strength', thumb: '', count: 5, sets: 2,
             estimatedTimePerCount: 5 },
           { label: 'Pullups', type: 'strength', thumb: '', count: 5, sets: 2,
             estimatedTimePerCount: 5},
           { label: 'Chin ups', type: 'strength', thumb: '', count: 5, sets: 2,
             estimatedTimePerCount: 5},
           { label: 'Plank', type: 'strength', thumb: '', time: 60, sets: 1}
           ]);
   }
}

if (!customElements.get('wkout-exercise-lib')) {
   customElements.define('wkout-exercise-lib', ExerciseLibrary);
}
```

Component definition module for the exercise library

```
// template.js
export default {
   render(exercises) {
       return `${this.css()}
               ${this.html(exercises)}`;
   },

   html(exercises) {

       let mkup = `<h1>Exercises</h1>
                   <div id="container">`;
       for (let c = 0; c < exercises.length; c++) {
           mkup +=
           `<wkout-exercise class="${exercises[c].type}" ></wkout-exercise>`;
       }
       return mkup + `</div>`;
   },

   css() {
   return `<style>
         host {
                display: flex;
                flex-direction: column;

            }

             #container {
                 overflow-y: scroll;
```

Template module for the exercise library, which holds our HTML and CSS

Loops through exercises and renders them

```
                height: calc(100% - 60px);
            }
        </style>`;
    }
}
```

You'll notice right away the big list of exercises we're feeding into the `Template.render` function. Each exercise has a label as well as a type of either `cardio` or `strength`. Depending on whether you count each rep or just do the exercise for a set amount of time, the exercise will have a number for `count` and `sets` or for `time`. If we're tracking count and sets, the only way we can estimate the total time of our workout is to estimate how much time each single rep of our exercise takes, so we use another property called `estimatedTimePerCount`.

Lastly, there is an empty `thumb` property on each exercise. Like I said at the beginning of this chapter, we'll just leave this blank to not show a thumbnail in this book. You can search for your own images or GIFs online to populate these or look at the GitHub repo for this book for ones I've found. Also in my GitHub repo are more exercises for our data model.

Our exerciselibrary/template.js file is mostly the same as the previous plan/template.js. Of course, the main difference is that we're accepting the list of exercises and rendering each one. Again, we're waiting to define the `<wkout-exercise>` for now while we focus on everything else, which gives us something that looks like figure 9.15.

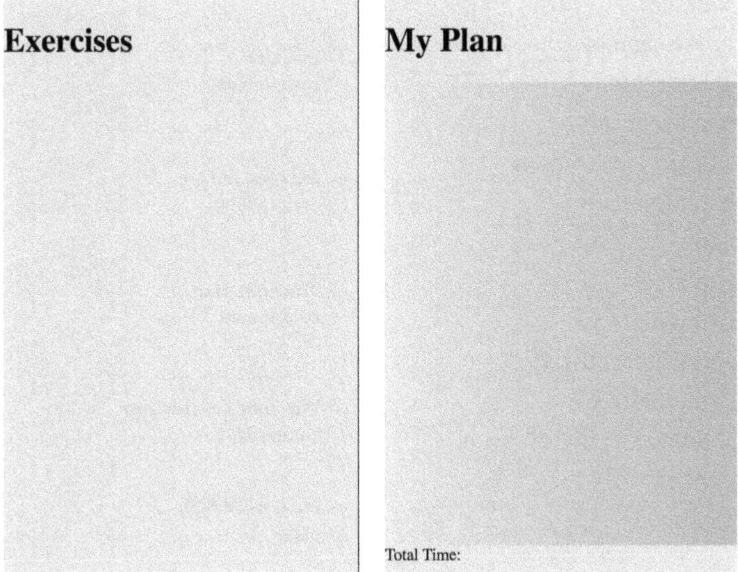

Figure 9.15 Filling in the components on the left and right sides of the application

You'll notice that even though we've rendered our exercises, they aren't showing up. That's because even though they are there in the DOM, they don't have a size or background—so, despite being present, they have a zero-pixel height and don't appear visually. We'll address this with the `<wkout-exercise>` component. It is the last one to cover, and it's actually pretty interesting.

9.4 Adaptable components

Why do I find this `<wkout-exercise>` so interesting? Well, it's because we're going to start on a component that needs to look slightly different depending on how it's used, and we'll learn an alternate way of using the `:host` selector. In the next chapter, we'll push even further on this adaptable component to make it look completely different in the workout plan container.

9.4.1 Creating the exercise component

Since our workout plan needs some interactivity to function, let's focus instead on the exercise library first, as it's easier to iterate on style for something that appears on page load instead of requiring the extra step of clicking to add. We're, of course, going to need to create the component files, and we'll end up with the file structure shown in figure 9.16.

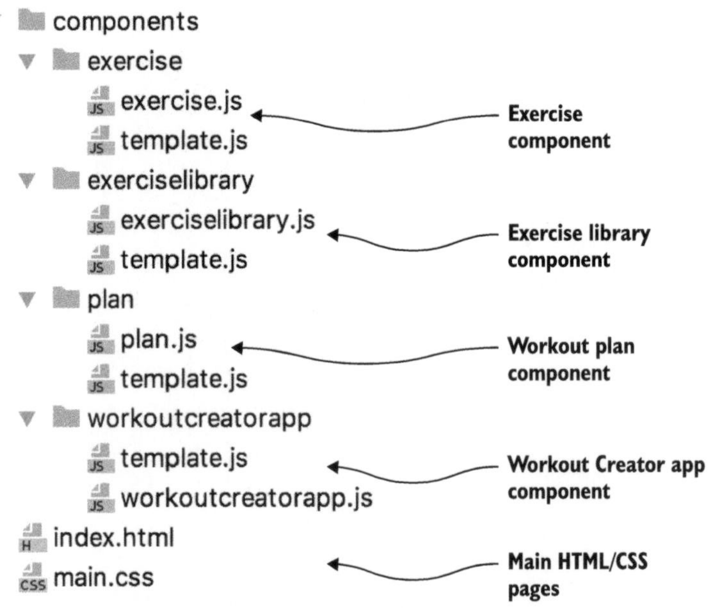

Figure 9.16 Final file structure for the application

Since both the workout plan and exercise library render the exercise component, we should place that import into both plan/template.js and exerciselibrary/template.js modules:

```
import Exercise from '../exercise/exercise.js';
```

Let's take a look at the Web Component definition for `<wkout-exercise>` in the following listing.

Listing 9.12 Component files for the exercise component

```
import Template from './template.js';

export default class Exercise extends HTMLElement {
   constructor() {
       super();
       this.attachShadow({mode: 'open'});

       const params = {
           label: this.getAttribute('label'),
           type: this.getAttribute('type'),
           thumb: this.getAttribute('thumb'),
           time: this.getAttribute('time'),
           count: this.getAttribute('count'),
           estimatedTimePerCount: this.getAttribute('estimatedtimepercount'),
           sets: this.getAttribute('sets'),
       };
       this.shadowRoot.innerHTML = Template.render(params);
   }

  get label() { return this.getAttribute('label'); }    <-- Getters/setters for each property

  set label(val) {  this.setAttribute('label', val); }

  // more getters/setters for thumb, type, time, count,
  // estimateTimePerCount, and sets
  serialize() {      <-- Function to serialize all properties into an object
       return {
           label: this.label,
           type: this.type,
           thumb: this.thumb,
           time: this.time,
           count: this.count,
           estimatedTimePerCount: this.estimatedTimePerCount,
           sets: this.sets,
       }
   }

   static toAttributeString(obj) {    <-- Function to assemble an attribute string for a cloned exercise component
       let attr = '';
       for (let key in obj) {
           if (obj[key]) {
               attr += key + '="' + obj[key] + '" ';
           }
       }
       return attr;
   }
```

```
}

if (!customElements.get('wkout-exercise')) {
   customElements.define('wkout-exercise', Exercise);
}
```

To save space here, I've eliminated all but one of my getters/setters. In this component definition, we're employing something we picked up in chapter 3. We're using reflection to use attributes and properties interchangeably. We can use either `element.setAttribute(property, value)` on the element or `element.property = value` to set a property. Either way, we're getting or setting some data that is internally based on the element's attribute. If I didn't cut it short for brevity, we'd have getters/setters for `thumb`, `type`, `time`, `count`, `estimateTimePerCount`, and `sets` as well.

The other two methods are ways to gather our data. First, we have `serialize`, which just assembles our data into one object we can pass around easily. The other static method, `toAttributeString`, is similar. It assembles all of our data like `serialize` does but creates a string that we can use to populate attributes. We'll end up with a string in the format of

```
property="value" property2="value2" property3="value3"
```

This extra method might not seem necessary, but we want to weed out those undefined properties. Remember that because of the variation of the exercises, some will have a rep count property, like when you lift weights, while others will have a duration property, like when you're jogging. So rather than having `property="undefined"` be an attribute on our tag when the actual undefined value gets converted to a string, or having to check for `undefined` on each property in our templates, making them a bit long and hard to read, this is a good alternative. All this is to explain why in exerciselibrary/template.js, we'll modify our loop in the `html()` function to be

```
for (let c = 0; c < exercises.length; c++) {
   mkup += `<wkout-exercise class="${exercises[c].type}"
     ${Exercise.toAttributeString(exercises[c])}></wkout-exercise>`;
}
```

With this, we can create attributes on our new element for each and every *valid* property in our data. As this is a static method (accessed from the class rather than the instance), we can use it either on the raw data objects we have in exerciselibrary/exerciselibrary.js before the component is created or against an already-created `<wkout-exercise>` component to copy those values. Whether a simple object or component, the properties are all there and can be used the same way by this method. The tag we get in the end looks like either of the following, depending on the exercise:

```
<wkout-exercise class="cardio" label="Jog" type="cardio" time="300"
     sets="1"></wkout-exercise>

<wkout-exercise class="strength" label="Pushups" type="strength" count="5"
     sets="2" estimatedtimepercount="5"></wkout-exercise>
```

9.4.2 Exercise component style

With all of the attributes we need set on the component, and the component definition created, there's just one last thing to do: create the HTML and CSS seen in the next listing.

Listing 9.13 First pass of the exercise component

```
export default {
   render(exercise) {
       return `${this.css(exercise)}
               ${this.html(exercise)}`;
   },

   html(exercise) {
       return `<div id="info">
                   <span id="label">${exercise.label}</span>
                   <span id="delete">x</span>
               </div>`;
   },

   css(exercise) {
       return `<style>
                   :host {        <-- Styles the overall component
                       display: inline-block;
                       background: radial-gradient(circle,
                       rgba(235,235,235,1) 0%, rgba(208,208,208,1) 100%);
                      /*background-image:
                      ➥url('${exercise.thumb}');*/
                       border-left-style: solid;
                       border-left-width: 5px;
                   }

                   :host(.cardio) {
                        border-left-color: #28a7ff;
                   }

                   :host(.strength) {
                        border-left-color: #75af01;
                   }

                   #info {
                       font-size: small;
                       display: flex;
                       align-items: center;
                       background-color: black;
                       color: white;
                   }

                   :host {
                       width: 200px;
                       height: 200px;
                       background-size: cover;
                   }

                   :host #info {
                       padding: 5px;
```

Annotations: "Commented out thumbnail background" (points to the `/*background-image: url(...)*/` lines); "Overall component style with a variation for a class on the component tag" (points to `:host(.cardio)` and `:host(.strength)`).

```
            }
        </style>`;
    }
}
```

With all of this now put together, our <wkout-exercise-lib> component renders all of the <wkout-exercise> components we have. Seen in figure 9.17, the first minor thing to notice is our component backgrounds:

```
background: radial-gradient(circle, rgba(235,235,235,1) 0%,
     rgba(208,208,208,1) 100%);
/*background-image: url('${exercise.thumb}');*/
```

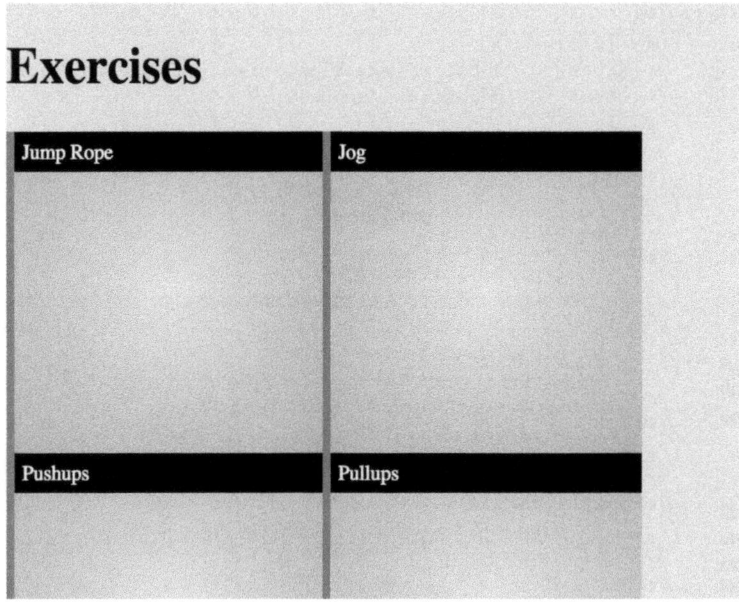

Figure 9.17 Newly styled exercise components

I've commented out the background image, but if you've searched online and found some great thumbnails for each exercise and added them to the data in the <wkout-exercise-lib> component, feel free to uncomment this line. If you didn't, we're simply showing a gradient gray background.

Notice as well how simple the HTML is. We're showing a 200 × 200 box with a black label at the top. This is fine for the library view, but you might imagine that this could all be a little problematic to display as a list view in the exercise plan.

Again, we're using some concepts we've covered before in this chapter. We're identifying and selecting elements using the ID attribute as well as using the `:host` selector for our component's shadow root context.

Note, however, that we have a small variation on the `:host` selector:

```
:host(.cardio) {
     border-left-color: #28a7ff;
}

:host(.strength) {
     border-left-color: #75af01;
}
```

Back when rendering each of these components, we did put a class of `strength` or `cardio` on each component:

```
mkup += `<wkout-exercise class="${exercises[c].type}"
  ${Exercise.toAttributeString(exercises[c])}></wkout-exercise>`;
```

This variation on the :host selector allows us to consider any classes on the component's tag itself and use that for more CSS specificity. To be clearer and more concise, `:host(.cardio)` enables us to style the element `<wkout-exercise class="cardio">` based on its `cardio` class. In practice, these differing border colors enable the user to differentiate between the two different types of exercises when browsing the library grid.

There are a few more CSS selectors you may have seen online that I didn't get to here, but they lack support or are deprecated. We'll finish up making the `<wkout-exercise>` component adaptable to different contexts in the next chapter, while talking about some Shadow DOM gotchas while we're at it.

9.5 Updating the slider component

Before exploring the Shadow DOM gotchas and updating the Workout Creator app some more, we've learned enough to update the slider UI component we've been working on throughout this book. What's nice is that not much needs to change!

First things first, let's start using the Shadow DOM. Previously, the component initialization code was in the `connectedCallback` function, but we know now about the ability to use the constructor because of the Shadow DOM. The following listing shows this constructor; keep in mind, we've removed the `connectedCallback` altogether, moving the setup code to here.

Listing 9.14 Slider component constructor

```
constructor() {                              <- Functionality in connectedCallback moved to constructor
    super();
    this.attachShadow({mode: 'open'});       <- Attaches the Shadow DOM
    this.shadowRoot.innerHTML =
       Template.render();                    <- Uses the shadowRoot property instead of this for scope
    this.dom = Template.mapDOM(this.shadowRoot);

    document.addEventListener('mousemove', e => this.eventHandler(e));
    document.addEventListener('mouseup', e => this.eventHandler(e));
    this.addEventListener('mousedown', e => this.eventHandler(e));
}
```

Also, because the constructor fires prior to the `attributeChangedCallback`, the timing issue we faced before with `connectedCallback` doesn't happen anymore. You'll notice that we no longer have the following lines in our constructor's setup code:

```
this.refreshSlider(this.getAttribute('value'));
this.setColor(this.getAttribute('backgroundcolor'));
```

We also don't need to check if the `this.dom` property exists anymore, like when we did this:

```
setColor(color) {
    if (this.dom) { . . .
```

Of course, this check doesn't hurt. But with all of the initialization happening prior to the incoming attribute changes when the component starts, it's just not needed.

The template.js module can change slightly as well. In addition to using the `:host` selector for the component root, we can use IDs now instead of classes for styling and selection. As I've mentioned, using IDs is a luxury we weren't afforded before without an encapsulated DOM like we have now. The next listing shows the new template.js file for the slider.

Listing 9.15 New slider template module

```
export default {
    render() {
        return `${this.css()}
                ${this.html()}`;
    },

    mapDOM(scope) {
        return {
            overlay: scope.getElementById(      <-- Using IDs now, we'll use getElementById instead of querySelector.
'bg-overlay'),
            thumb: scope.getElementById('thumb'),
        }
    },

    html() {
        return `<div id="bg-overlay"></div>      <-- References elements by ID instead of class
                <div id="thumb"></div>`;
    },

    css() {
        return `<style>
                   :host {      <-- Uses :host selector to style overall component
                       display: inline-block;
                       position: relative;
                       border-radius: 3px;
                   }

                   #bg-overlay {      <-- Uses IDs to style instead of class
                       width: 100%;
                       height: 100%;
                       position: absolute;
                       border-radius: 3px;
                   }
```

```
                #thumb {
                    margin-top: -1px;
                    width: 5px;
                    height: calc(100% - 5px);
                    position: absolute;
                    border-style: solid;
                    border-width: 3px;
                    border-color: white;
                    border-radius: 3px;
                    pointer-events: none;
                    box-shadow: 0 4px 8px 0 rgba(0, 0, 0, 0.2), 0 6px
                        20px 0 rgba(0, 0, 0, 0.19);
                }
            </style>`;
    }
}
```

With the Shadow DOM now working in the slider component, we've done just about all we need to do on that particular component. We won't abandon it yet, though! The slider will be an integral part of a bigger component that we'll create in the last chapters of this book, where we'll also explore testing, a build process, and running Web Components in IE11.

Summary

In this chapter, we learned

- How CSS styles can leak into and out of your Web Component just like anywhere else, if you're not using the Shadow DOM
- That the Shadow DOM completely protects your component's DOM from outside CSS
- That when using the Shadow DOM, we can be a lot less specific with our CSS selectors, taking full advantage of the separate DOM
- How to use specific Shadow DOM CSS selectors to style your component, and style it differently in different contexts

10 Shadow CSS rough edges

This chapter covers

- The widely unsupported `:host-context()` selector
- The deprecated `::shadow` and `/deep/` Shadow DOM CSS selectors
- CSS Variables
- Polyfilling the Shadow DOM
- Design systems

In the last two chapters, I painted a fairly rosy picture of the Shadow DOM. Don't worry, I won't take it back! As amazing as the Shadow DOM is, though, there are some caveats you should know about. Unfortunately, these caveats are likely the most confusing part of Web Components. Between deprecated features, features that lack support in certain browsers, or just needing to know how to navigate browsers that don't support the Shadow DOM at all, it can all be a bit tricky.

10.1 Contextual CSS

The first rough edge to get to know is the `:host-context()` selector. It's not deprecated per se—it's just not supported in any browser except Chrome. Also, it gets a little worse. Webkit/Safari stated back in 2016 that they will never support it because they claim it's an anti-pattern (https://bugs.webkit.org/show_bug.cgi?id=160038). The folks at Firefox likewise feel that it's not a great thing to implement in the Gecko engine because of the performance implications. Firefox has opened up a ticket (https://github.com/w3c/csswg-drafts/issues/1914) on the W3C specification that wonders what the best course of action is with a nod to the Chrome/Blink code base, pointing out the performance tradeoffs on their side.

So, we're left with a nice little selector that nobody but Chrome seems to want to support, but that still seems to be part of the Shadow DOM specification. Even worse, to find out what's actually happening, you'd need to search each browser's public mailing lists or issue trackers!

What does this mean? If I had to bet, the `:host-context()` selector will get kicked out of the Shadow DOM specification, and Chrome will probably remove it sometime in the distant future, if only to maintain sanity and a common Shadow DOM feature set across browsers.

Interestingly enough, Angular supports the `:host-context()` selector, and given that it is a framework, Angular doesn't necessarily need browser support to offer it. All in all, this selector presents a bit of a messy situation. Personally, I think it's important to think about what this selector offers and how we can overcome it if it's not available to us when we do want to use it. If you agree, read on! If not, feel free to jump to section 10.2.

WARNING The rest of section 10.1 talks about the `:host-context()` selector, which, while not deprecated yet, is likely to be in the future.

10.1.1 A small bit of interactivity

To jump into using this new but ill-fated selector, let's get back to exploring our Workout Creator app. In chapter 9, we left off in a pretty good state. Each exercise in our data set was visualized by a thumbnail in our library view on the left, while on the right, we have an empty container waiting to be used, as seen in figure 10.1.

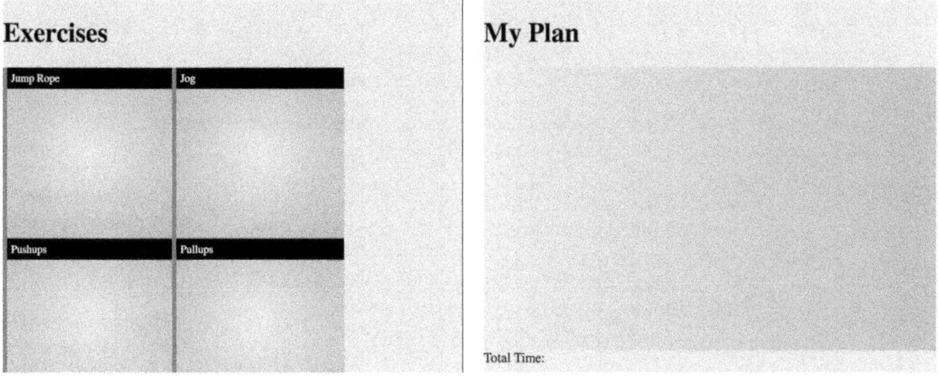

Figure 10.1 Where we left off in chapter 9

As you might imagine, the obvious next step is to allow the user to add exercises from the library on the left to their workout plan on the right. As we started to do in the last chapter with more subtle contextual styling, we'll use the same exercise component for both areas. The difference now is that instead of just differently colored lines to denote exercise types, our `<wkout-exercise>` component will look completely different in the two different containers.

With this in mind, we need to enable some interaction. Let's do a couple things to wire up the `<wkout-creator-app>`. For starters, we can cache element references for both containers (the library and the plan).

Inside workoutcreatorapp/template.js, let's add

```
mapDOM(scope) {
   return {
       library: scope.querySelector('wkout-exercise-lib'),
       plan: scope.querySelector('wkout-plan')
   };
},
```

It bears remembering that this `mapDOM` method is just my favorite custom way of saving references to elements, keeping `querySelectors` outside the main component class.

While we're here in this file, recall that to make things easier to see at the beginning, we added a background color to both components used here, so we could see them as progress was made. Now that we've built things up this far, let's remove it:

```
wkout-exercise-lib,
wkout-plan {
   flex: 1;
   height: 100%;
   background-color: #eaeaea;      <-- Remove this line
}
```

With element references mapped in this module, we can go back to workoutcreatorapp/workoutcreatorapp.js and add a click listener, as shown in the following listing.

Listing 10.1 Adding a click listener to allow exercise selection

```
import Template from './template.js';
import Plan from "../../plan/plan.js";
import Exercise from "../../exercise/exercise.js";

export default class WorkoutCreatorApp extends HTMLElement {
   constructor() {
       super();
       this.attachShadow({mode: 'open'});
       this.shadowRoot.innerHTML = Template.render();
       this.dom =                                         <-- Saves element references to an object for later use
               Template.mapDOM(this.shadowRoot);
       this.shadowRoot.addEventListener('click',          <-- Assigns a click listener to our component
           e => this.onClick(e));
   }
```

```
    onClick(e) {                                                  ◁── The click handler method
        const path = e.composedPath().reverse();
        for (let c = 0; c < path.length; c++) {
            if (path[c] instanceof Plan) {
                return;
            }
            if (path[c] instanceof Exercise) {
                const exercise = path[c];
                this.dom.plan.add(exercise);
            }
        }
    }
}

if (!customElements.get('wkout-creator-app')) {
    customElements.define('wkout-creator-app', WorkoutCreatorApp );
}
```

There are just two small additions in the constructor. First, we're calling the `mapDOM` method we just added from the template, so now `this.dom` holds all of our element references. Second, we're adding a click event listener to our component.

When you look at the contents of the `onClick` function and how the click listener is on the `<wkout-creator-app>` component rather than the exercise library component, you might question my methods. And you'd be right! The reason I'm doing things in this hacky way is so that we can properly explore events and some application design with this demo in chapter 14.

Even if you are familiar with events and custom events like I should have used here, the Shadow DOM does introduce some wrinkles. For now, this is a quick and dirty way to listen for events and act on them. Here, we're going through all of the elements that the click event went through to get to this function, and if it came from the component defined by the `Plan` class, then we exit from the function. But if it came from elsewhere, and there's a component defined by the `Exercise` class, then we know it can be added to the `<wkout-plan>` component.

That said, the line `this.dom.plan.add(exercise);` doesn't do anything yet. We'll need to add this functionality in the `<wkout-plan>` component. To do this, we can start with the template module at plan/template.js and add the contents of the next listing.

Listing 10.2 Adding new exercises to the workout plan component (template module)

```
mapDOM(scope) {
    return {
        exercises: scope.querySelector('#container')     ◁── Queries and saves a reference to the list container div
    }
},

renderExercise(exercise) {     ◁── Renders each exercise (returns a template literal string)
    return `<wkout-exercise class="${exercise.type}"
      ${Exercise.toAttributeString(exercise.serialize())}></wkout-exercise>`
}
```

Again, we're using the mapDOM method to store a reference to an element. This time, it's the container that should hold all of our exercises as we add them to the workout plan. The renderExercise method simply creates a new <wkout-exercise> component, as we did in the library component previously. This time, however, the data source is another <wkout-exercise> component that we're copying attributes from. This is done in an improved plan/plan.js class and reflected in the following listing.

Listing 10.3 Adding new exercises to the workout plan component (component module)

```
import Template from './template.js';

export default class Plan extends HTMLElement {
   constructor() {
        super();
        this.attachShadow({mode: 'open'});
        this.shadowRoot.innerHTML = Template.render();
        this.dom = Template.mapDOM(this.shadowRoot);       ❶
   }

   add(exercise) {                                        ❷
        this.dom.exercises.innerHTML += Template.renderExercise(exercise);
   }
}

if (!customElements.get('wkout-plan')) {
   customElements.define('wkout-plan', Plan);
}
```

❶ Saves the list container element reference to an object for later use

❷ Adds each exercise to our list container element

In this updated class, only two lines are added: the first is to get an object that contains our element references, as seen for annotation ❶ of listing 10.3. Second, an extremely simple add function, shown as annotation ❷, appends the new exercise onto our container's innerHTML by first rendering the HTML from the template module. After all this, refreshing our browser and clicking the Jump Rope exercise from the library, our application now looks like figure 10.2.

10.1.2 Contextual style

So far, so good! We're now showing an exercise library and allowing the user to click exercises and add them to a personal workout plan. The problem is, however, that we really want to show the personal workout plan as a list. We also want to allow users to customize the duration or reps/sets associated with the exercise they chose.

It wouldn't be so far-fetched to think that under these two different contexts, the exercise component uses are just too different, and we should create two different components for each context. But that would be a shame; we'd end up duplicating a significant amount of code, especially code that doesn't relate to the visual look. We can also use this opportunity to explore the :host-context() selector.

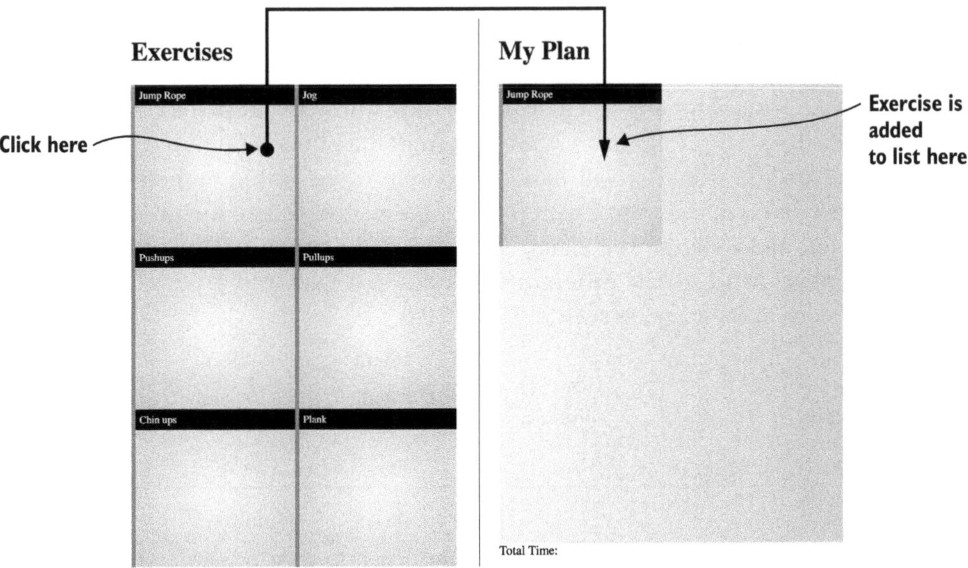

Figure 10.2 Application state after allowing exercises to be added to a workout plan

Let's first round out the HTML in exercise/template.js a bit more with some input fields to support the notion of customizing your exercise in the next listing.

Listing 10.4 Adding more functionality to the exercise component for the plan view

```
html(exercise) {
   return `<div id="info">
            <span id="label">    ◁— Exercise name
                   ${exercise.label}
            </span>
            <div id="customize">
               <label        ◁— Checks to see if property exists and, if not, hides the label/input
                   class="${exercise.time?'visible':'hidden'}">
                   <input type="number" max="999" style="width:35px;"
                   value="${Number(exercise.time)}"> seconds
               </label>
               <label class="${exercise.count?'visible':'hidden'}">
                   <input type="number" max="99" style="width:25px;"
                   value="${Number(exercise.count)}">
               </label>
               <label class="${exercise.sets?'visible':'hidden'}">x
                   <input type="number" max="9" style="width:20px;"
                   value="${Number(exercise.sets)}"> set(s)
               </label>
            </div>
            <span id="delete">x</span>    ◁— Delete button
        </div>`;
},
```

We've left the elements with IDs of `"info"` and `"label"` the same as how we had them before. These won't change. We have, however, added a `<div id="customize">` container holding a few `<input>` elements, as well as clickable `<span id="delete"> x</span>` to eventually delete this item from our workout plan.

Each `<input>` field has a `<label>` parent that, depending on whether the property exists on the exercise, will have a CSS rule to be visible or hidden. Now, with this added markup, the component is pretty messy no matter which context it's in. We can fix this, and we'll use the `:host-context` selector to do it! The `:host-context` selector allows us to specify different CSS rules that take into account where the component sits on the page, as seen in figure 10.3.

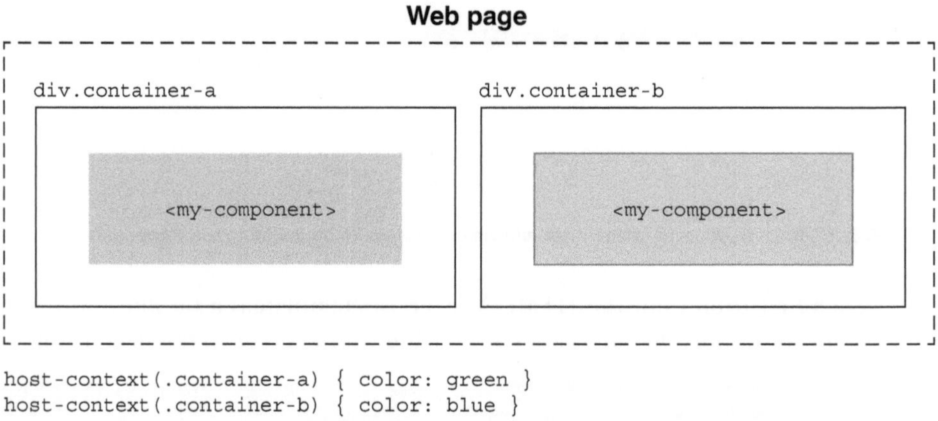

Web page

div.container-a

<my-component>

div.container-b

<my-component>

```
host-context(.container-a) { color: green }
host-context(.container-b) { color: blue }
```

Figure 10.3 Style differently depending on the context of the component with `:host-context()`.

As an example, let's look at the HTML we just added. Both the <div> and <span> should not be visible when the `<wkout-exercise>` component lives in the `<wkout-exercise-library>` component. Therefore, we can add the following CSS:

```
:host-context(wkout-exercise-lib) #customize {
   display: none;
}

:host-context(wkout-exercise-lib) #delete {
   display: none;
}
```

We can even start styling the component's shadow host itself with new sizing rules for when it appears in the `<wkout-plan>` component:

```
:host-context(wkout-plan) {
   width: 100%;
   height: 50px;
   margin-bottom: 1px;
   background-size: contain;
}
```

Here, instead of being a square 200 × 200 component, we're now saying that in the context of the <wkout-plan> element, we want it to be 100% wide and 50 pixels tall.

Now, with the ability to style according to our component's context, we can create a set of shared CSS rules, a set of rules for when we're under the <wkout-plan> component, and a set of rules for when we're under the <wkout-exercise-lib> component, as in the following listing.

Listing 10.5 Contextual style in the exercise component's CSS

```
<style>
    :host {
        display: inline-block;
        background: radial-gradient(circle, rgba(235,235,235,1) 0%,
        rgba(208,208,208,1) 100%);
        background-image: url('${exercise.thumb}');
        border-left-style: solid;
        border-left-width: 5px;
    }

    :host(.cardio) {
         border-left-color: #28a7ff;
    }

    :host(.strength) {
         border-left-color: #75af01;
    }

    #info {
        font-size: small;
        background-color: black;
        color: white;
        display: flex;
        align-items: center;
    }

    :host-context(wkout-exercise-lib) {
        width: 200px;
        height: 200px;
        background-size: cover;
    }

    :host-context(wkout-exercise-lib) #info {
        padding: 5px;
    }

    :host-context(wkout-exercise-lib) #customize {
        display: none;
    }

    :host-context(wkout-exercise-lib) #delete {
        display: none;
    }

    :host-context(wkout-plan) {
        width: 100%;
        height: 50px;
```

Component styling not dependent on context (annotation for `:host {`)

Component styling when in the context of the exercise library (annotation for `:host-context(wkout-exercise-lib) {`)

Component styling when in the context of the workout plan list (annotation for `:host-context(wkout-plan) {`)

```
        margin-bottom: 1px;
        background-size: contain;
    }

    :host-context(wkout-plan) input {
        background-color: #505050;
        padding: 5px;
        color: white;
        border: none;
    }

    :host-context(wkout-plan) #delete {
        width: 30px;
        height: 100%;
        line-height: 50px;
        font-size: 12px;
        font-family: Arial;
        text-align: center;
        background-color: #404040;
        cursor: pointer;
    }

    :host-context(wkout-plan) #delete:hover {
        background-color: #797979;
    }

    :host-context(wkout-plan) #info {
        width: calc(100% - 80px);
        height: 100%;
        margin-left: 75px;
        background-size: 75px 75px;
    }

    :host-context(wkout-plan) #customize {
        display: inline-block;
        flex: 1;
    }

    :host-context(wkout-plan) #label {
        padding-left: 10px;
        font-size: 16px;
        font-weight: bold;
        display: inline-block;
        flex: 1;
    }

    :host-context(wkout-plan) label.hidden {
        display: none;
    }
</style>
```

With all of this style in place, our component is finally starting to look finished! There are more things to do, like wire up some more interaction around the `<input>` fields, the Delete button, and so forth, but in terms of visual style and using the exercise component in different contexts, we're pretty good! The application as shown in figure 10.4 is just missing a couple of small details: some sort of font and color styling.

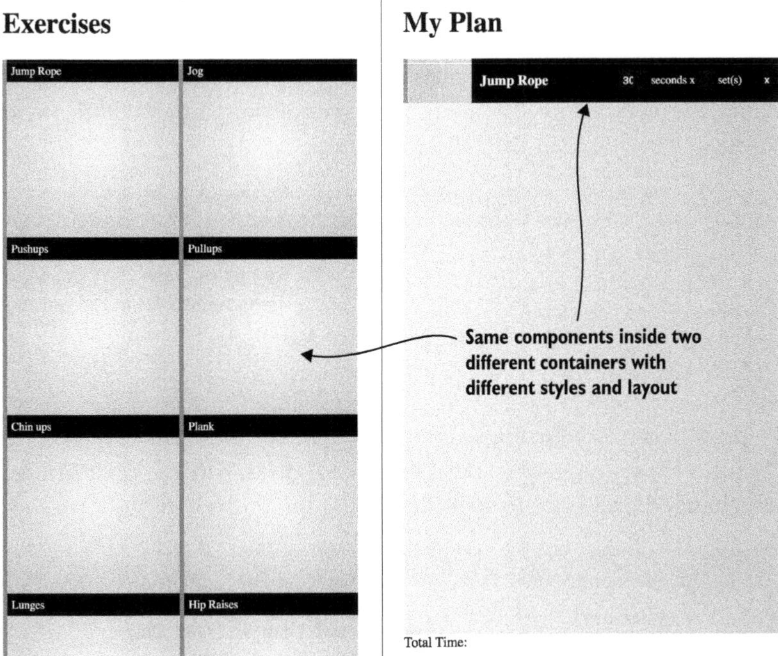

Figure 10.4 The exercise component has a different style, layout, and controls in different contexts.

10.1.3 Workaround for host-context

What I really like about the `:host-context()` selector is that it gets us thinking about how to use the same component in very different ways. But in the end, we don't actually need the selector to accomplish this level of different layout or styling. Sure, it's a tiny bit more work to achieve the same thing, but given the state of this selector as unsupported by everyone but Chrome, it's probably wise to pretend that it doesn't exist. What can we do instead?

One option is to just fall back to using `:host()` for the same purpose and add the context as a class on the component itself. To explain, we'll go back to the exercise library component's template module in components/exerciselibrary/template.js.

When we render our HTML, let's add one more class, as shown in the next listing.

Listing 10.6 Adding context via class name

```
html(exercises) {
    let mkup = `<h1>Exercises</h1>
                <div id="container">`;
    for (let c = 0; c < exercises.length; c++) {
        mkup += `<wkout-exercise
class="${exercises[c].type} library"
```

Adding the library class to indicate the component lives in the exercise library

```
${Exercise.toAttributeString(exercises[c])}></wkout-exercise>`;
    }
    Return
```

Let's do the same with our workout plan in components/plan/template.js. Recall that when adding the exercise to our plan, we're rendering some HTML for each one. We'll add the `plan` class, as in the following listing.

Listing 10.7 Adding a different context to the workout plan

```
renderExercise(exercise) {
    return `<wkout-exercise
class="${exercise.type} plan"                    <- Adding the plan class to indicate the
${Exercise.toAttributeString(exercise.serialize())}>   component lives in the workout plan
</wkout-exercise>`
},
```

Now, let's head back to the exercise component in components/exercise/template.js to kill all of the `:host-context()` selectors. We'll do this in the next listing, but only show a few changed CSS rules to avoid repeating the entirety of the style sheet.

Listing 10.8 Changing host-context selectors to host

```
:host(.library) #customize {    <- Two selectors changed from using
    display: none;                 :host-context to use .library,
}                                  directly on the component

:host(.library) #delete {
    display: none;
}

:host(.plan) {    <- Two selectors changed from :host-
    width: 100%;     context to use .plan, directly on
    height: 50px;    the component
    margin-bottom: 1px;
    background-size: contain;
}

:host(.plan) input {
    background-color: #505050;
    padding: 5px;
    color: white;
    border: none;
}
```

Of course, in this example, it was easy to add the `.library` or `.plan` class to the components to give them a different context. It gets a bit trickier if we have to replace `:host-context()` when the context we want to use is a parent of the parent of the parent of the component. In this case, you just can't reach as far back as this selector does. So, you'll need to get some kind of signal to your component through the DOM hierarchy to either add the desired class, or maybe just create some sort of API (perhaps a setter, an attribute, or both) in your application to switch the mode.

10.2 Component themes

Typically, when we talk about theming a web application, the way to do it is to use CSS, which makes its way into every aspect of our UI. In the last chapter, we discussed a themed button that came from a design system.

We're coming full circle now. When discussing this design system button before, the question was how we could stop the design system and the CSS rules behind it from coming in and destroying the buttons in our stepper component, shown again in figure 10.5.

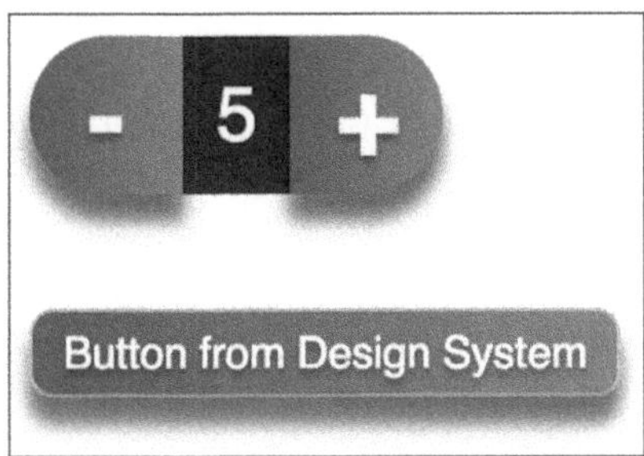

Figure 10.5 A reminder from chapter 9 on the dangers of style creeping into our component

Now, when using the Shadow DOM and successfully blocking those styles from creeping in, the question becomes, "What if we actually *want* those styles to creep in?" The answer is a little complicated.

10.2.1 Shadow and deep selectors

> **WARNING** Section 10.2.1 discusses some deprecated features. The `::shadow` and `/deep/` selectors are properly deprecated, unlike `:host-context()` in section 10.1. It can still be a bit confusing, though, because the deprecation is fairly recent. As a result, researching can lead you down the wrong path. Unfortunately, there's no great replacement for their functionality, so even if you don't care about deprecated features, we'll talk through some options here.

You've been warned—what we're getting into here is deprecated, but a little history helps.

To solve the problem of piercing the Shadow DOM when we actually want to, there used to be two CSS selectors: `::shadow` and `/deep/`. These selectors were designed to break through the Shadow DOM boundary in Google's first version of the Shadow DOM (v0). They never made it into v1, and were finally removed from Chrome in v63.

The `::shadow` selector would dive into the Shadow DOM and style anything inside. For example,

```
::shadow .example {
      color: red;
}
```

would make the <div> inside the following component (assuming a Shadow DOM is used) red:

```
<my-component>
    <div class="example">Some red text</div>
</my-component>
```

If, however, you also used the example class on something outside the Shadow DOM, the rule wouldn't be applied:

```
<div class="example">This text is not red</div>
<my-component>
    <div class="example">Some red text</div>
</my-component>
```

To style both, regardless of whether or not they appear inside the Shadow DOM, the `/deep/` selector could be used:

```
/deep/ .example {
        color: red;
}
```

When Chrome dropped support, people were understandably confused about what to do next. The reasoning behind dropping support is certainly well-intentioned. These selectors are basically Band-Aids—they allow you to go right back into enforcing your own style rules on an encapsulated component. The component itself loses control of its own style, as was the problem before the Shadow DOM.

One solution currently being suggested is the CSS Working Group (CSSWG) Shadow Parts draft. I won't cover the details here because it was just introduced in Chrome, along with a related selector, `::theme`, and will likely evolve. That said, if you'd like to keep tabs on it, you can follow it here: https://drafts.csswg.org/css-shadow-parts.

I'd like to quote one passage:

> *It's important to note that ::part() offers absolutely zero new theoretical power. It is not a rehash of the* `>>>`*combinator, it is simply a more convenient and consistent syntax for something authors can already do with custom properties.*

This quote is notable because the current recommendation of using Custom Properties is currently the *only* way to pierce the Shadow DOM. These Custom Properties, also known as CSS Variables, can combine with `::part` and `::theme` selectors, leading to brand-new ways of managing CSS, overcoming the deprecated features mentioned so far in this chapter.

This is a space you'll definitely want to keep an eye on, because once this gains adoption, I believe it will lead to new ways of making your components styleable and pave the way for the design systems of the future. Right now, though, it's just too early to predict how this will play out.

10.2.2 CSS Variables

If you skipped the last section due to the discussion of deprecated features, we're talking through a small problem. There is no good mechanism right now to carry CSS rules through to your component if that is indeed what you want. The best we have right now are CSS Variables.

You might already be familiar with CSS Variables, or Custom Properties. In fact, they are supported in all modern browsers (sorry, no IE without a polyfill), and don't have anything to do with the Shadow DOM other than the fact that they can cross over the shadow boundary.

You can probably imagine what they are. They enable you to define a variable that represents some CSS property somewhere and use that variable elsewhere in one or multiple places. Take for example, this listing.

Listing 10.9 Using CSS Variables

```
<head>
<style>
   body {
       --text-color: blue;     <-- Color var defined on body
   }

   .container {
       --text-color: red;
   }

   .child {
       color: var(--text-color);     <-- More specific color var defined on CSS class
   }
</style>

</head>
<body>
   <div class="container">
       <div class="child">Some Text</div>    <-- Uses the color variable
   </div>
</body>
```

We can define a variable scoped to the `container` class declaring that the variable `text-color` is red. Variables also have the concept of inheritance. This means that we can also have the same `text-color` variable defined on something less specific, like `body`. The variable scoped to `"container"` still takes precedence, but if this variable were removed, our body-scoped variable would kick in, and the text would now be blue. This behavior can be seen in figure 10.6.

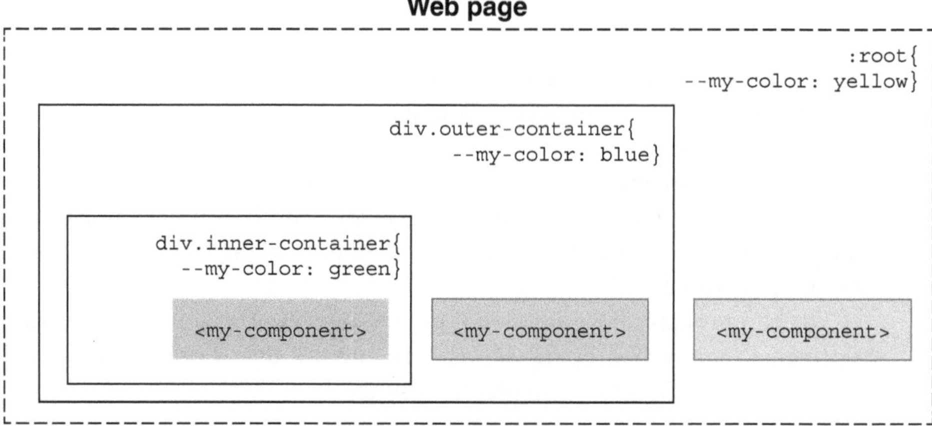

Figure 10.6 Using the same CSS Variable at multiple levels in your DOM

This works great in the Shadow DOM, too! The next listing shows a rule scoped to a custom component from the outside crossing right past the shadow boundary into our component.

Listing 10.10 Using CSS Variables in a Web Component's Shadow DOM

```
<style>
    sample-component {
        --text-color: blue;    <-- Declares a text color CSS Variable
    }
</style>
<script>
    class SampleComponent extends HTMLElement {
        connectedCallback() {
            this.attachShadow({mode: 'open'});
            this.shadowRoot.innerHTML = `<div class="inside-component">
                My Component
            </div>
            <style>
                .inside-component {
                    color: var(--text-color);    <-- Uses the text color CSS Variable
                }
            </style>`
        }
    }
    if (!customElements.get('sample-component')) {
        customElements.define('sample-component', SampleComponent);
    }
</script>
</head>
<body>
<sample-component></sample-component>
</body>
```

CSS Variables don't have to be scoped—they can be global using the `:root { . . . }` pseudo selector, which actually has an even lower specificity than `html { . . . }`. So, when we don't really want to worry about specificity or simply establishing a baseline of variables, `:root` is pretty good to use.

10.2.3 Applying CSS Variables to our demo

Let's get a simple theme started on our Workout Creator example! We can focus on just a few variables for now, but it's easy to imagine a bigger design system based on this.

First, I'd like to use a different font for our application, so we should modify our index.html file's <head> tag to load the font, as seen in the following listing.

Listing 10.11 Loading a font with our index.html

```
<head>
   <title>Workout Creator</title>
   <script type="module"
    src="components/workoutcreatorapp/workoutcreatorapp.js"></script>
   <link rel="stylesheet" type="text/css" href="main.css">
   <link href=
    "https://fonts.googleapis.com/css?family=Roboto+Slab" rel="stylesheet">
</head>
```

Font reference

Second, we can define some global variables inside main.css.

Listing 10.12 Defining global variables in CSS for text color and size

```
:root {
   --inverted-text-color: #eaeaea;
   --text-color: #3a3a3a;
   --label-color: #2a2a2a;
   --header-font-size: 21px;
   --font: 'Roboto Slab', serif;
}
```

Variables are scoped globally to :root, and define some key properties to use throughout.

Lastly, we can update each component's style as in the next listing (showing only the rules that changed).

Listing 10.13 Allowing light theming in the Workout Creator demo with CSS Variables

```
// exercise/template.js
:host {
   font-family: var(--font);
   display: inline-block;
   background: radial-gradient(circle, rgba(235,235,235,1) 0%,
   ➥rgba(208,208,208,1) 100%);
   background-image: url('${exercise.thumb}');
   border-left-style: solid;
   border-left-width: 5px;
}

#info {
```

CSS Variable theming in exercise/template.js

```
    font-size: small;
    background-color: var(--label-color);
    color: var(--inverted-text-color);
    display: flex;
    align-items: center;
}

// exerciselibrary/template.js
:host {
    display: inline-block;
    font-family: var(--font);
    color: var(--text-color);
}

h1 {
    font-size: var(--header-font-size);
}
```

Updating each component continues on to the following listing, where CSS Variables are added to the previous one.

Listing 10.14 More light theming with CSS Variables in the the workout plan component

```
// plan/template.js    <-- CSS Variable theming for plan/template.js
:host {
    display: flex;
    flex-direction: column;
    font-family: var(--font);
    color: var(--text-color);
}

h1 {
    font-size: var(--header-font-size);
}

// workoutcreatorapp/template.js
#divider-line {
    width: 1px;
    height: 100%;
    margin-right: 25px;
    background-color: var(--text-color);
}
```

With these text style changes, we can additionally tweak the CSS Variables to iterate our simple application theme. For example, we could switch to something a bit greener in this next listing, which themes our application, as shown in figure 10.7.

Listing 10.15 Changing variables to switch to a green theme

```
:root {
    --inverted-text-color: #daf8a1;
    --text-color: #47730c;    <-- Two CSS rules to change to shades of green instead of the original shades of grey
    --label-color: #59b624;
    --header-font-size: 18px;
    --font: 'Roboto Slab', serif;
}
```

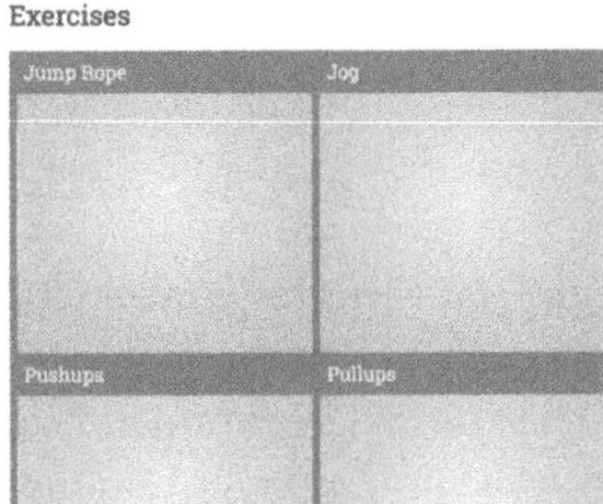

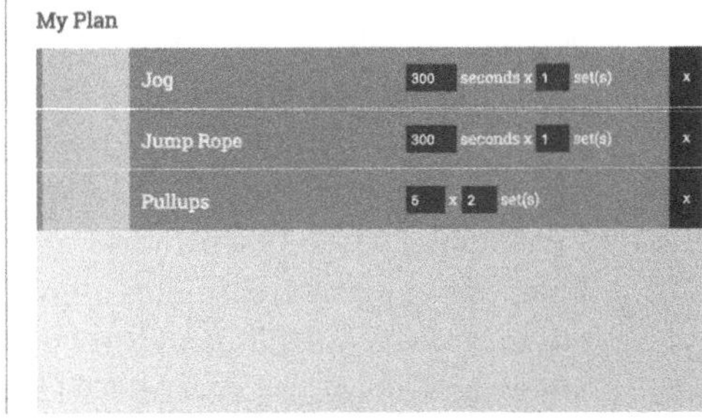

Figure 10.7 Simple change of root-level CSS Variables to adjust theme from black to green

10.3 Using the Shadow DOM in practice (today)

It wasn't too long ago that I was approaching the Shadow DOM with caution—so much so that my recommendation was not to use it quite yet and to develop your Web Components without it. Since then, some awesome things have happened, and we're finally in a really good position to use them. Of course, before you go all in, there are some things to consider!

10.3.1 Browser support

This is the main and most obvious concern. At first, only Chrome supported the Shadow DOM, and then came Safari. For a while, that's all we had! Then, in October 2018, Firefox shipped Web Components, which, of course, includes the Shadow DOM. We knew that Microsoft Edge was working on Web Components (https://developer.microsoft.com/en-us/microsoft-edge/platform/status/shadowdom). I greatly appreciate the note there that it will be supported on XBOX, Mobile, and Mixed Reality devices as well. When will it ship? Well, there's a developer preview out now, so perhaps we'll see a proper release just in time for this book to be published! Of course, that's just a guess, but regardless, it's looking like all of the latest versions of modern browsers (will) have support.

So, of course, the consideration here is to just keep up with Edge before all users have a chance to update to this new Chromium-backed version. If your project needs to support it, and you don't want to gamble on Microsoft's Shadow DOM ship date, then you may want to make your Web Components without the Shadow DOM for now.

10.3.2 Polyfilling

Of course, in the last section, I was talking about native support. More often than not, features can easily be polyfilled. This is likewise true for Web Components—with the exception of the CSS implementation of the Shadow DOM.

The problem here is that a mini-encapsulated DOM is hard to emulate. It's easier to protect your DOM from query-selecting and manipulation than it is to protect it from CSS rules creeping in. The former can be achieved by using the ShadyDOM polyfill. The latter, the CSS, can benefit from the ShadyCSS polyfill.

Unfortunately, while most every other polyfill is drop in and go, the ShadyCSS polyfill needs some handholding. Nevertheless, recent developments have increased my optimism.

The ShadyCSS polyfill was created by Google for use with the Polymer Library for Web Component creation. To give Google some credit, the company did its best to not lock these polyfills into the Polymer Library. They can all be found at https://www.webcomponents.org and on GitHub at https://github.com/webcomponents.

With ShadyCSS, the polyfill was a bit too tied into the Polymer Library, which itself was heavily based on the now-deprecated HTML Import workflow. As a result, the ShadyCSS documentation and proposed workflow was very focused on how to use the polyfill via the template you'd bring in with your HTML Import.

The Polymer team has since stopped feature development of the Polymer Library and is now recommending smaller and more targeted libraries that they've written and broken off, all under the umbrella of the Polymer Project. We've previously discussed lit-html as one of these. Another is the LitElement project, https://lit-element.polymer-project.org, which uses lit-html behind the scenes.

Fortunately for us, this new Web Component workflow they are proposing with LitElement works exactly like we've seen throughout the book: template literals in your JS to manage HTML and CSS, all managed with a simple Web Components lifecycle API. As a result, their usage of the ShadyDOM matches ours. Where we previously needed a template for our HTML, we still do, but that's all taken care of automatically by lit-html. What we would put in the shadow root now gets wrapped up as a template. As a template, ShadyCSS then rewrites our nonspecific CSS rules into something more unique that acts like an encapsulated Shadow DOM. ShadyCSS then adds this template as a child of our component.

The end result is that our Shadow DOM-enabled components work in all major browsers (yes, even IE). ShadyCSS has a list of known issues to be aware of, so don't expect quite everything to work: https://github.com/webcomponents/shadycss. In the next chapter, we'll create a battle-ready component with these concerns in mind, using polyfills where appropriate.

10.3.3 Design systems

Even just theming your application will require rethinking how we use design systems today. If you're not familiar with design systems, they are typically a CSS library for providing a consistent look across your project, including for commonly used UI elements like buttons, sliders, content containers, and so on. One of the more popular design systems, Bootstrap, for example, just won't work with the Shadow DOM as it is.

Design systems themselves tend to be fairly monolithic, meaning you'll likely include one core (and huge) CSS file on your main page. The included CSS will wind its way through your page and style all of your elements as it should.

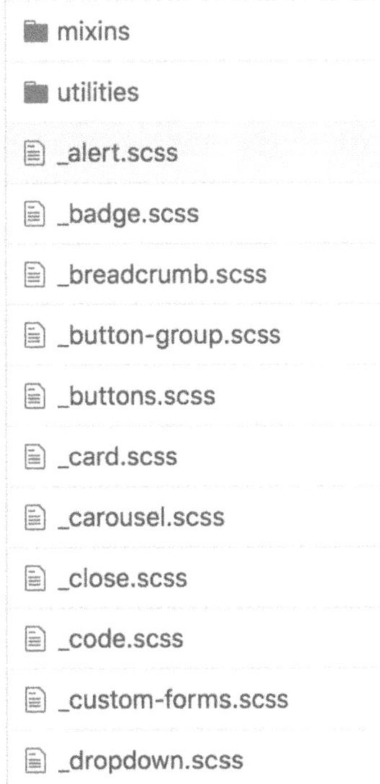

Figure 10.8 Bootstrap comprises these components and many more.

The problem, of course, is that the Shadow DOM will block all these styles defined for your page, protecting any elements enclosed in your component. The good news, however, is that a design system will likely comprise separate components. A snapshot of Bootstrap's components is shown in figure 10.8.

In the end, these CSS components all get built into that monolithic CSS file, but there is an opportunity in design systems like these to separate out each component as its own importable CSS, to be used by the exact Web Component that needs it. Things do get a little complex because, in Bootstrap's example, a carousel might depend on a button, which depends on some basic text, spacing, and color styling. So, dependencies do need to be managed to pull this off.

Already, though, some industrious folks are starting to create Web Component variations of popular design systems like Bootstrap, just as we've seen done with Angular and React variations of design systems. Google's Web Components variation of Material is already well underway (https://github.com/material-components/material-components-web-components). We should see lots of effort here, given that the Polymer team has moved on from the Polymer Library to these more generalized Web Component libraries.

There will definitely be challenges. Many times in design systems, you'll see an element's style be contextually dependent on who its parent element is, or go even farther up the ancestry chain. The `:host-context` selector sure would be useful here, but in lieu of that, we just have to be careful in creating or converting existing design systems.

It's certainly early days for using design systems in our Web Components, but we're starting to see some great progress. As we go forward, I expect to see lots more usage of CSS Variables and maybe even lots of CSS Shadow Parts usage, once that proposal is firmed up and shipped in browsers.

Summary

In this chapter, we've seen a lot of benefits to the Shadow DOM in terms of wrangling your CSS. But, with the downside being that it isn't quite fully supported everywhere yet, and never will be for IE, we know to proceed with caution. Going forward as browsers are updated, we're armed with some good foundational takeaways.

In this chapter, you also learned

- To watch out for common selectors that have since been deprecated as the Shadow DOM spec standardizes.
- That the Shadow DOM, when using CSS, can't easily be polyfilled. So, if using the Shadow DOM for CSS, be wary of which browsers support it, how to polyfill, and any unimplemented features.
- The design systems have a path forward for supporting the Shadow DOM, but support will take some time. While there are a few projects that are designed for the Shadow DOM right now, you may have to roll up your sleeves and do some adaptation work yourself.

Part 3

Putting your components together

The last part of this book is all about taking everything we've learned and making sure our components are production ready, tested, and working together as a group—everywhere.

Since the second chapter, we've been building and improving a very simple component. The first chapter in part 3 brings this component back to build something greater, with that simple component as a smaller, nested piece of a bigger Web Component. We put this new component through its paces by introducing a build and testing process, and finally refactoring it to make sure it works all the way down to IE11.

Orchestrating interactions and messaging throughout an entire application is no small feat either and, as such, is very important to the conversation, especially when deciding to use Web Components instead of a major framework. This part discusses some strategies around that before finally ending on some emerging technologies where Web Components could be useful, like Web 3D, Mixed Reality, and Machine Learning—all bringing simple examples from the book back to explore these futuristic subjects.

11 A real-world UI component

This chapter covers

- Building a brand-new component and refreshing our memories about what we've learned so far, including the Shadow DOM, modules, the Custom Element API, and reflection
- Breaking a design into multiple components and focusing on component reusability to use a single, smaller component for a dual purpose in a bigger context
- Using the `MutationObserver` feature to watch for attribute changes
- Event bubbling inside your component
- Component best practices as related to switching between using the Shadow DOM or not
- Using consistent and universal design rules provided by CSS vars and importable CSS modules

Now is a great time to step back and take stock of everything we've learned. We've done lots with Web Components throughout this book. At the same time, there haven't been many great examples of UI components that are good to share. One example of a UI component that we have been working on is the slider component.

Figure 11.1 gives a quick reminder of what that slider is capable of. This slider component has been built from the beginning with the intention of sharing and using it in a larger context. It is a bit of a simple component, so using it as a small piece of a larger, more useful and shareable UI component is a great next step!

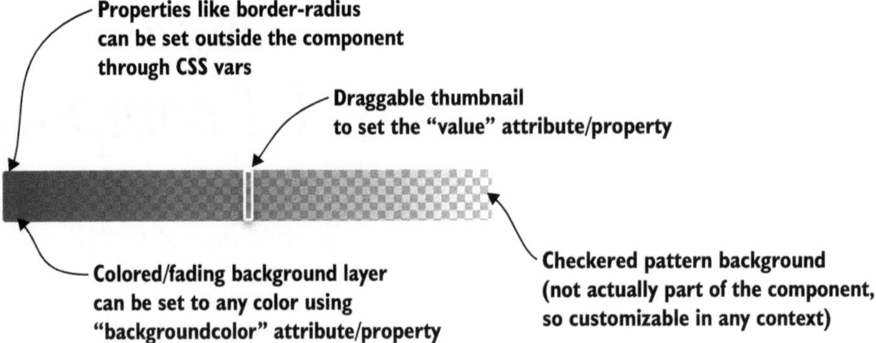

Figure 11.1 Slider UI component we've been building throughout the book

11.1 Crafting a color picker

So, what are we going to build? What is the larger context that we'll put the slider component in? Often when I need a gradient in my CSS, I use some of the simple but awesome tools offered online. The gradient creator at https://cssgradient.io and shown in figure 11.2 is one I really think is well-designed and easy to use. I also think it would make a nice color picker if we reduced the functionality and took out the gradient creation aspect.

You might be aware that there already exists an easy-to-use color picker provided by the `<input>` tag. We can simply add the element to our HTML:

```
<input type="color" value="#ff0000">
```

It gives us a nice, compact, clickable button that pops up a dialog when clicked, as in figure 11.3.

As convenient as this is, I happen to be working on a project in which this color picker would a bit too compact. Also, I'd like it to remain onscreen at all times, so I can continually tweak the object I'm coloring. Last, that object I'm coloring might be transparent as well, so I'd prefer a transparency control in addition to my colors.

With all this in mind, let's create a great-looking color picker, inspired by cssgradient .io, with Web Components!

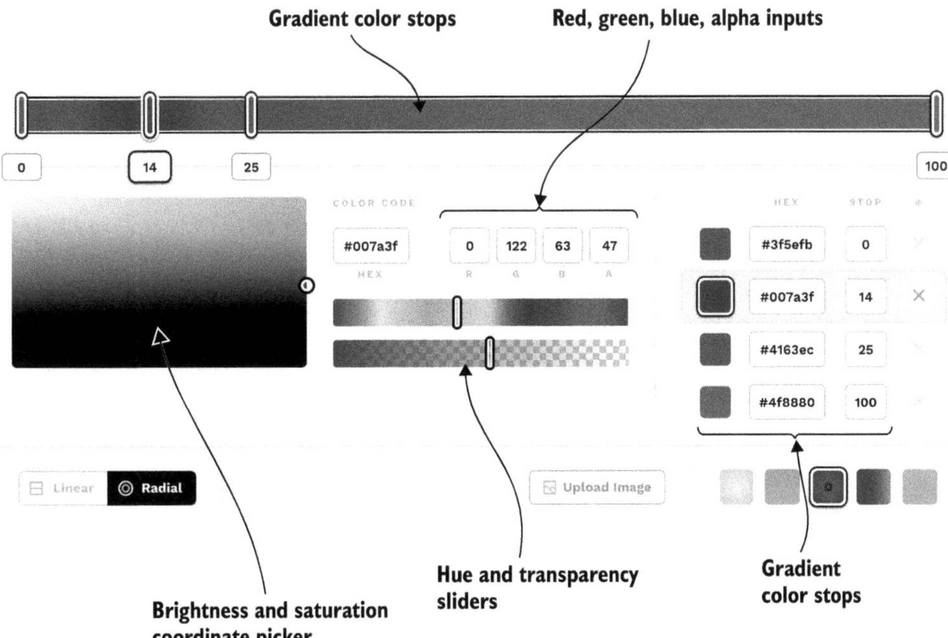

Figure 11.2 Gradient creator at cssgradient.io

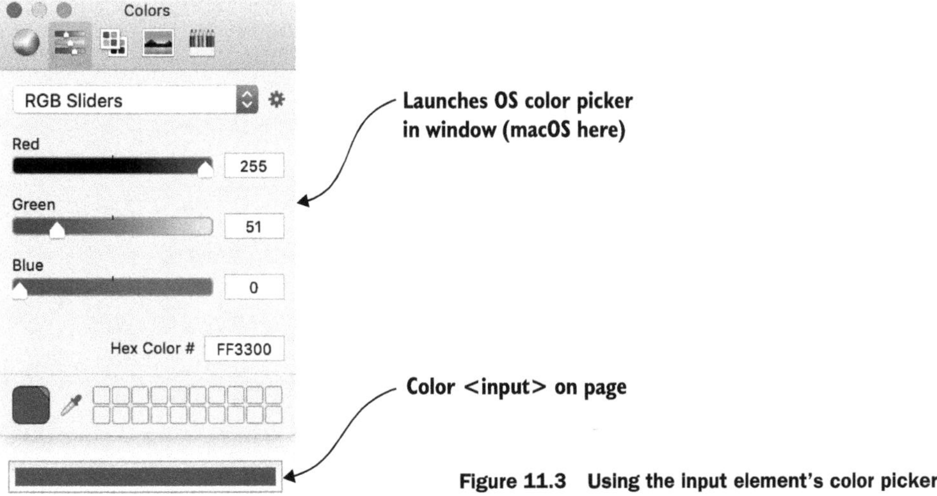

Figure 11.3 Using the input element's color picker

11.1.1 The components of our component

The first step here will be to break down what we need. We don't want our color picker component to be too complex, so we should think about which pieces of the UI are separate components of their own.

Referring to the gradient creator and figure 11.4, we can see two similar-looking and functioning sliders, one for the hue and one for the transparency. This is great, as we've been building that simple, reusable slider throughout this book explicitly for the transparency slider! The only real difference between what we built appears to be the images and colors used for the background in the hue slider versus the transparency. Recall that the slider component has a `<div>` inside that shows a single color that fades from 100% to 0% opacity. If the background color isn't set, this `<div>` never shows. This leaves a completely style-able component background. In the slider's demo.html, we use a checkered white and grey pattern to indicate transparency, but this can easily be swapped out for the rainbow-colored hue slider background.

Figure 11.4 Two very similar sliders that we can create one Web Component for

There's another piece of UI here that functions a lot like a slider, but it works both horizontally and vertically. Figure 11.5 shows the saturation and brightness picker. Dragging left to right adjusts saturation, or how intense the color is, while dragging

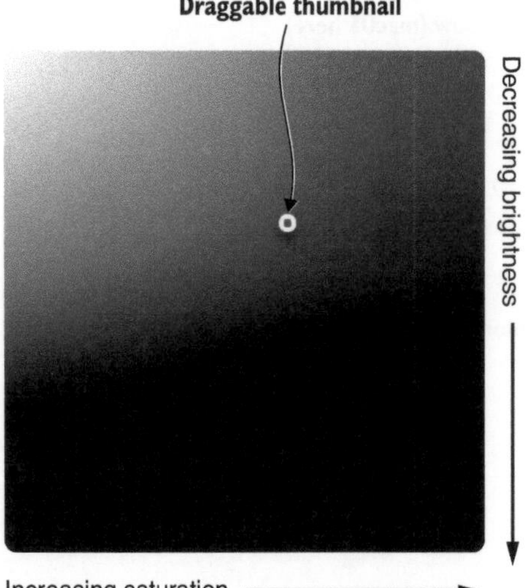

Figure 11.5 Saturation and brightness picker as a candidate for a web component

vertically adjusts brightness. The user would be able to drag in both directions simultaneously, picking the perfect mix of the two variables.

Unlike the slider, we only need one of these pickers; but similar to the slider, we need to be very comprehensive with how the user interacts with it. To make the picker and the slider respond correctly to user interaction, a number of edge cases must be handled; this two-directional picker is perfect to break out as its own Web Component, so we don't overburden our main color picker component with too much logic.

What other elements can we pick out? You might have your own ideas, but I think it's fine to stop there. Remember that even though we're inspired by the gradient creator at cssgradient.io, we're not creating gradients, just picking colors. The rest of the relevant UI elements are text and numeric inputs. We could certainly go more granular and wrap up all of them or sets of them as different components.

For example, we might make the numeric entry for the red, green, and blue fields one component. I'm not sure I see much benefit to that here, especially because when you step back, each piece of UI has a simple way to interact with it and offers an output value after interaction (or two, when you consider the horizontal and vertical picker).

To summarize, we have the following pieces of UI:

- Hue slider offers mouse interaction and outputs a single value
- Transparency slider offers mouse interaction and outputs a single value
- Saturation/brightness picker offers mouse interaction and outputs two values
- Red, green, blue, and alphanumeric inputs offer keyboard/mouse interaction and output a single value
- Hexadecimal input field offers keyboard interaction and outputs a single value

Like we discussed, we can combine the hue and slider into a single, reusable component. We'll also make that saturation and brightness coordinate picker a component as well. The rest—the text/numeric entry UI—will just live alongside our custom components in the master color picker component. Given this plan, let's create a project structure, as shown in figure 11.6.

Figure 11.6 Starting structure for our color picker component project

There will likely be more files as we go along, but we can assume these three components—the slider, the coordinate picker, and the overarching color picker—should each have three files. We'll want a class to define the component, a template that holds all the HTML/CSS, and, lastly, an HTML file to demo the standalone component. Since we've been working on the slider throughout this book, good news: it's done! It can be copied right into the components folder now.

11.2 Coordinate picker component

We'll cover the coordinate picker component quickly. The reason we can breeze right through is that in addition to being fairly simple, it functions in almost the exact same way as the slider component. The only difference is that the thumbnail can be dragged both vertically and horizontally over the component, as you saw in figure 11.5.

I call it a coordinate picker because you're dragging and selecting something on the *x* (horizontal) and *y* (vertical) axes. Specifically, we'll use the *y* axis to ultimately control brightness in the master color picker component, while saturation is controlled by the *x* axis.

11.2.1 The coordinate picker Web Component class

With the similarities in mind, let's talk about the one difference between the slider component and the coordinate picker. Instead of a `value` attribute, there are now two different values to use for horizontal and vertical percentages. We'll use attribute names of `x` and `y` to represent these. Additionally, when updating the visual thumbnail, we need to take the vertical position into account as well as the horizontal. We'll use the following listing to highlight the first part of the class with similar but slightly changed attributes and corresponding reflection.

Listing 11.1 Coordinate picker API

```
import Template from './template.js';

export default class CoordPicker extends HTMLElement {
    static get observedAttributes() {
        return ['x', 'y', 'backgroundcolor'];
    }

    attributeChangedCallback(
        name, oldVal, newValue) {
        switch (name) {
            case 'x':
            case 'y':
                this.refreshCoordinates();
                break;

            case 'backgroundcolor':
                this.style.backgroundcolor = newValue;
                break;
        }
    }

    set x(val) {
        this.setAttribute('x', val);
    }

    get x() {
        return this.getAttribute('x');
    }

// omitted y and backgroundcolor getters and setters for brevity
```

Annotations:
- Imports template module for HTML and CSS
- Defines what attributes to watch on this component
- Watches for changes to these attributes and responds accordingly
- Getters and setters for x, y, and backgroundcolor properties

You might notice that a lot of space is eaten up with reflection. It's also really boring, repetitive code—even more so when you consider there's very little difference between this component, the last component, or really . . . any other component. This is why it'll probably be increasingly rare to see explicit reflection like this in components you'll find in the wild.

Web Component libraries and utilities are popping up that aim to make reflection like this a feature that you don't have to implement yourself (in addition to other things). This can be accomplished via a base class that itself extends `HTMLElement` or, my personal preference, by a mixin approach where you can augment your class using the `prototype` keyword, so you can still be free to extend another base class. Here, though, I think it's good to show everything needed without hiding the more boring parts.

Another complexity that gets hidden a lot as you venture into recent Web Component libraries, like the Polymer Project's LitElement (https://lit-element.polymer-project.org/), is the initial component setup and HTML rendering. Indeed, the component's constructor in listing 11.2 looks exactly like the slider component, even down to the event listeners, given that we are duplicating the same dragging capability. When writing a lot of your own components, you might choose to attempt to hide this complexity as well with your own base class or helper utilities.

Listing 11.2 Constructor and mouse event handler

```
constructor() {
    super();
    this.attachShadow({mode: 'open'});
    this.shadowRoot.innerHTML = Template.render();
    this.dom = Template.mapDOM(this.shadowRoot);

    document.addEventListener('mousemove', e => this.eventHandler(e));
    document.addEventListener('mouseup', e => this.eventHandler(e));
    this.addEventListener('mousedown', e => this.eventHandler(e));
}

eventHandler(e) {
    const bounds = this.getBoundingClientRect();
    const coords = {
        x: e.clientX - bounds.left,
        y: e.clientY - bounds.top
    };
    switch (e.type) {
        case 'mousedown':
            this.isDragging = true;
            this.updateXY(coords.x, coords.y);
            this.refreshCoordinates();
            break;

        case 'mouseup':
            this.isDragging = false;
            break;
```

Annotations:

- **Component setup: Shadow DOM, rendering HTML/CSS, and element caching** (this.attachShadow line)
- **Adds mouse listeners for dragging** (document.addEventListener lines)
- **Captures mouse coordinates relative to component** (const coords line)
- **Updates the component x,y attributes as a percentage and moves the thumbnail** (this.updateXY line)

```
            case 'mousemove':
                if (this.isDragging) {
                    this.updateXY(coords.x, coords.y);
                    this.refreshCoordinates();
                }
                break;
        }
    }
```

Wrapping up the component, we'll again see very similar code to the slider component in the next listing. Yet again, the only real difference is handling two values, x and y, instead of a single value.

Listing 11.3 Updating the x and y attributes and the position of the thumbnail

```
    updateXY(x, y) {
        let hPos =                                    <-- Gets centered (against the
                x - this.dom.thumb.offsetWidth/2;         thumbnail) coordinates for
        let vPos = y - this.dom.thumb.offsetHeight/2;     both x and y
        if (hPos > this.offsetWidth) {                <-- Constrains x (or horizontal
            hPos = this.offsetWidth;                      value) to inside of
        }                                                 component bounds
        if (hPos < 0) {
            hPos = 0;
        }
        if (vPos > this.offsetHeight) {               <-- Constrains y (or vertical
            vPos = this.offsetHeight;                     value) to inside of
        }                                                 component bounds
        if (vPos < 0) {
            vPos = 0;
        }
        this.x = (hPos / this.offsetWidth) * 100;     <-- Updates both x and y
        this.y = (vPos / this.offsetHeight) * 100;        attributes through the
    }                                                     component's JS API

    refreshCoordinates() {                            <-- Updates the horizontal and vertical
        this.dom.thumb.style.left = (                     position of the thumbnail
        this.x/100 * this.offsetWidth - this.dom.thumb.offsetWidth/2) + 'px';
        this.dom.thumb.style.top =
        (this.y/100 * this.offsetHeight - this.dom.thumb.offsetWidth/2) + 'px';
    }
}

if (!customElements.get('wcia-coord-picker')) {
    customElements.define(                            <-- Defines the element and tag
        'wcia-coord-picker', CoordPicker);                from the component class
}
```

You'll note that at the top of the class, our method of setting the background color simply updates the overall component's background color. We'll peek next at the

HTML/CSS to see how to create a perfect, two-directional gradient, but setting the overall color is as simple as what we placed in the `attributeChangedCallback` handler:

```
this.style.backgroundcolor = newValue;
```

Why make this part of the API when we could set a CSS rule for background color outside the component? The simple answer is that we're making the coordinate picker API work exactly like the slider component API. It's much easier to set the `backgroundcolor` property on both the slider and this component at the same time with a similar API, rather than remember to interact with both of them differently, especially with both having very similar functionality.

11.2.2 Coordinate picker HTML/CSS

Moving on to our template.js, which holds the HTML and CSS for the coordinate picker, you'll again not notice much difference from the slider. The following listing shows the import.

Listing 11.4 Template.js for the coordinate picker component

```
export default {
   render() {                          <- Returns all HTML/CSS to render component
       return `${this.css()}
               ${this.html()}`;
   },

   mapDOM(scope) {
       return {
           thumb: scope.getElementById('thumb')   <- Only one element needs to be accessed by the class: the thumbnail
       }
   },

   html() {
       return `<div id="bg-overlay-a"></div>    <- HTML for component includes two layered backgrounds and a thumbnail
               <div id="bg-overlay-b"></div>
               <div id="thumb"></div>`;
   },

   css() {
       return `<style> . . . style to be continued . . . </style>`;
   }
}
```

As usual, the CSS proves a bit lengthy, so we'll continue it as follows.

Listing 11.4 Template.js for coordinate picker component (continued)

```
:host {
    display: inline-block;
    position: relative;
}

#bg-overlay-a {            <- First background contains a white gradient that fades to transparent from left to right
    width: 100%;
    height: 100%;
```

```
    border-radius: 3px;
    position: absolute;
    background: linear-gradient(to right, #fff 0%, rgba(255,255,255,0) 100%);
}

#bg-overlay-b {          <-- Second background contains a gradient that fades from transparent to black vertically
    width: 100%;
    height: 100%;
    border-radius: 3px;
    position: absolute;
    background: linear-gradient(to bottom, transparent 0%, #000 100%);
}

#thumb {      <-- Style for thumbnail
    width: 5px;
    height: 5px;
    position: absolute;
    border-style: solid;
    border-width: 3px;
    border-color: white;
    border-radius: 6px;
    pointer-events: none;
    box-shadow: 0 4px 8px 0 rgba(0, 0, 0, 0.2), 0 6px 20px 0 rgba(0, 0, 0,
     0.19);
}
```

As I mentioned, the overall color is set as the component's background color. To accomplish the effect of increasing saturation from left to right, we use a <div> with a white background color that fades from opaque to transparent as it goes from left to right. Layered on top of that is a similar gradient that fades from completely transparent to black as it goes from top to bottom. Put both of these layers on top of a completely solid background color (the background color of our component), and we have a nice little saturation and brightness map! But I should give credit where credit is due—like the slider background, I borrowed this approach from http://cssgradient.io.

11.2.3 Component demos

Let's finish up this component by creating a demo page for it. In fact, given that these demo pages are all so similar, let's knock out two at once. With the next listing, we can demo the coordinate picker component.

Listing 11.5 Coordinate picker demo page

```
<html lang="en">
<head>
   <title>Coordinate Picker Demo</title>
   <script type="module"          <-- Imports the coordinate picker component class
        src="coordpicker.js">
   </script>

   <style>
       wcia-coord-picker {     <-- Sets a specific size for the component with CSS
           width: 400px;
           height: 400px;
```

```
      }
    </style>
  </head>
<body>
  <wcia-coord-picker                              Places the coordinate picker
      backgroundcolor="#ff0000">                  on the page with an initial
  </wcia-coord-picker>                            background color of red
</body>
</html>
```

Just so I don't belabor this same point with the final color picker component and yet another very similar demo page, let's create the demo page for our final component while we're working on this one. Refreshing our memory with the project structure in figure 11.7, we'll now create a demo.html file in the components/colorpicker folder.

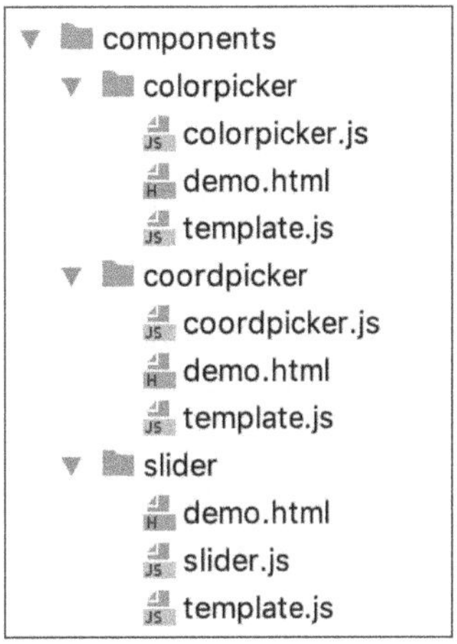

```
components
  colorpicker
    colorpicker.js
    demo.html
    template.js
  coordpicker
    coordpicker.js
    demo.html
    template.js
  slider
    demo.html
    slider.js
    template.js
```

Figure 11.7 A reminder of the files and folders for our component while adding a new demo

Unsurprisingly, we can just copy and paste the contents of the coordinate picker demo file into the color picker demo file. We can then just change a few things. First the title and script import changes from

```
<title>Coordinate Picker Demo</title>
<script type="module" src="coordpicker.js">
</script>
```

to

```
<title>Color Picker Demo</title>
<script type="module" src="colorpicker.js">
</script>
```

The size of the component demo is fairly arbitrary, and 400 pixels by 400 pixels will still work to demo the color picker. Only the CSS selector needs to be changed. Simply change `wcia-coord-picker` to `wcia-color-picker` in the <style> block.

Last, of course, the component is declared on the page differently:

```
<wcia-coord-picker backgroundcolor="#ff0000"></wcia-coord-picker>
```

becomes

```
<wcia-color-picker></wcia-color-picker>
```

Before moving on, however, it's important to reflect on what we've achieved thus far. We've now created the first steps for a color picker, or any number of UI components that might use the slider or the coordinate picker. Something as basic as either of these is a perfect example of an extremely simple component that could be used throughout an entire library.

We may well start a component library with an even simpler UI component: a button. Wherever you start, however, it's important to have some foresight to make things reusable and adaptable to the most scenarios. Our starter components only made it so far, here. In the slider, we've left the underlying background out of the component to be able to make a rainbow gradient for the hue slider or a checkered pattern for the opacity slider. But what about the <div> background inside the component? It only functions as a fading gradient, even though its color is customizable.

Perhaps we'll need the slider in another context, where we want this background layer to do something different, or maybe need more background layers! This is likewise true with the coordinate picker. Maybe instead of making the background a permanent part of our component, it might be better to allow backgrounds to be added via slots. The slider could even be turned into the gradient slider we were originally inspired by, requiring multiple thumbs to slide.

Starting these components as the beginnings of a set of UI components requires a lot of planning and a lot of refactoring, as different use cases come to light. In this book, we're considering only two use cases for the slider and only one for the coordinate picker, but if we were continuing on with a component library, there could be way more. With this in mind, let's move on to our primary use case: the color picker.

11.3 The color picker

We're now down to the third and final component, which holds the slider component, the coordinate picker component, and some input fields. Together, they form the overall color picker, as figure 11.8 shows.

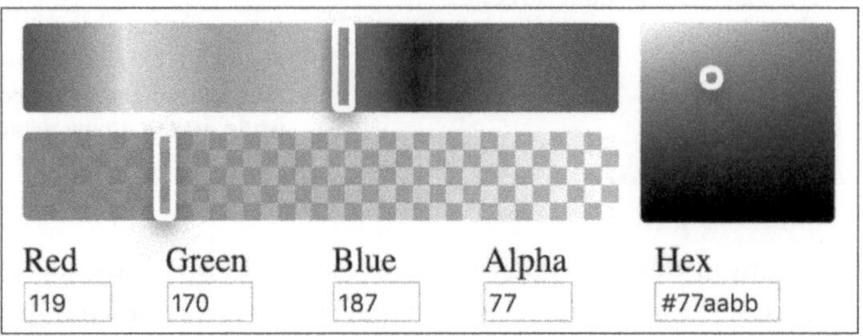

Figure 11.8 Color picker component

With the demo.html file done in place, let's focus on getting something up and running visually, even if we can't interact with it just yet. Also, we'll worry about the component's API later to focus on its internal workings right now. The first thing we should do is create the component class (components/colorpicker/colorpicker.js).

Listing 11.6 Component definition for the color picker

```
import Template from './template.js';          <- Imports HTML/CSS template module

export default class ColorPicker extends HTMLElement {

    constructor() {        <- Constructor that creates the Shadow DOM, renders the HTML/CSS, and caches the elements we'll need
```

```
        super();
        this.attachShadow({mode: 'open'});
        this.shadowRoot.innerHTML = Template.render();
        this.dom = Template.mapDOM(this.shadowRoot);
    }
}
if (!customElements.get('wcia-color-picker')) {
    customElements.define('wcia-color-picker', ColorPicker);
}
```

Defines the color picker component, mapping it to the <wcia-color-picker> tag

There's just enough there to now switch over to the template.js module to work on HTML and CSS. For the HTML in the next listing, we'll go ahead and lay out the slider component, the coordinate picker component, and the input fields with labels.

Listing 11.7 HTML for the color picker component

```
import Slider from '../slider/slider.js';
import CoordinatePicker from '../coordpicker/coordpicker.js';

export default {
    render() {
       return `${this.css()}
               ${this.html()}`;
    },

    html() {
       return `<div class="container">
                   <div class="row">
                       <div class="slider-container">
                           <wcia-slider
                                  id="hue-slider"
                              value="50">
                       </wcia-slider>
                       <wcia-slider
                              id="transparency-slider"
                              value="0">
                       </wcia-slider>
                   </div>

                   <wcia-coord-picker x="50" y="50"
                          id="saturation-brightness"></wcia-coord-picker>
               </div>

               <div class="row">
                   <div class="text-inputs">
```

Imports the slider and coordinate picker components

Returns the complete HTML/CSS markup string

Two instances of the slider, one for hue and one for transparency

Coordinate picker component

Continuing on with the HTML, we next encounter those input fields. Though they aren't custom-made Web Components, we'll be listening to user input from these in much the same way as we do our sliders and the coordinate picker.

Listing 11.7 HTML for the color picker component (continued)

Red, green, and blue numeric inputs (accept values of 0–255)

```
                <div>
                      <label class="top" for="textInputR">Red</label>
                      <input id="textInputR"
                              type="number" value="0"
                                max="255" size="4" min="0">
                </div>

                <div>
                    <label class="top" for="textInputG">Green</label>
                    <input id="textInputG"
                              type="number" value="0"
                              max="255" size="4" min="0">
                 </div>

                 <div>
                    <label class="top" for="textInputB">Blue</label>
                    <input id="textInputB"
                              type="number" value="0"
                              max="255" size="4" min="0">
                 </div>
```

Alpha/transparency input (accepts values of 0–100)

```
                 <div>
                    <label class="top" for="textInputA">Alpha</label>
                    <input id="textInputA"
                              type="number" value="0"
                               max="100" min="0" size="4">
                 </div>
```

Hexadecimal color input

```
                 <div>
                   <label class="top" for="textInputHex">Hex</label>
                   <input id="textInputHex"
                             type="text" width="50px" size="8">
                 </div>
              </div>
          </div>
      </div>`
    }
}
```

As the final visual step to see what we're working with, the next listing adds the CSS to this import module.

Listing 11.8 CSS for the color picker

Style on normal elements used for layout purposes

```
css() {
   return `<style>
            :host {
                width: 100%;
                display: inline-block;
            }

            .container {
                padding: 10px;
```

```
        }

        .text-inputs {
            display: flex;
            width: 100%;
            justify-content: center;
        }

        .row {
            display: flex;
        }

        .slider-container {
            flex: 1;
            padding-right: 10px;
        }
```

Continuing on with the CSS, the prior styles were all for layout and on standard, everyday elements. The next styles are all on our custom components and, in addition to simple style and layout, serve to differentiate the sliders through their backgrounds.

Listing 11.8 CSS for the color picker (continued)

```
        #hue-slider, #transparency-slider {
            width: 100%;
            height: 40px;
            margin-bottom: 5px;
            border-radius: 3px;
        }

        #saturation-brightness {
            width: 90px;
            height: 90px;
            border-radius: 3px;
        }

        #hue-slider {        <-- Special rainbow-like background for the hue slider
            background: linear-gradient(to right, red 0%, #ff0 17%,
            lime 33%, cyan 50%, blue 66%, #f0f 83%, red 100%);
        }

        #transparency-slider {        <-- Special checkered background to show transparency
            background-image: linear-gradient(45deg, #ccc 25%,
            transparent 25%),linear-gradient(-45deg, #ccc 25%,
            transparent 25%),linear-gradient(45deg, transparent 75%,
            #ccc 75%),linear-gradient(-45deg, transparent 75%,
            #ccc 75%);
            background-size: 16px 16px;
            background-position: 0 0, 0 8px, 8px -8px, -8px 0px;
        }
    </style>`;
}
```

Figure 11.9 shows what these sliders will look like once logic is wired up in the next steps to control these colored layers.

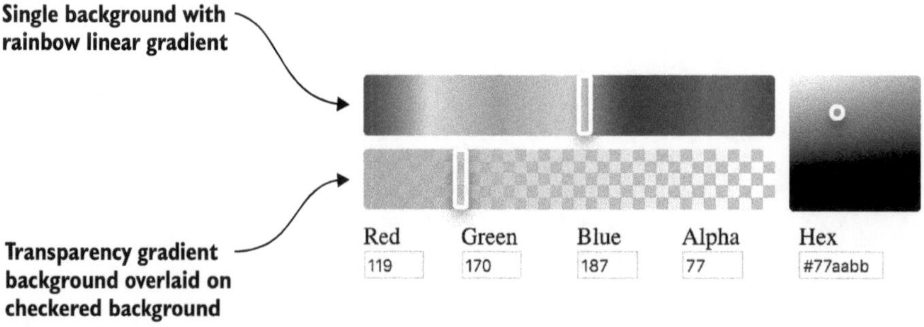

Figure 11.9 Hue and transparency slider backgrounds

As one last step in this import module, we'll cache some elements that are important to wiring up the interaction. The next listing shows these eight elements as we return references to them.

Listing 11.9 Important elements to cache and return references used for interaction

```
mapDOM(scope) {
    return {
        hue: scope.getElementById('hue-slider'),
        transparency: scope.getElementById('transparency-slider'),
        satbright: scope.getElementById('saturation-brightness'),
        textInputR:
scope.getElementById('textInputR'),
        textInputG: scope.getElementById('textInputG'),
        textInputB: scope.getElementById('textInputB'),
        textInputA: scope.getElementById('textInputA'),
        textInputHex: scope.getElementById('textInputHex'),
    }
}
```

Three of our Web Component elements cached

RGBA and hexadecimal input elements cached

We're working with a few more elements here than in the slider or coordinate picker components. We'll want to cache references here for those components, but we'll need to interact with each individual text field as well to listen and respond when users enter values by entering numbers and text.

11.3.1 Observing attribute changes for interaction

Many times when I'm working on a complex component like this, I'll add event listeners to every element and pair them with a handler to do something when that event happens. Though we could have done just that, Custom Events were not added to the slider and coordinate picker components. We'll cover using Custom Events in Web Components toward the end of the book, but for now, there's another way we can watch for and respond to changes.

You don't see the DOM Mutation Observer feature talked about that often, but I think Web Components are a perfect use case for it. When you set up a `MutationObserver`, you give it a specific chunk of HTML to watch or observe, as depicted in figure 11.10. You also set a handler to call when these changes occur.

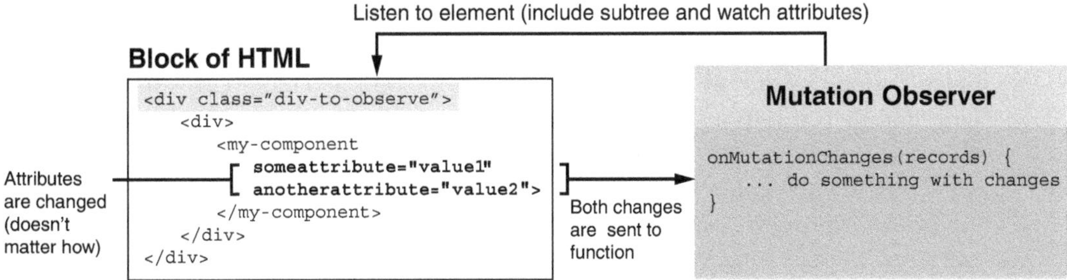

Figure 11.10 A Mutation Observer in action

While we won't need to watch the inner text contents of our HTML tags, our Web Component attributes are constantly updating as we use them. With some custom options, we can watch for attribute changes and react to them. Turning back to the component class (components/colorpicker/colorpicker.js) in the following listing, we can set up the `MutationObserver` to watch for these attribute changes.

Listing 11.10 Listening to attribute changes with a `MutationObserver`

```
constructor() {
   super();
   this.attachShadow({mode: 'open'});
   this.shadowRoot.innerHTML = Template.render();
   this.dom = Template.mapDOM(this.shadowRoot);
   const observer = new MutationObserver( e => this.onMutationChange(e));
   observer.observe(this.shadowRoot, { attributes: true, subtree: true });
}

onMutationChange(records) {
  records.forEach( rec => {
      this.data = Handlers.update({
          model: this.data,
          dom: this.dom,
          component: this,
          element: rec.target,
          attribute: rec.attributeName,
      });
  });
}
```

Creates a new MutationObserver with a handler to listen for changes

Observes the component's Shadow DOM, specifying to watch for attributes and also watch all the elements within

A custom handler not yet discussed

MutationObserver can report multiple changes, so we need to loop through an array to handle them.

Now, every time the slider value attribute is changed, or the coordinate picker's `x` or `y` value changes, we'll be notified! We'll also be notified of other things we don't necessarily care about, like the `class` attribute or even our `backgroundcolor` attributes, but we can ignore those changes.

To handle these change events, I've placed the logic away from the component class, so it doesn't grow too complex and unwieldly. The `Handlers.update` function comes from another import module. This function is passed two things the `MutationObserver` gives us: a reference to the changed element and which attribute changed. We're also feeding that handler a reference to `this`, or the color picker component itself, as well as `this.dom`, or the cached elements created in the template.js module. With access to all the elements we need, this update function can change attributes/properties on any of the elements. When the hue changes, for example, this new module can respond to the change by setting the background color of both the transparency slider and the coordinate picker, and can update all the input fields reflecting the new color.

Lastly, a property on this Web Component class, `this.data`, is passed into the `Handlers.update` function and returned. This property basically accumulates data.

Using the hue as an example again, the value would be stored and kept in this data. When the brightness or saturation changes, we don't want to lose that hue value, so we keep the `this.data` property as a persistent object.

Of course, none of this would work if we didn't import the module. Adding the import alongside the template.js module to the top of the Web Component class will do the job:

```
import Template from './template.js';
import Handlers from './handlers.js';
```

The `Handlers` import actually imports yet another separate module to do all the color math required. It offers conversion from hexadecimal to RGB, RGB to hexadecimal, and other handy utilities. I'm not going to cover the logic within either of these modules here. Neither teaches any Web Component concepts; they just provide logic for controlling the state of our UI. If you are curious, however, please refer to this book's GitHub repo.

With this extra functionality, our project structure grew by two files. Figure 11.11 shows all of the modules in our component and further details how the interaction works.

11.3.2 Responding to input fields

It would be super nice if, when the value changes on each `<input>` element, the attribute changed as well. Unfortunately, that's not how it works; the `value` attribute is just not updated when the user changes the contents of the input. So, another listener is needed—a simple `change` listener. You might think to wire each `<input>` element with its own event listener, but we can actually listen for change events that bubble up to our shadow root with a single listener, as figure 11.12 shows. Listing 11.11 puts that one event listener in practice.

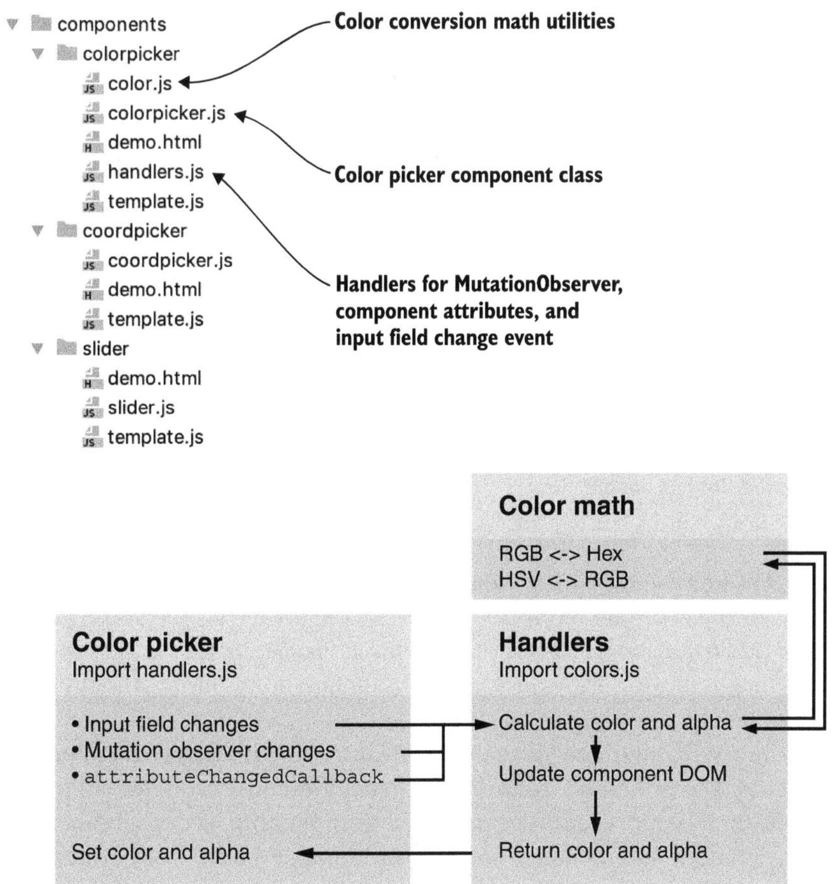

Figure 11.11 Project structure with new modules

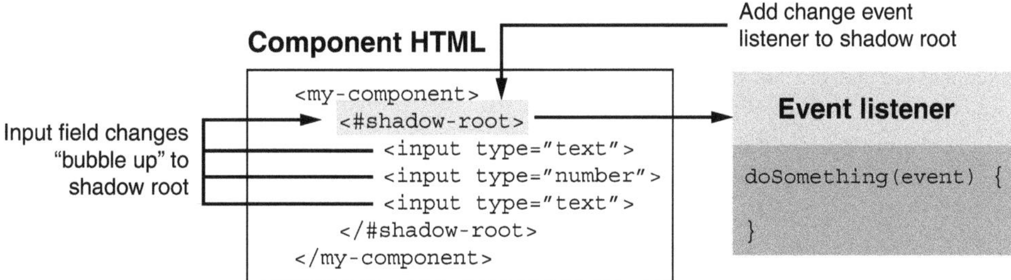

Figure 11.12 Events bubbling to the shadow root

Listing 11.11 Listening for change events inside the component's Shadow DOM

```
constructor() {
   super();
   this.attachShadow({mode: 'open'});
   this.shadowRoot.innerHTML = Template.render();
   this.dom = Template.mapDOM(this.shadowRoot);
   const observer = new MutationObserver( e => this.onMutationChange(e));
   observer.observe(this.shadowRoot, { attributes: true, subtree: true });
   this.shadowRoot.addEventListener('change', e =>
     this.onInputValueChanged(e));      <-- Change event listener for input fields
}

onInputValueChanged(e) {                <-- Change event handler
   this.data = Handlers.update( {
       model: this.data,
       dom: this.dom,
       component: this,
       element: e.target,
   });
}
```

Notice that we're sending the same exact objects to the `Handlers.update` function (except for the attribute name, as that doesn't apply here). All of the incoming data, whether it's from the change event or the `MutationObserver`, can be treated the same, which leads the `Handlers.update` function to be fairly straightforward. With all of the setup work done so far, it can be a good challenge to try to implement this module yourself along with the color math (http://www.easyrgb.com/en/math.php), which I used as a helpful resource to write the conversion functions. Again, the details of these import modules would be a bit lengthy to describe here and aren't Web Component specific at all; so while not included here, they are available in the GitHub repo for this book.

11.3.3 Responding to attribute changes

There is one last Web Components-related concept to make the color picker functional. Our component should update both color and transparency values for its own attributes. Color will be represented as a hexadecimal value, and transparency will be a percentage from 0 to 100. The attributes will be named `hex` and `alpha`, respectively.

To update these values after some aspect of the color has changed, whether it be a hue slider, the red input field, or the coordinate picker, the `Handlers.update` function takes a reference to the component, so it can easily update these attributes on the component. What needs to be accomplished, however, is listening for changes from the outside. Another part of the app that the color picker component lives in could set the color of the component, and it should respond by changing all of the applicable UI elements (updating the inputs, the sliders, and the coordinate picker). While the specific logic to achieve this can live in the `Handlers.update` function, we still need to respond to changes and send the information along to the module.

Since we've already defined the API as having both `hex` and `alpha` properties, it's obvious what we need to listen for and implement for reflection. The following listing shows implementations of the attribute change callbacks and the getters/setters in components/colorpicker/colorpicker.js.

Listing 11.12 Implementing the API for our component

```
static get observedAttributes() {
   return ['hex', 'alpha'];        <-- Defines which attributes to listen to changes for
}

attributeChangedCallback(name, oldVal, newValue) {
   switch (name) {
       case 'hex':
       case 'alpha':       <-- Listens for attribute changes
           if (oldVal !== newValue) {
               this.data = Handlers.update({
                   model: this.data,
                   dom: this.dom,
                   component: this,
                   element: this,
                   attribute: name,     <-- Responds to changes using Handlers import module, passing in the attribute name
               });
           }
           break;
   }
}

set hex(val) {       <-- Getters and setters for hex and alpha attributes
   this.setAttribute('hex', val);
}

get hex() {
   return this.getAttribute('hex');
}

set alpha(val) {
   this.setAttribute('alpha', val);
}

get alpha() {
   return this.getAttribute('alpha');
}
```

Though everything is in place now, one last issue with the API should be addressed. The color picker doesn't act quite right when loading up because there's no color or transparency value to start with if the attribute wasn't specified! To finish the functional implementation of the component, let's specify some default values. We can use two static getters at the top of the `ColorPicker` class:

```
export default class ColorPicker extends HTMLElement {
   static get DEFAULT_HEX() { return '#77aabb'; }
   static get DEFAULT_ALPHA() { return 100; }
```

The default values I used here are a bit arbitrary. Feel free to fill them in with whatever values you prefer. We can then populate these values when the component is added to the page. The next listing adds a `connectedCallback` for this purpose.

Listing 11.13 Setting color and transparency at the start if not defined

```
connectedCallback() {
   if (!this.hex) {                                  <- If no hexadecimal color
       this.hex = ColorPicker.DEFAULT_HEX;              attribute exists, uses the default
   }
   if (!this.alpha) {                                <- If no alpha attribute exists,
       this.alpha = ColorPicker.DEFAULT_ALPHA;          uses the default
   }
}
```

As the color picker component supports reflection, it's easy to simply set these properties through the JS API. As attribute changes are listened to, setting these two will flow through and make all of the appropriate changes in each piece of UI in the component. It's also important to note that this is on the `connectedCallback` handler instead of the constructor. When the constructor is called, it's just too early in the component lifecycle for attributes to exist yet!

11.4 Adding a common design language

We've done quite a bit so far! Three components are done, and they all work together in service of an overall color picker component we can use in a real project. While it's great to have a component demo, as we do in all three, it's even better to see the final component in a more real-world context. This is why I thought it would be good to set up a test page with the component in place, change the background color of the page, and set the opacity of some text. The next listing sets this up for us to give us the more comprehensive demo. We'll just create this in the root of our project as an index.html file.

Listing 11.14 A color picker demo that can affect elements on the page

```
<html lang="en">
<head>
   <title>Color Picker Component</title>
   <script type=
       "module" src="components/colorpicker/colorpicker.js"></script>   <- Imports the color picker component
   <style>
       h1 {
           font-family: sans-serif;
           font-weight: bolder;
           color: white;
           text-shadow:                      <- Gives the sample text a black border against a potential
                   -1px -1px 0 #000,            dark background when we use the color picker
                   1px -1px 0 #000,
                   -1px 1px 0 #000,
                   1px 1px 0 #000;
       }
   </style>
</head>
```

```
<body>
    <wcia-color-picker                      <-- Adds the color picker
        hex="#7687db"                           component to the page
        alpha="75">
    </wcia-color-picker>

    <h1>Transparency</h1>
    <script>
        document.body.style.backgroundColor =
            document.querySelector('wcia-color-picker').getAttribute('hex');   <-- Uses the color picker's initial values to set the sample text opacity and the background color of the page
        document.querySelector('h1').style.opacity =
            document.querySelector('wcia-color-picker').getAttribute('alpha');

        const observer = new MutationObserver(    <-- Observes attribute changes on the color picker and updates the sample text and page background
            function(records) {
              records.forEach( rec => {
                switch (rec.attributeName) {
                    case 'hex':
                        document.body.style.backgroundColor = rec.target.hex;
                        break;

                    case 'alpha':
                        document.querySelector('h1').style.opacity =
                            rec.target.alpha / 100;
                }
              });
        });
        observer.observe(document.querySelector('wcia-color-picker'),
            { attributes: true });
    </script>
</body>
</html>
```

While this new demo lets us interact with the color picker in a more meaningful way, it also highlights something else—it's kind of ugly! Figure 11.13 shows this new demo, and not much attention is paid to design details.

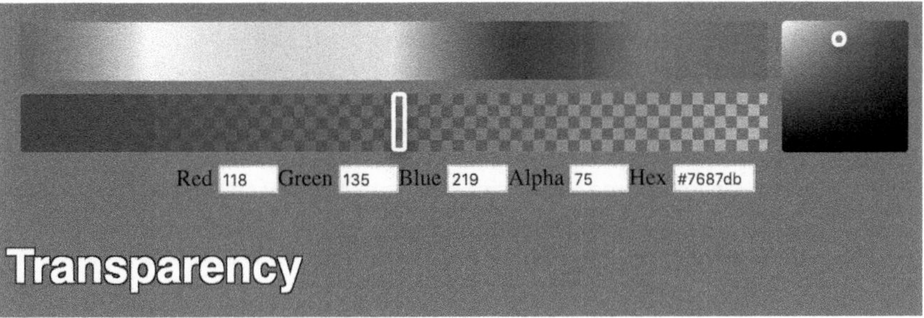

Figure 11.13 The new color picker demo, wired up to change page color and text transparency

11.4.1 Swapping in CSS vars for a consistent design

While there's not much that can go wrong with the slider and coordinate picker because there aren't many moving parts, the input fields are completely unstyled, and many of the finer details, like border radius (rounded corners), are pretty arbitrary.

These kinds of details should really be defined on a system-wide level. Thinking in terms of a larger application, you'll want to make sure all of these details are consistent. There might be not just a color picker but also a wide variety of components. If those components all have different style rules, things will look messier than ever!

Modern design systems are just catching up with Web Components now. Many, like Bootstrap, are built in such a way that the Shadow DOM will block their styles from the component altogether. Instead, let's go way more lightweight and create some common CSS of our own with JS imports. These rules can be imported into any component that needs them!

Before doing this, let's lay down some basic ground rules by using CSS Variables in listing 11.15. This could be a JS import module if we wanted it to be, but given that the larger context of an application or design system doesn't exist in our case, we'll simply place it at the root of our project in a vars.css file.

Listing 11.15 CSS vars to use throughout a hypothetical app and our components

```
:root {
    --text-xsmall: .5em;        <-- Defines various text sizes
    --text-small: .7em;
    --text-medium: 1em;
    --text-large: 1.3em;
    --text-xlarge: 1.5em;

    --color-pureblack: black;        <-- Various color variables
    --color-black: #2a2a2a;
    --color-lightblack: #4a4a4a;
    --color-darkgrey: #6a6a6a;
    --color-grey: #7a7a7a;
    --color-lightgrey: #9a9a9a;
    --color-darkwhite: #dadada;
    --color-white: #fafafa;
    --color-purewhite: #ffffff;

    --text-color: var(--color-lightblack);        <-- Maps color variables to specific items like text, border, and background
    --text-inverted-color: var(--color-white);
    --border-color: var(--color-lightblack);
    --border-color-light: var(--color-darkwhite);
    --border-inverted-color: var(--color-white);
    --background-color: var(--color-white);
    --background-inverted-color: var(--color-lightblack);

    --border-radius: 6px;        <-- Various spacing rules
    --border-width-thick: 3px;
    --border-width: 1px;
    --padding-medium: 5px;
}
```

It's true that I likely went a bit overboard here defining more than what our existing components might need, but these are good sample rules to lay down and build a common design language from for your application. We can even start replacing hard-coded values in the slider component (components/slider/template.js) in the following listing.

Listing 11.16 Replacing values with CSS vars in the slider component

```
css() {
   return `<style>
            :host {                 <-- Uses CSS vars on the component
            ...                         itself to control the border
                border-radius: var(--border-radius);
            ...
            }
            #bg-overlay {           <-- Uses CSS vars on the overlay background
            ...                         <div> to control the border
                border-radius: var(--border-radius);
                ...
            }
            #thumb {                <-- Uses CSS vars on the thumbnail
                ...                     to control the border
                border-width: var(--border-width-thick);
                border-color: var(--border-inverted-color);
                border-radius: var(--border-radius);
                ...
            }
        </style>`;
}
```

We can now do the same for the coordinate picker component (components/coord-picker/template.js).

Listing 11.17 Replacing values with CSS vars in the coordinate picker component

```
css() {
   return `<style>
            #bg-overlay-a {         <-- Uses CSS vars on the two overlay
                ...                     background <div> to control the border
                border-radius: var(--border-radius);
                ...
            }
            #bg-overlay-b {
                ...
                border-radius: var(--border-radius);
                ...
            }
            #thumb {                <-- Uses CSS vars on the thumbnail
                ...                     to control the border
                border-width: var(--border-width-thick);
                border-color: var(--border-inverted-color);
                border-radius: var(--border-radius);
                ...
            }
        </style>`;
}
```

Last, of course, we can do the same for the color picker component (components/colorpicker/template.js).

Listing 11.18 Replacing values with CSS vars in the color picker component

```
css() {
   return `<style>
            ...
            #hue-slider,                        <-- Uses CSS vars on the two
            #transparency-slider {                  sliders to control the border
               ...
               border-radius: var(--border-radius);
            }

            #saturation-brightness {            <-- Uses CSS vars on the
               ...                                  coordinate picker to
               border-radius: var(--border-radius);  control the border
            }

            ...
         </style>`;
}
```

With just these rules, design consistency goes a long, long way. There is no longer a risk of using inconsistent colors or rounded corners. These small details really add up. CSS Variables can only accomplish so much, though. We're limited to basically one CSS rule at a time.

11.4.2 Using imports for more complex CSS

Turning back to importable modules, we can cover the rest. What we'll do next is a drop in the bucket when thinking about every single need in a big design system like Bootstrap or Google's Material, but it's a start. Figure 11.14 indicates the new project structure with all of the imports for the "design system" in place.

First, in the following listing, we can start with defining some universal rules.

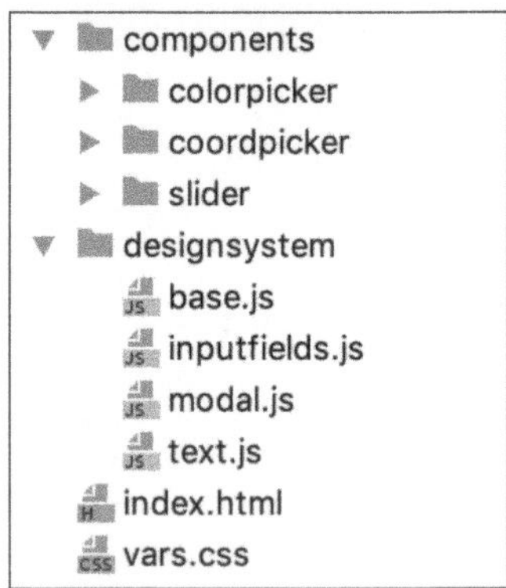

Figure 11.14 Our project file structure including the CSS vars and the design system imports

Listing 11.19 Universal text rules in designsystem/text.js

```
export default {
   normal() {                                    <-- Defines some normal text rules
       return `                                      with color, size, and font
           font-family: sans-serif;
           font-size: 1em;
           line-height: 1.2em;
           color: black;`;
   },
                                                     Alters the color when it
                                                     appears inverted over a
   inverted() { return `color: white;`; }       <-- dark background
}
```

This small set of text rules can then be imported into a module intended for use as a base rule set for any component (designsystem/base.js):

```
import Text from './text.js';
export default {
   common() { return `${Text.normal()}`; }
}
```

Since the extremely limited number of rules here don't happen to apply to the already pretty solid-looking slider or coordinate picker components, we can just use this base component style import in the color picker component (components/ colorpicker/ template.js):

```
import Base from '../../designsystem/base.js';
```

Using it is easy—it's just like using any other template literal:

```
:host {
   ${Base.common()};
   width: 100%;
   display: inline-block;
}
```

While it's great to have some basics down, the few that we have will make only a small impact on our fairly minimal component. No, the bulk of what needs to be styled are the input fields with their corresponding labels. We can take this on by defining some specific rules in a designsystem/inputfields.js module, shown in the following listing.

Listing 11.20 A module containing rules for input fields

```
// designsystem/inputfields.js

import Text from './text.js';          <-- Imports the text.js module, so we
                                           can use specific text CSS rules
export default {
   css() {
       return `
           .ds-form-input {         <-- Spacing for the input container
               margin-right: 5px;
           }
```

```
        .ds-form-input            <—— Styles the label for the input
        ➥.ds-input-field-label {
            border-top-left-radius: var(--border-radius);
            border-top-right-radius: var(--border-radius);
            background-color: var(--background-inverted-color);
            padding: var(--padding-medium);
            display: block;

            font-size: var(--text-xsmall);
            ${Text.inverted()}        <—— With a dark, inverted background color, use inverted text.
        }

        .ds-form-input                <—— For our demo, we're putting the label on top of the input, so
        ➥.ds-input-field-label.top {      specify top if we want to follow up in the future with variations.
            display: block;
        }

        .ds-form-input input {        <—— Styles the actual input field
            border-style: solid;
            border-width: var(--border-width);
            border-color: var(--border-color-light);
            padding: var(--padding-medium);
            font-size: var(--text-large);
        } `;
    }
}
```

As we did previously, we should import this module into the components/color-picker/template.js module:

```
import InputFields from '../../designsystem/inputfields.js';
import Base from '../../designsystem/base.js';
```

We can also add it to our CSS in the same module:

```
   css() {
        return `<style>
                ${InputFields.css()}
```

Note that we are importing complete CSS rules with selectors, so the function call can be embedded right in the `<style>` tag instead of inside a selector/block, as we did before with `:host`. And, as we are using new selectors, we'll need to add these to the HTML in the same file. It's an easy add that applies the same for all of our input fields, so I'll just highlight the first:

```
<div class="ds-form-input">
 <label class="ds-input-field-label top" for="textInputR">Red</label>
 <input id="textInputR" type="number" value="0" max="255" size="4" min="0">
</div>
```

Let's take a peek at our styled input fields in figure 11.15.

We're almost done! I don't like how all the UI elements seem to be floating in space in the layout on the demo page. I'd prefer the component have a white modal background to visually connect the elements and make it feel popped out from the

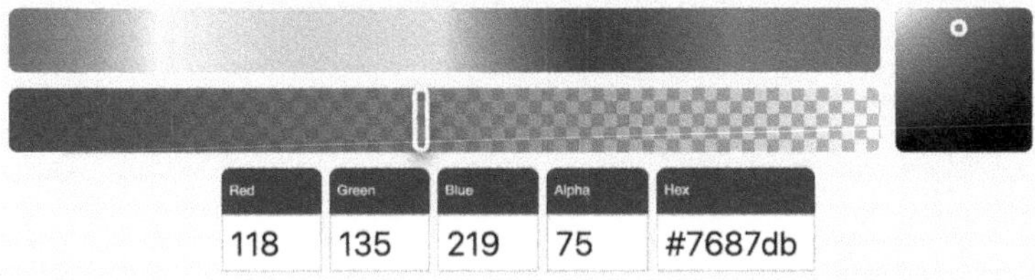

Figure 11.15 Style input fields after applying a rudimentary design system

page. So, with that, let's make one last CSS import module, designsystem/modal.js, as the following listing shows.

Listing 11.21 Modal CSS module

```
// designsystem/modal.js

export default {
   css() {
       return `
           .ds-modal {      <-- Selector and template literal
               ${this.rules()}   containing the CSS rules
           }
       `;
   },

   rules() {       <-- Just the CSS rules
       return `
           background-color: var(--background-color);
           border-radius: var(--border-radius);
           box-shadow: 0 4px 8px 0 rgba(0, 0, 0, 0.2),
           0 6px 20px 0 rgba(0, 0, 0, 0.19);      <-- A shadow around the
       `;                                             element to make it look
   }                                                  popped out from the page
}
```

I separate things out a bit here. The `.ds-modal` selector points to the `rules()` function to embed the actual CSS rules. The reason is that, ideally, I'd prefer to just tack the `.ds-modal` onto the color picker component and be done with it, like so:

```
<wcia-color-picker class="ds-modal" hex="#7687db" alpha="75">
    </wcia-color-picker>
```

Unfortunately, these CSS rules won't pierce the shadow boundary from outside the component (yes, even directly on the component tag itself is still outside the shadow boundary) and won't do anything to style the component.

Still, in other situations that don't involve a shadow boundary, having that selector would be nice, so we'll leave it in our design system. Breaking out those rules makes things dual-purpose, because in the context of our component, now we can just avoid calling `Modal.css()`and instead use our own CSS selector, as in the next listing.

Listing 11.22 Adding CSS style rules for a modal

```
css() {
   return `<style>
              ${InputFields.css()}

              :host {
                  ${Base.common()};
                  width: 100%;
                  display: inline-block;
              }

              :host(.modal) {
                  ${Modal.rules()}        <-- Styles any component with a .modal class assigned with the modal CSS rules
              }
```

As with all of our extra CSS modules, be sure to add the import in the components/colorpicker/template.js file:

```
import InputFields from '../../designsystem/inputfields.js';
import Base from '../../designsystem/base.js';
import Modal from '../../designsystem/modal.js';
```

Note the way we inserted the modal rules in our component. We've made having the modal treatment optional. Now, the modal style is only applied if the `modal` class is present on the component. We'll do this in the root index.html file to see it in the full context as we change the background color of the page with the color picker:

```
<wcia-color-picker class="modal" hex="#7687db" alpha="75"></wcia-color-picker>
```

Finally, we have a styled color picker component, as shown in figure 11.16.

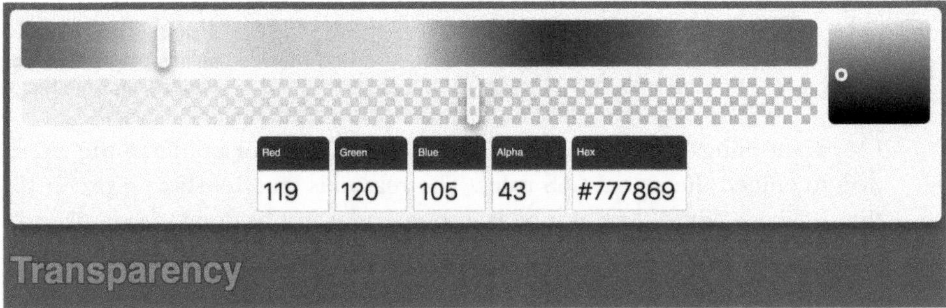

Figure 11.16 The color picker component style with a quick and dirty module-based design system

Not only did we make the component better looking here, but we can tweak things globally to give the component (and surrounding application, if we had one) a different look and feel. Let's give it a more playful look as shown in figure 11.17 simply by increasing the border radius all around. We can do this right in the vars.css file by changing `--border-radius: 6px;` to a value like 12 pixels.

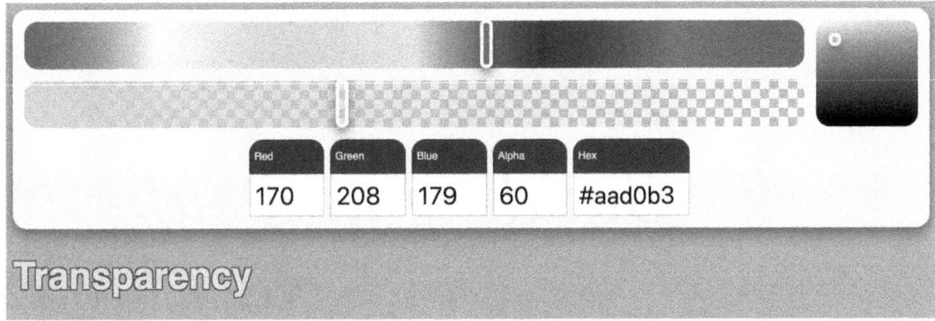

Figure 11.17 The color picker design is easily tweaked by changing the CSS modules or the CSS vars

If you're only worried about modern browsers that support Web Components, mission accomplished! We've created a nice-looking color picker thanks to design and technical inspiration from cssgradient.io. Certainly, the barebones design system we created has a lot of room to improve if we needed to build a larger application or platform, but for the purposes of the color picker component, there is plenty of room to style from the outside without changing a single line of any of our components.

In the next chapter, we'll be looking at what happens when the picture isn't so rosy, and a target browser we need to support doesn't offer Web Components natively. How outdated the browser is will dictate how far we'll need to go. Don't worry, this color picker will work just about everywhere!

Summary

In this chapter, you learned

- How to plan a semi-complex UI component by breaking an inspiration reference design down into multiple pieces, some of which become their own smaller components
- To break down a component into its inputs and outputs and plan an API around them, including using the concept of reflection to enforce a common API when using tag attributes or JS
- To create separate and universal styling rules, whether through CSS vars or importable modules that can be used in your components and in the larger system to enforce design consistency throughout

12 Building and supporting older browsers

This chapter covers

- Module bundling with Rollup
- Transpiling with Babel to allow Web Components in IE11
- Running and combining scripts with `npm` and package.json
- Using dev dependencies in package.json
- Ponyfilling CSS vars for IE11

In the last chapter, we finished building a reusable color picker component consisting of a few different custom components itself. It works pretty well, but the question now is whether this component works for all your target users. It certainly could, and we might stop here. The component we've built supports Chrome, Firefox, and Safari. This leaves only one *modern* browser left: Microsoft Edge.

As of now in this book, we've covered nearly every Web Component concept possible. Our learnings took us from creating Web Components with just Custom Elements to then capping everything off with the amazing Shadow DOM.

There is a good reason that we've tackled things in this order, and that reason is because there will be situations where you just can't or don't want to use the

Shadow DOM. I'm excited to say that these situations are becoming increasingly rare! The end of 2018 brought us some great news on that front. Web Components landed in Firefox, which makes Edge the only major browser we're waiting patiently for. We knew that the Microsoft Edge team was busy working on Web Component support, but then in April 2019, the team released a developer preview of a Chromium-based Edge. Browser diversity worries aside, this looks like great news for Web Components because this new version of Edge supports Web Components in the same way Chrome does (no worrying about weird things that Microsoft implemented in a slightly different way).

The big picture here is that there are currently two major browsers that don't support Web Components natively: pre-Chromium Edge and IE11. For some lucky web developers, these browsers just don't matter. For IE11, this is because on non-Windows 10 machines, it's already reached its end of life. On newer Windows 10 machines, Microsoft recommends that folks use Edge, despite having IE11 available. For Edge, it's now easy to assume that it's only a matter of waiting a few months before most normal consumers have a browser version available that has identical capabilities to Chrome.

Not all of us are that lucky, however. IE11 continues to be a thorn in the side of many web developers. Pre-Chromium Edge could also continue to exist for a while as users slowly upgrade.

Whatever the reason, when creating components, it's good to have a plan of action to take these issues on. So, in this chapter, we're going to take the real-world UI component from the last chapter and back up a bit to get it working on Edge with a polyfill and some small changes. Finally, we'll talk about specific build tools to get our component working in IE11.

12.1 Backward compatibility

So, do you wait for support? While a Chromium-based Edge developer preview is available today, how long before it's released to everyone using Windows? How long will it take for current users to upgrade to the latest? Right now, these questions don't have good answers, so it's worth talking strategy to make the color picker from the last chapter work for the current version of Edge. This strategy will also take us most of the way to supporting IE11 if you absolutely need to support that browser. For IE11, there is a build/transpile step, but, for now, let's focus on a hypothetical modern browser that doesn't support Web Components.

One great resource to help with this effort is the various polyfills provided at www.webcomponents.org/polyfills. To be honest, though, I'm not so much a fan of polyfilling the Shadow DOM. It's a bit too much like magic, meaning it does a good number of things behind the scenes that it doesn't make you aware of, like copying and rewriting your component's DOM elements with different unique classes. This would be fine if the polyfill handled everything seamlessly and had no limitations. The reality is that even when using the Shadow DOM polyfills, you really have to be aware of the limitations that come when the Shadow DOM isn't natively available and work around them. With this in mind, we can make a few changes to toggle on and off the Shadow DOM for our component that will make it compatible with Edge without polyfilling this specific feature.

Despite avoiding the Shadow DOM polyfill, the first step is to polyfill for another aspect of Web Components: Custom Elements. *This* polyfill is, in fact, drop-in. When we add the polyfill to our component, we don't have to worry about caveats or unsupported features. Custom Elements will just work in those browsers that don't support them yet.

The polyfill can be found at https://github.com/webcomponents/custom-elements. As per the documentation, you can build it yourself, install from NPM, or, as we will do now, just use it from a content delivery network (CDN). To be thorough, we should add the polyfill to all three of our demo.html files so that they all work. Simply add the script link to each—in the index.html demo, for example:

```
<title>Color Picker Component</title>
<link rel="stylesheet" type="text/css" href="vars.css">
<script type="module" src="components/colorpicker/colorpicker.js"></script>
<script src="https://unpkg.com/@webcomponents/custom-elements"></script>
```

12.1.1 Toggling the Shadow DOM

If the Shadow DOM was used but is then turned off, one of the great things that happens is that the shadow root isn't created; instead, you can fall back to the scope of your component (`this`). It works really well because the `shadowRoot` property can be interacted with in the same ways as your component. This means that in terms of using JS to interact with either, none of your code needs to change if you use a simple property to represent either scope interchangeably.

The major exception here is something we've covered before. This exception is the use of the constructor to do the heavy initialization work. Remember that when using the Shadow DOM, you're creating a separate, mini DOM inside your component. So, given that you're creating it right there in the constructor, this mini DOM is instantly available. When not using the Shadow DOM, you're relying on the DOM provided by the HTML page you're in. Access to this DOM isn't available yet in the constructor function, so the `connectedCallback` function is the best place to put DOM interaction like getting/setting attributes and setting the component's `innerHTML`.

Before we get into the workaround, chances are you're developing with Chrome, Firefox, or Safari. Instead of jumping over to Edge to test things where Web Components aren't supported, you can do the bulk of the work in your favorite browser by creating a toggle on the class that turns the Shadow DOM on and off. This will simulate Edge pretty well, and you can just do proper testing in that browser when you're done.

Using the slider component as a starting example, we'll add a static getter to control whether we opt in to the Shadow DOM:

```
export default class Slider extends HTMLElement {
   static get USE_SHADOWDOM_WHEN_AVAILABLE() { return false; }
```

We'll do this in components/slider/slider.js, as well as in the other two components found in components/coordinatepicker/coordinatepicker.js and components/colorpicker/colorpicker.js.

With this toggle in, we can now turn our attention to the constructor. Remember, we can't interact with the DOM here if we're not using the Shadow DOM, so we'll move some things around. Listing 12.1 shows what we started with, and listing 12.2 shows how it can be changed for toggling the DOM off and on.

Listing 12.1 Slider component before allowing Shadow DOM toggling

```
constructor() {
   super();
   this.attachShadow({mode: 'open'});
   this.shadowRoot.innerHTML = Template.render();
   this.dom = Template.mapDOM(this.shadowRoot);

   document.addEventListener('mousemove', e => this.eventHandler(e));
   document.addEventListener('mouseup', e => this.eventHandler(e));
   this.addEventListener('mousedown', e => this.eventHandler(e));
}
```

Creates a shadow root

Renders the HTML/CSS to innerHTML

Event listeners

To change this, we can move some code to the constructor and create (or not create) the Shadow DOM.

Listing 12.2 Enabling a Shadow DOM toggle

```
constructor() {
   super();

   if (Slider.USE_SHADOWDOM_WHEN_AVAILABLE &&
       this.attachShadow) {
       this.root = this.attachShadow({mode: 'open'});
   } else {
       this.root = this;
   }

   document.addEventListener('mousemove',
       e => this.eventHandler(e));
   document.addEventListener('mouseup', e => this.eventHandler(e));
   this.addEventListener('mousedown', e => this.eventHandler(e));
}

connectedCallback() {
   if (!this.initialized) {
       this.root.innerHTML = Template.render({
           useShadowDOM: Slider.USE_SHADOWDOM_WHEN_AVAILABLE &&
       this.attachShadow });
       this.dom = Template.mapDOM(this.root);
       this.initialized = true;

       if (this.backgroundcolor) {
           this.setColor(this.backgroundcolor);
       }
```

If opted into using the Shadow DOM and it's supported, creates a shadow root; otherwise sets the reference to the component (this)

Event listeners don't need to move because both the component and document are available from the constructor.

connectedCallback could happen multiple times (whenever the component is added to the page), so make sure initialization happens only once.

Indicates to the HTML/CSS Template module whether the Shadow DOM is being used

Updates component based on current attributes

```
        if (this.value) {
            this.refreshSlider(this.value);
        }
    }
}
```

The very first thing we're doing here is creating a property on the class called `this.root`. If we use the Shadow DOM, set this property to the shadow root. If not, simply set it as a reference to our component (`this`). Now, we can use `this.root` anywhere we need to manipulate the contents of our component, whether we're using the Shadow DOM or not.

We don't actually need to move the event listeners. We would if they were more specific. If, for example, we created an event listener on the thumbnail or some element that's not in the DOM yet, it wouldn't work here. In this example, it just so happens that the things we're listening to—the document and the component itself—are both available from the start.

The initialization code is moved to a new `connectedCallback` function, but remember, this handler is fired each time the component is added to the page. To make a truly bulletproof component, we should check if it's already been initialized with a custom `this.initialized` property, running code only if it hasn't been run yet. For our immediate needs with the color picker, we really don't need this check, but, again, if we want to make components that work in a variety of situations, this really should be prioritized.

Working with our `Template` import module is pretty straightforward. Instead of setting the `shadowRoot.innerHTML` to the HTML/CSS string returned from the import, we simply set `this.root.innerHTML`. Whether `this.root` is the shadow root or the component, it will work regardless. Similarly, when getting cached element references with `Template.mapDOM`, `this.root` works regardless of which reference it contains.

Lastly, we have to add one extra bit around our attributes. The reflection (attributes/getters/setters) strategy doesn't change, but there is a timing issue here. When we were using the Shadow DOM, we could initialize everything, including rendering all our HTML, getting element references, and so on, all in the constructor. By the time the `attributeChangedCallback` fired with our starting attributes, we'd be set up and ready to go. Now, however, the `attributeChangedCallback` fires before the `connectedCallback` handler, so our changes are lost without the ability to respond.

In fact, we do need to error-proof the `attributeChangedCallback`. Worse than losing these changes, we'll actually get an error. Since this callback causes code to run that changes the thumbnail and background, both of which don't exist yet, the following line, for example, will throw an error when the component starts up:

```
refreshSlider(value) {
    this.dom.thumb.style.left = (value/100 * this.offsetWidth -
     this.dom.thumb.offsetWidth/2) + 'px';
}
```

To take care of this issue, we can simply check if the component has been set up yet in the `attributeChangedCallback` and exit out if not:

```
attributeChangedCallback(name, oldVal, newValue) {
   if (!this.dom) { return; }
```

But then, of course, our component's starting attributes have not been used due to this timing issue, so we checked if they were present and acted on them in the last few lines of listing 12.2.

Though we've just focused on the slider component, the other two components can be modified in the exact same way. I won't spell it all out here, but it's a good exercise to fill these in on your own. If you get stuck, those components in their finished form can be found in this book's GitHub repo.

That said, there is one tiny consideration to make in the color picker component's specific implementation. I'm referring to the `onMutationChange` handler in components/colorpicker/colorpicker.js:

```
onMutationChange(records) {
  records.forEach( rec => {
      this.data = Handlers.update({
```

Here, we are handling any attribute changes to our inner DOM elements. Initially, we were watching for attribute changes on the `shadowRoot` and any elements within. Now, we're just listening for changes on `this.root`. When not using the Shadow DOM, we're observing attribute changes on the component itself! The problem is that we're already doing this using the `attributeChangedCallback`. So now we're double listening and double responding to events. To solve this, we'll simply ignore attribute changes coming from the component inside the `onMutationChange` handler:

```
onMutationChange(records) {
  records.forEach( rec => {
      if (rec.target !== this) {
```

Here, we're simply saying that if the target element identified by the change record (each record is a change recorded by the mutation observer) is not the color picker component, do all the normal stuff. If the target element *is* the color picker component, no action is taken.

12.1.2 Comparing to polyfills

While it wasn't overly complex to allow the components to operate without the Shadow DOM, it wasn't trivial. We couldn't just drop in a polyfill and go. In fact, the only thing a Shadow DOM polyfill would have really given us here is the ability to keep using `this.shadowRoot` in the component. It would also offer some encapsulation to prevent outside JS from manipulating the component's DOM like a real Shadow DOM would do. If that's important to you, the ShadyDOM polyfill might be worth looking into (https://github.com/webcomponents/shadydom).

The rest of the work we did, especially around breaking up the constructor to move the initialization to the `connectedCallback`, is something that would need to be done regardless. This one aspect is likely why the W3C spec recommends not having initialization code like this in the constructor at all (even when everyone else seems to ignore this rule). It's much easier to set things up right from the beginning and switch off the Shadow DOM if necessary. It's not a concern if your target browsers support Web Components natively, but when they don't, it's good to start your component with these best practices in mind.

12.1.3 Shadow CSS and child elements

Likely the most annoying part of moving back to a world without the Shadow DOM is HTML and CSS. In creating our HTML markup, I was overly enthusiastic and used IDs instead of classes to reference elements. Again, a polyfill won't save us here. Using the slider component's template as an example (components/slider/template.js), we simply need to go in and kill all the IDs. The following listing highlights this change.

Listing 12.3 Changing ID references to classes

```
mapDOM(scope) {
   return {
       // OLD //
       overlay: scope.getElementById(    <-- With the Shadow DOM, we could safely query by ID.
       'bg-overlay'),
       thumb: scope.getElementById('thumb')

       // NEW //
       overlay: scope.querySelector(     <-- Without the Shadow DOM, it's not safe anymore, so we should switch to classes.
       '.bg-overlay'),
       thumb: scope.querySelector('.thumb')
   }
},

html() {
   // OLD //
   return `<div id="bg-overlay"></div>       <-- Elements used ID to reference previously
           <div id="thumb"></div>`;

   // NEW //
   return `<div class="bg-overlay"></div>    <-- Change to use classes if no Shadow DOM is present
   <div class="thumb"></div>`;
},
```

For the limited context of our component on a demo page, we don't actually need this step. It just so happens that none of the IDs we were using clashed—they were all unique. So, if this step was missed, it's no big deal; everything would work fine. The problem is that if we kept referencing by ID and forgot about it, we'd have a ticking time bomb on our hands. Using this component in a larger application with other ID references could overrule what element gets returned here if more than one is using the same ID and could have some serious (and mysteriously acting) consequences.

Yet again, we have an instance of a best practice we need to worry about only if we're planning to use our components in a Shadow DOM-less context. If this is a possibility, it's just best to avoid ID altogether. If it's not a possibility—well, frankly, I really do enjoy the luxury of using ID as it was intended: to reference unique elements!

The last hurdle to overcome is CSS. The ShadyCSS polyfill does help here, but it comes with lots of baggage, to the point where I just don't feel like it's worth it for cases like this. The problem is that the `:host` selector doesn't exist. In fact, in Edge, it actually breaks your CSS if you even try to use it! Also, simple standalone selectors like `.thumb` that worked only on the scope of your Shadow DOM before can now affect your entire application.

The ShadyCSS polyfill works around this in the best way it can. You as a developer are responsible for putting your markup and CSS in a `<template>` tag. The polyfill then goes in and rewrites your elements and CSS to use unique selectors such that it appears the Shadow DOM still works. I'm inclined to think that the setup required here is the same or even more effort than just handling things ourselves. Yes, the Shadow DOM does provide protection from outside CSS creeping into our component, but the polyfill doesn't. So, there really doesn't appear to be much benefit to using it if we can do something more straightforward.

This is where our use of template literals comes in handy. Recall back in the component class, where we call the `Template.render` method:

```
this.root.innerHTML = Template.render({ useShadowDOM:
   Slider.USE_SHADOWDOM_WHEN_AVAILABLE && this.attachShadow });
```

Passing a boolean here indicates to the `render` function if we are using the Shadow DOM or not, and we can then modify the CSS to use the appropriate selectors. For example, if we were originally using `:host` as a selector, we should now use the component name for a selector. For the slider component, specifically,

```
:host { . . . } becomes wcia-slider { . . . }

:host .thumb { . . . }  or .thumb { . . . }  becomes wcia-slider .thumb { . . . }
```

With this in mind, and focusing on the slider component template module (components/slider/template.js), we can create some code in the next listing to use either one or the other.

Listing 12.4 Switching between Shadow DOM and non-Shadow DOM selectors

```
render(opts) {
   return `${this.css(opts.useShadowDOM)}
           ${this.html()}`;
},

createHostSelector(useshadow, host) {
   if (useshadow) {
       return ':host';
   } else {
       return host;
```

- Passes a boolean to the css function to indicate whether the Shadow DOM is used
- Returns the appropriate selector string for Shadow DOM or non-Shadow DOM usage

```
    }
},

css(useShadowDOM) {
    const comp = 'wcia-slider';
    return `<style>
            ${this.createHostSelector(
                useShadowDOM, comp)} {
              display: inline-block;
              position: relative;
              border-radius: var(--border-radius);
            }

            ${this.createHostSelector(useShadowDOM, comp)} .bg-overlay {
              width: 100%;
              height: 100%;
              position: absolute;
              border
```

Declares the component tag to use when generating the selector

Dynamically creates the selector based on whether using the Shadow DOM and the name of the component

The exact same thing can be done in the coordinate picker component and the color picker component. There is one selector that's a bit different in the color picker, however:

```
:host(.modal)
```

Remember that this selector simply states that if the color picker component has a class named `modal` on it, the background gets styled as a modal. To get what we want with no Shadow DOM, we'd want the following selector:

```
wcia-color-picker.modal
```

In this case, we'll add on more function to handle the case in components/color-picker/template.js, as seen in the next listing.

Listing 12.5 Handling a special case of class on component

```
createHostContextSelector(
        useshadow, host, clazz) {
    if (useshadow) {
        return `:host(${clazz})`;
    } else {
        return host + clazz;
    }
},

css(useShadowDOM) {
    const comp = 'wcia-color-picker';
    return `<style>
            ...
            ${this.createHostContextSelector(useShadowDOM, comp, '.modal')}
            {
              ${Modal.rules()}
            }
```

New function that accepts Shadow DOM boolean, component name, and class to use on component

Creates the selector :host(.modal) or wcia-color-picker.modal depending on if the ShadowDOM is used

A good JS homework challenge for you might to be to come up with a single function that handles all manner of `:host` variations and then build that into a base class that we can extend any Web Component's Template module from. Again, as we look to the future in Web Components, these kinds of optimizations will be where a lot of exciting work will be done, and we won't need new browser features to do it!

12.2 Building for the least common denominator

As you can see, there's a fair bit to consider when building a component that might potentially be used when native Web Components aren't available. It's great that the Custom Element API is so easy to polyfill, but the simplicity stops there. It's probably becoming apparent that components and, in fact, web development in general, play by different rules when using or not using the Shadow DOM.

When developing, whether using a polyfill or not, you'll need to develop your component for the least common denominator. If not using the Shadow DOM, or not certain you are, you must plan your component as if you are not using it. You'll also need to accept that polyfills have some major caveats. The most exciting aspect of the Shadow DOM is CSS encapsulation, but polyfills just don't solve that. CSS rules can still creep in. They can also creep out of your component if your selectors aren't properly set up to prevent this by making them specific to your component. Again, don't just use `.thumb`; use `my-component .thumb`.

There have been a lot of similarities and repeated code when preparing your component to go Shadow DOM-less. When considering this code in combination with the repetitious code for attribute/property reflection in your components, it might be tempting to try out a Web Component framework or library.

LitElement (https://lit-element.polymer-project.org) by the Google Polymer team is shaping up to be a strong Web Component base class to provide all of this functionality. It definitely forces you into a few development patterns and expands upon the Web Components API with some more functionality. You might be looking to put some of these concerns and limitations out of your mind, so LitElement can be nice, especially as it promises to support down to IE11. StencilJS (https://stenciljs.com) by Ionic offers a slightly different approach. A developer would create a component with the framework, and it gets compiled down to a vanilla Web Component.

I'm sure we'll see even more solutions going forward and solid future releases from LitElement and StencilJS. Personally, I'd rather avoid these solutions in my endeavors to avoid framework/library complexity, using only what I need. I also like to develop components without a build/compile step until releasing them, which both these solutions use during the development process.

At the end of the day, you should just use what works for your project. That said, all of the complexity we covered isn't necessary when developing for modern browsers with native support for Web Components. Edge will hopefully be less of a concern in short order, given that more and more developers are leaving IE11 out of their browser requirements.

What happens when we do need to push forward and support IE11, though? The Custom Elements polyfill still works, so making our own elements as we have been doing isn't a worry. The major problem left is a lack of support for newer JS features like `Class`. To move past this, we need to transpile and build! We'll explore this next.

Of course, there will always be browser inconsistencies that need to be solved. In fact, our color picker component doesn't quite work perfectly yet in Edge. To finish up here, let's fix it so the color picker works perfectly in all modern browsers. Refer back to the slider component class in components/slider/slider.js:

```
setColor(color) {
   this.dom.overlay.style.background = `linear-gradient(to right, ${color}
     0%, ${color}00 100%)`;
}
```

In this function, we can use the hexadecimal color right in the linear gradient when showing the transparency fade. All other modern browsers support adding an extra two digits for an eight-character color. Those last two digits indicate a 0% transparency. Unfortunately, Edge does not support this. We'll need to use RGBA-defined colors and get some conversion help from the `Color` utilities module, which we can import.

Listing 12.6 Fixing a linear gradient style rule for Edge

```
import Template from './template.js';
import Color from '../colorpicker/color.js';

export default class Slider extends HTMLElement {

...

setColor(color) {
   const rgb = Color.hexToRGB(color);
   this.dom.overlay.style.background = `linear-gradient(to right,
     rgba(${rgb.r}, ${rgb.g}, ${rgb.b}, 1) 0%, rgba(${rgb.r}, ${rgb.g},
     ${rgb.b}, 0) 100%)`;
}
```

Changes the style rule for IE/Edge

After adding these changes, our component can be tested in every modern browser, including Edge!

12.3 Build processes

So far in this book, we've been doing things with no framework and no complicated workflows that do a bunch of stuff under the hood you aren't aware of. It's just us, a browser, and some HTML, JS, and CSS.

This isn't the case with many modern web workflows. Many times, you won't be running the same code in your browser as you write in your editor. There may be a build step in between. From using tools like Sass and LESS to compile your CSS to generating a big HTML file from various snippets you have organized in many different files, there are many reasons for building.

I could go on and on with reasons for using one or several build steps without even talking about JS. Frontend tasks like these, whether for HTML, CSS, or JS, are almost always run with Node.js. But which specific system should you use? The major ones that promise to do it all are Grunt and Gulp, but even more specific systems that promise to do one thing well tend to overlap. For example, Webpack is designed to bundle assets, but for many tasks, it can overlap with ones that Grunt and Gulp can do themselves.

With the web developer community releasing new tools every day, and a plethora of really solid build systems that can do it all, it can be confusing which tools to include in your toolbelt and what systems to use to orchestrate everything. Lately, though, there's been bit of a trend toward simplicity when possible.

12.3.1 Using NPM scripts

Before delving into why we might want to include a build process in our Web Component workflow, let's talk about a simple way to run tasks. You've probably used Node.js, even if only to install something. To refresh your memory, `npm` is the piece of the Node.js ecosystem for installing the JS package of your choice.

For example, if you wanted to install the Web Component polyfills, you'd go to the root of your project directory, fire up the terminal, and run

```
npm install @webcomponents/webcomponentsjs
```

This package would get installed in your project root in a node_modules folder. Of course, as you add more and more packages, it's easy to lose track, which is why you'll want some record that keeps track of your dependencies like this as well as other details of your project. That's why the package.json file exists. It's easy to create a new one from scratch. Again in the terminal, at the root of your project, run

```
npm init
```

You'll be guided through some questions to fill in the details of your project, like name, email, package name, and so on. With a package.json in place, if you were to run the previous command to install `webcomponentsjs`, it would be added to the dependencies list in the JSON.

Or, if it's a dependency intended only for your project's developer workflow and not part of your production release, you'd run

```
npm install @webcomponents/webcomponentsjs --save-dev
```

Dependencies aside, the package.json file has another pretty powerful aspect. A `scripts` object can be added to run whatever you need. We can try running something simple pretty easily.

Listing 12.7 A simple package.json script

```
{
 "name": "wcia",
 "version": "1.0.0",
 "scripts": {
```

```
    "test": "echo 'Hello from package.json'"    <—— Script to run
  }
}
```

Basically, anything you might run in the terminal can be added here. The simple test in listing 12.7 uses the Linux `echo` command, which prints whatever message you give it as a line in your terminal. Windows users don't need to feel left out, either, thanks to the Windows Subsytem for Linux (WSL; https://docs.microsoft.com/en-us/windows/wsl/install-win10). With this, Windows users can run the same Linux commands as Mac or Linux users. Even prior to WSL, which is definitely not perfect yet, just installing Git for Windows (https://gitforwindows.org) allowed a limited set of Bash commands that might just be enough.

The reason to bring this up is that `npm` scripts are becoming more and more part of a developer workflow instead of big, complex build systems like Grunt or Gulp. There's absolutely nothing wrong with build systems like these for complicated and numerous tasks as part of a workflow. However, when just running a few simple tasks, there's no need for all of the complexity. Build systems tend to have a bit of a learning curve. Running many different tasks will require researching the plugins you need and ironing out kinks when they don't work together, but it also means you don't need to write every little task, like copying files, running CSS preprocessors, uploading to a server, file concatenation, HTML templating, and so on. But if you need only a few tasks, and they are very easy to code yourself, there's no reason you can't go simple.

Over the next two chapters, we'll be exploring a few basic ways to build and test. While the build and test tools themselves have various levels of complexity, the commands to launch them are incredibly simple. Even if you're on Windows without the aforementioned WSL and just using the Git Bash emulation, the commands we're running work, with one caveat when running tests that I'll mention in the next chapter. Hence, we'll be avoiding build systems as we explore build processes here, which allows us to focus on the specific tasks we're running while avoiding lots of setup that's not directly relevant to what we need to run. Most importantly, the choice of build system is up to you, should you want to use one.

12.4 Building components

Web Components are really no different than anything else in terms of how and why we'd use a build step for our JS. And just like anything else, complexity can grow as our project or component needs grow. What's not clear quite yet is why we should build at all.

12.4.1 Why we build

There are numerous reasons to run a JS build process. One increasingly common reason is that a developer might prefer another language besides JS to code in. CoffeeScript was a popular language for writing web applications years ago, though these days, Microsoft's TypeScript is the most popular non-JS language to create web applications with. TypeScript isn't a completely different language, however—it's a superset of JS with the addition of typed variables. It also offers the newest proposed JS features that haven't made it into browsers yet. In fact, the publisher of this book has two really solid books on TypeScript that recently came out:

- *Angular Development with TypeScript*, by Yakov Fain and Anton Moiseev (www.manning.com/books/angular-development-with-typescript-second- edition)
- *TypeScript Quickly*, by Yakov Fain and Anton Moiseev (www.manning.com/books/typescript-quickly)

TypeScript is becoming more and more relevant for Web Component work as well. In addition to its standing as a popular language to work with in general, the LitElement and lit-html projects by Google's Polymer team are written in TypeScript. Though writing your code with newer language features like decorators isn't required, it's strongly encouraged, as most of the examples are written this way.

It's not just CoffeeScript and TypeScript, either—there are tons of languages that developers use to run code on the web. All of these languages have one thing in common, however. They don't actually run in the browser. Your code is written in the language of your choice but then *transpiled* to JS so that it can run.

If transpiling sounds like a foreign concept, it's very similar to compiling. Both allow you to write code and transform it to something that runs on the platform of your choice, like the web. Compiling means you're targeting a lower level of abstraction, like bytecode. The output from a compiler is basically unreadable by human eyes.

Compilation can be almost thought of like capturing the audio of a spoken language and saving it as an audio waveform. It's impossible to make out what someone is saying by looking at an audio waveform in your favorite sound editor, but you can certainly play it back and understand what's being said perfectly fine.

Transpiling can be thought of more like translation, like from Spanish to English. Both Spanish and English are very readable languages if you know them, but, if not, a translation step helps you read in your native language.

Transpiling isn't even about writing things in an entirely new language, either. Over the years, JS has added many new and exciting features, especially in 2015, when the ES6/ES2015 standard was released. Developers couldn't use these features right away, though. Even if their favorite browser supported them, not all browsers did. Even now, while the major modern browsers have great support for ES6/ES2015 features, developers may want to target older browsers like IE. Even if that's not the case, there are some great, brand-new JS language features or even experimental ones that developers want to use that don't have any browser support just yet. For these types of use cases, Babel (https://babeljs.io) is likely the most widely used JS transpiler today.

Another big reason for modifying your JS code is to take many different source files and put them in a larger one. When the source code for your application starts growing into hundreds or thousands of lines of code, it's bad practice to put all of your JS in one big file. For one thing, when working with a team, it's easier to step on each other's toes when modifying the same file. Second, your project is way more organized when the JS is properly split up. Pieces of functionality are easier to find when you don't have to go hunting through one huge file. Additionally, when organized into smaller, well-named files, it's easier to look at a project's file structure and get a sense of what it does and how things work.

Despite the developer workflow improvements from smaller files, it's better for the browser to have everything together in one file or, even better, smartly bundled into files that are loaded when functionality is needed. When things are bundled together, there are fewer network requests for the browser to handle. This is important because browsers do have a maximum number of requests at a time. Also, scripts may be slow to load due to network conditions. You can start to imagine what weird things might happen to your application when some functionality is present to load it, but then another script isn't available yet because the network request is taking too long.

Prior to ES6/ES2015 modules, and ignoring similar solutions like RequireJS, JS code in separate files would be simply bundled together through concatenation tools. Essentially, concatenation just means putting the contents of each JS file into a bigger one in the order you specify. We still do something similar, but with modules, things need to be a bit smarter. Automated tools need to go through your code, track down the modules you reference through the `import` keyword, and bundle that into the final output. Even smarter, the better tools employ a method called *tree shaking*. If you import a module and don't happen to use it anywhere in your code, it won't bundle that particular module. Tree shaking is a smart way to ensure smaller JS bundles that include only the code you need.

Tools like Webpack (https://webpack.js.org) differentiate themselves even more by allowing you to create multiple output bundles and bundling more file types than just JS. These bundles are organized by functionality you'd need to run specific areas of your application. Web applications can be huge, and you may think of your application organized into different sections.

For example, if you were working on a banking web app, a user might view their recent transactions in one section but never visit another section to see their account info. There's no reason in this scenario to force the user to load a bundle containing JS related to account info. Therefore, while the banking application could be one big module, it's smarter to organize it into several bundles for each section of the application. Figure 12.1 highlights these main differences between simpler tools, like Rollup, and more complex tools, like Webpack.

Again, we're back to a plethora of tools we can use! Either way, both transpiling and bundling are two major motivators behind having a build process for your JS.

12.4.2 Module bundling with Rollup

Although there are a good many tools for module bundling, Webpack has historically been fairly tricky and complex to set up for the easiest of tasks, while Rollup has been the simple but not as configurable alternative. Recent Webpack releases have changed how steep the learning curve is for doing simple things, while newcomer Parcel.js (https://parceljs.org) has gained popularity as well!

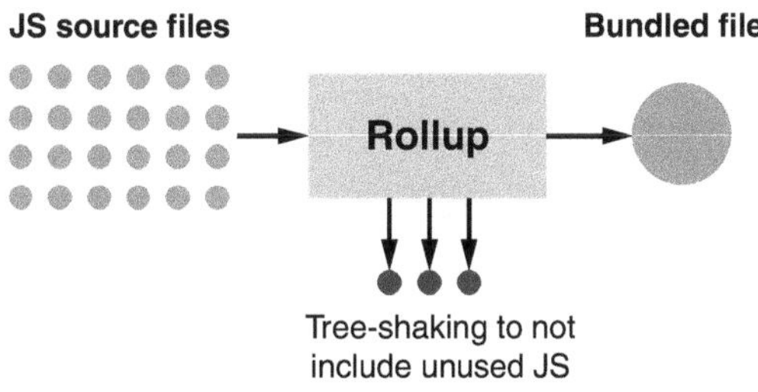

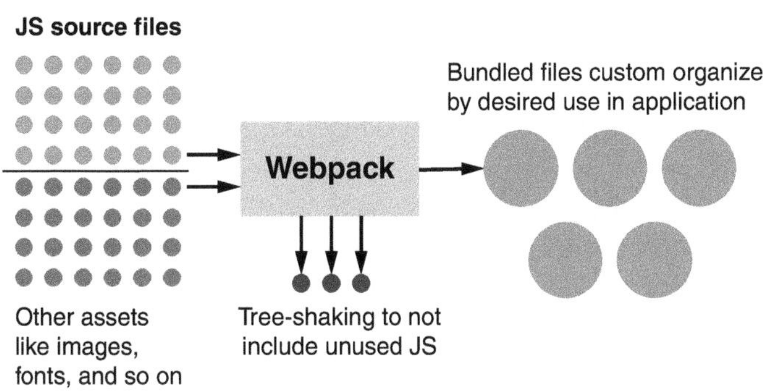

Figure 12.1 Rollup vs. Webpack

We just need to pick one to move forward with; and with these three great options in mind, I'd like to pick Rollup (https://rollupjs.org), as I have the most experience with it and appreciate its simplicity for getting up and running quickly. As with any `npm install` for a project, be sure to create a package.json file at the root of your project. Then, in the terminal, `cd` to your project root and run

```
npm install --save-dev rollup
```

Note that we used the `--save-dev` option here. Rollup will be added to your package .json as a dev dependency, meaning you don't intend to do anything with Rollup besides have it help you with your development and build process. It's not code that's intended to be shipped with your component. Once finished, your package.json looks like the following listing (varying, of course, by how you named and versioned your project).

Listing 12.8 A package.json file after installing Rollup

```
{
 "name": "wcia",
 "version": "1.0.0",
 "dependencies": {},
 "devDependencies": {
   "rollup": "^1.0.2"     <—— Rollup developer dependency
 }
}
```

Something interesting to note is that you could have installed Rollup (or any package in general) globally with the `-g` option, like this:

```
npm install rollup -g
```

When doing a global install, Rollup could be run directly from your terminal, anywhere on your computer, simply by issuing the `rollup` command with some parameters. Here, we installed locally instead, as part of the project. As a local install, Rollup can still be run in your terminal with the shorthand `rollup` command because the install path is likely added to your environmental variables. I still don't trust this! If you had several different Rollup installs on different projects, you'd be rolling the dice on which one you're actually using. Instead, I like to be a bit more exact and execute it from within my project at node_modules/.bin/rollup. This seems a bit more complicated, but is more widely accepted than having a global install.

The reason it's better is that if you wanted to get a team member set up with your project and tooling globally, you'd need to give them a handwritten list of everything they need to install to work with your project, which they'd install one by one. If there are a lot of dependencies, it's easy to forget certain things, and it becomes a pain to debug why their build process doesn't work. Instead, with a local install, everything they need is right there in the package.json and can be installed in one go with `npm install`.

It's still a bit of a pain to have to type that whole path every time you want to run a build. The command becomes even longer as we add the parameters to indicate where the main JS entry point is, where the output file should be, and what its name is. That's why we can make an entry in our package.json scripts object and add the command there.

Before we do that, however, we should change our Web Component structure a tiny bit. As an example, let's start with the slider component from the last chapter, which was a small piece of the color picker component. Figure 12.2 shows its simple file structure along with the other components and design system modules.

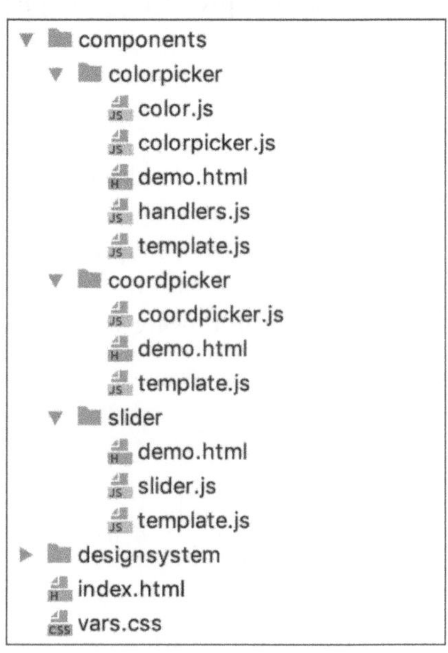

Figure 12.2 Slider component files

Again, though the slider component worked perfectly in our local development environment (and is honestly so small it would probably work fine on the web), we'll want to create a bundle such that the end user will load all the modules (slider.js, template.js, and all of the relevant bits of the custom-made design system). Those files should now be considered source files that aren't directly consumed by end users. As such, we'll create a src folder in

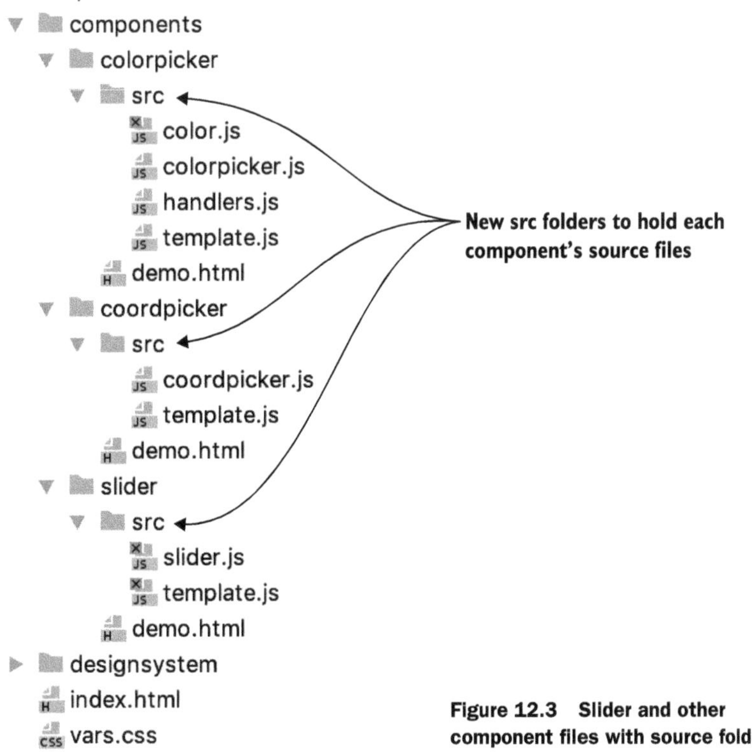

Figure 12.3 Slider and other component files with source folder

each component directory and put the slider.js and template.js inside. We'll do this for the other components as well. Figure 12.3 shows the new folder structure.

With this new folder structure, the input file for Rollup is now located at components/slider/src/slider.js. Nothing about the code inside this file changes except for one small detail. The good news is that our import paths are mostly relative to the component, so they shouldn't need to change. When we import the `Template` module, it's still located at ./template.js. The annoying bit is that when we fixed the transparency for Edge, we used the Color module from the color picker component. So now, instead of

```
import Color from '../../colorpicker/color.js';
```

we'll need to change to

```
import Color from '../../colorpicker/src/color.js';
```

In the end, the output can be created where the original slider.js used to be. Those two parameters are the main ones Rollup needs to function! The command we'll be running is

```
./node_modules/.bin/rollup chapter12and13/components/slider/src/slider.
   js --file chapter12and13/components/slider/slider.js --format umd
   --name slider -m
```

The complete directory path includes "chapter12and13" to match this book's GitHub repo. The very first parameter is the location of the slider component's source file. As the only required parameter, this first parameter is also the only one that doesn't need a flag.

Second, we'll need to specify the output file, passed by preceding the parameter with `--file`. Next is the output format, denoted by `--format`. There's no right answer here, but I suggest using Universal Module Definition (UMD). When bundling as UMD, the JS can be loaded in a variety of ways. Two of those ways are CommonJS and Asynchronous Module Definition (AMD), which can be used in a variety of different scenarios, including with RequireJS. The last method that UMD enables is via a simple global definition, where no JS loading mechanisms are assumed. UMD attaches the slider component to the `window` as a global variable accessible anywhere from your page.

What's the name of this global variable? That can easily be answered by using the `--name` parameter. We'll call ours `slider`. Now, as a global variable, `window.slider` exists, but we'll likely never use it since our component is set up automatically. You may want to be a bit more careful than me and use a name that could never be conflicted with in your application. Your component's namespace could be a good candidate to include here, like `MyNamespaceSlider`, or your application name could be used—just something to make it unique.

An obvious question is whether we're forgoing the ability to use the slider component as a normal ES6/ES2015 module, as we have been. We aren't! If the larger application that contains the slider wants to import the module, it could easily import src/slider.js and use it, ignoring the generated bundle. This larger application could then bundle the application itself plus all the components within, using Rollup or whatever module bundler it prefers.

The very last flag, `-m`, turns on "source map" generation. If you're not familiar with source maps, they bridge the generated output to the original source files. The "map" piece is a file with a .map extension, which is fairly unreadable by human eyes but contains lookup information to make this bridge possible. This might sound kind of meaningless without seeing it in action. You can try it yourself after we run the build, but figure 12.4 shows source maps in action. I've forced an error in my code. Though we're using the output bundle we'll generate next, our error shows the exact line where the error occurred in our source.

12.4.3 Running builds with npm

Now that we know how to build with Rollup, have planned the component's file structure a little better, and know what to expect for the bundled output, let's simplify bundling with Rollup. As discussed previously, we can easily add the Rollup bundle command to our package.json file. Normally, something simple would suffice. We could just call the task `build` and move on, like in the next listing.

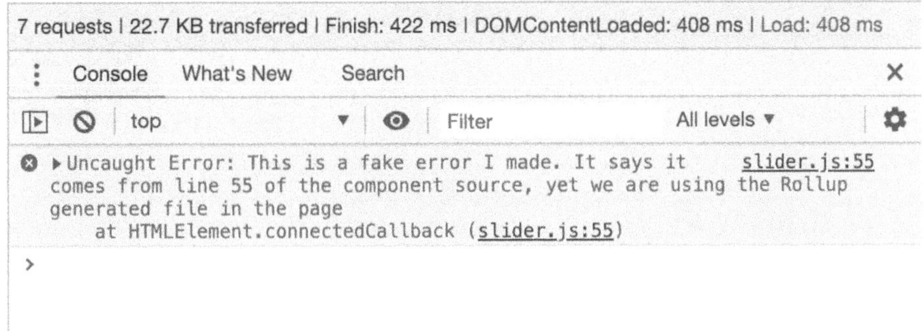

Figure 12.4 Source maps show where an error occurred in your source files, even when bundling output.

Listing 12.9 Adding a Rollup script in package.json

```
{
 "name": "wcia",
 "version": "1.0.0",
 "dependencies": {},
 "devDependencies": {
   "rollup": "^1.0.2"
 },
 "scripts": {
 "build": "./node_modules/.bin/rollup chapter12and13/components/slider/src/
   slider.js --file chapter12and13/components/slider/slider.js --format
   umd --name slider -m"
}
```

Rollup build script

So now, instead of typing a long and complicated command to build, we can simply run the new `build` command in the terminal at the root of the project:

```
npm run build
```

Ideally, the entire project would be this one slider component. We could then `npm install` the slider and use it in whatever project requires it (like the color picker). However, the way I set up the color picker project for this book, all of the components are together in the same project (and in the same chapter 12 folder). So, planning a strategy to accommodate this might be a bit of an odd challenge, but it actually exposes a neat way to run scripts.

We can start by adding two more build scripts into the package.json, as seen in the next listing. Since there are now three in total, we should be a little more specific in how we name them than just "build."

Listing 12.10 Scripts to run each component build

```
{
 "name": "wcia",
 "version": "1.0.0",
```

```
 "dependencies": {},
 "devDependencies": {
   "rollup": "^1.0.2"
 },
"scripts": {
   "build-slider": "./node_modules/.bin/rollup
     chapter12and13/components/slider/src/slider.js --file
     chapter12and13/components/slider/slider.js --format umd
     --name slider -m",
   "build-coordpicker": "./node_modules/.bin/rollup
     chapter12and13/components/coordpicker/src/coordpicker.js --file
     chapter12and13/components/coordpicker/coordpicker.js --format umd
     --name coordpicker -m",
   "build-colorpicker": "./node_modules/.bin/rollup
     chapter12and13/components/colorpicker/src/colorpicker.js --file
     chapter12and13/components/colorpicker/colorpicker.js --format umd
     --name colorpicker -m"
}
```

Rollup task for coordinate picker component

Rollup task for color picker component

You may now be thinking that we have three commands to run instead of the one, but we can combine scripts! The ampersand or double ampersand isn't strictly an `npm` thing. Instead, it's just standard Linux, and we can use ampersands to combine commands in the package.json scripts. A single ampersand runs commands in parallel, and a double ampersand runs them one after another. Additionally, we can reference other scripts by name in any new commands. We're going to add another build task after we finish covering Rollup, so let's not call this new script `build` just yet. Instead, we'll call it `build-rollup`:

```
"build-rollup": "npm run build-slider && npm run build-coordpicker && npm
    run build-colorpicker"
```

With `build-rollup` part of the `npm` scripts now, all three components can be built just by running

```
npm run build-rollup
```

Please note, however, that if you are on Windows, this ampersand approach won't work without using WSL, the Git Bash emulator, or something similar.

12.5 Transpiling for IE

I mentioned an additional build step for our components. As of now, the color picker and two child components work in all major browsers, including Edge if we toggle the Shadow DOM off. As mentioned before, Edge will soon be updated with Chrome behind the scenes and will natively support Web Components.

That leaves us with one problem browser: IE11. It's troubling because of its age and lack of updates. Modern browsers auto update, and web developers typically only have to worry about the latest few versions of each browser. So, we usually get to use the latest features in fairly short order, assuming all of the browsers keep up with each other. The thorn in our side here is IE. As IE11 is the last version that will ever be released, we're stuck with the features it currently has. Some of us web developers have been able to ignore it as a requirement because its usage is so low, and Microsoft recommends Edge now for Windows users. But not all web developers are that lucky, and it's still a requirement.

Not only does IE not support Web Components like the current version of Edge does, but it also does not support ES6/ES2015 language features like classes and fat arrow functions. We discussed transpiling earlier in this chapter as a way to do things like translate a language such as TypeScript or CoffeScript to JS, but we can use it now to solve the IE issue as well by transpiling newer JS to older JS.

12.5.1 Babel

The most popular tool to solve these issues is Babel (https://babeljs.io). We'll need to `npm install` a few packages to make Babel work:

- *Babel Core*—The main feature set of Babel.
- *Babel CLI*—Tooling to use Babel on the command line.
- *Babel preset-env*—Babel can get complicated; this standard setup takes the complicated setup out of Babel configuration.

Let's go ahead and install these as dev dependencies in the root of the project because, like Rollup, this is all just build tooling and won't be part of a component release:

```
npm install --save-dev @babel/core

npm install --save-dev @babel/cli

npm install --save-dev @babel/preset-env
```

After install, since they were saved, these dependencies get added onto the package .json. As of now, the following listing reflects the latest.

Listing 12.11 The latest package.json including Babel dependencies

```
{
 "name": "wcia",
 "version": "1.0.0",
 "dependencies": { },
 "devDependencies": {
   "@babel/cli": "^7.2.3",              <-- Babel command line tooling
   "@babel/core": "^7.2.2",             <-- Babel core library
   "@babel/preset-env": "^7.2.3",       <-- Babel preset environment for easy setup
   "rollup": "^1.0.2",
 },
 "scripts": {
   "build-slider": "./node_modules/.bin/rollup
     chapter12and13/components/slider/src/slider.js --file
     chapter12and13/components/slider/slider.js --format umd
     --name slider -m",
   "build-coordpicker": "./node_modules/.bin/rollup
     chapter12and13/components/coordpicker/src/coordpicker.js --file
     chapter12and13/components/coordpicker/coordpicker.js --format umd
```

```
    --name coordpicker -m",
  "build-colorpicker": "./node_modules/.bin/rollup
    chapter12and13/components/colorpicker/src/colorpicker.js --file
    chapter12and13/components/colorpicker/colorpicker.js --format umd
    --name colorpicker -m",
  "build-rollup": "npm run build-slider && npm run build-coordpicker && npm
    run build-colorpicker",
 }
}
```

With the requirements installed, Babel is super easy to use. Again, like Rollup, since we installed as a local instead of a global dependency, the Babel executable can be found in node_modules/.bin/babel.

Babel does not, however, solve module bundling. For this, we need an extra step. Plugins exist to take care of this extra step as part of the Rollup process. However, we're starting to venture into territory where this entire setup is very opinionated and really depends on the needs of your project. For these components, my opinion is that we should make a different build for IE than what we'd deliver to modern browsers. The reason I think we should have different builds is that it's unnecessary to overburden modern browsers with bulky transpiled code when there's no reason to. But maybe having multiple builds hurts the simplicity of component delivery for you and your team. Ultimately, the choice is up to you, but for right now, I'm deciding on delivering two versions.

Since the Rollup bundle already exists, we can simply use that as a pre-bundled source that gets fed into Babel, so long as we're careful to build it first in the build process. If you're of the different opinion that these components would be better served by a single output file, Rollup can be configured to add this step with some extra configuration. It really depends on your use case and how your component will be consumed. For us, figure 12.5 represents our build pipeline.

A Babel configuration file is needed, however, to use the `preset-env` settings. It's really simple, though. At the root of the project, just create a .babelrc file containing the following:

```
{
 "presets": ["@babel/preset-env"]
}
```

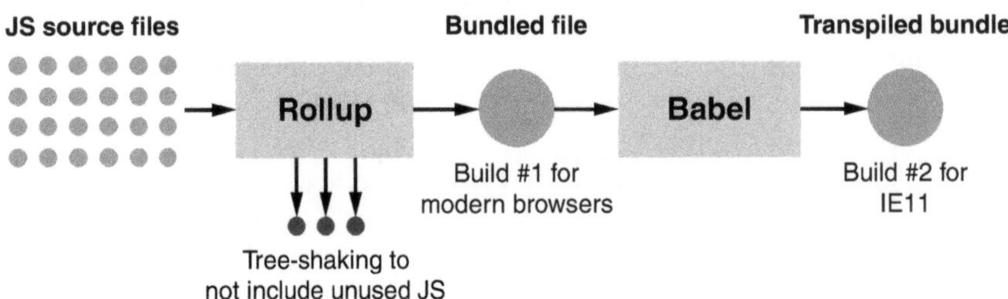

Figure 12.5 The color picker build pipeline includes two builds, one for modern browsers and the other for IE11.

That last bit is all the setup needed to run a Babel transpile. We're just telling it to use the preset Babel settings in one line. Next, to run the command with that setting in place, you'll just need to run the Babel command with an input file and an output file:

```
./node_modules/.bin/babel chapter12and13/components/slider/slider.js
   --out-file chapter12and13/components/slider/slider.build.js
```

The first parameter is the input, and, again, it's the bundled output from Rollup. We'll put the output in the same place, just called something slightly different, like slider.build.js. Surprisingly, unlike many commands you might run, this won't produce any output in your terminal. You can easily verify that this is working by the file it creates.

Just like we did with the three Rollup scripts in the package.json file, we can add scripts for transpiling with Babel. The next listing shows the three new build scripts.

Listing 12.12 A Babel transpile step for each component

```
"build-slider-ie": "./node_modules/.bin/babel
  chapter12and13/components/slider/slider.js --out-file
  chapter12and13/components/slider/slider.build.js",
"build-coordpicker-ie": "./node_modules/.bin/babel
  chapter12and13/components/coordpicker/coordpicker.js --out-file
  chapter12and13/components/coordpicker/coordpicker.build.js",
"build-colorpicker-ie": "./node_modules/.bin/babel
  chapter12and13/components/colorpicker/colorpicker.js --out-file
  chapter12and13/components/colorpicker/colorpicker.build.js",
```

Again, like we did with Rollup, these commands can be combined into a single transpile step using ampersands:

```
"build-ie": "npm run build-slider-ie && npm run build-coordpicker-ie &&
npm run build-colorpicker-ie"
```

Of course, to transpile all three, we could use the terminal and run

```
npm run build-ie
```

Even better, let's create a single script that bundles and transpiles. The next listing shows the complete package.json with a new "build" script.

Listing 12.13 Current package.json with Rollup bundling and Babel transpilation

```
{
 "name": "wcia",
 "version": "1.0.0",
 "dependencies": { },
 "devDependencies": {
   "@babel/cli": "^7.2.3",
   "@babel/core": "^7.2.2",
   "@babel/preset-env": "^7.2.3",
   "rollup": "^1.0.2",
 },
 "scripts": {
   . . . previously added scripts . . .
```

```
    "build": "npm run build-rollup
    ➥&& npm run build-ie"
  }
}
```

New build script that bundles and transpiles all the components

And now, we're back to a sane and easy-to-remember build process. Just use `npm run build` in your terminal, and all three components will be bundled and transpiled so IE can run perfectly!

Since I made the decision to have two different outputs, it makes sense to have two different HTML files, one for IE and the other for everything else. Of course, the file structure has changed with the addition of the source folder. Personally, I think it makes sense to use the original source files instead of the bundled Rollup output, so we can get instant feedback during development. Adding a Rollup "watch" task could do the job as well in a more complex system that's constantly running while you develop, but in the interest of keeping things basic, we'll just change the path slightly in demo.html:

```
<script type="module" src="src/slider.js"></script>
```

To get the IE demo to run, the `<script>` tag needs to be changed even more. As modules aren't supported, it cannot contain `type="module"` anymore. We'll create a different demo file for IE only called demo-ie.html. The `<script>` tag will be the only thing that changes so far:

```
<script src="slider.build.js"></script>
```

Of course, this step will be repeated for the other two components. Figure 12.6 shows the one component's structure with output files.

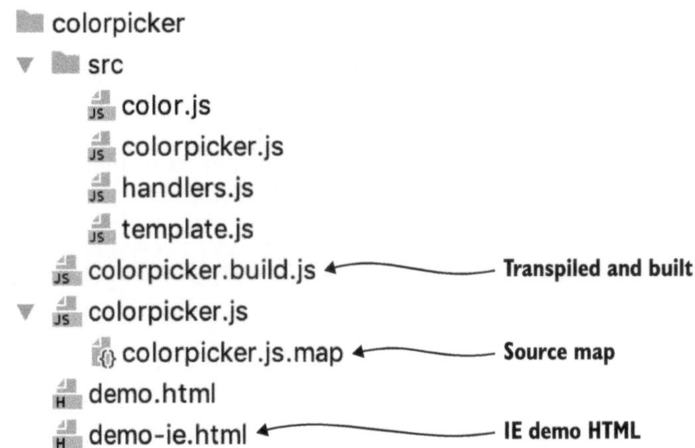

Figure 12.6 Project file structure with bundled and transpiled output. Tools like Webstorm, pictured here, make the JS file look like a directory to hide the complexity of generated files like source maps, even though it's actually a flat file structure.

12.5.2 CSS vars ponyfill

On further review of the components when testing in IE11 using the new demo file, things are a little less than perfect. Figure 12.7 shows some visual discrepancies. Otherwise, everything works just fine.

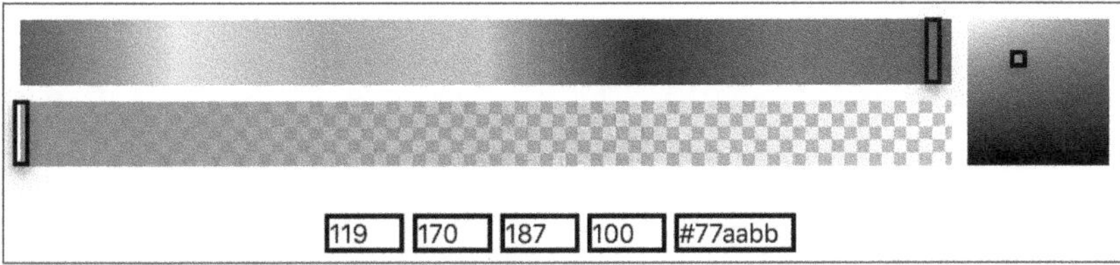

Figure 12.7 Looking a little broken in IE11

This isn't a Web Components problem at all, but we did use CSS vars to make the components flexible in terms of style. CSS vars enabled us to tweak a global border radius, text color, and so on and affect everything on the page. The downside is that it's a newer feature. Even with widespread browser support for CSS vars, IE11 just hasn't added features lately, so it will fail to use them. Does this mean we need to back off CSS vars? Nope—like many features, we can make do. Normally I'd say "polyfill," but in this case, I'll be using a "ponyfill."

To be honest, I hadn't heard of ponyfills prior to researching how to handle CSS vars in IE11. Polyfills tend to modify the runtime environment of the browser. For example, when polyfilling Web Component Custom Elements, a global is created called `customElements` to match modern browsers where this is already present. Adding this global means that we're modifying the browser, specifically adding the features provided to its global space. Ponyfills promise to not modify the browser environment when making unsupported features work.

The CSS vars ponyfill isn't completely drop-in, meaning we'll need to call a function to make it run. First, now that we have a package.json file, let's install the ponyfill with `npm`. Since it is a client-side dependency, we'll save it, but not as a dev dependency like the other build tools:

```
npm install css-vars-ponyfill
```

With this installed, the ponyfill can be added to each demo-ie.html file:

```
<script src="https://unpkg.com/@webcomponents/custom-elements"></script>
<script src="https://cdn.jsdelivr.net/npm/css-vars-ponyfill@1"></script>
<script src="slider.build.js"></script>
```

I'll note that in my `<script>` tag, I'm using an online version just to give some awareness that it exists, but you could use that one or swap in the one that just installed at node_ modules/css-vars-ponyfill/dist/css-vars-ponyfill.js.

As mentioned, the `css-vars-ponyfill` isn't a drop-in solution. We still need to call a function for it to do its job. It works by processing `<style>` tags on the page and swapping in CSS that IE will be able to understand. Since the component CSS isn't available until after setting the `innerHTML` in each one, we'll run the ponyfill after that. The next listing shows the slider component's `connectedCallback` with the CSS vars ponyfill in place.

Listing 12.14 Adding the CSS vars ponyfill to allow existing CSS vars to work in IE

```
connectedCallback() {
   if (!this.initialized) {
        this.root.innerHTML = Template.render({ useShadowDOM:
          Slider.USE_SHADOWDOM_WHEN_AVAILABLE && this.attachShadow });
        this.dom = Template.mapDOM(this.root);
        if ( typeof cssVars !== 'undefined') {
            cssVars();
        }
        this.initialized = true;

        if (this.backgroundcolor) {
            this.setColor(this.backgroundcolor);
        }

        if (this.value) {
            this.refreshSlider(this.value);
        }
   }
}
```

Tests if the ponyfill exists as added through the <script> tag on the demo page

Calls the cssVars function to replace CSS vars in the browser

As we've just placed the script on the page, our usage just dictates that the `cssVars` function is attached to the global space (the opposite of how I described a ponyfill). This solution does exist as a module, however, that we could import and run that way. Here, though, we're giving component consumers an opportunity to use the ponyfill or not based on if they added the script or not. Note that the syntax of how I check is a *little* weird. If I simply checked `!cssVars` when it didn't exist, we'd get an error stating that `cssVars` is undefined, since it's not a property of anything and could be just an undefined variable in the scope we're checking in. So we're being a little more careful in order to not throw the error by looking at its type.

Summary

In this chapter, you learned

- A simple way to run scripts using `npm` and your package.json without having to rely on more complex build systems that require lots of setup
- Reasons for a build step, whether bundling your code for production or transpiling to let newer JS features work in older browsers
- How bundling is good for combining your code into one or more files, while intelligently leaving out unused imports

13 Component testing

This chapter covers

- Running tests with the Web Component Tester (WCT)
- Using Mocha and Chai for creating tests
- Alternate test running with Karma and Karma Web Components

Before we consider the color picker component finished, there is one additional step that should really be taken into account. It's not a step that everyone puts effort into, but testing can go a long way in terms of how much the component can be trusted and how easy it is to maintain. The same can be said for almost anything you make in software development.

Testing can be broken down in many ways, but one of those ways is functional versus unit testing. The lines between these can get fairly blurry, but unit testing typically involves taking a piece of code that does one single thing, or a unit, and running a series of tests on it to make sure it doesn't fall down for some edge case that wasn't considered during development. Functional testing, on the other hand, involves testing a specific piece of functionality that is expected by the user—it's not making sure the code does the right things, only that the application does.

13.1 Unit testing and TDD

In the color picker component, the color conversion utilities in components/color-picker/src/color.js are the perfect candidates for unit testing. For example, in the module, a function exists to convert RGB color to a hex value. A single test might be to ensure that an object that looks like `{ r: 255, g: 0, b: 0 }` produces the output of `#ff0000`. It could work perfectly and in all the right ways, but doesn't error correct when invalid values (like those over 255 or negative numbers) are passed. The practice of writing unit tests is a great way to think of these edge cases.

Unit tests would throw a wide variety of cases at this function, and, if any of them failed, you as a developer would know you have something to fix. Of course, if you did fix it and made lots of changes to do so, you might want to have confidence that you didn't break anything else. So, you'd re-run the unit tests. If they all passed, you'd have confidence that this piece of functionality works as it always has.

Test running can also track code coverage. For example, if there was an `if/then` block in your code, and your unit tests didn't cover a case that happened over both of those conditions, a report would be generated indicating that you didn't cover those specific lines of code.

When people normally think of unit testing, especially outside of web development, unit tests don't often include the UI. Modern web development is where those lines can tend to get blurred. If you think of a component, whether a Web Component or one in React, Vue, Angular, and so on, it will have an API. This API can be thought of as a unit that can be tested. Moreover, lots of JS functionality like this needs to be tested and can't be run without a DOM.

A recent and popular solution to this problem is to completely virtualize the DOM. JSDOM (https://github.com/jsdom/jsdom) offers a completely virtual DOM that runs without a browser or even a graphical interface right in Node.js or the browser. Unfortunately, Web Components aren't yet supported in JSDOM, so it's not a solution that can be used unless you picked apart and tested pieces of your Web Component without actually running it as a component.

Because of this, when testing Web Components specifically, we'll need to fall back to actually using browsers to run the tests. Despite introducing a browser and UI into testing, we can still test discrete "units" of functionality.

Another point of blurriness comes in when thinking about functional testing. These types of tests can be thought of from the user's perspective. When the user clicks a button, something happens that is meaningful to the user, and the output can be tested. These tests can sometimes be mixed right into unit testing, if desired, and if the browser is used to run the test, it's that much easier to do this.

The reason to bring this up is that there are many different testing methodologies and tools. What we'll be discussing here are tools and methods typically thought of as unit tests, or tests that a developer would typically write from the perspective of Test-Driven Development (TDD). These are tests that a developer writes as they write code.

In an ideal world, a developer would create a piece of functionality and would write tests to back up that piece of functionality.

Testing is a broad subject, with many books written about its various aspects. As far as Web Components are concerned, however, I think TDD and unit tests are the most relevant to discuss, given the nuance that we must currently rely on the browser for this, though the expectation might be that a solution like JSDOM could be used.

13.2 Web Component tester

Another reason to explore this type of testing is that Google's Polymer team created a TDD testing tool of their own explicitly for Web Components. This tool is called the Web Component Tester (WCT) and can be found at https://github.com/Polymer/tools/tree/master/packages/web-component-tester. What's great about WCT is that a lot of things are built into it by default, and it's really easy to get up and running.

Testing tools like these are often broken up into a few different parts. For WCT, browser automation is handled by Selenium. Browser automation simply means that the browsers you intend to host your tests in need to be automatically launched from the terminal with the HTML/JS/CSS that runs your tests, and these browsers need to report back to your terminal with the results.

The test framework—Mocha, in WCT's case—is what you'd use as a developer to organize and write your tests. With Mocha, you'd create *suites*, or groups of tests in which each group is filled in with the actual singular tests. Mocha provides hooks to set things up before your tests, hooks to tear things down when your tests finish, so you can run the next test from a clean slate, and lots more functionality.

The last major piece of WCT is the assertion library—in this case, Chai. Assertion libraries are a small but central piece of any testing solution. Basically, an assertion is a question that you ask and expect the answer to be true. A plain English example would be "I expect 1 + 2 to equal 3." That assertion could be paraphrased with Chai by writing

```
assert.equal(1 + 2, 3);
```

Of course, 1 + 2 is always 3, so this assertion would never fail. In practice, you won't see hardcoded values (at least on both sides of the assertion). You'll likely test that a variable or the result of a function equals another variable or another result. For example, you might have a simple function that doubles numbers. Your `doubleNum(num)` function could take a value and double it. To know that it works, you'd want to run a number of assertions, such as

```
assert.equal(doubleNum(2), 4);
```

More complicated functions can and do fail for various reasons, and testing is a great way to catch these cases.

Chai offers different ways to do assertions, but in a nutshell, Chai does this one thing and does it well. Figure 13.1 shows the entire WCT flow.

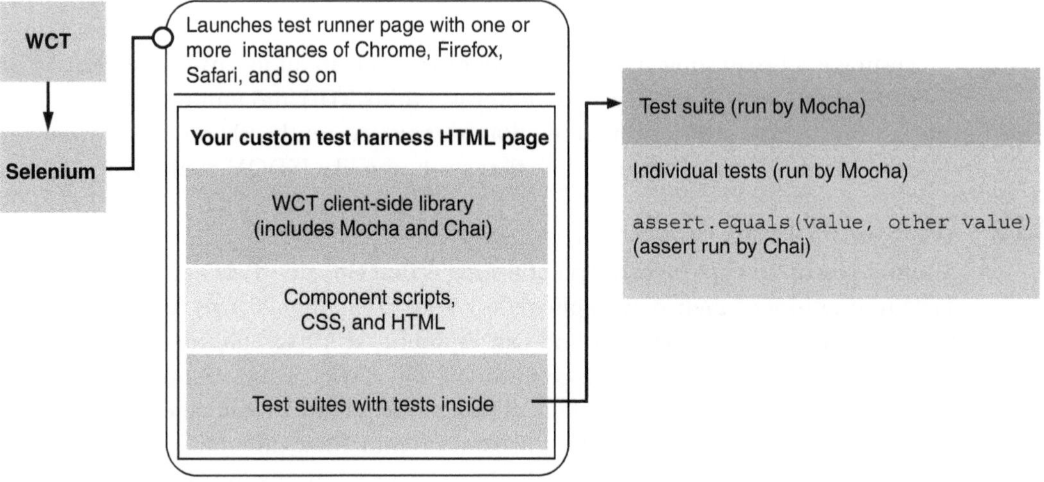

Figure 13.1 The WCT running flow

Installing WCT is easy:

```
npm install --save-dev web-component-tester
```

This is yet another dev dependency that we'll want to run locally from the node_modules/bin folder. I should note, however, that because Selenium is a dependency and uses Java, one of the sharp technical reviewers of this book found that on his Windows 10 setup, running WCT wasn't possible until he downgraded to Java 8. I have a feeling that running different versions of Java will be a moving target on different platforms as multiple dependencies are updated when new versions of WCT and Selenium are released. Ideally, you'll have luck similar to mine and won't even need to think about Java when installing WCT—but in case you don't, your installed Java version is something to pay attention to.

We'll need to run tests against some files, however, so now is the time to create a test folder with a test HTML file for each component. Figure 13.2 shows the new folder structure with new test files.

The HTML file in the new test folder will normally be called something like index.html or index.test.html. But throughout this chapter, we'll be exploring a few different ways to test; so to be clear which is which, I've named this first HTML file wct-test.html. Before creating the actual tests in the file, let's add the script to the package.json file. The following listing shows the latest package.json file after installing WCT and adding the script.

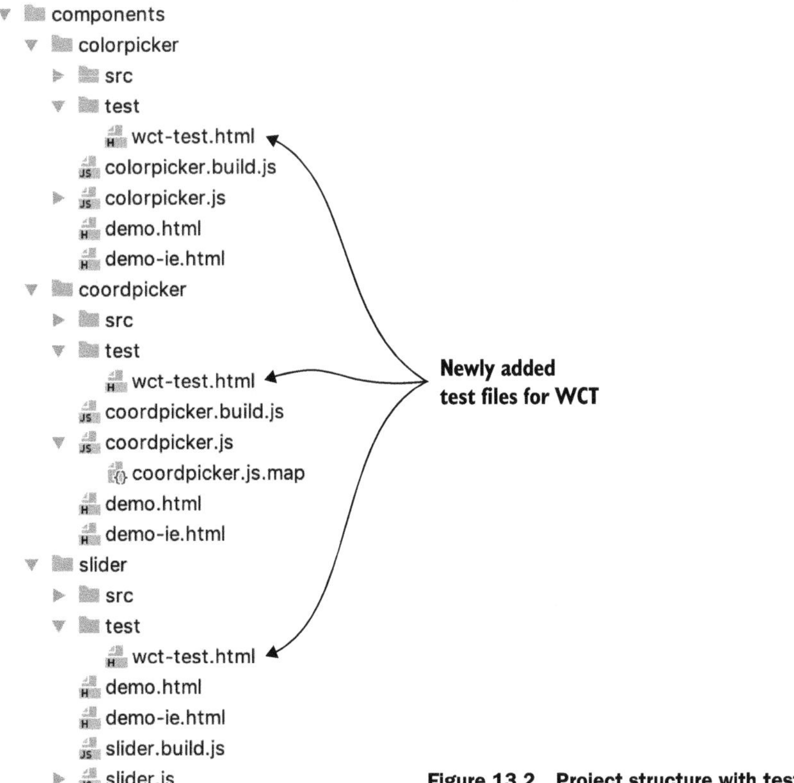

Figure 13.2 Project structure with test files

Listing 13.1 Adding WCT testing to our project's package.json

```
{
 "name": "wcia",
 "version": "1.0.0",
 "dependencies": {
   "css-vars-ponyfill": "^1.16.2"
 },
 "devDependencies": {
   "@babel/cli": "^7.2.3",
   "@babel/core": "^7.2.2",
   "@babel/preset-env": "^7.2.3",
   "mocha": "^5.2.0",
   "rollup": "^1.0.2",
   "rollup-plugin-babel": "^4.2.0",
   "web-component-tester": "^6.9.2"    <-- WCT package
 },
 "scripts": {
   "wcttest": "./node_modules/.bin/wct    <-- WCT script
--npm chapter12and13/components/**/test/wct-test.html",
```

```
    "build-slider": "./node_modules/.bin/rollup
     chapter12and13/components/slider/src/slider.js --file
     chapter12and13/components/slider/slider.js --format umd
     --name slider -m",
    "build-coordpicker": "./node_modules/.bin/rollup
     chapter12and13/components/coordpicker/src/coordpicker.js --file
     chapter12and13/components/coordpicker/coordpicker.js --format umd
     --name coordpicker -m",
    "build-colorpicker": "./node_modules/.bin/rollup
     chapter12and13/components/colorpicker/src/colorpicker.js --file
     chapter12and13/components/colorpicker/colorpicker.js --format umd
     --name colorpicker -m",
    "build-rollup": "npm run build-slider && npm run build-coordpicker &&
     npm run build-colorpicker",
    "build-slider-ie": "./node_modules/.bin/babel
     chapter12and13/components/slider/slider.js --out-file
     chapter12and13/components/slider/slider.build.js",
    "build-coordpicker-ie": "./node_modules/.bin/babel
     chapter12and13/components/coordpicker/coordpicker.js --out-file
     chapter12and13/components/coordpicker/coordpicker.build.js",
    "build-colorpicker-ie": "./node_modules/.bin/babel
     chapter12and13/components/colorpicker/colorpicker.js --out-file
     chapter12and13/components/colorpicker/colorpicker.build.js",
    "build-ie": "npm run build-slider-ie && npm run build-coordpicker-ie &&
     npm run build-colorpicker-ie",
    "build": "npm run build-rollup && npm run build-ie"
  }
}
```

WCT is an extremely easy command to run. Simply run the WCT executable with a file path to one or multiple tests. For our test setup, the HTML files are always found at a specific location within each component folder. Since we want to run all the components with one command, we'll swap the component name with a directory wildcard: `components/**/test/wct-test.html`. Lastly, since we're using `npm` to run, WCT needs the `--npm` flag.

13.2.1 Writing tests

Each HTML test file will have a very familiar setup. Without tests yet, the setup in the next listing looks no different than any other HTML file. The only dependency beyond our component are the browser.js files, which provide all the features and client-side loading of WCT.

Listing 13.2 WCT test file setup

```
<html>
<head>
  <script src="../../../../node_modules/web-component-tester/browser.js">
  </script>     <-- Required WCT testing scripts
  <script       <-- Slider component import
       type="module"
       src="../src/slider.js">
  </script>
```

```
    <style>
        wcia-slider {
            width: 500px;    ◁── Gives the slider some width to
        }                        run size-dependent tests
    </style>
</head>
<body>
<wcia-slider value="50"></wcia-slider>    ◁── The slider component
<script>
// tests go here    ◁── Placeholder for tests
</script>
</body>
</html>
```

As we start writing tests, remember we're being specific to our test framework and assertion library here, Mocha and Chai. Mocha actually has two different styles: TDD and Behavior-Driven (or functional style) Development (BDD). WCT defaults to TDD, which are ideally unit tests you'd write as you create your component. With that said, let's define a group, or suite of tests for the slider component.

Listing 13.3 A start to a test suite for the slider component

```
suite('slider value getting/setting', function() {
    const sliderWidth = 500;
    const thumbCenterOffset = 5/2 + 3; // width/2 + left border
    const slider = document.body.querySelector('wcia-slider');
```

- Defines the width of the slider in preparation for tests (`const sliderWidth = 500;`)
- Defines the slider center to aid in future tests (`const thumbCenterOffset = 5/2 + 3;`)

The first parameter passed to Mocha's `suite` function is the name of the suite of tests. It's really handy to be specific here. The better you name a test, the easier you'll find it when a named test and suite reports a failure in your terminal.

Second is the function containing the tests. While we haven't gotten to defining a single test yet, there is some light setup to do. This is a good chance to step back and think about what functionality needs testing. A slider component doesn't do all that much, really. Given that it's a Web Component, and we spent time to support component reflection, we should be able to set the slider's value with an attribute or with the JS API. Beyond that, the component really only ties its visual state (the thumbnail position) to the numeric percentage value. We can test this aspect, but the position (in pixels) of the thumbnail will depend on the slider component's size.

This is what these two variables enable. First, we specify the slider width, which has already been defined in the CSS on the HTML page. Second, we'll define how much the slider is offset to center it in position by subtracting half its width and the left border size. Lastly, we'll grab a reference to the slider for the tests.

We'll label the first test "slider get initial value." The component, as set up on the page, has a `value` attribute set to 50:

```
<wcia-slider value="50"></wcia-slider>
```

So, with 50% as the initial slider value, the thumbnail should appear in the center of the slider. We can assert three things in this first test, shown in the following listing.

Listing 13.4 A single slider test

```
test('slider get initial value', function () {
   assert.equal(slider.value, 50);
   assert.equal(
     slider.getAttribute('value'), 50);
   assert.equal(slider.root.querySelector('.thumb').style.left, sliderWidth *
     50/100 - thumbCenterOffset + 'px');
});
```

Tests that the slider value as observed by JS is 50

Tests that the slider thumb is in the middle of the component

Tests that the slider value as observed by attribute is 50

First, we're checking that getting the value with JS returns 50. We also need Chai to assert that we're getting the same value from the attribute to prove that reflection works. Next, we'll test the slider's position. Given the value of 50, we can calculate where the thumbnail should be given the component, thumbnail, and border size. Since we know how the slider internally works, we know that the `left` property of the style should be 500 * 50/100 – (5 / 2 + 3), or 244.5 pixels.

There is something very interesting to call out here. Recall back to when we learned about the Shadow DOM. There was some discussion of an "open" versus a "closed" shadow root. Remember that with a closed root, the intended functionality was that no matter how hard we tried, we'd never be able to reach into the component and work with the DOM. The open shadow root was a bit more forgiving because we could get in through the component's `shadowRoot` property, knowing that this back door wasn't the component developer's intention. This back door comes in very handy here. If we couldn't break through the shadow boundary of a Web Component, we couldn't query-select the thumbnail and test it.

The next listing continues on through the remaining few tests for this component.

Listing 13.5 Slider component test suite

```
suite('slider value getting/setting', function() {
    const sliderWidth = 500;
    const thumbCenterOffset = 5/2 + 3; // width/2 + left border

    const slider = document.body.querySelector('wcia-slider');

    test('slider get initial value',
        function () {
            assert.equal(slider.value, 50);
            assert.equal(slider.getAttribute('value'), 50);
            assert.equal(slider.root.querySelector('.thumb').style.left,
              sliderWidth * 50/100 - thumbCenterOffset + 'px');
    });

    test('set slider value with JS',
        function () {
            slider.value = 20;
```

Tests the initial slider value

Tests setting a new value with the JS API

```
            assert.equal(slider.value, 20);
            assert.equal(slider.getAttribute('value'), 20);
            assert.equal(slider.root.querySelector('.thumb').style.left,
              sliderWidth * 20/100 - thumbCenterOffset + 'px');
    });

    test('set slider value with attributes',
        function () {
            slider.setAttribute('value', 30);
            assert.equal(slider.value, 30);
            assert.equal(slider.getAttribute('value'), 30);
            assert.equal(slider.root.querySelector('.thumb').style.left,
              sliderWidth * 30/100 - thumbCenterOffset + 'px');
    });
});
```

Tests setting a new value with attributes

We can now run these tests with `npm run wcttest`. Figure 13.3 shows an example of what you'd see in the terminal when running with a few more tests that we'll add in a bit. Note that the passing tests are nice and green!

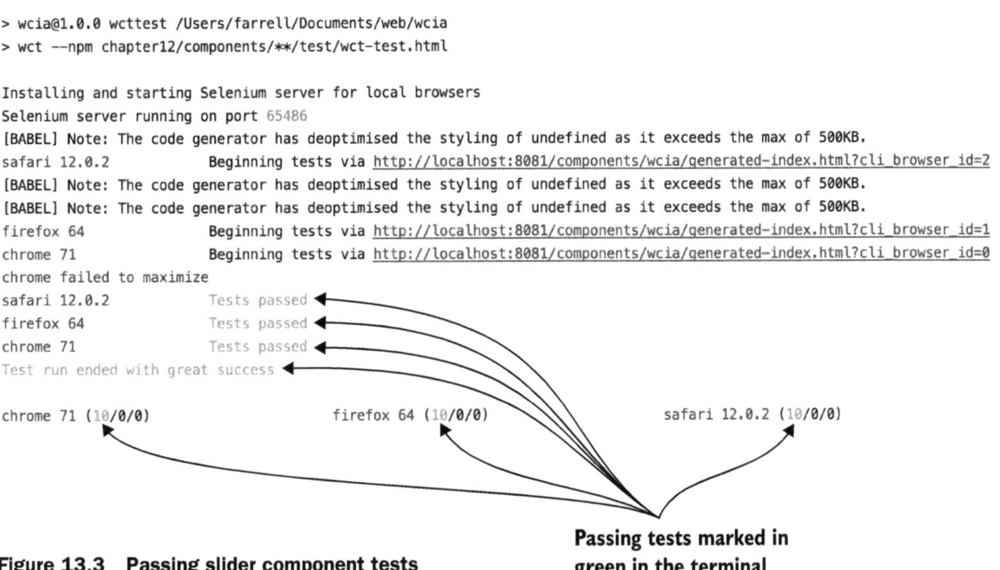

> wcia@1.0.0 wcttest /Users/farrell/Documents/web/wcia
> wct --npm chapter12/components/**/test/wct-test.html
Installing and starting Selenium server for local browsers
Selenium server running on port 65486
[BABEL] Note: The code generator has deoptimised the styling of undefined as it exceeds the max of 500KB.
safari 12.0.2 Beginning tests via http://localhost:8081/components/wcia/generated-index.html?cli_browser_id=2
[BABEL] Note: The code generator has deoptimised the styling of undefined as it exceeds the max of 500KB.
[BABEL] Note: The code generator has deoptimised the styling of undefined as it exceeds the max of 500KB.
firefox 64 Beginning tests via http://localhost:8081/components/wcia/generated-index.html?cli_browser_id=1
chrome 71 Beginning tests via http://localhost:8081/components/wcia/generated-index.html?cli_browser_id=0
chrome failed to maximize
safari 12.0.2 Tests passed
firefox 64 Tests passed
chrome 71 Tests passed
Test run ended with great success
chrome 71 (10/0/0)
firefox 64 (10/0/0)
safari 12.0.2 (10/0/0)
Passing tests marked in green in the terminal

Figure 13.3 Passing slider component tests

It's also helpful to show some failed tests! The practice of writing these tests as you develop forces you to start thinking of weird edge cases to test. The slider component is a simple one, but there are some easy ways to make it fail. Think of what would happen when setting the slider value to more than 100 or less than 0. Doing this makes no sense in terms of the slider's visual display—so, ideally, we should restrict the slider with max and min values. Let's add two more tests in the next listing to make it fail, assuming this restriction is in place.

Listing 13.6 Failing slider tests because max and min values aren't yet implemented

```
test('set slider value too big', function () {
   slider.setAttribute('value', 110);
   assert.equal(slider.value, 100);
   assert.equal(slider.getAttribute('value'), 100);
   assert.equal(slider.root.querySelector('.thumb').style.left, sliderWidth *
     100/100 - thumbCenterOffset + 'px');
});
```

Slider value is over 100, so it should be coerced back to 100.

```
test('set slider value too small', function () {
   slider.setAttribute('value', -10);
   assert.equal(slider.value, 0);
   assert.equal(slider.getAttribute('value'), 0);
   assert.equal(slider.root.querySelector('.thumb').style.left, sliderWidth *
     0/100 - thumbCenterOffset + 'px');
});
```

Slider value is less than 0, so it should be coerced to 0.

With the tests failing, as figure 13.4 shows, we've defined some functionality that we need to implement. A good exercise for you to try later is to tweak the slider component in a way that these and the previous tests all pass.

In addition to the homework I just gave you, there are three other components to get cracking on! I've written some tests myself if you get stuck. If so, feel free to visit this book's GitHub repo.

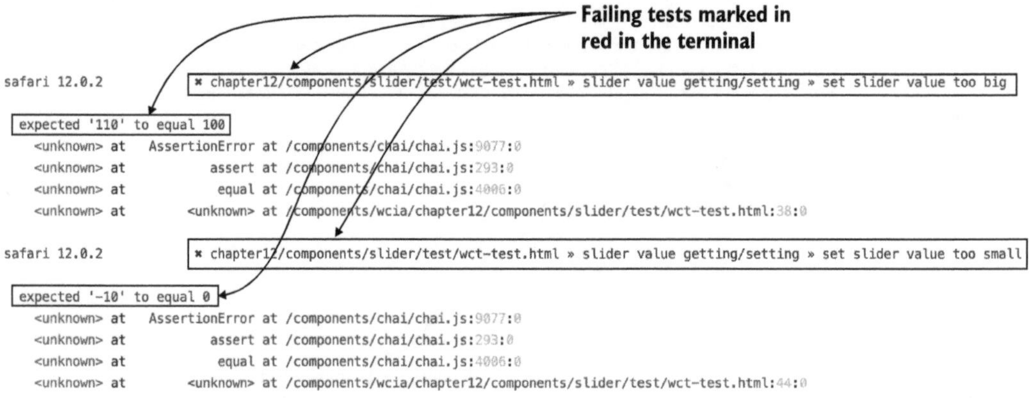

Figure 13.4 Failing slider tests

13.3 Comparing to a standard test setup with Karma

WCT is fairly nice! The setup was extremely minimal and allowed us to focus on writing tests without fumbling over complicated configurations, though a configuration could be added if there were defaults you didn't care for. More details can be found at https://github.com/Polymer/tools/tree/master/packages/web-component-tester.

The bottom line, though, is that WCT is intended for Web Components, and bundles some key things to test them. For one, the Web Component polyfills are bundled in and automatically included, should they be needed in your HTML test fixtures. WCT also waits for your components to be ready by waiting for the browser's `WebComponentsReady` event. Also provided is a helper for using `<template>` tags in your tests.

WCT is still new, though, and a work in progress. If it works for you, great! If it doesn't work for you, and you'd rather use a different setup, that's OK too. What's great is that with modern browsers now supporting Web Components, there really aren't any gotchas with simple Web Component tests. They just work like any other web feature.

With this in mind, let's try swapping out test runners. We'll replace Selenium with Karma but keep Mocha and Chai. This keeps all our tests the same and gives us all the flexibility and plugins that come with the Karma ecosystem. Figure 13.5 highlights our new test runner flow with Karma.

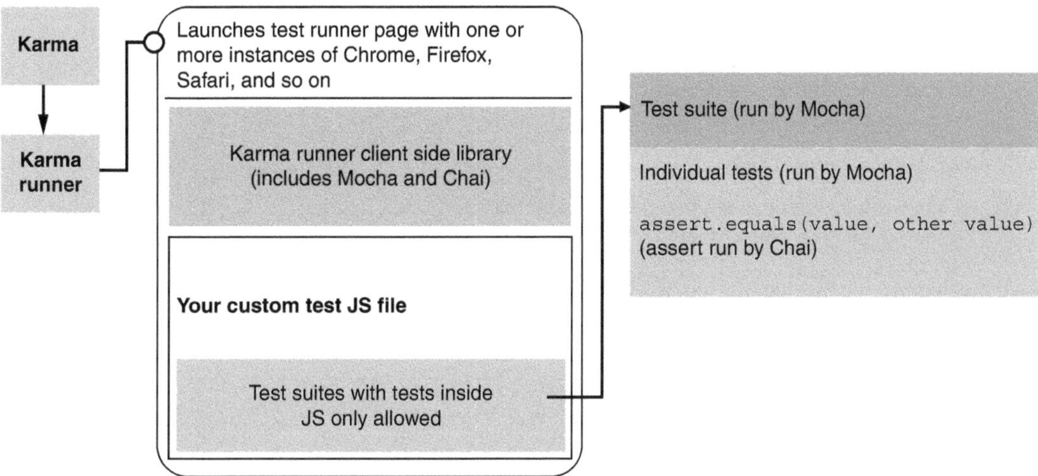

Figure 13.5 A new test runner flow with Karma

The downside of a Karma-based setup, however, is that we'll need to deal with a bit of complexity to set it up. For starters, let's install a few things with `npm`:

```
npm install --save-dev karma
npm install --save-dev mocha
npm install --save-dev chai
```

Mocha and Chai won't run in Karma without a plugin to bridge the gap, so we'll install those as well:

```
npm install --save-dev karma-mocha
npm install --save-dev karma-chai
```

Karma also needs plugins to launch browsers and run our tests:

```
npm install --save-dev karma-chrome-launcher
npm install --save-dev karma-firefox-launcher
```

There are a few other dependencies as we get rolling, but these are the basics. One last thing to do is to again install Karma, but globally, and I'll explain why:

```
npm install -g karma
```

This global install has nothing to do with running your tests. Instead, it provides a command line utility to generate a configuration file. Running `karma init` from your project root after the install gives a series of prompts and questions, as figure 13.6 shows.

```
Which testing framework do you want to use ?
Press tab to list possible options. Enter to move to the next question.
> mocha

Do you want to use Require.js ?
This will add Require.js plugin.
Press tab to list possible options. Enter to move to the next question.
> no

Do you want to capture any browsers automatically ?
Press tab to list possible options. Enter empty string to move to the next question.
> Chrome
> Firefox
>

What is the location of your source and test files ?
You can use glob patterns, eg. "js/*.js" or "test/**/*Spec.js".
Enter empty string to move to the next question.
>

Should any of the files included by the previous patterns be excluded ?
You can use glob patterns, eg. "**/*.swp".
Enter empty string to move to the next question.
>

Do you want Karma to watch all the files and run the tests on change ?
Press tab to list possible options.
> no
```

Figure 13.6 Karma init questions

It's not imperative that you follow what I did exactly, because we'll be changing some options around as we go. The good thing here is that we have a karma.conf.js baseline file to work with. The next listing shows the initial configuration.

Listing 13.7 Initial Karma config (condensed by removing blank lines and comments)

```
module.exports = function(config) {
 config.set({
   basePath: '',
   frameworks: ['mocha'],
   files: [],
   exclude: [],
   preprocessors: {},
   reporters: ['progress'],
   port: 9876,
   colors: true,
   logLevel: config.LOG_INFO,
   autoWatch: false,
   browsers: ['Chrome', 'Firefox'],
   singleRun: false,
   concurrency: Infinity
 })
}
```

The very first thing to worry about is the use of modules in our Web Components. WCT allowed us to ignore this part of setup, but when we roll a testing setup ourselves, it's our problem now. Modules and imports don't work easily because Node.js is working for us behind the scenes to handle a lot of test running. Node itself doesn't support modules yet. So, we'll need to run a "preprocessing" step before components get loaded on the page and run tests.

Rollup was covered in the last chapter, so let's use it again! As I write this, Rollup has just moved beyond a 1.0 release. Ordinarily, I'd recommend installing `karma-rollup-preprocessor`. Unfortunately, we're at an inconvenient gap in support where this module doesn't support the latest Rollup version. This can happen every so often when packages fall out of sync with each other, especially with so many working parts. Luckily, I was able to hunt around and find that someone forked this original project and made something that *does* work with the latest version. Perhaps soon, we won't have to use this fork, but until then, you can install

```
npm install --save-dev @metahub/karma-rollup-preprocessor
```

Because of the `@metahub` package namespace, the default loading of any plugin with a name starting with "karma-" doesn't work here. As annoying as this might be, it does walk us through a piece of nonstandard setup, which is par for the course when working on a Karma configuration from scratch. With this in mind, a `plugins` entry needs to be added to the config file:

```
plugins: ['@metahub/karma-rollup-preprocessor', 'karma-*']
```

As we're overriding defaults here, karma-* needs to be added back into the list as well. We'll also add an entry to the preprocessors list to map the JS files to Rollup:

```
preprocessors: {
    './chapter12and13/components/**/*.js': ['rollup']
}
```

Here, we're likely rolling up more than necessary, as there are multiple JS files but only one JS entry point for each component. The path could be more exact, but I'm not too worried about shaving a few microseconds off of the preprocessing time.

Rollup, or plugins in general, needs to be configured as well. The following listing shows a Rollup configuration that will work for us in the karma.conf.js file.

Listing 13.8 Rollup plugin configuration in Karma

```
rollupPreprocessor: {
 options: {
      output: {
          // To include inlined sourcemaps as data URIs
          sourcemap: true,    <-- Turns on sourcemaps
          format: 'iife',     <-- Bundles format
          name: 'testing'     <-- Bundles package name
      }
 }
},
```

Source maps might not sound necessary here, but that's only if your tests pass. If they fail and need debugging, you'll really want to know what line failed in your original, nonbundled source. Bundling as IIFE literally means "immediately invoked function expressions." Do we want our bundle to immediately invoke after loading and create the Web Component definition right away? Yes, please. This works great for testing and is inclusive of how the component was built previously with Rollup. With UMD-style bundling before, this option and more were allowed (hence the "universal" part of the name). The bundle name doesn't matter too much here, but it's required, so "testing" works fine.

Two last simple adds are Chai to the frameworks we need to use,

```
frameworks: ['mocha', 'chai'],
```

and also a configuration to tell Mocha to use TDD-style testing:

```
client: {  mocha: {  ui: 'tdd'  } }
```

Now, as we get back to not-so-simple stuff, there needs to be a plan for what files Karma will serve. With WCT, it was really nice that tests could run from an HTML file. We'll loop back around to that in a bit, but as is, Karma only sort of supports HTML tests like this. The problem is that Karma loads HTML files using HTML Imports. Since Chrome is the only browser that supports this deprecated feature (and soon won't), it's also the only browser that could run our HTML test pages. With this in mind, if no other plugins are used, we'll need tests as JS files, and the file patterns to serve will look like this:

```
files: [
  './chapter12and13/components/**/test/karma-test.js',
  './chapter12and13/components/**/*.js'
],
```

This file pattern serves all component JS files and also component tests named karma-test.js, which we still need to create. Even though we're using a different runner, we're still using Mocha and Chai, so all the tests previously made can be copied over. There is just a bit more setup in the next listing with a JS-only test file, and that is to programmatically attach the component scripts, create the component, and add it all to the page body.

Listing 13.9 A JS-only test file created in the test folder for each component

```
suite('slider value getting/setting', function() {
   const sliderWidth = 500;
   const thumbCenterOffset = 5/2 + 3; // width/2 + left border
   const container = document.createElement('div');
   container.innerHTML = `<script type="module" src="../src/slider.js">
                          </script>
                          <wcia-slider style="width: ${sliderWidth}px"
                           value="50"></wcia-slider>`;      <- Puts the component and component script inside a container
   document.body.appendChild(container);                    <- Adds everything to the page body for testing
   const slider = container.querySelector('wcia-slider');

   test('slider get initial value', function () {
       assert.equal(slider.value, 50);
       assert.equal(slider.getAttribute('value'), 50);
       assert.equal(slider.root.querySelector('.thumb').style.left,
     sliderWidth * 50/100 - thumbCenterOffset + 'px');
   });
});
```

You can refer to this book's GitHub repo to see all of these new JS tests in place for all the components, but listing 13.9 does highlight the only real differences using the slider component as an example.

Now is a great time to try running the tests! As before, a script called `test` added to the package.json file would be a more apt name, but since we're giving a few different types of tests a spin, it can be called `karmatest`:

```
"karmatest": "./node_modules/karma/bin/karma start karma.conf.js"
```

This script simply tells Karma to start test running against the config file we just created. We need to flip one thing in the configuration to get it running normally. Before we do, running `npm start karmatest` kicks off the browsers in the `browsers` entry inside the Karma configuration and shows figure 13.7 while the browser is paused in place after running the tests.

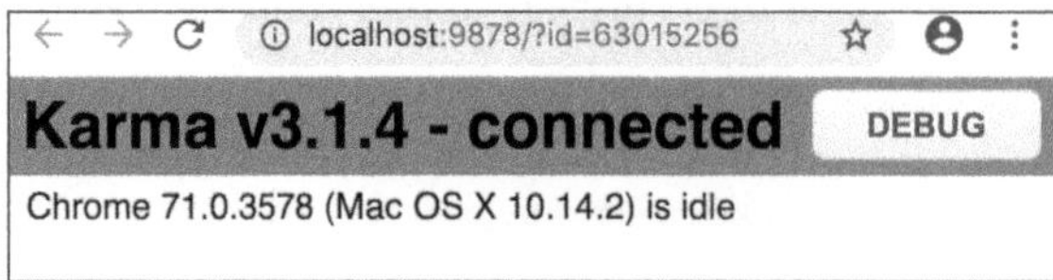

Figure 13.7 Karma test runner page

The reason to pause here is that it gives us an opportunity to press the Debug button and see the tests running in context. We can open up the browser's dev tools like normal and see test output, look at the elements on the page, and debug any errors shown. Figure 13.8 shows this debug mode, though, again, it's really just the browser with dev tools open.

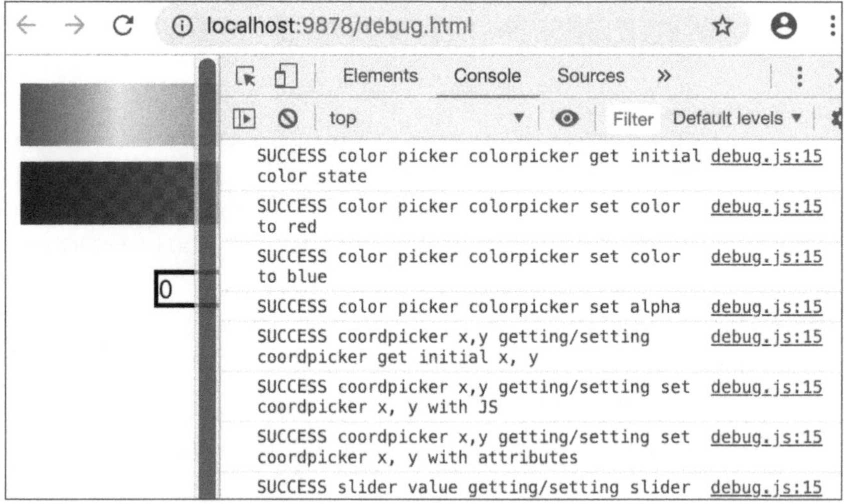

Figure 13.8 Karma debug page

Assuming everything works, and we don't need to debug, it's desirable to have Karma fire up the browsers, run the test, and then quit everything. To do this, we just need to flip the `singleRun` entry in the Karma configuration from false to true:

```
singleRun: true
```

Even better, we have the option to not see the browsers pop up on the screen at all if the "headless" versions are supported by the Karma launchers like Chrome and Firefox are. Note that it's not Karma alone that supports this. Both normally installed versions of these browsers offer a headless mode, and the Karma launchers are simply tapping into this:

```
browsers: ['FirefoxHeadless', 'ChromeHeadless'],
```

The next listing reviews all of the options we changed in the Karma configuration to make the Karma/Mocha/Chai tests possible.

Listing 13.10 Final Karma configuration

```
module.exports = function(config) {
 config.set({
   basePath: '',
   plugins: [          <-- Added plugins for Rollup and re-added default karma-*
       '@metahub/karma-rollup-preprocessor',
       'karma-*'],
   frameworks: ['mocha', 'chai'],   <-- Added Chai
   files: [                         <-- Added specific files for our setup
     './chapter12and13/components/**/test/karma-test.js',
     './chapter12and13/components/**/*.js'
   ],
   exclude: [],

   preprocessors: {     <-- Added Rollup preprocessor and configuration
       './chapter12and13/components/**/*.js': ['rollup']
   },

   rollupPreprocessor: {
     options: {
         output: {
             sourcemap: true,
             format: 'iife',
             name: 'testing'
         }
     }
   },
   reporters: ['progress'],
   port: 9876,
   colors: true,
   logLevel: config.LOG_INFO,
   autoWatch: false,
   browsers: [       <-- Changed to headless versions of browsers
        'FirefoxHeadless',
        'ChromeHeadless'],
   singleRun: true,        <-- Changed to true
   concurrency: Infinity,
   client: {          <-- Added TDD testing
       mocha: {
           ui: 'tdd'
       }
   }
 })
};
```

Now hopefully when running `npm start karmatest`, you'll see all green—successful output in your terminal! There were quite a few moving parts to get right here, and it takes a bit of trial and error when configuring it all by yourself; but the benefit over WCT is that you have a lot more control and a significant number of compatible plugins with a testing setup like this that's been around for a while.

The only part that's a little sad in this is the lack of being able to use an HTML test file like in WCT. Personally, that's my favorite piece of the WCT ecosystem. Fortunately, there's a Web Component-specific Karma plugin!

13.3.1 Karma Web Components

The `karma-web-components` plugin does a few things, but mostly it allows us to use HTML test files again like WCT does. We happen to have done well with load-timing issues in the tests run so far; but `karma-web-components` also listens for your browser's `WebComponentsReady` event before tests start, just to ensure everything is in place for tests to succeed.

The first thing to do is install the plugin:

```
npm install --save-dev karma-web-components
```

Next, we can add on to each component's test folder an extra file called karma-wc-test.html. For the slider component, the next listing shows what's inside.

Listing 13.11 HTML test file for use by the `karma-web-components` plugin

```
<html>
<head>
    <script          <- Component module import
        type="module"
        src="../src/slider.js">
    </script>
    <script src="../../../../node_modules/karma-web-components/framework.js">  <- Framework provided by karma-web-components
    </script>
    <style>
        wcia-slider {
            width: 500px;
        }
    </style>
</head>
<body>
<wcia-slider value="50"></wcia-slider>   <- Slider component on page
<script>
// Same exact tests and test suite we've had in the others
</script>
</body>
</html>
```

Like WCT, the `karma-web-components` plugin needs to load client-side. But that one script file is the only thing that needs to change on this page versus the WCT test page. It's a different library to load, but the entire test setup can remain the same. Figure 13.9 shows the updated test runner flow. It looks a lot like the WCT setup again.

Back in the Karma configuration file, we'll need to add the plugin to our existing list:

```
frameworks: ['mocha', 'chai', 'web-components'],
```

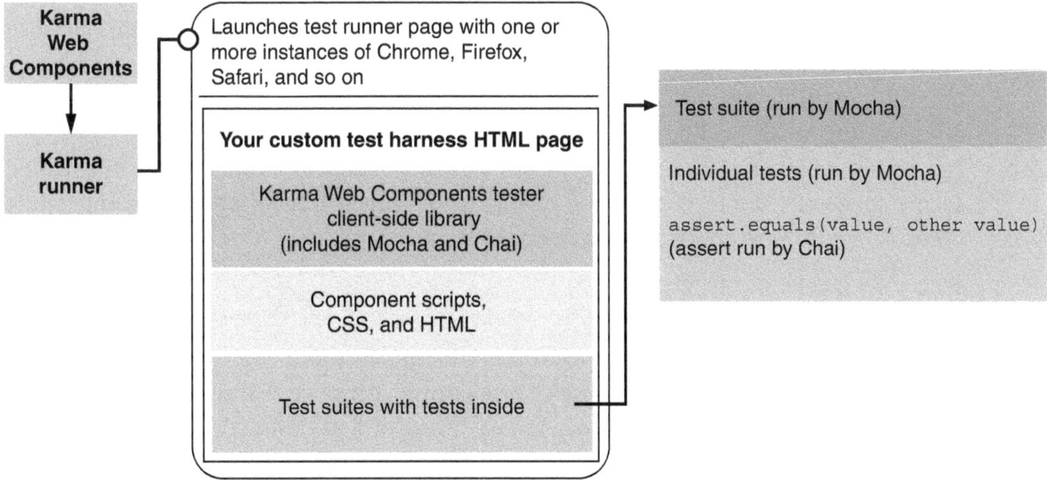

Figure 13.9 Karma Web Components test runner flow

The only other difference is that the files will need to be served in a slightly different way, as the following listing shows.

Listing 13.12 File-serving Karma configuration to use `karma-web-components`

```
files: [
  './chapter12and13/components/**/src/*.js',
  './node_modules/karma-web-components/framework.js',
    {
        pattern: './chapter12and13/components/**/test/karma-wc-test.html',
        watched: true,
        included: false
    }
],
```

Of course, the existing Web Components files need to still be served. Also required is the `karma-web-components` client-side framework. Lastly, the HTML file containing the tests needs to be served, but we'll also need to adjust a couple of settings. The `included` flag should be `false`, so the HTML files aren't automatically loaded in the browser. Previous examples have been a bit lazy and inexact in including files that don't need to be loaded before. The difference here is that, if it's included, your test run will break.

13.3.2 Multiple tests in the same project

That last `karma-web-components` example meant modifying the Karma configuration slightly. Instead of modifying the default one, I wanted to leave both Karma configurations in place. In this book's GitHub repo, you'll be able to run WCT, the Karma test runner, and the Karma test runner with `karma-web-components`, all from the same project.

It's a lot to cover, and while one of these would suffice, there's no single standard way to set testing up. Every project has different needs and will likely require a bit of work to tweak everything to your liking. Covering a few different methods in this chapter will hopefully get your setup far enough along that you'll at least be able to research any tweaks you'll need to make.

That's why, in my repo, the `karma-web-components` setup is in a file called karma.conf.webcomponents.js. The `npm` script to run it has yet another name, while pointing to this new configuration in the parameters:

```
"karma-wc-test":
  "./node_modules/karma/bin/karma start karma.conf.webcomponents.js",
```

You won't have all these similar tests in the same project, but you could have different types of tests running different things. For example, for pure JS unit tests only, with no need to rely on the browser, I like to use Tape and JSDOM. And I might have a Karma/Mocha/Chai setup for the tests that I do need to run in the browser. My point is that while I've gone out of my way to include redundant tests in this project, the notion of having several separate test runs in one project is fairly normal.

13.3.3 A note on Safari

There is one last thing to call out here. Windows developers won't be able to run tests on Safari anyway, but macOS users should expect to. In my examples, I did not install `karma-launcher-safari`. Typically, "Safari" is another browser you can add to the Karma configuration file. Currently, this Karma launcher is a bit broken when running on Apple's newest OS, Mojave. Safari will launch, but will require user intervention to give permission to load Karma's test harness. This is an open issue as I write this chapter (https://github.com/karma-runner/karma-safari-launcher/issues/29). In this book's GitHub repo, I'm now using karma-safarinative-launcher instead of karma-safari-launcher as a workaround. To use this custom launcher, the only thing necessary to add to the karma.conf.js file is the following:

```
customLaunchers: {
  Safari: {
      base: 'SafariNative'
  }
},
```

With this in place, you can now test with Safari in your karma.conf.js browsers list:

```
browsers: ['FirefoxHeadless', 'ChromeHeadless', 'Safari'],
```

Ideally, though, this workaround will not be needed as the issue gets resolved in the original launcher package. Until then, we can roll with this!

Summary

In this chapter, you learned

- What the different styles of testing are and the benefits of TDD when writing components
- Three different ways of test running to show the diversity of options available
- Ways to think of your code in units and develop tests for each unit

14 Events and application data flow

This chapter covers

- Creating your own Custom Events versus using the DOM's native events
- Event bubbling for the two event types, including using the `composed` option to bubble through the Shadow DOM
- The `WebComponentsReady` event and the `customElements.isDefined` promise for handling timing
- Using a centralized data model and an event bus to handle data flow throughout an application

As we get closer to the end of our Web Component journey together, there really isn't much left to cover in terms of Web Component features. That said, when contrasting what we've learned thus far in this book against a modern framework, Web Components may feel a little lacking in some areas.

14.1 Framework offerings

While Web Component features are now part of standard web specifications, things like data binding, routing, and model-view-controller (MVC) style application design patterns are not! To be honest, it would be kind of silly if they were. The web is a big place, and we're not all doing applications. Even if we were, application developers will typically pick the right design pattern for a specific project. Native features that favor certain ways of doing application development would likely not be a welcome addition.

In fact, we almost had some incredibly basic native underpinnings for data binding with the JS feature `Object.observe`, which allowed listening to changes on a JS object (figure 14.1). Popular frameworks, however, ended up not adopting it because it didn't fit with their specific solutions for data binding and application state management.

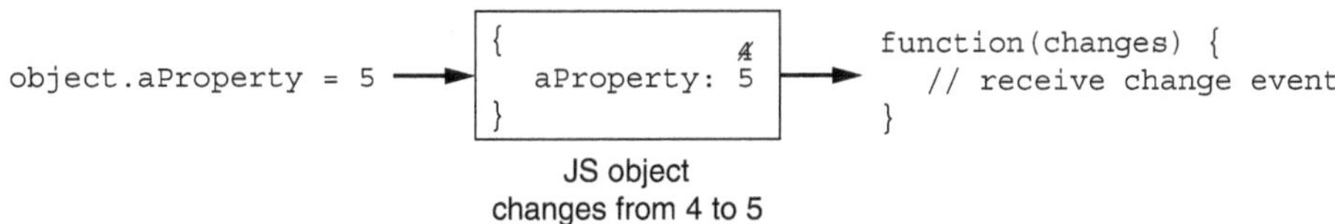

Figure 14.1 Deprecated data binding feature: `Object.observe`

Even though it makes sense that these types of features aren't part of plain JS Web Components, a framework can and will pick a favorite way to offer them, especially when the typical application-oriented user needs some or all of them. This enables some great tutorials and amazing examples that are in lockstep with each other and are great for beginners.

Given the diverse nature of Web Component usage, it's likely there will never be one application design pattern to rule them all. You won't see massive numbers of blog takes on the same design patterns being used for Web Components, at least not anytime soon. This lack of crystal-clear direction is why Web Components can feel a bit lacking to some, especially when making a project decision and inevitably comparing a framework to any no-framework solution, including Web Components.

There is good news, however. Common features of modern frameworks are now more interchangeable than ever. Take the application state management library Redux. Redux is so strongly associated with React that it might lead you to believe that the two can't be separated. Some assume that if you use React, you have to use Redux. Conversely, people might assume that Redux can't be used anywhere besides React. This is an artifact of those amazing demos, blog posts, and tutorials created by the React community pairing the two. In fact, some React developers have started using other state management libraries, like MobX.

My point is that there is a wide variety of interchangeable solutions that the major frameworks use already; it's just not immediately obvious when researching a framework. This ongoing effort to make a library like Redux work in React, Angular, Vue, and plain JS will only help us Web Component developers.

Even better, you might not need a complex library like Redux to help manage your application. In this chapter, we'll improve chapter 10's exercise planner to adopt some extremely simple and custom-built application design patterns. You might wonder why you'd put thought into design patterns, or even where to start. Like any solution, it starts with a problem that needs to be solved.

14.2 Events

I think it's fair to say that underneath every complicated application architecture or framework, there is some sort of custom message passing. It could have lots more moving parts built on top of that, but at a very basic level, it all starts with some kind of event, like the click of a button or the change of an input field. A message is generated to communicate this change, and then something happens as the result of that event. So, let's start at the beginning.

14.2.1 Native events and WebComponentsReady

Not much needs to be said about native events. We've been using them throughout the book when we listen to button clicks, input element changes, and so on. These are events that the browser generates itself by way of the DOM.

Since you're already familiar with native events, I want to give a questionable example of a native event that relates to some code you might find when researching Web Components. It hasn't been mentioned because it's not needed much for daily use; it's not officially even a Web Component feature but is only available through a polyfill. It's used like a native event, however, so let's explore! The following listing shows an extremely basic example to test the `WebComponentsReady` event.

Listing 14.1 `WebComponentsReady` event

```
<html>
<head>
   <title>Web Components Ready</title>
   <script src="https://unpkg.com/@webcomponents/webcomponentsjs@2.0.0/
              webcomponents-loader.js"></script>
   <script>
       document.addEventListener(
              'WebComponentsReady', function(e) {
           console.log('components ready');
       });

   </script>
</head>
</html>
```

Web Components polyfill

WebComponentsReady event listener

This event simply allows you to be notified when Web Components as a whole are ready on the page. Readiness really just means that any Web Component definitions created can be applied to the elements on the page. For example, a custom

`<sample-component>` element you've made is an `HTMLUnknownElement` without defining it with `customElements.define`.

I did say that this was a questionable example, however. True native events are generated by the browser. While this event is used as if it were generated by the browser, it's not. It's generated by the polyfill. Can this be called a native event if it is used like one and looks like one? What's more, it might be a bit confusing that it looks like such a core feature of Web Components when used—you would expect it to fire even without the polyfill. Why is it only available when polyfilling?

When the browser natively supports Web Components, specifically the Custom Element API, components are ready instantaneously. When not supported and using a polyfill, however, it takes time to load the polyfill and allow the Web Components to define themselves. An even worse situation was when HTML Imports were the preferred way to create Web Components. It takes time to load the desired HTML Import as well. While waiting for these things, it might not be wise to interact with components on your page. The `WebComponentsReady` event lets you know when it's safe.

This sounds useful, but in reality, it's rarely used. For one, when using a modern browser where polyfills aren't needed, Web Components will instantly be ready. Second, these timing issues just don't seem to come up much. We've been organizing our Web Components in this book by creating one big component that represents the application and comprises child components. Though we do interact with these child Web Components and assume they are ready from the start, they wouldn't even exist if the main application component wasn't already created. And, of course, that main application component gets instantiated only when Web Components are ready.

Additionally, the `WebComponentsReady` event is not part of the Web Components specification. Without including the polyfill, the ready event won't be triggered, simply because it doesn't exist normally!

Despite its lack of everyday usefulness (though it has been helpful for some testing setups), I did want to bring it up for a few reasons. First, it comes up fairly often in online searches, to the point where it's a bit confusing to determine whether it's a real Web Component event or just from the polyfill. Second, it demonstrates a "native event." Though it might be a bit weird to call it native due to the fact that it's generated from a polyfill, it still comes from the DOM—specifically, the `document` object in our example. We'll contrast this to Custom Events next. Lastly, it gives us a good segue into a related Web Component function (a real one this time).

14.2.2 When custom elements are defined

I'm stretching things a bit to include a "promise" under a section on events. But if you know what a promise is, it accomplishes a similar thing as an event; and this particular promise lets us talk about a better way to handle Web Component timing issues if we run into them.

Promises are pretty basic JS functionality. Creating them from scratch is easy, but using one that already exists is even easier. We've explored two out of the three features of the Custom Element API in this book so far:

- `customElements.define(<tag name>, <class>, <options>)` lets us give life and assign behavior to a custom element name.
- `customElements.get(<tag name>)` returns the class associated with an existing custom tag. We've used this to determine if a custom element has already been defined. Hint: if it returns undefined, it's not defined.
- `customElements.whenDefined` is the last one, and we'll discuss it now.

Instead of getting a ready event for when Web Components as a whole are generally ready, it might make more sense to listen for when a specific Web Component has been defined, especially when we may want to delay the loading of JS modules or entire bundles because we're not using a particular set of components just yet. We might want to be alerted when particular components are ready, even when other components have been running for quite some time.

With this in mind, we can see an example of `customElements.whenDefined` in action in the next listing.

Listing 14.2 Using a promise to detect when a specific component is defined

```
<html>
<head>
   <title>Custom Elements When Defined</title>
   <script>
       class SampleComponent        <—— A very simple component class
               extends HTMLElement {
           constructor() {
               super();
               this.attachShadow({mode: 'open'});
               this.shadowRoot.innerHTML = 'my component';
           }
       }                                Waits 2 seconds, then
                                        defines the component
       setTimeout( function() {    <—
           if (!customElements.get('sample-component')) {
               customElements.define('sample-component', SampleComponent);
           }
       }, 2000);

   customElements.whenDefined(   <——  Creates a promise that alerts
     'sample-component').then( ()=>{   us when the web component
       console.log('defined now!');    has been defined
   });
   </script>
</head>
<body>
<sample-component></sample-component>
</body>
</html>
```

Thanks to this last `customElements` feature, we have a real way to take or delay action until we know that a specific Web Component is properly working.

14.2.3 Custom Events

Native events are great, but if you do web development, you've likely been using them as a daily part of your work for ages for things as simple as listening to a mouse click. So, there's really nothing exciting about them.

Custom Events are several years old, and they are far from a secret; but if they aren't part of your web development repertoire, they probably should be! Before getting into message passing throughout an application where we'll be using Custom Events, let's quickly cover some basic usage.

What exactly do they enable you to do? Well, just like native events, they allow you to receive messages and take action. Like a mouse click event, I could listen for a Custom Event and do something when the event fires. Unlike with native events, we can generate and trigger the event ourselves. In the last chapter's color picker, for example, instead of watching for attribute changes as we did, we could instead create our own event that triggers when the component's color or alpha changes as a result of us using the component. With Custom Events, we control the contents of the event, the name of the event to listen for, and the timing of when it gets fired.

There are three basic things to do when it comes to working with Custom Events. The first is to create the event. We'll create it by using the `CustomEvent` constructor. The constructor takes the name of the event as the first parameter and then another, optional object with event options and details as the second parameter:

```
const event = new CustomEvent('myevent', { detail: { message: 'hi', number: 5 } });
```

Just like native events, we have the same `detail` object for custom key/value pairs. The `detail` property likely isn't widely used by most people with native events. Since the browser generates native events, it's all planned ahead of time with specific key/value pairs on the event object itself. For example, we can get the click location from the `clientX` and `clientY` properties with a normal native click event:

```
document.addEventListener('click', function(e) {
   console.log(e.clientX, e.clientY)
})
```

We can get `e.detail` as well. This property, for the mouse click specifically, holds the number of times the element is clicked. It seems kind of random to have this value be in a variable named `detail`, and that's exactly what it is: random. It would seem that the `detail` property just contains whatever custom property data is needed and maybe wasn't properly planned for from the start.

This seems a bit weird for native events, where the browser controls everything. But the `detail` property is a core concept for Custom Events, where we do have custom data that needs to be passed, like our previous sample data.

With the event created, it's not going anywhere until we trigger or, more formally, *dispatch* it. Like native events, Custom Events are dispatched from the DOM (the document or elements within). With this in mind, let's dispatch from the document:

```
document.dispatchEvent(event);
```

The last basic step for working with Custom Events is to finally listen for the event! This is where we can treat it like any native event you've ever worked with, just with a unique event name and custom data in the detail object. We should set up the listener before we dispatch the event, so we have that listener in place when it's triggered. The following listing shows the entire simple example.

Listing 14.3 Custom Event creation, dispatching, and listening

```
<html>
<head>
   <title>Custom Events</title>
   <script>
       document.addEventListener(            <- Event listener and callback function
               'myevent', function(e) {
          console.log('The message', e.detail.message, 'with number',
                        e.detail.number);
       });

       const event = new CustomEvent(         <- Creates the new Custom Event
               'myevent', {
                   detail: {   <- Custom detail object holding properties we are passing through
                    message: 'hi',
                    number: 5 }
       });

       setTimeout( function() {  <- Triggers/dispatches the event, but waits 2 seconds to prove that the callback waits for the event
           document.dispatchEvent(event);
       }, 2000);

   </script>
</head>
<body>

</body>
</html>
```

Since we're logging output to our console in this example, if you try to run this, open it in your browser's dev tools as you do. The custom properties of `message: 'hi'` and `number: 5` get carried over all the way through to the console.log when the event callback is triggered. We can also dispatch the event using a timer. The timer just better proves to us in this example that the event callback is actually being triggered from the event itself.

14.2.4 Custom Event bubbling

Dispatching and listening for an event all from one element is fine and all, but one nuance with Custom Events is that they don't "bubble" by default. When we say *bubble*, it means that the event passes through many DOM layers, and any of them could be listened to for the event. For example, when clicking on a button, the click goes through the button and then to its parent, to the parent's parent, and all the way up to the page's root. Each element that the click passes through could generate its own click event if you chose to listen for it.

Native events, like a click event, do this by default. Custom Events don't. So, we'll need to help them along. We'll show this in practice with the next listing by adding an additional element for the Custom Event to pass through.

Listing 14.4 Custom Event bubbling

```
<html>
<head>
   <title>Custom Event Bubbling</title>
   <script>
       document.addEventListener('myevent', function(e) {
           console.log('The message', e.detail.message, 'with number',
                        e.detail.number);
       });

       const event = new CustomEvent('myevent', {
           bubbles: true,          <-- Turns on bubbling
           detail: {
               message: 'hi',
               number: 5
           }
       });

       setTimeout( function() {
           document.getElementById('target')      <-- Dispatches the element
                       .dispatchEvent(event);          through another <div>
       }, 2000);

   </script>
</head>
<body>
   <div id="target"></div>      <-- The additional <div> to
</body>                              pass the event through
</html>
```

Listing 14.4 will work, but only because we've added the `bubbles: true` option to the Custom Event's second parameter. Without it, if you chose to comment it out in this example, the event would start and stop at the `<div>` with the ID of `"target"`. If the event listener were added to that `<div>` instead of the document, the example would work fine because it wouldn't need to bubble up to get captured.

14.3 Passing events through Web Components

While native events and Custom Events are fairly simple concepts when considered at a feature level, event-passing strategies in general can be numerous and complex. One of those complexities arises when working with Web Components and the Shadow DOM.

The following listing starts with a simple Web Component example that does not use the Shadow DOM. It only contains a clickable button.

Listing 14.5 Web Component example with a click listener on the containing document

```
<html>
<head>
   <title>Web Component Events</title>
   <script>
       class SampleComponent extends HTMLElement {
           connectedCallback() {
               this.innerHTML =          <— Button inside Web Component
                   '<button>Click me</button>';
           }
       }

       customElements.define('sample-component', SampleComponent);

       document.addEventListener(        <— Click event listener on document
               'click', function(e) {
           console.log('was clicked', e.target, e.currentTarget,
                       e.composedPath());        <— Console logs the event
       });                                           origin and path
   </script>
</head>

<body>
<sample-component></sample-component>
</body>
</html>
```

Typically, in this book, we've been listening to click events and similar things within the component itself. However, in listing 14.5, we're listening to the click event on the overall document, but this event originated inside the component. We're relying on the ability of the click event to bubble through the component to the document.

Clicking anywhere in the page would trigger the callback. But if the event can come from anywhere, can this extremely nonspecific event listener be useful if you don't know where the click came from?

It turns out that we can know exactly where it originated. When clicking on the button in our Web Component, the `event.target` property is logged as `<button> Click me</button>`. This `target` is the first stop of the click before it bubbles up through the rest.

It's also not always useful to know where the click came from—rather, we want to know the actual element that we added the event to. We can get this by using `event .currentTarget`. In our example, we add the event to the document, and that's exactly what we get when we log `event.currentTarget`.

Also interesting is `event.composedPath()`. Note that this is a function rather than a property. Calling this function will return the complete path that the event bubbles through. In our example, this gives us

```
[button, sample-component, body, html, document, Window]
```

Note that it starts on the button we clicked, passes through the Web Component, through the `body` and `html` elements and `document` object, and ends on the very root of everything: the `Window` object. Again, however, note that we aren't using the Shadow DOM just yet!

14.3.1 *Native event propagation through the Shadow DOM*

Recall the two Shadow DOM modes mentioned earlier in this book, closed and open. If you remember, closed wasn't recommended because it makes things a bit more difficult to work with while not offering any real security as was intended. Despite this, it's worth mentioning another minor difference between closed and open.

In the next listing, we've changed the simple Web Component slightly to include the Shadow DOM. Everything else is the same, including the button and the event listener on the document.

Listing 14.6 Web Component with Shadow DOM and a click listener on the document

```
<html>
<head>
  <title>Shadow DOM Events</title>
  <script>
      class SampleComponent extends HTMLElement {
          connectedCallback() {
              const shadow = this.attachShadow(    <- Uses Shadow DOM this time
                      {mode: 'open'});
              shadow.innerHTML = '<button>Click me</button>';
          }
      }

      customElements.define('sample-component', SampleComponent);

      document.addEventListener('click', function(e) {
          console.log('was clicked', e.target, e.currentTarget,
                          e.composedPath());
      });
  </script>
</head>

<body>
<sample-component></sample-component>
</body>
</html>
```

Looking at the console log now, `event.currentTarget` is still the same: the document that we added the event listener to. Different, however, is `event.target`. This shows as the Web Component element `<sample-component>`. The Shadow DOM is hiding the fact that the click originated from the button inside the component. It's not completely hiding it, though. When we look at `event.composedPath()`, we see

```
[button, document-fragment, sample-component, body, html, document, Window]
```

With the exception of the additional document fragment layer that represents the shadow boundary, everything is still the same. We see that the event originates on the `<button>` inside the component and propagates through.

If we change the Shadow DOM mode to `closed`, though, we don't even get the full `composedPath`. It starts at the `<sample-component>` element:

```
[sample-component, body, html, document, Window]
```

This seems par for the course when dealing with the closed versus open Shadow DOM, right? The open mode closes things off enough to not do anything bad accidentally, but is open enough to have workarounds if you know you are going against the intended workflow. Recall that we can't query-select elements inside the Shadow DOM from the outside, except when we go through the `shadowRoot` property. This seems pretty similar. We can look at the `event.target` to see where the event originates, but when the Shadow DOM prevents us from getting the full picture, we can look at `event.composedPath()`. The closed mode doesn't make any of this easy, despite not really being secure.

14.3.2 Custom Event propagation through the Shadow DOM

Custom Events have one more thing to do to escape the Shadow DOM. In addition to needing to set `bubbles` to `true` to bubble up through the DOM, we'll also need to set a property called `composed` to `true` as well. Without setting `composed` to `true`, the event just won't bubble out of the Shadow DOM and hit any parent components or elements.

The next listing builds on the last example, where we passed a click event through the Shadow DOM. Instead of directly passing the click event on, we'll listen for the event in the component and generate a custom event that we'll pass instead.

Listing 14.7 Passing a Custom Event through the Shadow DOM

```
<html>
<head>
  <title>Shadow DOM Custom Events</title>
  <script>
     class SampleComponent extends HTMLElement {
        connectedCallback() {
           const shadow = this.attachShadow({mode: 'open'});
           shadow.innerHTML = '<button>Click me</button>';
           shadow.querySelector('button').addEventListener(
                 'click', e => {
                    const customEvent = new CustomEvent('myclick', {
                    bubbles: true,
                    composed: true,
                    detail: {
```

When button is clicked, generates a new Custom Event to dispatch

```
                                message: 'hi',
                                number: 5
                            }
                    });
                    shadow.dispatchEvent(customEvent);
                })
            }
        }

        customElements.define('sample-component', SampleComponent);

        document.addEventListener(        <—— Listens for the custom myclick event
                'myclick', function(e) {
            console.log('was clicked', e.target, e.currentTarget,
                        e.composedPath());
        });
    </script>
</head>

<body>
<sample-component></sample-component>
</body>
</html>
```

While the example works just fine, and the message gets logged, removing either `bubbles: true` or `composed: true` would disable everything. We've covered `bubbles: true` previously in this chapter. As Custom Events don't bubble by default, they'd never make it out of the Web Component, Shadow DOM or no.

The `composed` boolean is required in addition to `bubbles`. Just because the event bubbles does not mean it will make it through the shadow boundary. This property enables breaking through the boundary.

What actually gets logged is exactly the same as before, except for the composed path when using the open Shadow DOM mode. The button is no longer part of the path, of course, because the Custom Event is now being generated from the component's shadow root. So now, the logged `event.composedPath()` is

```
[document-fragment, sample-component, body, html, document, Window]
```

Event bubbling is great, but it can have some major shortcomings when trying to pass messages to objects that aren't part of the same ancestry. We'll explore this in a bit, as it's really an application architecture problem. As a beginning step, let's improve on the Workout Creator application from chapter 10 to make it usable as a real application.

14.4 Separate your data

Let's recap what we accomplished so far on the Workout Creator application in chapter 10. As that chapter highlighted, working with the Shadow DOM and CSS, the functionality within was mostly visual. We had created a list full of exercises to choose from on the left half of the application. Each exercise in the list was an exercise Web Component populated with unique data. Clicking on any one of them would add that exercise to the plan on the right side of the application.

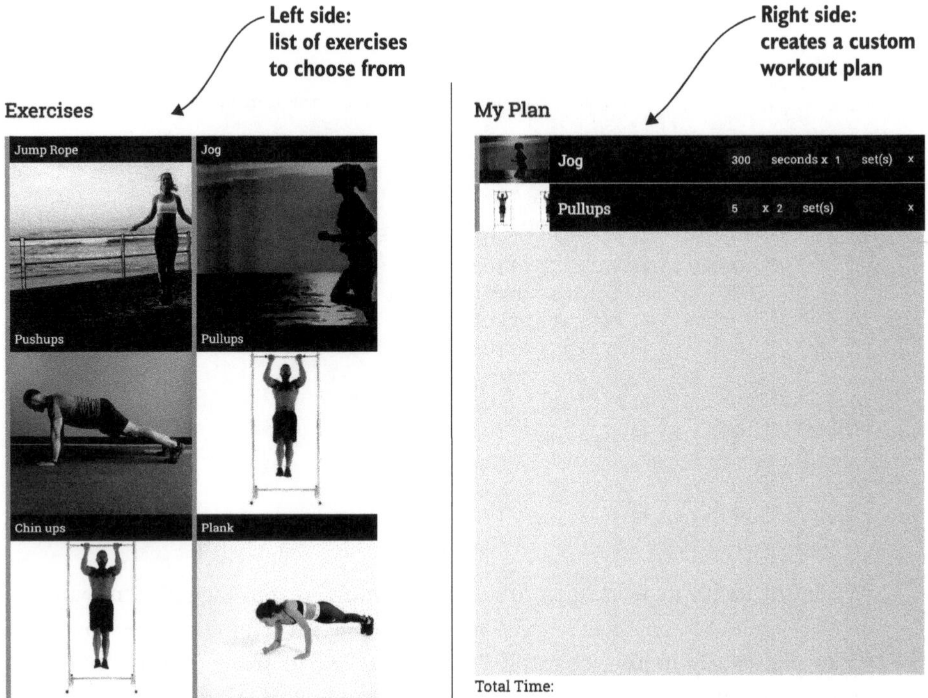

Figure 14.2 Workout Creator application recap

Once in the workout plan, each exercise had some UI for adjusting the number of times to do each rep or set or adjusting the overall number of seconds to do the exercise. There was also a button on the right of the exercise to delete it from your plan. Not much of this UI was functional yet, though!

If you look back at the `exerciselibrary` component, shown on the left side of figure 14.2, it didn't do all that much. It simply rendered a list of available exercises. Any clicks to add the exercise weren't handled here, either—the event was bubbled up to the `workoutcreatorapp` component. We'll change this soon and actually handle the event properly, but the point is that this `exerciselibrary` component barely does anything. The following listing shows this component, though it cuts the big exercise list short for brevity.

Listing 14.8 Exercise library component

```
import Template from './template.js';

export default class ExerciseLibrary extends HTMLElement {
   constructor() {
       super();
       this.attachShadow({mode: 'open'});
       this.shadowRoot.innerHTML = Template.render([
```

```
            { label: 'Jump Rope', type: 'cardio', thumb: '', time: 300, sets: 1}, <-
            ... more exercises ...  ]);
        }
}

if (!customElements.get('wkout-exercise-lib')) {
    customElements.define('wkout-exercise-lib', ExerciseLibrary);
}
```

Shortened exercise list

Although placing this huge array of exercises inline as a parameter to the function that renders the HTML does work, it's bad practice. When you think about it, if you wanted to add another exercise or edit what you have, how would a person who is not familiar with the project know where to look? Why would this list necessarily be in this particular component versus the `workoutcreatorapp` component, or exist as a static getter from the exercise component?

14.4.1 Model-view-controller

None of these components are especially good for storing data like this. A core practice of a design pattern like MVC is that it separates your model, view, and controller. While we haven't paid close attention to MVC in this book, we've already separated out the view from our controller logic.

To define some terms, the *view* is presentational. It's the visual aspect of your application, component, or however you slice things up. Given that we are dealing with a web application, the view will likely be HTML and CSS. We've been using a separate Template import in our recent Web Component, which only holds the HTML/CSS, or the view.

The *controller* is the piece in the middle. It will handle all the logic between your model and view. It reacts to changes in the UI like button clicks or input field changes and updates the model accordingly. The *model* in this case is simply our list of exercises.

Models typically hold a bunch of data, provide access to that data, or both. A JSON object *could* be a data model, but then it's up to the developer to know how to interface with the underlying data. For example, listing all the users' names from a hypothetical model might sound easy, until you realize that the JSON object is a bit weird, and you'd need to loop through lots of objects and child objects, finding the name object, and then concatenating a first name and a last name property. In this case, a data model could provide a nice function to do that for you. Or, if the data needs to come remotely through a REST API, the data model could handle the network requests for you to get exactly what you need through some sort of asynchronous function that looks like a simple targeted function.

MVC, and design patterns in general, aren't always (or usually, in my experience) so clear cut. We use them as references to draw from, inspire our application architecture, and communicate those ideas to our team, but never adhere to them at all costs or at the expense of common sense.

In this component, for example, our controller doesn't react to any UI changes (yet). Our data doesn't change, either. So really, in this particular example, the controller just doesn't do much to the view or model other than pass it on. That doesn't mean we can't take inspiration from the MVC design pattern, however. We can remove the data from our controller or component class to have a proper separation of concerns.

Let's create a new folder in our project source called data. We'll create a new JS file here called exerciselibrary.js. Figure 14.3 shows the new project structure, and listing 14.9 shows the new exerciselibrary.js data model.

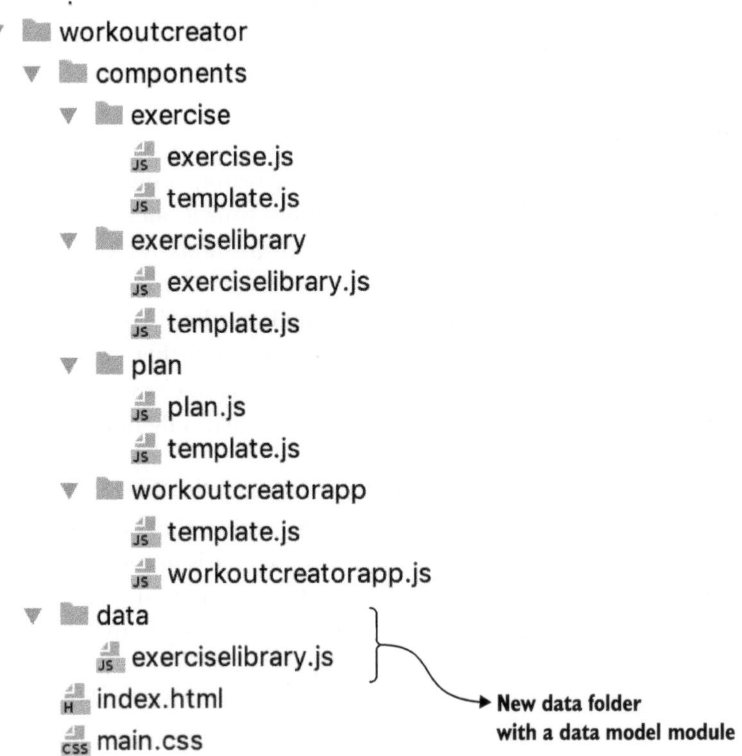

Figure 14.3 Project structure with the new data folder

Listing 14.9 Data model for the exercise library

```
export default {
   get all() {        <— Getter function to retrieve exercises
        return [      <— Actual (shortened) list of data
            {
                label: 'Jump Rope',
                type: 'cardio',
```

```
                thumb: '',
                time: 300,
                sets: 1
            }
        ... more exercises here ...
        ]
    }
}
```

When we separate this file out to the new data folder, it becomes pretty obvious where another developer would go to edit the exercises. Also important is that we could grow the component more, adding new features as we need them, and it wouldn't become a code spaghetti mess of a logic and data. We can also feel free to space things out a little more in the data file using more lines. As the file now just contains data, readability of this data is the most important thing here, unlike before, where component setup and logic were the most important things.

You might ask yourself why this needs to be JS. Why can't it be a JSON file we load at runtime? Well, it certainly could be! However, we've already started a bit of an API with that first `all` getter function. If we had way more exercises, we could use this data model to include some filters, search, pagination, and more. Also, given that it's not a class and is globally accessible, we could easily use this data model as a single source of the exercise library from anywhere in the application.

We could also include a load function within this module to load up that JSON file as well, or even pull from a REST-based API. While we won't introduce these extra features here, it paves the way for editing our workout plan.

14.4.2 Local storage

While extra features might be nice in the exercise library, it goes a little above and beyond a simple demo for this book. It really can be a static, non-changeable list to make our application function. The workout planner, on the other hand, actually does need some extra attention.

Recall that the workout planner is an editable and customizable list containing a personal workout routine. Given that the data represents just a single workout routine for the entire application, it can also be a single centralized data model available everywhere, just like the exercise library. The extra attention required will be to provide ways to add, remove, and edit items, as well as save the entire list, making it possible to reload a previously saved plan after you've closed the browser.

To make saving and loading possible, we'll use a feature that's been around for a while called *local storage*, or *web storage*. Using it is simple. We take a string of data (yes, strings only) and save it using a specific name, or a key:

```
localStorage.setItem("mykey", "a string");
```

Reading is equally simple:

```
localStorage.getItem("mykey");
```

Any key name used is unique to an *origin*. An example origin would be http://mysite.com, which includes the protocol, the domain name, and the port number (default port if not specified). A key named `mykey` would return different data if used on http://mysite.com than on http://anothersite.com. This means that we can also list all the keys for the current site and won't get back lots of stuff that is not relevant to us:

```
Object.keys(localStorage);
```

With this in mind, let's create a data model like the workout library, but which allows us to save, edit, load, add, and remove data. Listing 14.10 has all these features, but most importantly, it keeps track of the current core exercise list used anywhere in the application that needs it. This aspect will become super important in a bit as we add the ability to view and play back the workout.

Listing 14.10 Central data model for workout plan

```
export default {
   get saved() {        // Method to get a list of all saved exercise plans
       const savedplans = [];
       Object.keys(localStorage).forEach(function(key){
           savedplans.push(key);
       });
       return savedplans;
   },

   save(name) {         // Saves current workout plan to local storage
       localStorage.setItem(name, JSON.stringify(this._currentWorkout));
   },

   load(key) {          // Loads a workout plan from local storage by name
       this._currentWorkout = JSON.parse(localStorage.getItem(key));
   },

   edit(id, key, value) {   // Edits a specific workout plan using a unique ID for reference
       let exercise;
       for (let c = 0; c < this._currentWorkout.length; c++) {
           if (id === this._currentWorkout[c].id) {
               exercise = this._currentWorkout[c];
               exercise[key] = value;
           }
       }
   },

   add(exercise) {      // Adds an exercise to the workout plan and assigns it a unique ID for later reference
       if (!this._currentWorkout) {
           this._currentWorkout = [];
       }
       exercise.id = this.createID();
       this._currentWorkout.push(exercise);
   },

   remove(id) {         // Removes an exercise from the plan, referenced by ID
```

```
        if (!this._currentWorkout) { return; }
        for (let c = 0; c < this._currentWorkout.length; c++) {
            if (this._currentWorkout[c].id === id) {
                const deleted = this._currentWorkout.splice(c, 1);
                return;
            }
        }
    }
}
```

Let's also add on a few more convenience methods that will help elsewhere in the application, as we continue this listing.

Listing 14.10 Central data model for workout plan (continued)

```
clear() {                                  <-- Clears all exercises
    this._currentWorkout = [];                 from the plan
},

get exercises() {                          <-- Read-only getter for
     if (!this._currentWorkout) {              current exercise plan list
         this._currentWorkout = [];
     }
     return this._currentWorkout;
},                                         Method to create a unique
                                           ID for each exercise
createID() {  <--
         return 'xxxxxxxx-xxxx-4xxx-yxxx-xxxxxxxxxxxx'.replace(/[xy]/g,
         function(c) {
         var r = Math.random()*16|0, v = c == 'x' ? r : (r&0x3|0x8);
         return v.toString(16);
    });                                    Getter for total duration of
 },                                        the exercise list to display
                                           the time in the UI
get totalDuration() {  <--
  let ttlTime = 0;
  for (let c = 0; c < this._currentWorkout.length; c++) {
      ttlTime += this.getDurationOfExercise(this._currentWorkout[c]);
  }
  return ttlTime;                          Formats the number of seconds into
},                                         an easier-to-read format including
                                           hours, minutes, and seconds
formatTime(seconds) {  <--
  return new Date(1000 * seconds).toISOString().substr(11, 8);
}
```

The prior save, edit, delete, and load functionality was a fairly standard set of things to help manage a list. This next set of functions in the continued listing are there to add some additional help functions used both inside and outside this data model.

Creating a unique ID is important because when adding multiple exercises that could be exactly the same type, it's important to be able to differentiate between them when removing or editing a specific one—thus we generate a unique ID every time an exercise is added. To create a unique ID, I've simply copied some code from online that generates UUIDs (universally unique IDs). These IDs have a standard format and an extremely high probability of being unique no matter how many you generate. Having something that is so long and that has this exact formatting is probably overkill for this application, but it's easy enough to copy over and include here.

Convenience methods like getting the total duration for the set of exercises and formatting time consistently are important to centralize here as well. No, it's not that hard to do either of these, but they will be done quite a bit from multiple places. It's important to not repeat code like this, or else different implementations might accidentally become inconsistent as code gets tweaked over time. Plus, if we suddenly wanted a different time format, we could change it once in this central location.

Clearing the data seems a bit too simple to have a separate function here when all it does is set the data to an empty array. But it paves the way to do more complex things in the `clear` function when your application grows while still allowing users of this data model to perform the same action.

Now that the underlying data model has been created, it's a great time to improve our UI to interact with it! To save time and space in this chapter, I'll say that this is a great opportunity to add on to the component class yourself, though if you get stuck, the final project is available in this book's GitHub repo. That said, I'll cover the major points right now.

14.4.3 Wiring UI to the data model

Buttons to save, load, and clear the list of exercises can be added to this component's HTML, found in components/plan/template.js. Additionally, we can even render a menu to allow the user to choose from available workout plans in this same template file. By importing the module WorkoutPlanData from `'../../data/workoutplan.js'`, a function can generate all the names of saved plans and put them in a list for the user to choose from, as seen in the following listing.

Listing 14.11 Function to generate saved plans from the data model

```
renderSavedPlans() {
   const saved =
     WorkoutPlanData.saved;     <-- Gets a list of saved workout plan names
   let options = '<option value="none">Load a saved plan</option>';
   for (let c = 0; c < saved.length; c++) {     <-- Loops through each plan name and creates an option
       options += `<option value="${saved[c]}">${saved[c]}</option>`;
   }
   return `<select id="menu">     <-- Returns the final select menu full of options
             ${options}
           </select>`;
},
```

Once the buttons and the menu are made available in the HTML, we can add event listeners to them in components/plan/plan.js. By importing the `WorkoutPlanData` module from `'../../data/workoutplan.js'` here as well, we can add the click events in the next listing.

Listing 14.12 Workout plan click listeners for saving, loading, and clearing the plan

```
this.dom.saveButton.addEventListener(
     'click', e => {
   WorkoutPlanData.save(this.dom.planName.innerText);
});

this.dom.clearButton.addEventListener(
     'click', e => {
   WorkoutPlanData.clear();
});

this.dom.menu.addEventListener('change', e => {
   WorkoutPlanData.load(this.dom.menu.value);
});
```

Saves the current exercise list with a specific name that the user specified

Clears the current list of all exercises

When the user selects a menu item from the list of saved plans, loads that plan

Figure 14.4 shows the state of the workout plan after adding this additional UI, but what hasn't changed from chapter 10 is how the exercise is added to the visual list. Clicking on an exercise adds it just fine to the component, but since the data model is new, it is out of sync with the visuals. Attempting to remove an added exercise, for example, wouldn't actually do anything because the exercise doesn't exist there. This model will be where all the different pieces of our application are tied together, so making everything go through this central place is a must!

This is easy to fix. Formerly, the `workoutcreatorapp` component (components/workoutcreatorapp/workoutcreatorapp.js) contained a click listener and `onClick` method that used the `add` function on the workout plan component to add a new exercise. Back in chapter 10, I said this would be temporary. We can take it out right now.

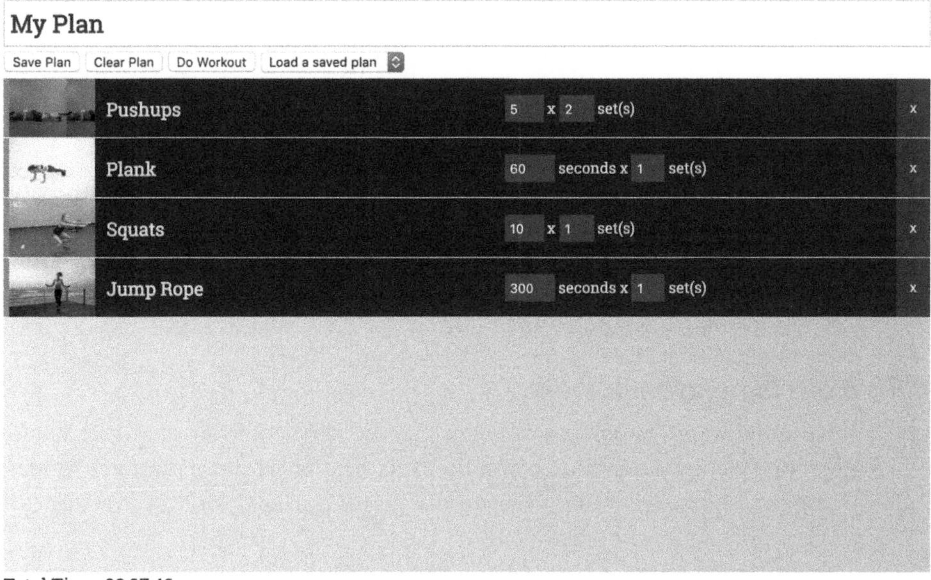

Figure 14.4 Additional UI to manage the plan list

Instead, let's add this click listener to the exerciselibrary component and use the data model this time to add it. The next listing shows this new component (components/exerciselibrary/exerciselibrary.js).

Listing 14.13 Exercise library listening for clicks on exercises and adding to the plan

```
import Template from './template.js';
import Library from                      <-- Imports the exercise library data model
'../../data/exerciselibrary.js';
import WorkoutPlanData from '../../data/workoutplan.js';

export default class ExerciseLibrary extends HTMLElement {
   constructor() {
       super();
       this.attachShadow({mode: 'open'});
       this.shadowRoot.innerHTML = Template.render(Library.all);
       this.shadowRoot.addEventListener(      <-- Listens for clicks from the exercise library that bubble up to this component's shadow root
         'click', e => {
           if (e.target.constructor.name === 'Exercise') {
               WorkoutPlanData.add(      <-- Serializes the data from the clicked exercise and adds to the data model
                    e.target.serialize());
           }
       })
   }
}

if (!customElements.get('wkout-exercise-lib')) {
   customElements.define('wkout-exercise-lib', ExerciseLibrary);
}
```

Let's pause for a second and reflect on what we've done so far. Creating a centralized data model that we can access from anywhere is great, but could we deal without it? Absolutely! Each component could own its own data as it did before. Do you want to query all available exercises in the library? Talk to the exerciselibrary component. Likewise with the workout plan list and the workout plan component.

Thus far in our application, with just a few components, it's very easy to listen for events and interact with each component's API. Figure 14.5 shows how easily data flows among the existing components due to their nature in the DOM's hierarchy.

Things can and do get complex, however. What if we had another component that needed this same data but wasn't part of the same hierarchy?

14.5 Exercise playback view

What good would creating a workout plan be if we couldn't play it back and get some exercise? We need one final component to offer an exercise playback mode. As shown in Figure 14.6, we're going to make the player a modal window that appears over the entire application when activated.

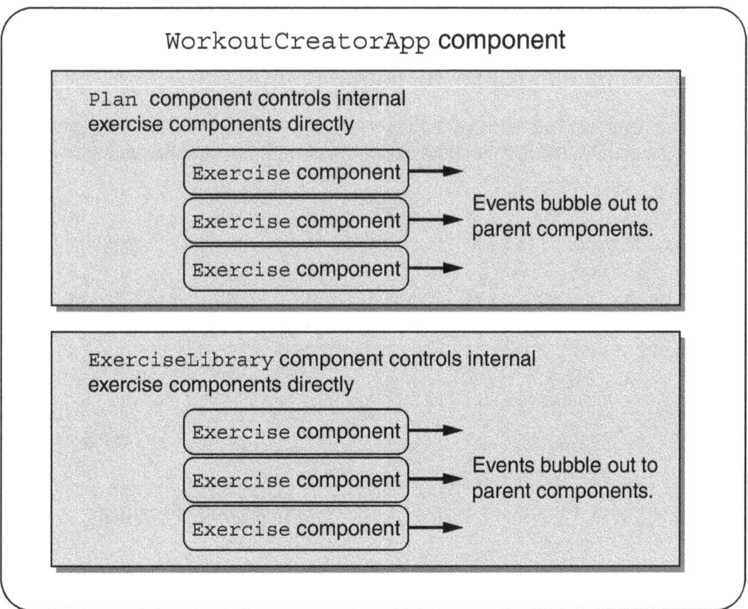

Figure 14.5 Easy data flow with existing component hierarchy

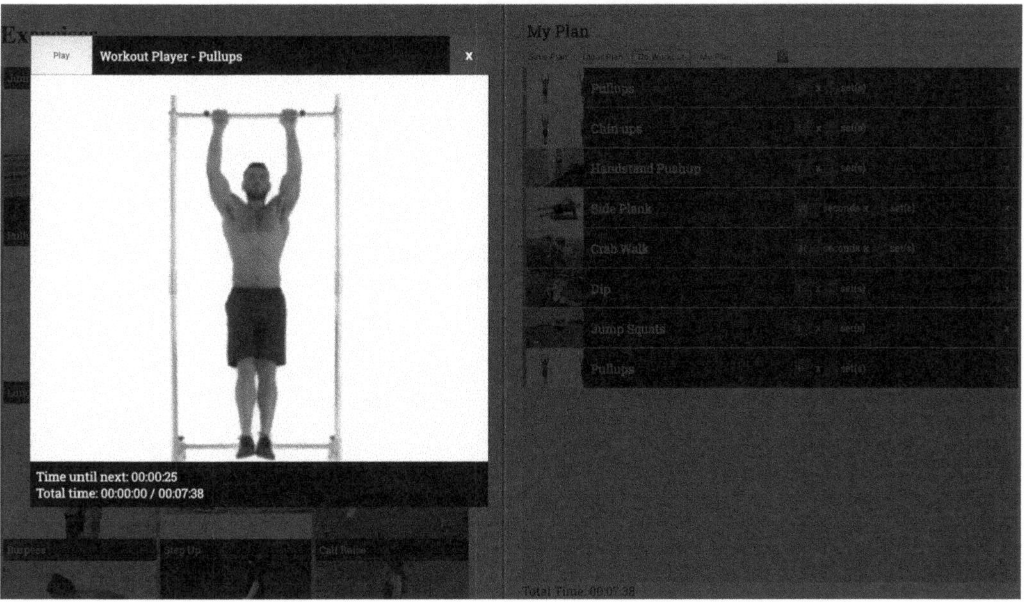

Figure 14.6 Workout playback modal

As this component is an element that should overlay everything on the page, it might make sense to break it out of the existing application altogether. Our new index.html for the entire project might look like the following listing.

Listing 14.14 New project's index.html with workout playback overlay

```
<html>
<head>
   <title>Workout Creator</title>
   <script type="module"
      src="components/workoutcreatorapp/workoutcreatorapp.js"></script>
   <script type="module" src="components/playback/playback.js"></script>   <-- Workout playback component definition
   <link rel="stylesheet" type="text/css" href="main.css">
   <link href="https://fonts.googleapis.com/css?family=
      Roboto+Slab" rel="stylesheet">
</head>
<body>
   <wkout-creator-app></wkout-creator-app>
   <wkout-playback></wkout-playback>   <-- Workout playback on page
</body>
</html>
```

The internal workings of the playback component rely on being able to play and pause the entire exercise list in sequence, like a music playlist. To get this working, we should add some playback controls in the workout plan data model (data/workout-plan.js). The next listing shows these additional functions.

Listing 14.15 Additional methods to support workout plan playback

```
play() {                      <-- Starts playback using a timer
   if (!this._seconds) {
       this._seconds = 0;
   }
   this._timer = setInterval( () => {
       this._seconds ++;
       this.updateTime(this._seconds);
   }, 1000);
},

stop() {   <-- Stops playback, cancelling timer and setting current time to 0
   this._seconds = 0;
   clearInterval(this._timer);
},

pause() {
   clearInterval(this._timer);   <-- Pauses playback by cancelling the timer
},

updateTime(seconds) {   <-- Timer callback to update the current time and current exercise for time
   let exercise = this.getExerciseForTime(seconds);
   let exerciseChanged = false;
   if (this._currentExercise !== exercise) {
       this._currentExercise = exercise;
       exerciseChanged = true;
   }
},
```

The previous functions are core to providing some playback controls for starting up and playing an exercise session. Playing starts a timer and makes the more-complicated `updateTime` function do the work of figuring out which exercise is happening at the current time. Pausing stops the timer, while the `stop` function stops the timer and resets the time.

Next, we'll need to provide common functionality to get some basic info for anywhere that needs it. Even the `updateTime` function needs to know what exercise is currently playing for a certain time. And that function will, in turn, need to know the duration of a specific exercise. So, let's create some of this common functionality.

Listing 14.15 Additional methods to support workout plan playback (continued)

```
getExerciseStartTime(exercise) {
   let time = 0;
   for (let c = 0; c < this._currentWorkout.length; c++) {
       if (this._currentWorkout[c].id === exercise.id) {
           return time;
       }
       time += this.getDurationOfExercise(this._currentWorkout[c]);
   }
},

getExerciseForTime(seconds) {
   let startTime = 0;
   for (let c = 0; c < this._currentWorkout.length; c++) {
       let duration = this.getDurationOfExercise(this._currentWorkout[c]);
       if (seconds <= startTime + duration && seconds >= startTime) {
           return this._currentWorkout[c];
       }
       startTime += duration;
   }
},

get currentExercise() {
   if (!this._currentExercise) {
       this._currentExercise = this._currentWorkout[0];
   }
   return this._currentExercise;
},

getDurationOfExercise(exercise) {
   if (exercise.time) {
      return exercise.time * exercise.sets;
   } else {
       return exercise.estimatedTimePerCount *  exercise.count *
     exercise.sets;
   }
}
```

Annotations:
- getExerciseStartTime: Gets overall start time, in seconds, of exercise
- getExerciseForTime: Function to find an exercise for a specific time
- currentExercise: Getter for the current exercise
- getDurationOfExercise: Gets duration of the exercise passed as a parameter

With the data model updated to allow playback, we can easily use those functions from the playback component. By importing the workout plan data model into this component, we can easily call `WorkoutPlan.play()`, `WorkoutPlan.pause()`, and `WorkoutPlan.stop()`. See this book's GitHub repo for the full component source code.

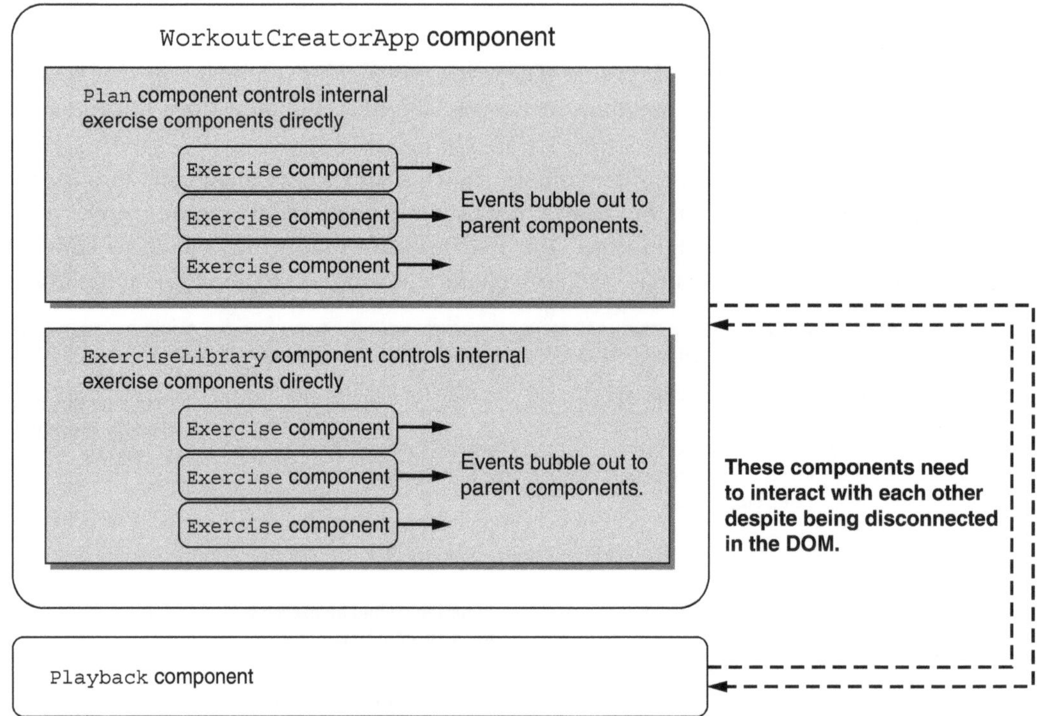

Figure 14.7 Component interaction after adding the player and with no global data model

Given the placement of this new component in the DOM—outside of the main application right on the page—this single and global data model makes a lot of sense.

Now, things are a bit more complicated! Figure 14.7 shows how we'd need to listen for events and interact with component APIs with the workout player now in the picture.

It's entirely possible to deal with things this way, but it's definitely annoying. Without the Shadow DOM, we could bubble events up to the main page and then use query selection to select the right component to perform actions on. With the Shadow DOM, we are blocked from query-selecting anything inside the child components. To work around this, we could create an API for each component that needs to give access to its children. This is fairly brittle because every time we reorganize things in the DOM to make visual changes, we make sure that API holds up with the new DOM structure.

For this use case, and similar use cases, using a global data model like this can be a good way to go! A data model definitely doesn't have to be global, either. Each component could have its own data model if it makes sense for your application. So far in the simple exercises in this book, there hasn't been an overwhelming need to separate data out like this, but certainly your components could be a lot more complex, and that's when, depending on your project, it can make sense to really start enforcing an MVC or similar pattern on a component level.

As I said earlier in this chapter, using more robust solutions like Redux or MobX can be a great solution as well. Like any DIY solution, as you start needing more features, it starts making more and more sense to go with tried and tested solutions. In our simple example, however, a data model is almost enough.

14.6 Passing events with an event bus

Note that I said a data model is *almost* enough. Sure, we can directly interact with the data model, but take playback, for example. We can call `WorkoutPlan.play()`, but once the timer kicks in and playback begins, the elapsed seconds will change, and the current exercise will change every so often. It's not just playback—it's almost every aspect of the application. Changing the duration of a single exercise should cause the total time for your workout to update, and so too should adding and removing exercises from the plan. The list of events we need to listen for is long.

Earlier in this chapter, we discussed bubbling Custom Events through the DOM. Again, prior to the new workout player view, we were mostly OK. It just so happened in our application that the events we needed to listen for would bubble up to where we needed them because the DOM hierarchy we had matched the data flow we needed.

The new workout player complicates things. We'd need to bubble any events up to the index.html page and pass them somehow to the component, as events don't bubble *down* to children. Perhaps making an API on the workout player would accomplish this goal.

An alternative is to do something similar to our global data model. An event bus is a single, global object for passing events throughout your application. Moreover, we can use the same Custom Events we've been using. Instead of calling `dispatchEvent(mycustomevent)` from the component, we can call `EventBus.dispatchEvent(mycustomevent)`.

An event bus, at minimum, needs a way to subscribe to events and a way to send events. The next listing shows both in a new module saved in data/eventbus.js.

Listing 14.16 A simple event bus

```
export default {
   addEventListener(type, cb) {          <-- Adds an event listener; passes in an
       if (!this._listeners) {               event type and a callback function
           this._listeners = [];
       }

       let listener = { type: type, callback: cb };
       this._listeners.push(listener);        <-- Adds the listener data onto
       return listener;                           an array to reference when
   },                                             dispatching events
   dispatchEvent(ce) {
       this._listeners.forEach( function(l) {   <-- Loops through all listeners
           if (ce.type === l.type) {
```

```
                l.callback.apply(this, [ce]);
            }
        });
    }
}
```

If the Custom Event type matches the listener type, calls the function and passes the event

The function names I used, addEventListener and dispatchEvent, should look familiar. They have the same names as the methods you'd use to do the same things with the DOM. The same parameters and return values are used as well. Even though this is a custom solution, I think it's important to keep consistency when you use the event bus or events that occur on the DOM; it just makes usage that much easier to remember. The following listing shows a snippet from the workout player, where the event listener is added after importing the EventBus module.

Listing 14.17 Add event listener in workout player to receive time updates

```
EventBus.addEventListener(
    'onPlaylistTimeUpdate', e => {
    if (e.detail.exercise) {
        if (e.detail.exerciseChanged) {
            this.dom.currentExercise.innerHTML = e.detail.exercise.label;
            this.dom.window.style.backgroundImage =
               `url("${e.detail.exercise.thumb}")`;
        }
        this.dom.timer.innerHTML =
            Template.renderTime(e.detail.time, e.detail.exercise);
    }
});
```

Adds the event listener to the event bus

Looks at a custom property on event.detail to see if the exercise changed, and updates the display

Updates the time display in the component

Of course, the event needs to be dispatched from somewhere. Given that all of the playback logic is in the workout plan data model, the next listing shows it added there.

Listing 14.18 Dispatching events to the event bus from the workout plan data model

```
play() {
   if (!this._seconds) {
       this._seconds = 0;
   }
   this._timer = setInterval( () => {
       this._seconds ++;
       this.updateTime(this._seconds);
   }, 1000);
},

updateTime(seconds) {
   let exercise =
     this.getExerciseForTime(seconds);
   let exerciseChanged = false;
   if (this._currentExercise !== exercise) {
       this._currentExercise = exercise;
       exerciseChanged = true;
   }

   let ce = new CustomEvent(
```

Calls the timer function to internally update the seconds elapsed

Calculates what the current exercise is and if it changed

Creates the event and dispatches it from the event bus

```
        'onPlaylistTimeUpdate', {
          detail: {
              exercise: this._currentExercise,
              exerciseChanged: exerciseChanged,
              exerciseIndex: this._currentWorkout.indexOf(this._currentExercise),
              time: seconds,
          }});
    EventBus.dispatchEvent(ce);
},
```

While we won't rewrite the entire application here, this book's GitHub repo will show all the events added throughout. Aside from UI-related events, like mouse clicks, the application has been refactored to use the event bus for all event passing. I do have one last improvement, however, related to the event types.

14.6.1 Static getter event types

In the previous example, sending time updates, the event type used a string. The exact string was `'onPlaylistTimeUpdate'`. A name like `onUpdate` might suffice, too, but as your application grows in complexity, and an event bus or even just the DOM has lots of events flowing through, it can get harder to maintain the uniqueness of your Custom Event types. Citing an extreme example, naming something `change` is a bit dangerous because it's a native DOM event that regularly happens from input fields; so your callback function might be confused about which event it's actually getting if you were to name your Custom Event type `change` as well.

Similarly, you might have multiple Custom Events that happen when something updates in the application. It can be tempting to just name them all `onUpdate`, but this will lead to confusion as well. That's why it helps to have event types that are a bit longer and more specific.

On the other hand, maybe it doesn't matter that your event type is differentiated. Listening for `change` can be acted upon regardless of whether it's a Custom Event or native event, and just knowing the element that fired the event using `event.currentTarget` or `event.target` can tell you all you need to know. Either way, event types can be nonspecific like this or as specific as helps your use case. Remember, these are just strings that represent the type of event and not functions themselves, so they can be as flexible as you need without worrying about an API.

Having unique events that don't get confused is exactly why the name `onPlaylistTimeUpdate` was used. The problem with these longer event names is that when reaching across components, it can be difficult to remember what each event is named. Worse, it can be easy to misspell! The problem with misspelled event types is that they won't give an error. The intended listener just won't be called because you're either dispatching or listening to the wrong event.

We learned about static getters in chapter 3, when discussing the Web Component's `observedAttributes` function. Custom Events are another perfect use for them. As the data model isn't a class and is already static, we can just use a simple getter here:

```
get PLAYLIST_UPDATE_EVENT() { return 'onPlaylistTimeUpdate'; },
```

If it were a class, like a component class we are dispatching Custom Events from, we could mark it `static`:

```
static get PLAYLIST_UPDATE_EVENT() { return 'onPlaylistTimeUpdate'; },
```

Now, when dispatching events or listening for events, we can avoid the typo-prone string. The listener can change to

```
let ce = new CustomEvent(WorkoutPlanData.PLAYLIST_UPDATE_EVENT, {
```

Adding listeners can be done similarly:

```
EventBus.addEventListener(WorkoutPlanData.PLAYLIST_UPDATE_EVENT
```

Because these getters are static, the instanced class or component doesn't need to be anywhere in sight to be able to use the getter. These event types are all available globally. Now if you make a typo, an error will be thrown, immediately alerting you to your mistake. Even better, if using an IDE like VS Code or WebStorm, the code editor will automatically suggest the static getter name for you, so you don't make the mistake in the first place.

14.6.2 Design patterns as suggestions

I can't emphasize enough that design patterns like the event bus are merely suggestions. If they help your application, great! If not, don't use them. There is always debate and renewed interest over application patterns current and old. And these debates can get heated. New and popular frameworks tend to reinforce certain design patterns. Some developers can run with these ways that are new to them and view them as the only way to solve a problem.

Just like those patterns aren't the ultimate answer, the patterns presented in this chapter aren't the ultimate answer, either. For example, overusing the event bus can be bad as well, making your application confusing. Passing UI events through a global bus that are only relevant to your component can severely impact its share-ability and how much it can function alone.

There are much better resources than this chapter that discuss application design and patterns. The goal here is just to show that Web Components aren't limited compared to other modern frameworks. All the features aren't baked into the browser, but there are countless JS libraries to pull in to help—that is, if a simple custom solution like the ones outlined in this chapter isn't enough.

Summary

In this chapter, you learned

- How to create Custom Events and how they differentiate from native events as they bubble through the DOM, especially the Shadow DOM
- To work with Web Component timing by listening to when they are ready or defined
- How to use static getters to avoid typos when working with Custom Events
- Some example design patterns, with an emphasis on working with an MVC paradigm

15 Hiding your complexities

This chapter covers

- Using A-Frame to create a VR-enabled immersive scene
- Using Google's `model-viewer` component to preview 3D models onscreen and in AR
- Manipulating a live camera feed with WebGL
- Using Babylon.js to create a 3D scene component
- Tracking your hands with Tensorflow.js via handtrack.js

While this book is coming to a close, Web Components are really just getting started. It took a while to create their foundations and even longer to get browser support, but all the same, the last of the modern browsers (Microsoft Edge) is on the verge of full support.

The path to get here was a bit fraught with obstacles and dead ends at times. We've seen a few features come and go. Among the deprecated was HTML Imports, which somewhat coincided with the deprecation of the Polymer Library, the first Web Components library. I'm sure this wasn't coincidental, as the Polymer Library was heavily influenced by HTML Imports as a starting point for every new Web Component.

It was sad to see HTML Imports go away, but that's just how it goes when working on a web standard with stakeholders from multiple browser vendors. As much as I love using JS modules and template literals within to hold HTML and CSS, it's not a perfect solution for everyone. For me, as a developer, it's great, but not everyone likes HTML and CSS inside JS.

15.1 Looking to the Web Component future

We've been able to do some amazing things on the web with just HTML and CSS for ages. Requiring JS as a way to create these visual aspects in your component will be a bit of a sore spot. That's why I'm excited that the Chrome team has announced its intention to ship HTML and CSS modules!

I personally feel like these new module types will be one of a few big next steps for Web Components. Being able to craft a small snippet of HTML and CSS outside of your larger application, and outside of the complexity of your Web Component, will go that much further in making Web Component development accessible to people who may not be up to speed with the latest in JS techniques. It will allow better focus on component structure and style, leaving logic and interactivity a truly separate concern. If you're like me and love HTML, CSS, and JS all the same, this might not be a big deal to you. But allowing people to focus on the thing they are good at and use their individual talents to create the same component as a team is going to be amazing!

CSS modules could be even more important. Allowing imports of small style sheets into components begins to address what I see as the biggest rough edge of Shadow DOM-enabled components. Without styles being able to pierce the Shadow DOM, years of CSS workflows have gone out the window. The biggest CSS workflow we're missing is the concept of an entire design system being able to style your component or set of components.

Design systems are already fairly modular in their source code. It's only when they are built that they become a monolithic, or semi-monolithic, CSS file that is intended to style your entire application from the top down. As CSS modules enter our workflows, perhaps we'll have a reliance directly on the tiny, modular source files. Couple this with (already released in Chrome) *shadow parts* and the upcoming *shadow themes*, and we might have an extremely robust solution in our near future that creates an even better workflow for design systems in general.

I predict that design systems and application theming with these new features are another next big game changer for Web Components. Though, really, it's not just Web Components that will benefit. Given that most modern frameworks work with some form of component (some even using Web Components), these features could be equally relevant to all of them.

This is fantastic news for everyone, really. Already we are seeing a trend toward framework-agnostic solutions. Redux, MobX, lit-html, and more all solve a small, targeted problem. While Redux is popular for React users, and lit-html is popular for LitElement Web Component users, these solutions can be used anywhere. Going forward, I see this continuing. We may all be using the same solutions for similar problems no matter which foundational framework—or lack thereof—our project is built on. Even better, Web Components themselves are agnostic and can be used in other frameworks, just like any other element.

Speaking of LitElement, this Google Polymer Project library seems to be catching on quite nicely. Just recently, LitElement has reached a production-ready 1.0 . . . er, rather 2.0. The lit-element package was already claimed on NPM (www.npmjs.com/package/lit-element). Though the Polymer team was able to snag the name from the previous author, they also wanted to avoid confusion and not get their 1.0 release confused with the previous project. So, LitElement was finally released as 2.0, skipping right over 1.0. Not to mention, Ionic has had StencilJS for a little while as well. Stencil has its own ecosystem of sorts, but compiles to a native, no-dependency Web Component.

It can be exciting looking to the future, but it's also important to recognize what we can do right now and how future changes to Web Components impact us as we go forward. And that's the exciting thing. It really does look like the foundational basics of Web Components aren't going to be changing anytime soon. Everything in this book should remain relevant for years to come.

The things that will change aren't the fundamental building blocks; instead, the change will come with the developer workflow for dealing with layout, style, application design patterns, and so on. Yet, all of these details will not be visible to developers who just want to use your component. Even if you are using old and outdated 2019 methods in your component when using it in 2025, it should still work because the complexities inside your component aren't really important to usage outside your component.

I heard one statistic from the Polymer team in February 2019 about Web Component usage. That statistic is that 10% of all page views in Chrome use Web Components in some way. This number underscores the biggest takeaway for me, and why I'm such a big Web Components fan.

To explain, that 10% is a little surprising, to be honest. It means that we're all likely using Web Components and don't even know it. A Web Component is just another element on a page. They are incredibly simple to use and consume, but on the inside, components can be doing incredibly complicated things!

The hidden complexity of Web Components is what's so exciting for me. We can wrap up something potentially insanely complex and expose it to users as an element with a well-documented API or just a few attributes. The encapsulation provided by the Shadow DOM lets us sleep at night knowing that despite whatever complexities lie within, the outside page won't inject any surprises.

To be fair, components in any modern framework can offer this. When the first version of Angular was introduced, I would write some pretty nifty "directives," essentially the components of the time. The problem is that when Angular v1 fell out of fashion, the components/directives I had just weren't relevant anymore, and I had to rewrite if I wanted to keep using the same intended functionality.

So, this notion of hidden complexities is what I'd like to end *Web Components in Action* on. The projects and components we've created have been fun, but I've made every effort to keep them small so we could discuss most if not all the code in the pages of this book. Now, however, I'd like to push these artificial boundaries and explore some more out-there topics!

15.2 3D and mixed reality

I'm not sure there's much on the web today that's more complex than 3D and mixed reality! I'm betting we're all familiar with 3D. With real-time 3D, we can look at an object or scene from any angle we choose. Until recently, most of us have only been able to interact with a 3D scene with traditional UI modalities, perhaps using our arrow keys to walk around in a game or using a mouse to drag and spin an object to look at it from any angle.

This started to change in 2013 with virtual reality. I was one of the Oculus Rift DK1 backers on Kickstarter, and 2013 is when the first units started to ship. Also, around this time you could purchase a small, inexpensive cardboard kit that held your phone right in front of your eyes, taking up your entire viewing area.

Also, because you've now stuck a phone on your face, the relative movement of your head can be tracked. When you look around in the real world, this information can be sent to the 3D scene. So now, instead of looking around by dragging your mouse across a flat interface, as we've done since the first-person shooter video games of the '90s, your own head and eye gaze are how you look around.

How is this possible? How does a phone know how your head is moving? Standard now with any phone are accelerometer, gyroscope, and magnetometer sensors. An accelerometer detects how fast your phone moves in a certain direction, while your gyroscope can tell how fast your phone rotates in a certain direction. A magnetometer is the sensor most commonly known as your compass. It can tell which direction your phone is facing in the world in terms of north, east, west, or south. *Sensor fusion algorithms* take all of these sensors together and can accurately determine how your head moves! Combined with a split screen 3D scene where the left viewpoint is slightly off from the right and then placed over your eyes, you get a full 3D stereo effect, as if you're actually in this virtual world.

You might wonder what relevance this has to the web and Web Components. But all of these capabilities have been part of the web for a while as separate pieces, even without VR, and Web Components can definitely encapsulate and hide these complexities.

Tons of math and code for sensor fusion head-tracking aside, 3D in general is super hard! While 3D graphics using normal code on your CPU are possible, they're pretty slow. That's why any modern and serious effort for real-time 3D uses your GPU. On the web, the only way to take advantage of the GPU is with WebGL.

WebGL is incredibly low-level code, and it's not JS. The following listing shows an example WebGL shader that can take an image and do a radial fade to black around the middle.

Listing 15.1 An example WebGL shader

```
attribute vec2 a_position;
attribute vec2 a_texCoord;
uniform vec2 u_resolution;
varying vec2 v_texCoord;
uniform vec2 offset;

void main() {
   vec2 zeroToOne = a_position / u_resolution;
   vec2 zeroToTwo = zeroToOne * 2.0;
   vec2 clipSpace = zeroToTwo - 1.0 + offset;
   gl_Position = vec4(clipSpace.x * 1.0, clipSpace.y * -1.0, 0.0, 1.0);
   v_texCoord = a_texCoord;
}
```

- Incoming and shared variables to help calculate the vertex points
- Main function to calculate and set vertex positions based on canvas size

Note that the aforementioned shader is a so-called "vertex" shader. Vertices are heavily used as interconnected points in space on a 3D model. For us, since we're going extremely simple and using this only to manipulate pixels, our points in space are simply a flat square the exact size of our canvas.

The following fragment shader complements the vertex shader. Whereas before, we were drawing vertices and creating a flat canvas of sorts in the WebGL context, we can now set each color of the pixel we're drawing in that canvas.

Listing 15.1 An example WebGL shader (continued)

```
precision mediump float;
varying vec2 v_texCoord;

uniform sampler2D u_image0;

void main(void) {
    vec4 sourcePixel =
    ➥texture2D(u_image0, v_texCoord);
    float multiply = 1.0;
    vec2 center = vec2(0.5, 0.5);

    float dist = distance(v_texCoord, center);
    gl_FragColor = (0.6-dist) * sourcePixel;
}
```

- The coordinate of the pixel we're operating on
- Incoming texture (like from a photo we've provided to the shader)
- Gets the pixel from the texture at the current pixel location
- Sets the darkness of the pixel as a function of how far it is from the center

Of course, a simple effect like this is a far cry from a scene full of 3D models. Yet, the previous code is a good example of what you have to work with for rendering your graphics. There is lots of 3D math involved, and orchestrating it all is an HTML <canvas> element and JS. Given all this underlying complexity, it's standard practice to use a higher-level 3D library, like Three.js (https://threejs.org) or Babylon.js (www.babylonjs.com). At least with these, you aren't forced to handle the nitty gritty graphics rendering, writing shaders that are way more complex than those in listing 15.1. Instead, you can work with virtual objects like spheres, cubes, and any 3D models you load.

Even then, moving things around in 3D space is still hard! We're dealing with transform matrices, quaternions, and more. Web Components can help with specific things here to hide all of this insane complexity, depending on your use case.

15.2.1 A-Frame

Technically speaking, A-Frame does not use proper Web Components. If you peek at its source code, you can get a sense of how much of a technicality this statement really is. I want to bring it up, however, as an offbeat, yet extremely relevant, Web Component use case.

A-Frame (https://aframe.io) describes itself as "a Web framework for building virtual reality experiences." This is great, but to me, it's more than that. I think the power and appeal of A-Frame is its ability to allow developers and nondevelopers alike to create 3D scenes on the web that also work in VR.

The reason that it's so easy to create with A-Frame is because you're not really coding when you start with it. The library lets you create scenes with tags on an HTML page. Take the next listing, for example. It's a simple "hello world" 3D scene that A-Frame has as its first example of many.

Listing 15.2 A-Frame hello WebVR scene

```
<html>
<head>
   <title>Hello, WebVR! • A-Frame</title>
   <script src="aframe.min.js"></script>        ◁ Includes A-Frame library
</head>
<body>
<a-scene background="color: #ECECEC">           ◁ Element that contains entire 3D scene
        <a-box position="-1 0.5 -3" rotation="0 45 0" color="#4CC3D9" shadow>
        </a-box>                                 ◁ Example 3D object; a box/cube
        <a-sphere position="0 1.25 -5" radius="1.25" color="#EF2D5E" shadow>
        </a-sphere>
        <a-cylinder position="1 0.75 -3" radius="0.5" height="1.5" color=
        "#FFC65D" shadow></a-cylinder>
        <a-plane position="0 0 -4" rotation="-90 0 0" width="4" height="4"
        color="#7BC8A4" shadow></a-plane>
</a-scene>
</body>
</html>
```

This little bit of HTML gets us an entire 3D scene! Figure 15.1 shows everything that appears in the browser. Even better, you can see a little VR goggles icon on the lower right.

This icon, when pressed, takes you into immersive mode. On a desktop, this isn't so interesting—it just goes full-screen. On a phone, it *does* get more interesting. Normally, when entering immersive mode, A-Frame splits the screen to show slightly

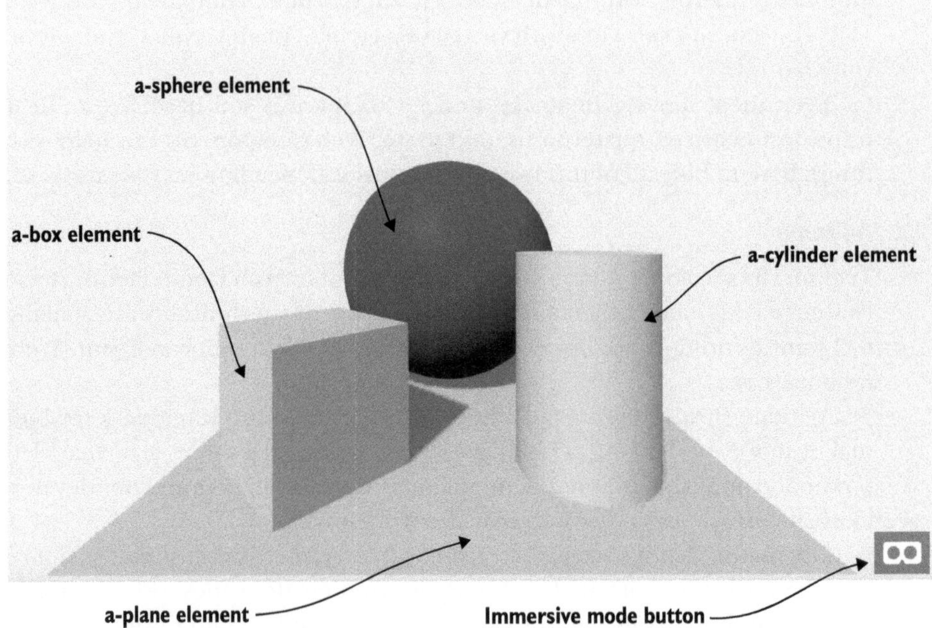

Figure 15.1 Example A-Frame scene

different content on the left and right for stereoscopic 3D. It also distorts each view for lenses that you'd find on something like a Google Cardboard, where the lenses enlarge these views to take up your entire field of view when the phone is millimeters from your eyes.

If you have Google Daydream installed on your phone, immersive mode gets even more interesting, where the Daydream's Bluetooth controller is now supported as well. Daydream is Google's VR platform, which runs on smartphones with an accompanying headset and controller. By default here, entering immersive mode will automatically start Daydream.

Desktop browsers are supported too, as are new VR-focused desktop browsers like Supermedium and Firefox Reality. This is a bit more complicated than a phone, because now your browser has to support a number of actual VR headsets and controllers. All the same, immersive mode works similarly here using your real headset and controllers, such as the Oculus Rift, Oculus Go, HTC Vive, and Vive Focus.

WebVR is such a new and emerging standard that it's already out of date. WebVR essentially defines a JS API that browsers implement for displaying VR and accepting positional and rotation input that informs where your hand controllers and headset are. Given the new excitement around AR, WebVR's next version is now being called WebXR to be inclusive of as many different immersive modalities as possible. This situation feels a lot like Web Components several years ago. Some browser vendors went ahead and tried to implement what they thought would be great standards.

Experiments in the web dev community around WebVR proved that some things worked, and some things didn't, and now we're entering a new round of standards with WebXR.

What does A-Frame have to do with Web Components? Well, let's revisit the markup. Declaring a 3D scene is done quite easily with what looks like an `a-scene` Web Component:

```
<a-scene background="color: #ECECEC"></a-scene>
```

When opening up the DOM inspector in your dev tools, as in figure 15.2, you can see that this component encloses elements in the scene as well as a `<canvas>` tag for rendering the 3D scene. Interestingly enough, though, elements like `<a-box>` that represent the cube or box in the 3D scene are zero height and width and are positioned nowhere in particular.

That's because these elements that represent objects in the `<a-scene>` element aren't actually used visually. A-Frame is using HTML elements as nonvisual data models to be created in 3D. This is interesting, isn't it? On one hand, we have the `<a-scene>` component handling the incredible complexity of a full 3D scene and also allowing it to work in a variety of VR settings and hardware.

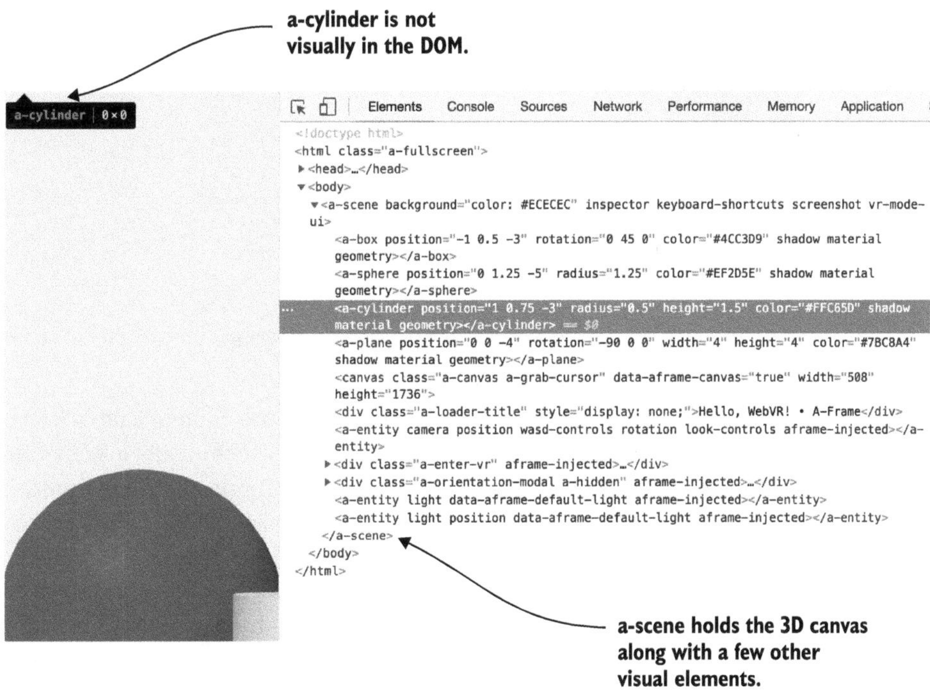

Figure 15.2 Inspecting the A-Frame scene

On the other hand, we have a variety of nonvisual components inside `<a-scene>` that do nothing but help create the 3D scene. I think the notion of nonvisual components is super interesting. I go back and forth on whether they are useful or not. As a decent JS developer, anything that's not visual I tend to think of as something you should just do with JS, leaving HTML out of it. Yet, there is a nice approachability to nonvisual Web Components. Anyone without JS knowledge can just place something nonvisual, like a background audio player, on the page without having to worry about instantiation, JS libraries, or any other concerns.

Here, since these nonvisual components and the visual `<a-scene>` tag help each other out to create the entire scene and look like one consistent thing in your HTML markup, I'm definitely a fan! It's just fun to start editing the scene live in your dev tools and watch the 3D scene instantly change, like in figure 15.3, where I change the box color and rotation.

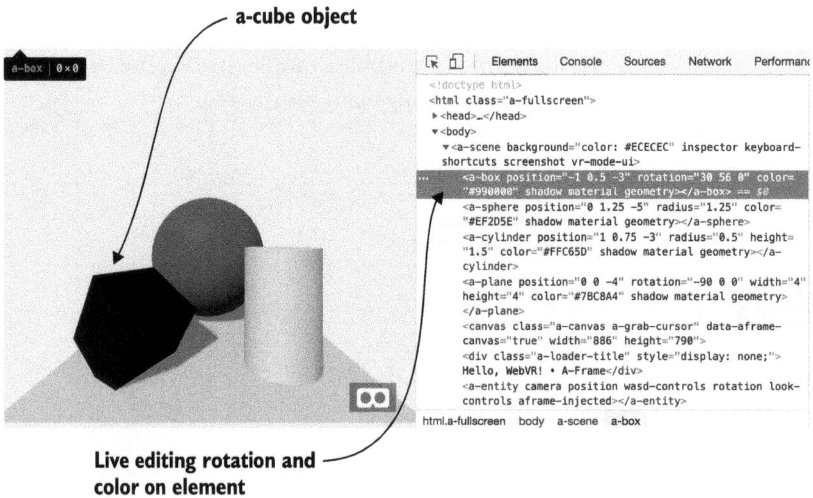

Figure 15.3 Changing A-Frame objects live in the browser's dev tools

In summary, we have custom element creation, attribute change callbacks, connected callbacks, and likely more. I did state that this wasn't technically a Web Component under the hood at the beginning. The reason why is simple. A-Frame doesn't use the Custom Element API at this point. It is using the old API of `document.registerElement` with a polyfill to ensure it works everywhere. One of the lead A-Frame authors has stated they will start using the Custom Element API soon (https://github.com/aframevr/aframe/issues/3923), but for all intents and purposes, I do consider A-Frame a great use case for Web Components. Additionally, it isn't using the Shadow DOM. Here, there's really no reason to do so, since the elements aren't styled, and it's preferable to allow unrestricted access to the inner DOM inside `<a-scene>` to manipulate the scene however a developer wants. As a result, we don't have to manage the nonvisual inner child nodes as anything but normal elements. If using the Shadow DOM, these child nodes would have to be managed as slots.

15.2.2 Model-viewer component

One narrow but popular use case for 3D on the web is simply being able to preview a 3D model—allowing a user to drag to spin it around and zoom in. Google has created a Web Component for just that called `model-viewer`. Documentation and examples can be seen at https://googlewebcomponents.github.io/model-viewer, but I think it's worth pulling it down and playing with it a little.

In this book's GitHub repo, I've done just that. In an HTML file called simpledemo.html, we can see this component in action. We'll build up to interactivity and adding a background color as in the demo as we go along. There's really nothing to it beyond linking to the component's JS, doing a little style to set the component size, and finally putting the component on the page, as shown in the next listing.

Listing 15.3 A `model-viewer` component demo

```
<html>
<head>
   <script src="model-viewer.js"></script>        <-- Model-viewer component JS
   <title>Simple Demo for Model Viewer</title>
   <style>
       body {
           margin: 0;
       }
       model-viewer {        <-- Sizes the component to be the
           width: 100vw;         entire size of the page
           height: 100vh;
       }
   </style>
</head>
<body>
     <model-viewer src="Astronaut.glb"></model-viewer>    <-- Adds the component to
</body>                                                       the page showing the
</html>                                                       Astronaut model
```

There's not much you couldn't do here on your own; but for your convenience, I've downloaded the Astronaut 3D model and the component JS into this book's GitHub repo, so you can follow along without hunting things down yourself. The 3D model is actually a brand-new 3D format called glTF. Compressed as a binary bundle, the file format ends up as .glb. This is yet another complexity, as 3D formats need to be unpacked and parsed to actually create the 3D model in the 3D engine.

Once it's up and running, it doesn't look that impressive with no interaction! It may as well be an image. The `model-viewer` component gives us a whole bunch of attributes to work with. Probably the least impressive is the ability to add a background color, shown in figure 15.4. Let's start with a lavender background:

```
<model-viewer src="Astronaut.glb" background-color="#9999bb"></model-viewer>
```

Figure 15.4 Astronaut model over a colored background

Next, let's make this 3D context useful. The `model-viewer` allows autorotation, as if the astronaut was on a slowly rotating turntable:

```
<model-viewer src="Astronaut.glb"
              auto-rotate
              background-color="#9999bb"></model-viewer>
```

Or perhaps you'd like it to be a little more interactive, allowing it to rotate by dragging across the element:

```
<model-viewer src="Astronaut.glb"
              controls
              background-color="#9999bb"></model-viewer>
```

Note the attention to detail when you drag to rotate. There's a little acceleration when you drag, and it drops off pretty quickly after release, but it does ease out, so it doesn't feel too jarring.

Consider this tiny usability detail when also thinking about every other little thing this component does, from rendering geometry to using a WebGL canvas to loading a 3D model with geometry, materials, and textures. A component like this takes time to create, which is why it's great that Google already did it and shared it via open source.

The `model-viewer` ends up being just one more component that we can include on our page without having to understand all of the complexities underneath. It frees us up to turn our attention to other aspects of our application.

15.2.3 model-viewer + Poly search

Remember back in chapter 3, when we created a 3D model search with Google Poly? Displaying a 3D model and being able to interact with it was a bit too much to get into back then, and it still is now. But we don't need to get into those details; we can simply make our search function and find a real result, previewed in full 3D with the `model-viewer` component.

The next listing shows this search example augmented to include the glTF URL as an attribute of each image thumbnail. We can listen to clicks on each thumbnail, grab that URL, and update the `model-viewer` component.

Listing 15.4 Poly search component with a `model-viewer` component to preview

```
<html>
<head>
    <title>Poly Search with Preview</title>
    <script src="model-viewer.js"></script>        <-- Imports poly-search component and includes model-viewer component
    <script src="poly-search.js" type="module"></script>

    <style>
        model-viewer {
            width: 50vw;
            height: 50vh;
        }
    </style>
</head>
<body>
<model-viewer src="../Astronaut.glb" controls></model-viewer>

<label>Enter search term: </label>
<input type="text" onchange="updatePolySearch(event)" />
<br /><br />

<poly-search apikey="<enter your API key here>"    <-- Be sure to enter your own API key from chapter 3 to get this example working.
            format="GLTF2"    <-- Tells poly-search to only include glTF results (for model-viewer component compatibility)
            thumbheight="50"
            backgroundcolor="#99ffff"
            baseuri="https://poly.googleapis.com/v1/assets"
            searchterm="parrot">
</poly-search>

<script>
    function updatePolySearch(event) {
        document.querySelector('poly-search').searchTerm = event.target.value;
    }

    document.querySelector('poly-search').addEventListener('click', e => {
        const model =    <-- On click, gets the glTF URL and updates the model-viewer component
                e.target.getAttribute('gltf');
        document.querySelector('model-viewer').setAttribute('src', model);
    });
</script>

</body>
</html>
```

For brevity here, I've wrapped up the Poly search component as its own module and used a template literal inside to manage its own CSS. We didn't do either before because chapter 3 was prior to introducing these concepts. Feel free to try this yourself or visit this book's GitHub repo.

The only logic change within was filtering those results to include only glTF files and grabbing the URL of the result. The next listing shows this change.

Listing 15.5 Filtering results by glTF, including the URL on the result image element

```
for (let c = 0; c < assets.length; c++) {
   for (let d = 0; d < assets[c].formats.length; d++) {
       if (assets[c].formats[d].formatType ===
                      this.getAttribute('format')) {     <- Filters by format (glTF as specified on the component attribute)
           html += '<img gltf="' +
             assets[c].formats[d].root.url +            <- Adds a special attribute to the image result for the glTF URL
             '" src="' +
             assets[c].thumbnail.url +
             '" width="' +
             this._thumbwidth + '" height="' + this._thumbheight + '"/>';
       }
   }
}
```

The resulting demo loads up "parrot" models initially, but anything we type into that search box, we'll likely find a 3D model for. Of course, clicking each result gives a full interactive preview. In figure 15.5, I've typed "spaceship," and chapter 3's Poly search component shows the corresponding results. Clicking any one result passes an event onto the surrounding HTML page, which sets the `src` attribute to the result's glTF web address.

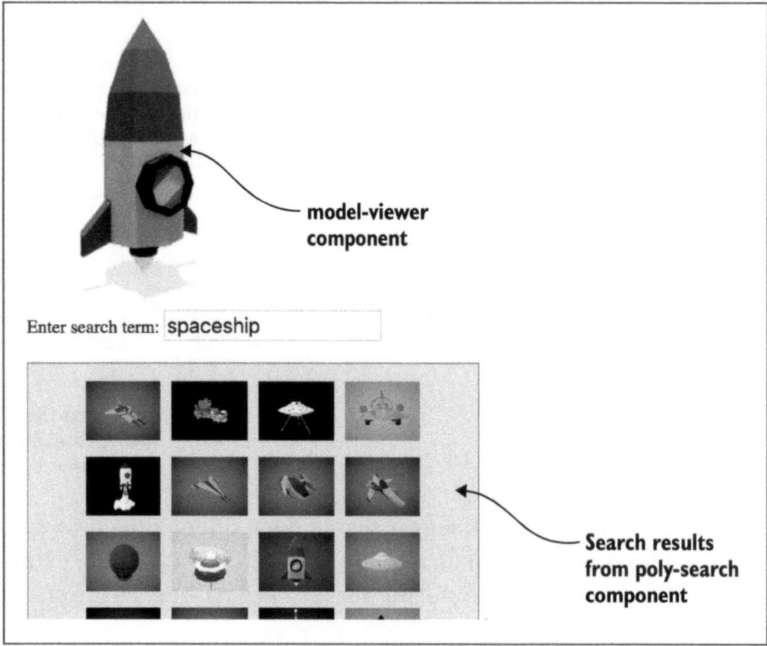

Figure 15.5 Poly search component with `model-viewer` preview

Think about what we just did! We took an early simple component from before we learned much of anything Web Component-related, combined it with a complex Google Web Component that we have no idea, really, how it works, and made something super useful in a very simple way. Again, this is my favorite part of Web Components—hiding complexity inside a few simple tags and making something greater than the sum of its parts.

15.2.4 AR with model-viewer

As complex as 3D is, we can go deeper. AR is the next immersive step beyond VR. While VR lets you view an entirely fake and virtual world, AR allows placement of virtual objects in the real world. This is extremely challenging just in terms of hardware. Screens that you can't see through are all around us. On the other hand, creating a screen that a user can see through while it's also mounted on their head is a big challenge that some huge, well-funded companies are struggling to take on right now.

Notably, the biggest efforts to create hardware like this come from Magic Leap and Microsoft's HoloLens. These devices cost thousands of dollars and, frankly, don't live up to what you might imagine because of their limited field of view. What I mean by this is that when you experience one of these devices, the virtual objects in your scene are limited to an area of your view similar to holding up an 8.5 × 11 sheet of paper at arm's length, as in figure 15.6. When these virtual objects are viewed at a distance, it's amazing what you can see and how these objects seem to live in the real world. However, when you get closer, and objects are bigger than that limited field of view, they get clipped! It really tends to break the immersion of the experience.

This and similar challenges along with price are why folks are taking a step back from such devices and going full steam ahead with AR on their everyday phones while we wait for the ultimate AR headset. Separately (or possibly in conjunction with futuristic glasses in their secret hardware labs), Apple and Google are working on their

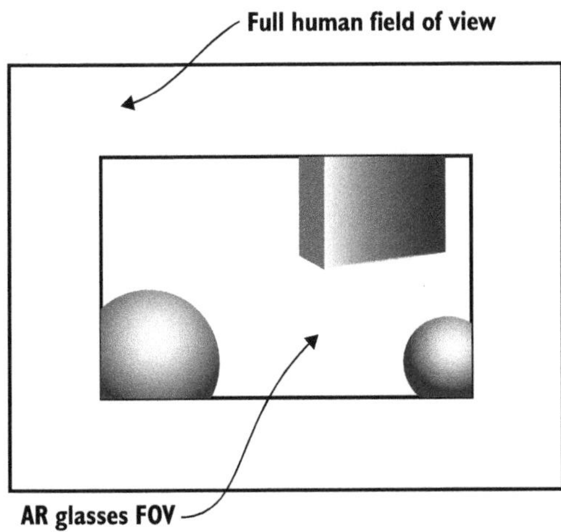

Figure 15.6 Example AR glasses field of view

smartphone libraries—ARKit and ARCore, respectively—to give developers a leg up for creating AR smartphone experiences.

The complexity that these libraries solve is with attempting to "see" the world. Using computer vision, ARKit/ARCore find interesting "features" in the real world through your phone's camera. These features manifest as 3D points that it finds. When these 3D points are found, they can be linked together and manifest as a found surface, like a floor, a table, or a wall. When a surface is found, a 3D object or scene can be placed on it, as seen in figure 15.7, courtesy of Google's ARCore Quickstart (https://developers.google.com/ar/develop/java/quickstart).

Figure 15.7 Placing a virtual object in the real world using ARCore

These hidden complexities keep piling up! The `model-viewer` component attempts to take this on as well. Unfortunately, at the time of this writing, pure web-powered AR is not supported in your phone. This is because an experimental version of Chrome (Chrome Canary) with WebVR was needed to try this out. With WebXR now in development, Chrome Canary no longer supports the features that `model-viewer` was using to give us AR.

Early days for sure, but you can still try AR out with the `model-viewer` component if you have either a Magic Leap device with its "Hello" browser or a newer iPhone with iOS 12+. If this is you, it's really easy to try (though I'll admit, I haven't tried with a Magic Leap).

For the Magic Leap, it's as easy as setting the corresponding attribute `<model-viewer src="Astronaut.glb" magic-leap>` and including the @magicleap/prismatic library on your page. Since I don't have a Magic Leap, and you probably don't either, the iPhone option is the most approachable for us.

Recall that I said that pure web-powered AR isn't supported right now with `model-viewer`. This is because, as it is currently, `model-viewer` cheats a bit on iOS. To enable AR, the component uses Apple's Quick Look feature, which now supports 3D and AR. When entering immersive mode from your web page, the Quick Look application opens with your 3D model. Despite the hoops jumped through by the component, it's really easy to try, provided you have a newer iPhone. The following listing shows a simple alteration to our last example.

Listing 15.6 AR with the `model-viewer` component

```
<model-viewer src="Astronaut.glb"
            background-color="#45aa22"
            ios-src="Astronaut.usdz">
</model-viewer>
```

New ios-src attribute with USDZ file to enable AR on iOS 12+

To support Quick Look, the model needs to be provided in Apple's new 3D format, USDZ. I've downloaded and provided this model in this book's GitHub repo, so you can easily check it out.

15.2.5 Your own 3D component

Of course, sometimes you know full well how a complex component works because you've coded it yourself. It's just helpful to hide that complexity from the rest of the app, so you can worry about developing one component at a time. Developing for 3D is such a different context, it can definitely give you a bit of developer whiplash when the rest of your application is a 2D UI.

Wrapping up your 3D work in a component containing the `<canvas>` tag for display and all the JS needed to run a full 3D scene with a render loop can be a great way to go. Mixing 3D and 2D sounds like a great use of the color picker we made a few chapters ago!

This demo, specifically, will have a 3D scene that holds a simple primitive, like a sphere, cube, or low-polygon sphere. This scene will include a custom camera and lights and will feature drag interaction that allows a user to spin the camera to look at the scene from any angle they wish.

On the 2D UI end, the color picker will allow changing the 3D primitive's color and transparency. Also, we'll have some really simple buttons that allow a user to choose whichever 3D primitive they'd like to view. Figure 15.8 shows what we'll end up with.

In total, there will be three components, including the color picker we've already done. The other two are the 3D scene component and the application component that holds both the 3D scene and color picker. Figure 15.9 shows the folder structure of the entire application.

There are a few things to call out that might be a bit abnormal. We've been using two files for each component throughout this book—one for the component class and one to hold HTML/CSS. This is still true. The `scene` component has an extra file containing the Babylon.js library.

As I mentioned earlier in this chapter, 3D is hard to do, and WebGL is a bit too low-level for us to be productive in. This is why a 3D library is pretty standard fare when working on similar things. Three.js is probably the most popular 3D library right now and, in fact, is used in both the `model-viewer` component and A-Frame. It's a

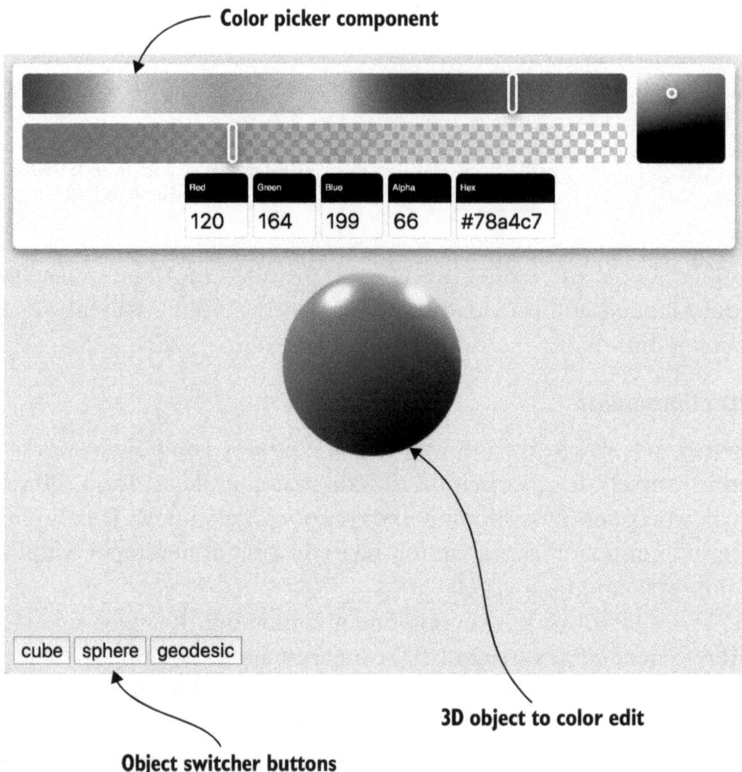

Figure 15.8 A 3D color picker application

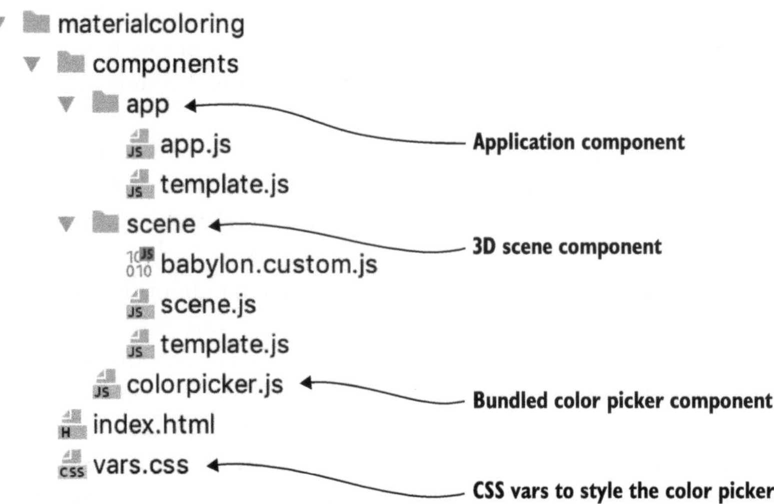

Figure 15.9 3D color picker project structure

great library, but lately, I've simply been preferring Babylon.js. It's an entirely personal preference, though. I like how much of a complete package Babylon.js is, whereas Three.js is more plugin-based if you need anything beyond extremely simple functionality. There's absolutely nothing wrong with this—each has its time and place, and I would say both are equally awesome.

Aside from the extra library, the color picker component folder doesn't exist! I simply copied over the component build file that we created in chapter 12 with Rollup. The only other thing to call out that you may have forgotten is the CSS file at the project root containing the CSS vars that helped style the color picker component.

Let's start simple and work our way up to the 3D part last. First, the next listing shows a basic HTML page hosting the application.

Listing 15.7 3D color picker index.html

```
<head>
  <title>Material Coloring</title>
  <script                                    Includes the main
    type="module"                            application component
    src="components/app/app.js">
  </script>
  <script                                    Includes the
    src="components/scene/babylon.custom.js">   Babylon.js 3D library
  </script>
  <script                                    Includes the color
    src="components/colorpicker.js">         picker component
  </script>
  <link                                      Includes CSS vars to
    rel="stylesheet"                         theme the color picker
    type="text/css"
    href="vars.css"/>

  <style>
      body {
          margin: 0;
          padding: 0;
          overflow: hidden;
      }

      mc-app {                               Makes the application
          width: 100vw;                      fill the entire page
          height: 100vh;
      }
  </style>
</head>
<body>
  <mc-app></mc-app>                          Places the application
</body>                                      on the page
</html>
```

There are two script references that stand out a little here. First, we've included Bablyon.js here instead of in the component where we're using it. While I'd prefer to import it as a module, it's a bit much for our simple example to grab the entire

Babylon source and deal with that. Alternately, it would be nice to include the <script> tag when setting the innerHTML of the 3D scene component. Unfortunately, due to security concerns, scripts aren't allowed to load like this. Instead, we'd have to create a new script element with JS, set the source, and manually append it. Listing 15.7 is just easier to show you now.

Second, you'll notice that the color picker component isn't imported as a module, either. Yet again, this is for convenience. Instead of copying the entire component source over or importing a source where we'd need to back up several levels, and up through a chapter again in this repo, it's easier to copy over the build file that we packaged up as something we'd drop in on an HTML page like this.

Moving on to the application component in components/app, we'll start with the template.js file to review the HTML and CSS. The next listing shows these details.

Listing 15.8 Application template module for HTML/CSS

```
import Scene from '../scene/scene.js';

export default {
   render() {
       return `${this.css()}
               ${this.html()}`;
   },

   mapDOM(scope) {
       return {
           scene:
               scope.querySelector('mc-scene'),
           colorpicker: scope.querySelector('wcia-color-picker')
       }
   },

   html() {
       return `<mc-scene
                     object="cube">
               </mc-scene>
               <div id="model-buttons">
                   <button class="object-button">cube</button>
                   <button class="object-button">sphere</button>
                   <button class="object-button">geodesic</button>
               </div>
               <wcia-color-picker class="modal" hex="#99224A">
               </wcia-color-picker>`;
   },

   css() {
       return `<style>
              . . . CSS here
               </style>`;
   }
}
```

Annotations:
- scene: — Caches references to the scene component and the color picker component
- <mc-scene — 3D scene component with a default primitive object of cube
- <div id="model-buttons"> — Buttons to click and change the primitive object that the 3D scene shows
- </wcia-color-picker> — Color picker component with a default color already set

The CSS is rather simple. But it's a bit different than our usual layout, as we overlay all of the elements on top of the scene through absolute positioning, as the following listing shows.

Listing 15.9 Absolutely positioning elements over the 3D scene

```
:host {
   display: inline-block;
}

#model-buttons {
   position: absolute;
   width: 100%;
   bottom: 10px;
   left: 10px;
}

#model-buttons button {
   font-size: 20px;
}

mc-scene {
   position: absolute;
   width: 100%;
}

wcia-color-picker {
   position: absolute;
   width: calc(100% - 20px);
   margin: 10px;
}
```

- Model buttons are at the bottom and over the 3D scene. (`#model-buttons`)
- The 3D scene takes up the entire component, but layered underneath everything else. (`mc-scene`)
- The color picker sits at the top of the page, over the 3D scene and with some margins at all sides. (`wcia-color-picker`)

Next, since we're only tying these two components together (the color picker and 3D scene), the JS in components/app/app.js is very simple as well. It's no different than any other component we've done, and the next listing highlights the parts that aren't boilerplate Web Component setup.

Listing 15.10 Application component JS

```
import Template from './template.js';

export default class App extends HTMLElement {
   constructor() {
       super();
       this.attachShadow({mode: 'open'});
       this.shadowRoot.innerHTML = Template.render();
       this.dom = Template.mapDOM(this.shadowRoot);

       const observer = new MutationObserver( e => this.onMutationChange(e));
       observer.observe(this.dom.colorpicker, { attributes: true });
       this.shadowRoot.addEventListener('click', e => this.onClick(e));
       this.dom.scene.color =
               this.dom.colorpicker.hex;
       this.dom.scene.alpha = this.dom.colorpicker.alpha;
   }
```

- Listens to attribute changes by the color picker (`const observer = new MutationObserver(...)`)
- Listens for clicks to capture when the 3D object buttons are pressed (`this.shadowRoot.addEventListener('click', ...)`)
- Initially sets the color and alpha of the 3D scene based on color picker defaults (`this.dom.scene.color = ...`)

```
    onClick(e) {
        if (e.target.classList.contains(
                'object-button')) {
            this.dom.scene.object = e.target.innerText;
        }
    }

    onMutationChange(changes) {
        for (let c = 0; c < changes.length; c++) {
            switch (changes[c].attributeName) {
                case 'hex':
                    this.dom.scene.color = this.dom.colorpicker.hex;
                    break;

                case 'alpha':
                    this.dom.scene.alpha = this.dom.colorpicker.alpha;
                    break;
            }
        }
    }
}

if (!customElements.get('mc-app')) {
    customElements.define('mc-app', App);
}
```

With all clicks captured from the component, filters by class, only listening to the 3D object buttons

Sets color or alpha depending on the mutation change

Having to use a MutationObserver again for such a simple task hurts a bit here. It's overly complicated, so I wish the color picker component had a custom event built in, as we covered in the last chapter. It might be some great homework for you to go back and do this yourself and refactor the previous code as well to use it.

Moving on, though, we now come to the 3D scene component. Given how little HTML/CSS is here because we're just using a <canvas> element to show the 3D, we'll show components/scene/template.js first.

Listing 15.11 HTML/CSS for the 3D scene component

```
export default {
    render() {
        return `${this.css()}
                ${this.html()}`;
    },

    mapDOM(scope) {
        return {
            scene: scope.querySelector('canvas')
        }
    },

    html() {
        return `<canvas touch-action="none">
                   </canvas>`;
    },

    css() {
        return `<style>
                  :host {
```

Caches the canvas element for use in the component class

Only element here is the canvas, and touch-action="none" enables Babylon mouse interaction

CSS here only serves to size the component and canvas to fill the page

```
                display: inline-block;
                width: 100%;
                height: 100%;
              }
              canvas {
                width: 100%;
                height: 100%;
              }
            </style>`;
    }
}
```

Like I said, really simple stuff where we just need to show a <canvas>. In terms of 3D coding in general, we're not doing anything too complicated in the component class in components/scene/scene.js. Still, though, there is a bit of setup for the scene, lights, and camera. Splitting up the JS module, let's cover the standard Web Component bits first in the next listing.

Listing 15.12 Web Component setup for the 3D scene component

```
import Template from './template.js';

export default class Scene extends HTMLElement {
   static get observedAttributes() {
       return ['object', 'color', 'alpha'];
   }

   set color(val) {
         this.setAttribute('color', val);
   }
   get color() {  return this.getAttribute('color'); }
   set alpha(val) { this.setAttribute('alpha', val); }
   get alpha() { return parseFloat(this.getAttribute('alpha')); }
   set object(val) {  this.setAttribute('object', val); }
   get object() { return this.getAttribute('object');  }

   attributeChangedCallback(
     name, oldVal, newValue) {
       switch (name) {
           case 'alpha':
               this.updateColor();
               break;

           case 'color':
               this.updateColor();
               break;

           case 'object':
               this.switchMesh(newValue);
               break;
       }
   }

   constructor() {
       super();
       this.attachShadow({mode: 'open'});
```

Annotations:
- Attributes we're observing (3D object, color, and alpha)
- JS methods to support component reflection
- Attribute change callback handles color/alpha and 3D object changes with methods not shown yet

```
        this.shadowRoot.innerHTML = Template.render();
        this.dom = Template.mapDOM(this.shadowRoot);
        this.initScene();          <-- Initializes the 3D scene, not shown yet
    }
}

if (!customElements.get('mc-scene')) {
    customElements.define('mc-scene', Scene);
}
```

Yet again, we have lots of space eaten up with reflection. I've condensed the code a little more than I normally would here because of how much space it takes up. As I said in a previous chapter, this boring, repetitive code is exactly the type of thing a nice utility function or library will solve!

Now, in the next listing, we'll cover the 3D setup JS. These functions are just more in the same class.

Listing 15.13 3D scene setup code

```
initScene() {
    this.engine = new BABYLON.Engine(        <-- Babylon.js engine and scene setup
      this.dom.scene, true);
    this.scene = new BABYLON.Scene(this.engine);
    this.scene.clearColor = new BABYLON.Color3(0.894, 0.894, 0.894);

    const camera = new BABYLON.ArcRotateCamera(     <-- Camera and lighting setup
      "Camera",
      Math.PI / 2,
      Math.PI / 2, 4,
      BABYLON.Vector3.Zero(), this.scene);
    const light1 = new BABYLON.HemisphericLight("light1",
      new BABYLON.Vector3(1, 1, 0), this.scene);
    const light2 = new BABYLON.PointLight("light2",
      new BABYLON.Vector3(0, 1, -1), this.scene);
    camera.attachControl(this.dom.scene, true);    <-- Attaches interaction controls to the camera to drag and rotate

    this.engine.runRenderLoop(        <-- Babylon needs a render loop to constantly re-render and update the scene when things change.
      () => this.render() );
    window.addEventListener(          <-- Changes the 3D scene size when the overall page resizes
      'resize', () => this.onResize());
}

render() {
    this.scene.render();
}

onResize() {
    this.engine.resize();
}
```

Likely the biggest thing you wouldn't expect here if you're used to traditional web development is the render function. This is common to 3D and 2D game engines. The scene needs to be rendered every several milliseconds. The `scene.render()` function basically gathers up everything in the scene; transforms it, materials and all; and re-renders everything to the <canvas> based on that point in time. If not done repeatedly, things just get stuck in place, unmoving. This function is also a good place to add custom code that continually updates every frame. For example, if you were moving an object from point A to point B, you might continually increment the position here, so it appears to move smoothly.

The last of the code can be seen in the following listing, where we update the 3D object primitive (or mesh) to a new type if changed, as well as any color or alpha changes.

Listing 15.14 Functions to update the 3D object, color, and alpha

```
updateColor() {
    if (!this.currentMesh) {
        return;
    }
    const material = new BABYLON.StandardMaterial('material', this.scene);
    if (this.color) {
        material.diffuseColor = new
      BABYLON.Color3.FromHexString(this.color);
    }
    if (this.alpha) {
        material.alpha = this.alpha/100;
    }
    this.currentMesh.material = material;
}

switchMesh(mesh) {
    if (this.currentMesh) {
        this.currentMesh.dispose();
    }
    switch (mesh) {
        case 'sphere':
            this.currentMesh = BABYLON.MeshBuilder.CreateSphere
            ("sphere", {}, this.scene);
            break;

        case 'cube':
            this.currentMesh = BABYLON.MeshBuilder.CreateBox
            ("cube", {}, this.scene);
            break;

        case 'geodesic':
            this.currentMesh = BABYLON.MeshBuilder.CreateSphere
            ("sphere", { segments: 2 }, this.scene);
            break;
    }
    this.updateColor();
}
```

Creates a brand-new material (or a sort of 3D style) for the object

Sets the color of the material with the current color property of the component

Sets the alpha/transparency of the material

Sets the mesh (3D object) material with the new material we've created

When creating a new mesh, throws out the current one we have in the scene

Creates a new mesh, adding it to the scene

With a new mesh, the material needs to update as well.

With those last changes, we've just created a nice little 3D material designer application! Maybe you'd like to take it further and add more functionality, like textures, reflections, bump maps, scene importing and object selection, and so on. That's more features than will fit here, but we have a decent start.

We've certainly run a good gamut of some wildly different 3D use cases. I've done a fair bit of 3D application development recently myself, and Web Components have been instrumental in helping organize a project and in separating concerns. As a prototyper, I've needed to constantly change these applications from day to day as we redesign. Many times, it's as easy as moving a component from one location in my HTML markup to another. Even if that component represents an entire 3D scene, it's not a big deal. And, of course, when I need to work on a major 3D feature, I can mentally switch contexts from all my 2D UI, open my 3D component project structure, and do my work there.

15.3 Video effects

One thing I like about mixed reality is having a window to see the world in a different way. While AR adds virtual objects to the real world, I've always liked completely altering how you see the world. We've had video effects in films and television for a long time, and being able to do these digitally is nothing new, but it can be really fun to tweak a live video feed in weird ways.

Processing pixels can be complex on its own, but if that's the fun you want to have, setting up the video feed over and over again can be a drag. In this way, we're faced with two different types of complexity. Manipulating pixels from a video feed is a complexity that we aren't hiding. Instead, we're hiding the somewhat boring complexity of getting the stream running and exposing the frame data.

15.3.1 Processing pixels with JS

A while back, I got interested in playing with video and crafted a video component of my own. I won't get into the underlying code here, but just use it as a final *Web Components in Action* component to experiment and have some fun! I've put this component in this book's GitHub repo to play around with.

There are actually two components for this purpose. The first is a really straightforward video component that simply uses normal, single-threaded JS to manipulate video pixels. The following listing is a copy of videofx/demos/video-simple.html.

Listing 15.15 Simple video playback demo

```
<html>
<head>
   <title>Demo: Simple Video Playback</title>
   <script        <-- Imports video component module
     type="module"
     src="../video.js">
   </script>

   <style>
       wcia-video {        <-- Sets video component size
           width: 500px;
           height: 500px;
       }
```

```
  </style>
</head>

<body>
<h2>Demo: Simple Video Playback</h2>
<p>
  Simple video playback
</p>
<wcia-video useCamera></wcia-video>     <-- Includes video component on page
</body>
</html>
```

While the component can take a `src=path/to/video` attribute, it's easier (and more fun) showing a live camera feed from your computer rather than uploading a big video somewhere, and that's exactly what the `useCamera` attribute does. This live camera feed is exactly what'll you'll see when loading the page.

Even though it's technically working, it's not altering the video frames yet. For this, let's switch rendering to the component's internal canvas and tell it how often to render each frame. Let's set a couple more attributes:

```
<wcia-video useCamera useCanvasForDisplay canvasRefreshInterval="50">
</wcia-video>
```

Here, we've chose to refresh the canvas every 50 milliseconds. If we go with something like 500, we'll see a very choppy video. If we go too low, our browser will struggle to keep up. Either way, now that we're using the internal canvas, we can draw to it!

I've included a set of filters that can be used fairly easily just by setting the filter on the component with another `<script>` block on the page, as seen in the next listing.

Listing 15.16 Setting a video filter

```
<wcia-video useCamera useCanvasForDisplay canvasRefreshInterval="50">   <-- Adds the video component to the page using the camera
</wcia-video>

<script type="module">
  import Filters from                       <-- Imports a filter library provided in the component
    '../filters/canvas/filters.js';
  document.querySelector('wcia-video').canvasFilter =
    Filters.toBlackAndWhite;   <-- Sets the filter of the component to a specific black and white filter
</script>
```

The black and white filter renders every pixel either black or white and produces a live video stream looking like figure 15.10—though it's much cooler live and in motion!

The file videofx/demos/video-filters.html contains the black and white filter plus a few more, but I think it's better to make the frame data available right on the page. Listing 15.17 shows changes to the demo and is found at videofx/demos/video-customfilter.html.

Figure 15.10 A live video stream with a black and white filter

Listing 15.17 Custom filter demo to introduce video "snow"

```
<wcia-video
       frameDataMode="imagedata"            ◁— Sets attribute to allow
       canvasRefreshInterval="50"              frameData event from
       useCamera                               video component
       useCanvasForDisplay>
</wcia-video>

<p>Amount of snow</p>
<input type="range" min="0" step=".01" max="1" value="0.7"
   oninput="snow = event.target.value">     ◁— Range slider to change
                                                amount of video snow
<script>
   var snow = .7;
   const customfilter = function(pxs) {     ◁— Custom function to
       for (var c = 0; c < pxs.data.length; c+=4) {   process and change pixels
           if (Math.random() < snow) {                 in each video frame
               pxs.data[c] = Math.random() * 255;
               pxs.data[c+1] = Math.random() * 255;
               pxs.data[c+2] = Math.random() * 255;
           }
       }
       return pxs;
   };

   document.querySelector('wcia-video').addEventListener
       ('frameupdate', function(event) {    ◁— Listens to frame update events,
       var data = event.detail;                 processes the pixels, and redraws
       data.canvascontext.putImageData(         to video component canvas
       customfilter(data.framedata), 0, 0, 0, 0, data.width, data.height );
   });
</script>
```

So, these video frames are fairly easy to process—we just loop through the data. Each pixel uses four values, one each for red, green, blue, and alpha. Alpha (`pxs.data[c+3]`), while not used here, could be cool to experiment with if you were to change the component to not have a black background.

Anyway, this custom filter is simply for adding randomly colored pixels at random locations in each frame. How many randomly colored pixels is determined by the slider value. The output, shown in figure 15.11, looks like when TV signals were still analog and had snow or noise when the signal wasn't strong.

Figure 15.11 Live camera feed with "snow" effect

Getting real video frame data can be a powerful thing! We'll circle back to this at the very end with a real application for it that doesn't just change pixels. Before we do though, it's worth noting that while processing pixels with JS is pretty neat, it's also fairly slow. While my browser easily kept up with refreshing the canvas every 50 ms, our image processing was fairly simple. In general, using your CPU is not the best way to go for this. Even worse is doing this in JS in your browser. Since JS is single threaded (until you get into Web Workers; https://developer.mozilla.org/en-US/docs/Web/API/Web_Workers_API/Using_web_workers), doing these intensive operations can block your UI and make things seem sluggish.

15.3.2 WebGL shaders

Offloading your pixels to the GPU is exactly how to avoid this sluggishness when needing to run image processing such as this. Now that GPUs are standard in every device, it's becoming more common to offload graphics drawing here. In fact, it was several years back that many CSS effects got a GPU bump to make everything run much smoother.

The way to access the GPU in your browser is to use WebGL. You might recall that at the beginning of this chapter, I mentioned that 3D on the web, including VR and AR, was powered by WebGL, but that it was too low-level to be productive for the ordinary person.

I still hold to that! But I did extend the video component to accommodate WebGL. Again, what's great with Web Component classes is that while your class extends

`HTMLElement`, you can further extend your Web Component class. With the WebGL version of the video component, I layered some additional functionality to handle the low-level shader code, as well as changed the internal canvas to a WebGL context instead of the typical 2D canvas context. The next listing shows the demo located at videofx/demos/videogl-filters.html and contains a few different WebGL filters.

Listing 15.18 WebGL video component demo

```
<html>
   <head>
       <title>Demo: Copy to Canvas</title>
       <script                        <-- Links to WebGL flavor of
               type="module"              the video component
               src="../glvideo.js">
       </script>

       <style>
           wcia-glvideo {         <-- Be sure to use the new
               width: 250px;          CSS selector for the
               height: 250px;         different component tags.
           }
       </style>
   </head>

   <body>
       <h2>Demo: Apply WebGL Filter</h2>
       <p>
           Apply WebGL Filter - possible glfilters are "sepia",
           "greyscale", "sobel_edge_detection", "freichen_edge_detection",
           "freichen_inverted", and "sobel_inverted"
       </p>
       <wcia-glvideo      <-- Adds the WebGL video
               useCamera      component to the page
               useCanvasForDisplay
               canvasRefreshInterval="10"
               useWebGL='{"filter": "freichen_inverted"}'>     <--
       </wcia-glvideo>
   </body>                        Specifies WebGL options,
</html>                           including the filter to use
```

Technically speaking, the Freichen and Sobel shader is used to bring out edges of objects in your video. When you wash out everything but edges, you start approaching the basics of computer visualization where, if taken further, objects can start to be recognized in your video frames. That's way more advanced than we can cover here. But at its rawest form, if nothing else, it does produce a nice rendition of a line art effect, so you can be in a version of your own "Take On Me" A-ha music video, as figure 15.12 shows!

Writing WebGL shaders (the tiny programs that manipulate pixels) is really complicated and infuriating sometimes. Shaders are written as plain strings in JS, with no great way to debug. It can also be pretty hard to set up an environment where you can write your own shaders. Once again, however, Web Components like this can

Figure 15.12 Edge detection effect with a WebGL-based video Web Component

make it easier. This same component also allows custom shaders to be written, as in the next listing.

Listing 15.19 Custom shaders used in the WebGL video component

```
<html>
<head>
   <script type="module" src="../glvideo.js"></script>

   <script                      <-- Script tag to hold custom
     id="2d-vertex-shader"          vertex shader
     type="x-shader/x-vertex">
// Use any shader here, or the Vertex shader included in Listing 15.1
   </script>

   <script                      <-- Script tag to hold custom
     id="2d-fragment-shader"        fragment shader
     type="x-shader/x-fragment">
// Use any shader here, or the Fragment shader included in Listing 15.1
   </script>

   <style>
       wcia-glvideo {  <-- Sizes the video component
           width: 640px;
           height: 480px;
       }
   </style>

</head>

<body>                       Places the video
<wcia-glvideo          <--   component on the page
       useCamera
       useWebGL
       useCanvasForDisplay
       canvasRefreshInterval="10">
</wcia-glvideo>

<script type="module">
   import Shaders from '../filters/webgl/shaders.js';
```

```
    import Constants from '../filters/webgl/constants.js';

    var video = document.querySelector('wcia-glvideo');
    video.webglProperties.vertexShader =
        document.getElementById('2d-vertex-shader').text;
    video.webglProperties.fragmentShader =
        document.getElementById('2d-fragment-shader').text;
</script>
</body>
</html>
```

Sets the video's WebGL shaders to the script tag contents

The output is subtle, but it creates an effect shown in figure 15.13; the subject at the center of the photo (my cat) has perfect clarity, but as the photo gets farther away to the outer edges all around, it slowly fades to black.

Figure 15.13 Radial fade around the edges of a live camera feed

15.4 Hand tracking and machine learning

As I was writing this final chapter, I knew I wanted to do one last thing with the Web Harp demo from chapter 5. I had some ideas for generic computer vision and motion tracking, but then a rather exciting article was posted on hand tracking in JS: https://hackernoon.com/handtrackjs-677c29c1d585.

The relatively new field of machine learning involves training a set of data, or model, against right and wrong things. In the case of hand tracking, this particular model was trained to recognize images of hands. While all the training for this experiment was performed with Google's TensorFlow machine learning framework in Python, the trained model can then be used in our browser with Tensorflow.js.

The details don't matter so much, except to explain how it works under the hood. Also, because of the hard work that went into it, the author really needs to be credited. His name is Victor Dibia, and Handtrack.js along with a great demo can be found here: https://github.com/victordibia/handtrack.js/.

Crediting the author and learning about the technology aside, we can hide his amazing library and all of the complexities that went into this project by creating a hand-tracking Web Component! In fact, given that the library uses a source video element and renders tracking details to another canvas, Handtrack.js is a lot like the inner workings of the video Web Component we've been working on. Just as with the WebGL flavor, the video component class can be extended to create a specialized `handtracker` component. The next listing shows this relatively simple extension.

Listing 15.20 Hand-tracking Web Component

```
import Video from './video.js';

export default class HandTracker extends Video {          <-- Extends the base video component class
    static get HAND_LOCATION() { return 'onHandLocation'; }
    constructor() {
        super();
        const modelParams = {
            flipHorizontal: true, // flip e.g for video
            maxNumBoxes: 20,      // maximum number of boxes to detect
            iouThreshold: 0.5,    // ioU threshold for non-max suppression
            scoreThreshold: 0.6,  // confidence threshold for predictions.
        };
        handTrack.load(modelParams)        <-- Loads the Handtrack.js Tensorflow model
           .then(lmodel => {
                this._model = lmodel;
        });
    }

    runDetection() {
        if (!this._model) { return; }
        this._model.detect(this.dom.video).then(predictions => {
            const pts = [];
            for (let c = 0; c < predictions.length; c++) {
                const centerpoint = {};
                centerpoint.x = (predictions[c].bbox[0] +
                  (predictions[c].bbox[2] / 2));
                centerpoint.y = (predictions[c].bbox[1] +
                  (predictions[c].bbox[3] / 2));
                pts.push(centerpoint);
            }
            this._model.renderPredictions(predictions, this.dom.canvas,
                this.canvasContext, this.dom.video);

            const ce = new CustomEvent( HandTracker.HAND_LOCATION,
                { detail: { points: pts }, bubbles: true, composed: true });
            this.dispatchEvent(ce);    <-- Dispatches Custom Events for center point of hand locations found
        });
    }

    init() {                           <-- Runs normal video component initialization plus starts the hand tracking
        super.init();
        handTrack.startVideo(this.dom.video).then((status) => {
            this.onResize();
            console.log(this.visibleVideoRect)
            if (status) { this.runDetection();  }
        });
    }
```

```
    getCurrentFrameData(mode, noredraw) {     <-- Keeps running detection every
        this.runDetection();                      frame by taking over the original
    }                                             component's canvas redraw
}

if (!customElements.get('wcia-handtracker')) {
    customElements.define('wcia-handtracker', HandTracker);
}
```

You might be asking, "Is that it?" Well, it's definitely small, but there is a missing piece. The library that the author distributes isn't a module (the source is, but it has TensorFlow dependencies, and I want to keep this example simple); so instead of jumping through hoops to include it in this component, we'll simply include it on the demo HTML page, which I'll show in the following listing.

Listing 15.21 `Handtracker` demo HTML file

```
<html>
<head>                          Imports handtracker
    <script                 <-- Web Component
        type="module"
        src="../handtracker.js">
    </script>                                          Includes Handtrack.js
    <script src="../handtrack.min.js"></script>   <-- library

    <style>
        wcia-handtracker {
            width: 500px;
            height: 500px;
        }
    </style>
</head>

<body>
    <h2>Demo: Hand Tracker <span id="loc"></span></h2>
    <wcia-handtracker useCamera useCanvasForDisplay         Places handtracker
      canvasRefreshInterval="50"></wcia-handtracker>   <-- component on page

    <script>
        document.addEventListener('onHandLocation', function(e) {
            if (e.detail.points.length > 0) {
                document.getElementById('loc')
➥.innerText = e.detail.points[0].x + ',' + e.detail.points[0].y;
            }
        })
     </script>
</body>
</html>
```

Updates text in the header to show where the first hand found is

For such a complex and useful thing, there's not much here, but it does work like a charm! Figure 15.14 shows the demo page in action.

As neat as this is, Victor already has this demo up and running. In isolation, my component demo doesn't add anything to this conversation. However, as a Web Component with a Custom Event being dispatched to notify any listeners of hand locations, we can now use this component in the Web Harp application from chapter 5.

Demo: Hand Tracker 256,173

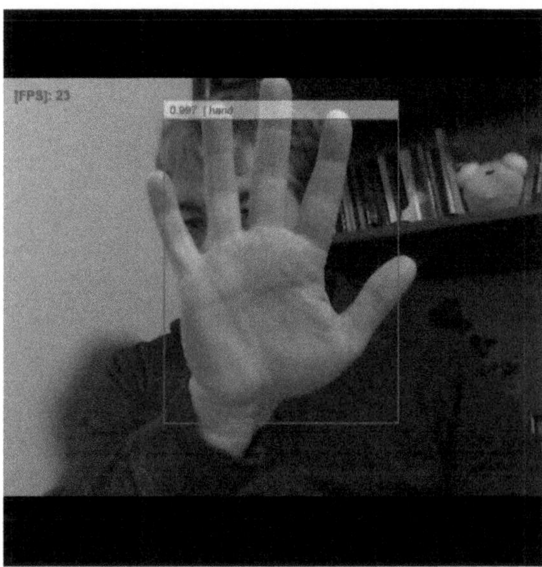

Figure 15.14 Hand-tracker Web Component demo

Not only can we use it, it really isn't that much effort to integrate! First, go into the index.html for the Web Harp application and add the hand-tracker library:

```
<script src="../videofx/handtrack.min.js"></script>
```

As I've copied the Web Harp code right into the chapter 15 folder of this book's GitHub repo, we can link inside the video component folder we were just using. From there, we simply have to alter webharp/components/app/app.js.

Remember, chapter 5 was before we started separating out CSS and HTML into a template.js file, so we'll add it to the string that we're setting `innerHTML` with. Another small change is to no longer listen to the mouse move event, but instead directly tap into the component's hand-tracking Custom Event. The next listing shows how we've changed this component class.

Listing 15.22 Web Harp app component integrated with the `handtracker` component

```
import Strings from '../strings/strings.js';
import HandTracker from '../../../videofx/handtracker.js';

export default class WebHarpApp extends HTMLElement {
    connectedCallback() {
        this.innerHTML = `
            <style>
                wcia-handtracker {
                    position: absolute;
                    background: none;
                    width: 100%;
```

```
                height: 100%;
            }
            webharp-strings {
                position: absolute;
                width: 100%;
                height: 100%;
            }
        </style>
        <wcia-handtracker useCamera useCanvasForDisplay
           canvasRefreshInterval="50"></wcia-handtracker>
           <webharp-strings
              strings="${this.getAttribute('strings')}">
           </webharp-strings>`;

        this.stringsElement = this.querySelector('webharp-strings');
        this.addEventListener(HandTracker.HAND_LOCATION, e =>
        this.onMouseMove(e));
    }

    onMouseMove(event) {
            if (event.detail.points.length > 0) {
                this.stringsElement.points = { last: this.lastPoint,
                current: { x: event.detail.points[0].x, y:
                event.detail.points[0].y } };
                this.lastPoint = { x: event.detail.points[0].x, y:
                  event.detail.points[0].y };
            }
    }
}

if (!customElements.get('webharp-app')) {
    customElements.define('webharp-app', WebHarpApp);
}
```

New HTML string including the handtracker and CSS to position it behind the strings component

Changes event listener from mouse move to hand location

Sets the points to the first hand found instead of the mouse location

You can probably start to imagine all sorts of ways to improve this application—perhaps by getting rid of the demo hand display bounding box info. Most of all, you might want to get rid of the restriction of only one hand being tracked and use the full list of points to strum the harp with both hands. That could be a great homework assignment to continue on with. Right now, though, figure 15.15 shows the Web Harp as it stands, complete with hand tracking.

I have to admit that I had a bit too much fun playing with the Web Harp. In fact, this chapter was really all about playing with fun Web Component examples that I've either created or come across over the past couple of years.

While I hope you had fun too, I also hope that what you take away from this last chapter is a bit of the excitement I'm feeling from Web Components. We started in chapter 2 by building the simplest of all components: a slider. We're still using that slider in this last chapter inside a color picker inside a 3D material-editing application. We've gone from an image carousel in a component to creating mixed reality scenes viewable on an Oculus Rift or Magic Leap headset, and then ended with a video effects processing component that uses machine learning to track your hands.

Figure 15.15 Web Harp with hand tracking

We've done all of this, and it doesn't really matter what your experience level is. Any of these components can be added to any ordinary HTML page. It doesn't matter if you're too timid to look inside any particular component—you can just use it. On top of that, Web Components really do have a simple API, such that any beginner JS developer can start working with them right away.

We'll certainly have more complex workflows get popular as component developers grow beyond the initial standards. But these initial standards won't change anytime soon. With Web Components, we'll be left with what I've always loved about the web. It's a place where anyone can contribute by building on the basic building blocks within, or on top of the shoulders of experts and creatives alike. However you proceed, I sincerely wish you the best, and I do hope Web Components and this book are a stepping stone to some amazing things that you create. Above all, please share! It's one of the benefits of people like you creating for the web today. Thank you for reading!

Summary

In this chapter, you learned

- What may happen in the Web Component future
- How Web Components can make intimidating technologies like mixed reality and machine learning approachable
- How to hide your own complex systems, like a full 3D scene in a Web Component
- How to use components created throughout this book for emerging technologies

appendix ES2015 for Web Components

A.1 What is ES2015?

It used to be that changes to the JavaScript language were few and far between. What you might not know is that "JavaScript" really isn't the official name—it's just something we've been calling it since 1996, when Java was king, and Netscape wanted to give its LiveScript language a boost. That was also the year that Netscape submitted JavaScript to ECMA International (www.ecma-international.org) for standardization.

After acceptance as a new language standard, we should have been calling it ECMAScript, but the name just doesn't roll off the tongue. So, for more than 20 years, it's been known as JavaScript (or JS), while the standard is referred to as ECMAScript. When ECMAScript 3 came out in 1999, that was pretty much it in regard to changes for a while.

It wasn't until 2009 that the fifth edition of ECMAScript was finalized. The fourth edition was, unfortunately, scrapped after being based on Adobe Flash's ActionScript and proving to be a bit too ambitious of a language change in many people's minds. With ECMAScript 5 being a decade old, it's the standard most of us are familiar with. People also referred to this version as ES5.

So, of course, in 2015, when the sixth edition of the language was finalized, folks were referring to it as ES6—which was, unfortunately, a bit inaccurate! ECMAScript version 6 was the first edition that the standards committee decided to call by the year it was released, hence ES2015.

Since 2015, we've seen a new version every year. With the short turnaround, the changes have been fairly steady and small. These days, it's more helpful to see if the language feature you want to use has been adopted by the browsers you are targeting.

Despite some great JS language features since 2015, I like to focus on a few core ES2015 (ES6) language features that really make Web Component development so much better.

A.2 Rethinking variables with ES2015

Strictly speaking, you're free to keep using `var` whenever you want. Declaring variables this way has worked for as long as JS has been in existence, and it's not changing anytime soon.

A.2.1 Variable declaration with let

ES2015 brings us two more ways to declare your variables: `let` and `const`. In terms of usage, not much has changed—things are just a bit stricter and a little saner. With `let`, you may declare your variables, just as you always have with `var`:

```
var x = 5; // old way
let x = 5; // new way
```

The difference between `let` and `var` is a matter of scope. Variable declarations made with `let` are a bit more familiar to users of other programming languages. The variables will exist only in the block they were created with, as well as any nested blocks within. Blocks are basically lines of code surrounded by curly braces, like an `if/then`, a `for` loop, or a function declaration.

Consider the following listing.

Listing A.1 Declaring a `var` inside a `for` loop block

```
for (var c = 0; c < 5; c++) {
     var message = 'hi' + c;
}

console.log(message);
```

The message variable is declared inside the for loop.

With the `var` declaration, we're repeatedly setting `message` to "hi" along with the current iteration of the loop. As we limit `c` to less than 5 in this loop, our console log prints out "hi4." The fact that our `message` variable contains anything at all after this loop is a bit unique to JS.

Typically, in other languages, our `message` variable would be scoped to the block that it lives in, namely, this `for` loop. In practice, the variable just wouldn't exist outside this scope! Using `let` for variable declaration makes this scoping behavior default.

Let's change `var` to `let` in the next listing.

Listing A.2 Declaring a variable with `let` inside a `for` loop block

```
for (let c = 0; c < 5; c++) {
    let message = 'hi' + c;
}

console.log(message);
```

Same variable declaration as before, except now with "let" instead of "var"

Not only is message undefined now, but JS throws an error:

```
Uncaught ReferenceError: message is not defined
```

Another interesting behavior of `let` is that it can't be used before it's declared, unlike `var`. Yes, there's a little bit to unpack here because if you're not used to JS, you might be thinking, "How can I use a variable before it's declared?!" Well, you can, thanks to something called *hoisting*. Hoisting has implications outside of simple variable declaration, but when a variable is declared, it is "hoisted," or moved up to the top of the block.

Consider the following:

```
x = 5;
var x;
console.log(x);
```

With variable hoisting, the declaration is actually moved to the top of this block prior to execution. So, in reality, x is declared prior to it being set to 5, despite what the code says. Using `let` to declare x, on the other hand, will cause the following error:

```
Uncaught ReferenceError: x is not defined
```

Does this mean that `let` does not hoist? No—in fact, x would still be hoisted, but a so-called "temporal dead zone" is created between the start of the block and when the code defines the variable. Inside this dead zone, variables cannot be accessed or set. Figure A.1 highlights this temporal dead zone with `let` versus simple variable hoisting with `var`.

Now, the next question you might be asking yourself is, "How is this useful?" Everything I've described about `let` is more restrictive than `var`! Why strive to introduce errors? It's really the code readability that matters here, and the intent you are declaring with your code to anyone who comes and reads it later.

When folks come in to read your code, with `let` they will automatically know that you aren't using your variable inside any other block besides where they are seeing it. Are they seeing your variable declared inside a `for` loop? A reader will be 100%

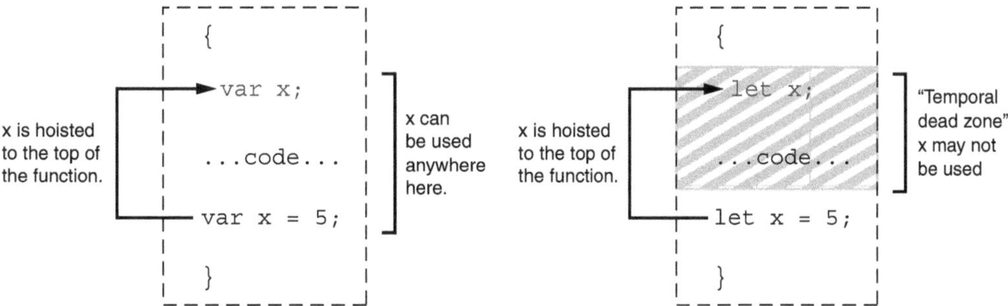

Figure A.1 Difference between variable access prior to declaration with `var` vs. `let`. Using `let` introduces a "temporal dead zone" where the variable cannot be accessed.

assured that your code isn't using the same variable reference anywhere else. Even if it has the same name in another block, they are completely sure that the variables aren't referencing the same thing. Using `let` also reassures the reader of your code that you aren't accessing or setting the variable before you declare it.

Having this very strict behavior with errors helps keep your code to these promises you are making. If you break this promise, your code just won't function! On the other hand, using `var` for variable declarations makes no such promises, and your code is pretty ambiguous about what your intent is.

A.2.2 Variable declaration with const

Declaring a variable with `const` is virtually identical to declaring with `let`. You are making the same promises to folks who read your code that you aren't using the variable before declaring it and that the variable is undefined outside the block that it lives in.

The one difference with `const` is that when you declare a variable with `const`, it cannot be set to a different value after it is first set. Let's try it out:

```
const x = 5;
console.log(x);
x = 6;
```

In this example, we set x to 5. The variable logs fine as 5, but when we set x to 6, we get an error:

```
Uncaught TypeError: Assignment to constant variable.
```

So, with `const`, can a variable really not be changed? It looks like it cannot, but it depends on what you mean by "changed." It's true that we can't just set x to something else entirely, but we can certainly edit x, so to speak. If our variable isn't a primitive type like a string or a number, but instead an object that has properties of its own, we can edit those properties:

```
const x = { a: 5 };
x.a = 6;
```

The previous example does not throw an error. However, if we set x to another object altogether, it would definitely throw an error.

A.2.3 Important by convention but not functionality

As you can see, both `let` and `const` don't give you more functionality. With this in mind, using these new JS features isn't required in the least. If you still prefer using `var` after reading all of this, you really won't run into any trouble (aside from the readability aspects mentioned). That said, given that you are creating Web Components, you'll need to be using at least one ES2015 feature. Because of this, there isn't much of an excuse to opt out of using `let` and `const`. If other people are reading your code, they'll likely be wondering why you're still using `var`.

A.3 Classes

In other languages, classes can be thought of as blueprints or templates. When you create this blueprint, you're creating a well-defined construct that you can instantiate objects from. The class doesn't really serve to do anything besides be this template. Despite just being a blueprint, classes serve to plan out how objects we create from them will act. Any instance or object created from a certain class will always act a certain way because the programmer has defined all of the methods, properties, and logic within the class.

A class usually looks something like this:

```
Class MyClass {
        . . .
}
```

You would instantiate, or create, an instance of the class like the following line of JS, shown in figure A.2:

```
const myInstance = new MyClass();
```

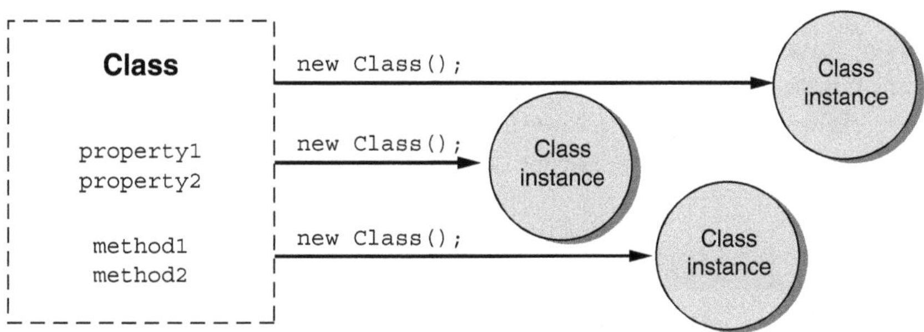

Figure A.2 In object-oriented programming languages, class instances are typically made from a class, kind of like a blueprint.

In JS, however, classes are a bit different. As JS is a prototype-based language, true classes don't really exist like they do in object-oriented languages. Instead, the new ES2015 class feature offers some nice syntax that makes JS look a little more object-oriented. Under the hood, there really is no "blueprint"—you're simply creating a runtime object with the class feature that you clone to create the instance.

With this in mind, even though they look similar and offer some great functionality, classes in JS don't offer all the same things that classes in other languages do. There are good resources for learning all about both object-oriented programming and classes in JS. This section will serve to cover some of the basics to help you learn concepts relating to Web Components without getting too deep.

A.3.1 Constructor

The constructor is a fairly simple concept but is used and referred to anywhere the discussion of classes comes up. From a usage standpoint, there's really no difference between a constructor in JS and a constructor in most other languages.

A constructor is a function that describes any user-defined logic that happens when a class is instantiated. For example, we can define a class in JS with a constructor that does a simple `console.log` when the class is instantiated, as shown in the following listing.

Listing A.3 Using the constructor method of a class

```
<script>
    class MyClass {
        constructor() {        <— The constructor method
            console.log('hi from my class');
        }
    }

    let instance = new MyClass();        <— Instantiates the class
</script>
```

Simply by instantiating this class, our `console.log` is executed. Typically, any logic initialization is put in the constructor.

One extra rule when using inheritance on a class is that you must call `super();` as the very first line, even if the parent class has no constructor. Let's take a look in the next listing.

Listing A.4 Calling `super()` is required in a subclass's constructor

```
<script>
    class MyParentClass {        <— Declares base class
    }

    class MyClass extends MyParentClass {        <— Inherits the base class
        constructor() {
            super();                          <— Calling super() is required in
            console.log('hi from my class');     the constructor if inheriting.
        }
    }

    let instance = new MyClass();
</script>
```

Calling `super();` is a way to call the constructor of the inherited class—in this case, `MyParentClass`.

A.3.2 Properties

In most languages, a class will generally serve as a blueprint for both method definitions *and* property definitions. A generic example can be seen in this listing.

Listing A.5 A generic class example for any language

```
class MyClass {
    property1: . . .;       <-- A property declared on the class
    property2: . . .;           (does not work in vanilla JS)

    method1() {     <-- A method declared on the
        . . .           class (does work in JS)
    }

    method2() {
        . . .
    }
}
```

In JS, only methods are defined on the class. Properties are a different story. If you'd like to create a variable that exists in your class's scope, you'd need to create it in one of the methods as a property of `this`, which represents the scope of your class instance. Unfortunately, this difference means that your JS code might get a little hard to read. In other languages, where variables are declared on the class itself, it's easy to know exactly what properties are available in your class because they are typically declared at the top.

With JS, I usually like to declare my variables inside the constructor to attempt to make up for this shortcoming. If I wanted to leverage my constructor to make my class properties a little easier to read, I might try the approach outlined in the next listing.

Listing A.6 Declaring your properties in the constructor instead of on the class itself

```
class MyClass {
    constructor() {
        this.property1;     <-- Declares a property on a
                                class that starts as undefined
        this.property2 =        <-- Declares a property on a class
            'a starting value';     with an initial value
    }

    method1() {
      . . .
    }

    method2() {
      . . .
    }
}
```

Another thing you might find yourself missing if you come from other languages is the notion of private, protected, and public properties in your class.

A.3.3 Private properties in JS

In traditional object-oriented programming languages, in addition to being able to declare properties on a class, developers may also specify *how* these variables are accessed. There are typically three types of properties on a class in these types of languages:

- Private
- Protected
- Public

Figure A.3 demonstrates each type of property as an attempt is made to access it from outside the class.

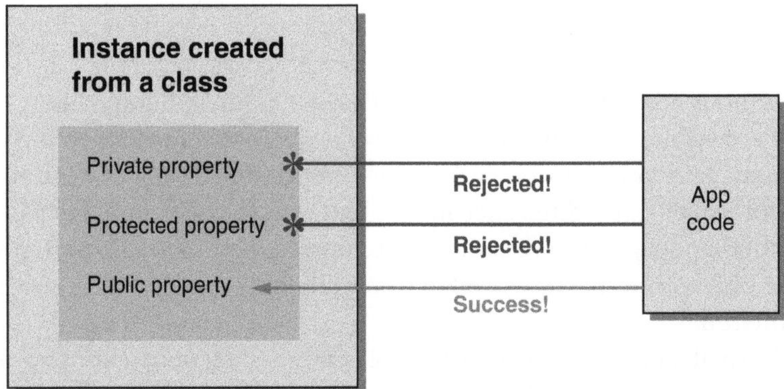

Figure A.3 Non-JS example of the differences among public, private, and protected variables

A private variable is one that is only accessible from within your class. This means that if you instantiated the class with `new` and then tried to access the property, it would be undefined or throw an exception, as seen in the following listing.

Listing A.7 Pseudocode for private class properties in other languages

```
Class MyClass {
        private x;        <— Declares a private variable on a class

        constructor() {
           x = 5;
        }
}

instance = new MyClass();
instance.x = 6;        <— Fails because the property is private
```

Private variables offer your class some protection against consumers of the class coming in and changing its internal workings. As a class creator, you get to define how that class gets used and how it doesn't.

Say, for example, that there is a variable you are using inside the class to track something. For example, you might be tracking the number of times a user clicked a button. Inside the class, we set `counter = 0`. Every time a user clicks, we increment the counter: `counter ++`. Typically, in many languages, this counter might be a private or protected variable. This would prevent a developer from setting `myinstance .counter` from the outside to whatever they wanted, completely destroying the actual count!

Private variables in other languages are also unable to be accessed by a parent class. Consider the two classes in the next listing.

Listing A.8 Showing bad access of private property in subclass (pseudocode)

```
Class MyParentClass {
     private x;          <-- Private variable is declared in base class

     constructor() {
         x = 5;          <-- Variable is set in the base class's constructor
     }
}

Class MyClass extends MyParentClass {
       constructor() {
         super();
         x = 6;          <-- Throws an exception because x is
       }                     private and not declared in this class
}
```

In this example, even though `MyClass` inherits from `MyParentClass`, variable `x` can't be accessed by `MyClass`. If `x` were protected instead of private, this wouldn't be the case. With JS, however, these distinctions go out the window. As properties aren't declared and are all accessible on the scope of the class using `this`, there really is no distinction—all properties are public. This means that after you instantiate your object from the class, any property or method that can be used inside the class can be referenced outside the class.

JS developers have dealt with this for a while, even before classes were a thing. Some have created some fairly genius, as well as ugly looking, workarounds for this. I'm a proponent of going simple and using an underscore to prepend my variable names. Something like this is what I use:

```
this._property2 = 'a starting value';
```

An underscore in your variable name doesn't actually *do* anything. Instead, it's a convention many of us use to pretend it's not public and can't be accessed from outside. It's true that a developer might set `myobject._counter` from outside of the class, but by using that underscore, it's obvious that anyone who reads the code knows they are doing a "bad" thing.

Though I do favor the underscore for simplicity and use it in this book, a more modern approach is to use another ES2015 feature called `WeakMap`. `WeakMap` and `Map` are two similar concepts in JS. Both are used as a key/value store. Not only do Map and WeakMap have an arguably nicer API than a simple object, they also accept nonprimitive data types as keys (in fact, WeakMap requires nonprimitive keys).

What this means is that we can actually use an entire class instance as a key for either of our maps. As we want automatic garbage collection for our maps, we'll use a WeakMap for our private variable implementation instead of a Map in the next listing.

Listing A.9 Using WeakMap to simulate private properties in JS

```
const vars = new WeakMap();          <-- Initializes the WeakMap

const _private = obj => {            <-- Object to access private variables,
    if (!vars.has(obj)) {                organized by class instance
        vars.set(obj, {});
    }
    return vars.get(obj);
};

class MyClass {
    constructor() {
        _private(this).test =        <-- Sets a private variable from inside the class
                'hi from my class';
    }
}
```

This might look a bit confusing at first but bear with me. First, we create the WeakMap to store collections of our private variables. Remember that one class can have many instances, so we use each instance as a key for the WeakMap managed by the class itself.

So, if the key is the instance, what is the value? Each value is a JS object that contains even more key/value pairs. Each of these key/value pairs is the name of the private variable and the value of the variable itself, as outlined in figure A.4.

Lastly, we also declare a function, _private, to help manage usage of this WeakMap and make getting and setting private variables easy. In addition to getting the correct private variable for an instance, this function creates objects to hold an individual instance's private variables.

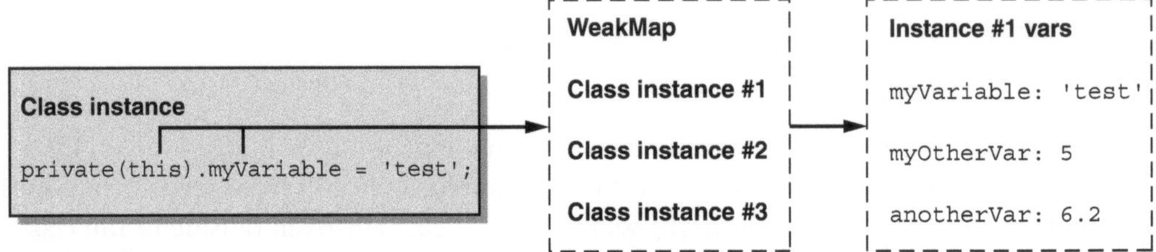

Figure A.4 An implementation that uses private variables going through a WeakMap with keys based on class instances, with each key referencing an object holding the private variables

This method seems like a popular, modern way to make your variables private. Unlike simply using underscores to denote private variables, this method actually makes variables inaccessible through the instance of the class. There are quite a few workarounds like this. Perhaps soon, we'll really have private variable support (private class fields are already in Chrome Canary), but in the meantime, we can only choose the solution that suits our needs by weighing ease of use and true inaccessibility from outside the class instance.

A.3.4 Getters and setters

Another set of class features that will be relevant in our Web Component pursuit are getters and setters. Getters and setters are methods that look like properties from the outside. Let's pretend in the next listing that we have a class with a click counter that we'd rather not let be changed from the outside, but that we'd still like to make available to read.

Listing A.10 An internally tracked mouse-click counter

```
class MyClass {
        constructor() {
                this._counter = 0;     <-- Initializes a counter in
        }                                  the class's constructor

        mouseClickHandler() {
                this._counter ++;     <-- Increments the counter in a
        }                                 hypothetical mouse-click handler
}
```

As detailed in the last section on private variables, using the underscore for `this._counter` is a naïve implementation for marking this variable as private. Again, it's by convention, meaning it's understood that we shouldn't be accessing `_counter` like this:

```
let myInstance = new MyClass();
let myCounter = myInstance._counter;
```

To make our variable readable but not writeable, we need to define access to it via a getter method. Again, getters and setters aren't really properties we can access. Instead, in the following listing, we are creating a method on our class that acts like a property.

Listing A.11 Creating a getter method to allow read but not write access to a property

```
class MyClass {
        constructor() {
                this._counter = 0;
        }

        get counter() {          <-- Getter for counter variable
                return this._counter;
        }
```

```
        mouseClickHandler() {
                this._counter ++;
        }
}
```

Now we have a way to query counter, but since we've not added a setter, setting counter will not actually accomplish anything. The internal value will still be 0:

```
let myInstance = new MyClass();
let myCounter = myInstance.counter; // works
myInstance.counter = 5;
console.log(myInstance.counter) // logs 0
```

This is exactly what we want! We want to provide a way to access how many times a mouse was clicked but, like in figure A.5, don't want someone to come in and assign counter to any number. Of course, in the next listing, we can also add a setter as well by using set instead of get in our method definition.

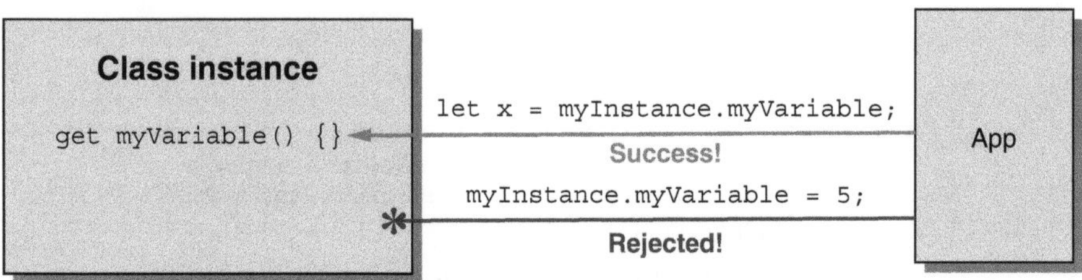

Figure A.5 Example of declaring a getter on a class with no setter. The outside application can get the variable, but cannot set it.

Listing A.12 Defining both getters and setters on a class

```
class MyClass {
        constructor() {
                this._counter = 0;
        }

        set counter(val) {        <-- A setter to complement the counter getter
                this._counter = val;
        }

        get counter() {
                return this._counter;
        }
        mouseClickHandler() {
                this._counter ++;
        }
}
```

Of course, in the context of this example, a setter doesn't make much sense. Moreover, using both getters and setters to read and write from a simple property is a bit verbose. Why not just make counter an actual public property?

Defining both getters and setters is useful when you want to perform some logic in addition to, or in lieu of, reading or writing a variable. For example, perhaps setting our `counter` property updates a graphic as well. Here, we can imagine a bar from a bar chart that grows to the value of the counter, and it's all done by simply using the counter setter:

```
set counter(val) {
        this.counterElement.style.height = val + "px";
        this._counter = val;
}
```

A.3.5 Static methods

Let's move on to *static* methods. Static methods are also called *class methods* because they are run on the class itself, rather than on an instance of the class.

Let's start with a simple but useless example: adding two numbers and returning a result. Of course, normally you'd just use the + operator and add them, but let's make it a method in our class.

Listing A.13 An add method on a class

```
class MyClass {
        constructor() {
        }
        add(a, b) {     <-- An addition method defined inside a class
               return a + b;
        }
}
```

To use our new `add` method, we'd need to instantiate the class first:

```
let myInstance = new MyClass();
let total = myInstance.add(5, 6); // total is set to 11
```

If you think about it, though, we aren't using any properties of the instantiated class. Previously, in our getter/setter click-counter example, we recorded the count as a property of the class. Without using the instance created from our class to increment our counter, we'd have no way to know what it was before we tried to increment.

In this case, however, we aren't tracking anything—we don't actually need the instance of the class; we just want to call a function and get a result.

Listing A.14 Example of a class method using the `static` keyword

```
class MyClass {
        constructor() {
        }

        static add(a, b) {
               return a + b;
        }
}
```

The function in listing A.14 can now be run from the class itself (hence the name class method):

```
let total = MyClass.add(5, 6);
```

Static or class methods are fairly useful, but they are also directly applicable to how we listen for attributes in Web Components, as you can see in chapter 4, where `observedAttributes` is used to tell your Web Component which attributes to watch for changes.

Static methods can additionally be combined with getters and setters. Using a static getter can be a great way to define constant values that need to be shared across your application.

Listing A.15 Static getter to share constant values across your application

```
class MyClass {
        static get URL() {
               return "http://myserviceurl/api/v2";
        }
}
```

With this static getter, the URL can be shared anywhere, even without instantiation of the class:

```
let url = MyClass.URL;
```

A.4 Modules

To explore what modules are, we should take a peek at a common feature from other languages: the import. Consider the following class in Java, adapted from a tutorial at www.javatpoint.com/java-swing.

Listing A.16 Example of a Java import

```
import javax.swing.*;

public class SwingHelloWorld {
     public static void main(String[] args) {
               JFrame f=new JFrame();
               JButton b=new JButton("click");      // Creates instance of button
               b.setBounds(130,100,100, 40);        // Sets x axis, y axis, width, height
               f.add(b);                            // Adds button to UI
               f.setSize(400,500);                  // Sets button size
               f.setLayout(null);
               f.setVisible(true);
     }
}
```

In this Java-based example, we're programmatically creating a button and placing it in a window. If you don't know Java, this looks pretty easy, right? We could actually do something pretty similar and concise with HTML and JS. The difference with JS is that we would be using the `document` namespace to create our button:

```
document.createElement('button');
```

A.4.1 Top-level objects in JS

Have you ever thought about all of the methods we use every day from `document` or `window`? There are lots, and even though it can be a bit overwhelming, it's manageable once you get used to it. These top-level, or global, objects are designed to control the DOM and your visual elements within. Meanwhile, there are other global objects that deal with other concerns. We print logs to our console with `console.log` and can parse JSON with `JSON.parse`. We also have a top-level `Math` object, which we can use to do trigonometry, create random numbers, and more.

When you think about all of these top-level objects that we, as JS developers, should just know, it can seem a bit chaotic. Alternately, when you consider the Java example in listing A.16, you'll notice objects like `JFrame` and `JButton` to create the window and button, respectively—but where did those objects come from?

To answer this, consider that graphic interfaces aren't necessarily something that Java developers do. Many do, but many will be happy doing all backend work. Given the wide breadth of everything Java needs to do and deal with when it comes to third-party libraries, Java, as well as most other languages, has an `import` feature.

Note the import `javax.swing.*;` at the top of the class. This is actually shorthand. To be more concise, we could expand this to be

```
import javax.swing.JFrame;
import javax.swing.JButton;
```

Using the `.*` syntax imports all classes or nested classes in `javax.swing` and makes them accessible by their name in the class you imported them in, which is why `JButton` has the smarts to create a visual button.

A.4.2 Module syntax for importing and exporting

Until now, browser-based JS has never had a built-in way to manage external dependencies other than by using a `<script>` tag. Third-party libraries like require.js have tried to fill this gap, but this was never adopted as a specification. Now, though, we officially have the native JS feature of modules. In order to use modules, which enable imports just like other languages, there's a small bit of setup.

First, let's prepare a little JS to be usable as an importable module. In a separate JS file, we can write just a few lines:

```
export default function demo() {
   console.log('demo');
}
```

Breaking this down, it's obvious that we are defining a function named `demo` that logs "demo." The keyword `export` is what makes this function able to be imported. The keyword `default` is simply declaring to any JS that imports this script that this function is the default variable, object, or function that is used when importing the script.

To be a little clearer, let's look at how we import in the following listing. To do so, we need to declare that the `<script>` tag that we're using is of type `module`.

Listing A.17 Setting the `<script>` tag type to enable JS modules

```
<script type="module">                                   ← Uses script type of module
   import DemoModule from "./moduledemo.js";             ← Imports a script
   DemoModule();
</script>
```

We can simply import the few lines of JS we just made. The name `DemoModule` is a made-up name in this case. With this import, we could call what we import most anything we wanted, like in figure A.6. Because we've declared our function as `default` in the imported JS, we don't need any further specificity.

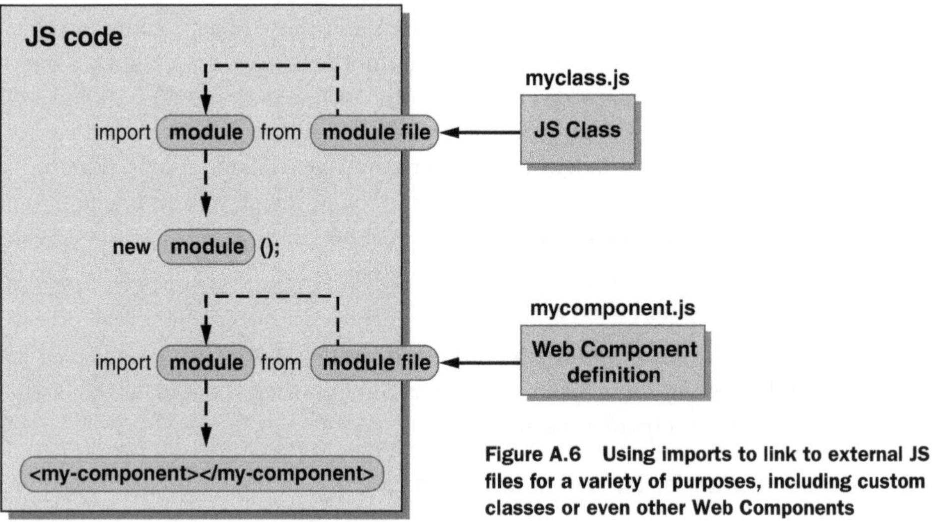

Figure A.6 Using imports to link to external JS files for a variety of purposes, including custom classes or even other Web Components

A.4.3 *Working with multiple functions in the same module*

We do need a bit more specificity if there are multiple things to import from a JS file, like the example in the next listing.

Listing A.18 Exporting multiple functions in the same module

```
export function hi() {          ← A function exported
   console.log('hi');              from a module
}

export function bye() {         ← An additional function exported
   console.log('bye');             from the same module
}
```

Before, we could use shorthand and make up any name we wanted. In the next listing, we need to use the real names of the functions we defined in the modules as we import them.

Listing A.19 Importing specific and multiple functions from the same module

```
<script type="module">
   import { hi, bye } from "./multiplemoduledemo.js";    <-- Imports two exports from the same module
   hi();    <-- Uses the first of the two exports
   bye();
</script>
```

That's not to say we couldn't invent our own names if we really wanted to. To accomplish this, we can use the as modifier.

Listing A.20 Aliasing functions from a module

```
<script type="module">
   import { hi as SomeName, bye as SomeOtherName } from
     "./multiplemoduledemo.js";    <-- Uses the "as" keyword to reference the imports by a custom name
   SomeName();
   SomeOtherName();
</script>
```

Lastly, we can simply scope both the hi and bye methods to an object with the as modifier.

Listing A.21 Aliasing functions as a group from a module

```
<script type="module">
   import * as Greeting from    <-- Uses * to import everything under the object of "Greeting"
     "./multiplemoduledemo.js";
   Greeting.hi();
   Greeting.bye();
</script>
```

Modules are fantastic for use in Web Components. Chapter 5 details how they can be used to keep your Web Components completely self-reliant, managing all of their own dependencies.

A.5 Template literals

Templating is long overdue in JS as a core language feature. While it's true that there have been many libraries and frameworks offering something similar, it's nice that we can now do something without an external library.

Prior to template literals, JS developers have used single or double quotes to define strings. Inserting variables in strings as well as creating multiline strings have always been fairly ugly. This tension is outlined in chapter 6 as I introduce template literals as a better way to insert markup into our Web Components.

What does templating do for us in general? Consider the following string:

```
`Hi, my name is Ben Farrell and I live in Oakland, CA`
```

A.5.1 Inserting variables into a template literal

This is good if you happen to be me (and also if I don't move to a new city), but how do you personalize this string a bit? To start with, we can use a few variables:

```
const firstName = 'Ben';
const lastName = 'Farrell';
const city = 'Oakland';
const state = 'CA';
```

Here, we've pulled out the information that personalizes this string into variables—the idea, of course, being that you can swap any name, city, and state into this string. Previously, we could do this with string concatenation methods like

```
const greeting = 'Hi, my name is ' + firstName + ' ' + lastName + ' and I
     live in ' + city + ', ' + state;
```

This way has always been a bit of a chore. It's not terrible, but remembering to add spaces in all the right places around your variable, coupled with the fact that it's JS code to represent your template, means it's not really an expression you can bring in from elsewhere.

Instead, we can use template literals to do the same thing:

```
const greeting = `Hi, my name is ${firstName} ${lastName}
     and I live in ${city}, ${state}`;
```

Note how this is all one string, variables included. We can see a variety of uses in figure A.7.

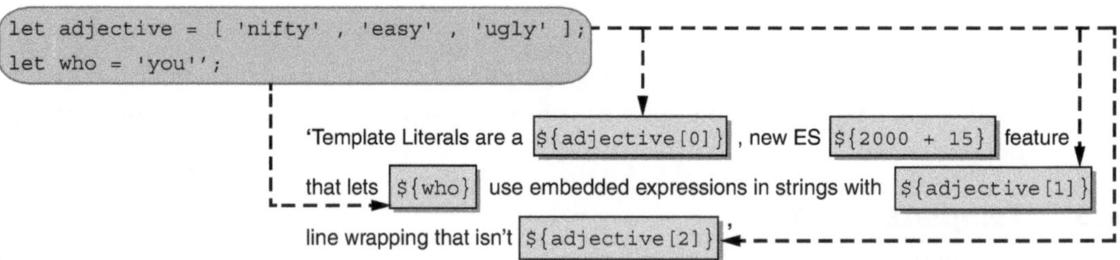

Figure A.7 When combining our variables and our template literal string, we get "Template Literals are a nifty, new ES2015 feature that lets you use embedded expressions in strings with easy line wrapping that isn't ugly."

A.6 The fat arrow

The fat arrow is a newer JS feature that solves a long-standing problem in the language. JS's `bind` method, in addition to `apply`, solved this prior to ES2015. The fat arrow, or the arrow function, now solves the scope problem in a more readable way. This problem isn't unique to Web Components, or classes, for that matter. The fat arrow allows us to preserve scope anywhere we need to. For Web Component classes specifically, it makes our event listeners and callbacks much more readable and easier to use.

A.6.1 The callback scope problem

You're probably familiar with event listeners, as we use them all the time when checking for mouse events, keyboard input, as well as lots of other things. Typically, you'll use them with two parameters, the first being a string describing the event to listen for and the second being the function to call when the thing you're listening for dispatches an event.

Ignoring the fat arrow syntax for now, the syntax is typically

```
target.addEventListener('mousemove', function(event) {
        ...do something
});
```

Or, if you have a function already set up to handle the event:

```
target.addEventListener('mousemove', myFunction);
```

In each of these cases, a rather unfortunate thing happens: we've lost our original scope, and in the function that gets called, we have a brand-new scope. To explain, let's take a peek at the next listing for an example.

Listing A.22 A timer example showing loss of scope within a class

```
class ScopeTest {
   constructor() {
       this.message = 'hi';
       setInterval(this.onTimer, 1000);      <-- Starts a timer with the onTimer function being called on every timeout
   }

   onTimer() {
       console.log(this.message);      <-- Undefined, because "this" is no longer in the class scope
   }
}
let test = new ScopeTest();
```

With this example, we instantiate a class. Right off the bat, in the constructor, we set a string called `message` to "hi". We also start a timer that fires every second. The timer calls a function called `onTimer`, which console-logs our `message` variable.

A.6.2 Losing scope in classes

The problem is that when you run this code, `undefined` is logged to the console. Why doesn't "hi" get logged? What would happen if we changed our constructor to directly call the function?

Listing A.23 Directly calling a function to avoid scope loss

```
class ScopeTest {
   constructor() {
       this.message = 'hi';
       this.onTimer();      <-- Calls the onTimer function directly instead of through setInterval
   }

   onTimer() {
```

```
        console.log(this.message);   <-- Will log "hi" because "this"
    }                                    is still in the class's scope
}
let test = new ScopeTest();
```

In this case, our message of "hi" is indeed logged, but the difference between these two methods is a matter of scope.

Scope is the context in which we can access variables, functions, and objects. In fact, the reference `this` is that context. Try adding the following console log to your constructor:

```
  constructor() {
       console.log(this);
       this.message = 'hi';
       this.onTimer();
   }
```

What gets logged is this:

```
ScopeTest {message: "hi"}
```

And, of course, if you expand in your dev tools, you'll be able to see the `onTimer` function in there as well. Logging `this` in your class's scope gives you a reference to your class! Exactly what we need for managing code in our class, and it's why we can access variables through `this` or call functions on `this`.

On the other hand, if we set up a proper timer in the constructor using `setTimeout(this.onTimer, 1000)` and log `this` from our timer callback, like so,

```
   onTimer() {
       console.log(this);
   }
```

we find ourselves inside an unrecognizable scope:

```
Window {postMessage: f, blur: f, focus: f, close: f, frames: Window, . . .}
```

In fact, if you were to run `onTimer` from the constructor without the timer, your scope would still be that of your class.

So, as you can probably see, when you pass a function to something like an event listener, a timer, or similar to be called back at a later time, your callback function is suddenly in a new scope! Of course, this is problematic, because the question then becomes how to reference your class's scope again from your callback.

With our example, within our timer callback, we can't access our `message` variable. What if, instead, we wanted to take action on our Web Component's DOM? A mouse click wouldn't be terribly useful to listen for if we couldn't take some kind of contextual action on it.

A.6.3 Managing scope with the fat arrow

There have been many ways to tackle this problem over time in JS, but we finally have a new JS feature specifically for it, and that is the fat arrow. Of course, we affectionately refer to this as the fat arrow because the syntax of => is an arrow with a thick stem.

To use the fat arrow in the next listing, we pass an arrow function containing an expression that calls our method instead of the function itself.

Listing A.24 Using the fat arrow to maintain scope

```
class ScopeTest {
  constructor() {
     this.message = 'hi';
     setInterval(() => this.onTimer(), 1000);   <-- Passes a fat arrow expression instead of a function
  }

  onTimer() {
     console.log(this.message);   <-- Class scope is preserved; the message "hi" is logged
  }
}
let test = new ScopeTest();
```

Using the fat arrow here, we can log `this.message`, and it's not `undefined`; more importantly, we are preserving the scope of our class even through a callback. Oftentimes, you won't see the empty parentheses in a fat arrow expression. Here, it denotes that we're not passing parameters, since `setInterval` callbacks don't take them.

If there were parameters for a given method, those parentheses would be filled in as you might expect:

```
callback((x, y, z) => this.onCallback(x, y, z));
```

For an example that directly applies to us, let's circle back to our mouse-move listener:

```
this.addEventListener('mousemove', e => this.onMouseMove(e));
```

In this case, an event listener passes an event into the callback, and we're choosing to use it. We could still ignore this event and use the function with the empty parentheses, like this:

```
this.addEventListener('mousemove', () => this.onMouseMove());
```

Either way, we can use the fat arrow to properly preserve scope, as figure A.8 shows, where we contrast this against the other methods we discussed. More importantly for

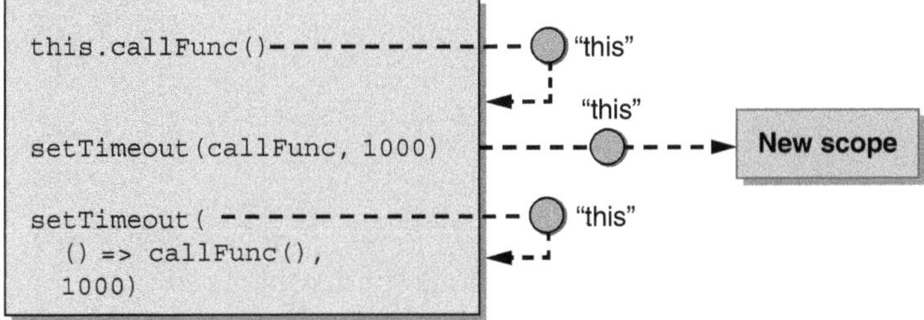

Figure A.8 Showing loss of scope or context when using a callback with no way to get back, and how the fat arrow can map scope back to where the function was called, just like calling a normal function

our Web Component use cases, we can keep scope directly to the Web Component itself, and writing code for our component is kept easy without becoming a maze of mixed scopes we need to manage.

index

Numerics

A

B

C

D

E

F

G

H

I

J

K

L

T

U

V

W

X

Y